Operating Systems
and Middleware
Supporting Controlled Interaction

Max Hailperin

THOMSON

COURSE TECHNOLOGY

Australia • Canada • Mexico • Singapore • Spain • United Kingdom • United States

THOMSON
COURSE TECHNOLOGY™

Operating Systems and Middleware: Supporting Controlled Interaction
by Max Hailperin

Senior Product Manager:
Alyssa Pratt

Managing Editor:
Mary Franz

Development Editor:
Jill Batistick

Senior Marketing Manager:
Karen Seitz

Associate Product Manager:
Jennifer Smith

Editorial Assistant:
Allison Murphy

Senior Manufacturing Coordinator:
Justin Palmeiro

Cover Designer:
Deborah VanRooyen

Compositor:
Interactive Composition Corporation

For permission to use material from this text or product, submit a request online at http://www.thomsonrights.com
Any additional questions about permissions can be submitted by e-mail to thomsonrights@thomson.com

Disclaimer
Thomson Course Technology reserves the right to revise this publication and make changes from time to time in its content without notice.

ISBN 0-534-42369-8

To
My Family

BRIEF

Contents

TABLE OF
Contents

Preface

Suppose you sit down at your computer to check your email. One of the messages includes an attached document, which you are to edit. You click the attachment, and it opens up in another window. After you start editing the document, you realize you need to leave for a trip. You save the document in its partially edited state and shut down the computer to save energy while you are gone. Upon returning, you boot the computer back up, open the document, and continue editing.

This scenario illustrates that computations interact. In fact, it demonstrates at least three kinds of interactions between computations. In each case, one computation provides data to another. First, your email program retrieves new mail from the server, using the Internet to bridge space. Second, your email program provides the attachment to the word processor, using the operating system's services to couple the two application programs. Third, the invocation of the word processor that is running before your trip provides the partially edited document to the invocation running after your return, using disk storage to bridge time.

In this book, you will learn about all three kinds of interaction. In all three cases, interesting software techniques are needed in order to bring the computations into contact, yet keep them sufficiently at arms length that they don't compromise each other's reliability. The exciting challenge, then, is supporting controlled interaction. This includes support for computations that share a single computer and interact with one another, as your email and word processing programs do. It also includes support for data storage and network communication. This book describes how all these kinds of support are provided both by operating systems and by additional software layered on top of operating systems, which is known as middleware.

Audience

If you are an upper-level computer science student who wants to understand how contemporary operating systems and middleware products work and why they work that way, this book is for you. In this book, you will find many forms of balance. The high-level application programmer's view, focused on the services that system software provides, is balanced with a lower-level perspective, focused on the mechanisms used to provide those services. Timeless concepts are balanced with concrete examples of how those concepts are embodied in a range of currently popular systems. Programming is balanced with other intellectual activities, such as the scientific measurement of system performance and the strategic consideration of system security in its human and business context. Even the programming languages used for examples are balanced, with some examples in Java and others in C or C++. (Only limited portions of these languages are used, however, so that the examples can serve as learning opportunities, not stumbling blocks.)

Systems Used as Examples

Most of the examples throughout the book are drawn from the two dominant families of operating systems: Microsoft Windows and the UNIX family, including especially Linux and Mac OS X. Using this range of systems promotes the students' flexibility. It also allows a more comprehensive array of concepts to be concretely illustrated, as the systems embody fundamentally different approaches to some problems, such as the scheduling of processors' time and the tracking of files' disk space.

Most of the examples are drawn from the stable core portions of the operating systems and, as such, are equally applicable to a range of specific versions. Whenever Microsoft Windows is mentioned without further specification, the material applies to Windows NT, Windows 2000, Windows XP, Windows Server 2003, and (so far as can be determined from pre-release information) Windows Vista. All Linux examples are from version 2.6, though much of the material applies to other versions as well. Wherever actual Linux source code is shown (or whenever fine details matter for other reasons), the specific subversion of 2.6 is mentioned in the end-of-chapter notes. All Mac OS X examples are from version 10.4, also known as Tiger. However, other than the description of the Spotlight feature for indexed file search, all the material is applicable to earlier versions.

Where the book discusses the protection of each process's memory, one additional operating system is brought into the mix of examples, in order to illustrate a more comprehensive range of alternative designs. The IBM iSeries, formerly known as the AS/400, embodies an interesting approach to protection that might see wider application within current students' lifetimes. Rather than giving each process its own address space (as Linux, Windows, and Mac OS X do), the iSeries allows all processes to share a single address space and to hold varying access permissions to individual objects within that space.

Several middleware systems are used for examples as well. The Oracle database system is used to illustrate deadlock detection and recovery as well as the use of atomic transactions. Messaging systems appear both as another application of atomic transactions and as an important form of communication middleware, supporting distributed applications. The specific messaging examples are drawn from the IBM WebSphere MQ system (formerly MQSeries) and the Java Message Service (JMS) interface, which is part of Java 2 Enterprise Edition (J2EE). The other communication middleware examples are Java RMI (Remote Method Invocation) and web services. Web services are explained in platform-neutral terms using the SOAP and WSDL standards, as well as through a J2EE interface, JAX-RPC (Java API for XML-Based RPC).

Organization of the Text

Chapter 1 provides an overview of the text as a whole, explaining what an operating system is, what middleware is, and what sorts of support these systems provide for controlled interaction.

The next nine chapters work through the varieties of controlled interaction that are exemplified by the scenario at the beginning of the preface: interaction between concurrent computations on the same system (as between your email program and your word processor), interaction across time (as between your word processor before your trip and your word processor after your trip), and interaction across space (as between your email program and your service provider's email server).

The first of these three topics is controlled interaction between computations operating at one time on a particular computer. Before such interaction can make sense, you need to understand how it is that a single computer can be running more than one program, such as an email program in one window and a word processing program in another. Therefore, Chapter 2 explains the fundamental mechanism for dividing a computer's attention between concurrent computations, known as threads. Chapter 3 continues with the related topic of scheduling. That is, if the computer is dividing its time between computations, it needs to decide which one to work on at any moment.

With concurrent computations explained, Chapter 4 introduces controlled interactions between them by explaining synchronization, which is control over the threads' relative timing. For example, this chapter explains how, when your email program sends a document to your word processor, the word processor can be constrained to read the document only after the email program writes it. One particularly important form of synchronization, atomic transactions, is the topic of Chapter 5. Atomic transactions are groups of operations that take place as an indivisible unit; they are most commonly supported by middleware, though they are also playing an increasing role in operating systems.

Other than synchronization, the main way that operating systems control the interaction between computations is by controlling their access to memory. Chapter 6 explains how this is achieved using the technique known as virtual memory. That chapter also explains the many other objectives this same technique can serve. Virtual memory serves as the foundation for Chapter 7's topic, which is processes. A process is the fundamental unit of computation for protected access, just as a thread is the fundamental unit of computation for concurrency. A process is a group of threads that share a protection environment; in particular, they share the same access to virtual memory.

The next three chapters move outside the limitations of a single computer operating in a single session. First, consider the document stored before a trip and available again after it. Chapter 8 explains persistent storage mechanisms, focusing particularly on the file storage that operating systems provide. Second, consider the interaction between your email program and your service provider's email server. Chapter 9 provides an overview of networking, including the services that operating systems make available to programs such as the email client and server. Chapter 10 extends this discussion into the more sophisticated forms of support provided by communication middleware, such as messaging systems, RMI, and web services.

Finally, Chapter 11 focuses on security. Because security is a pervasive issue, the preceding ten chapters all provide some information on it as well. Specifically, the final section of each chapter points out ways in which security relates to that chapter's particular topic. However, even with that coverage distributed throughout the book, a chapter specifically on security is needed, primarily to elevate it out of technical particulars and talk about general principles and the human and organizational context surrounding the computer technology.

The best way to use these chapters is in consecutive order. However, Chapter 5 can be omitted with only minor harm to Chapters 8 and 10, and Chapter 9 can be omitted if students are already sufficiently familiar with networking.

Relationship to Computing Curricula 2001

Operating systems are traditionally the subject of a course required for all computer science majors. In recent years, however, there has been increasing interest in the idea that upper-level courses should be centered less around particular artifacts, such as operating systems, and more around cross-cutting concepts. In particular, the recently adopted *Computing Curricula 2001* (CC2001) provides encouragement for this approach, at least as one option. Most colleges and universities still retain a relatively traditional operating systems course, however. Therefore, this book steers a middle course, moving in the direction of the cross-cutting concerns while retaining enough familiarity to be broadly adoptable.

The following table indicates the placement within this text of knowledge units from CC2001's computer science body of knowledge. Those knowledge units designated as core units within CC2001 are listed in italics. The book covers all core operating systems (OS) units, as well as two elective OS units. The overall amount of coverage for each unit is always at least that recommended by CC2001, though sometimes the specific subtopics don't quite correspond exactly. Outside the OS area, this book's most substantial coverage is of Net-Centric Computing (NC); another major topic, transaction processing, comes from Information Management (IM). In each row, the listed chapters contain the bulk of the knowledge unit's coverage, though some topics may be elsewhere.

Knowledge unit (italic indicates core units in CC2001)	Chapter(s)
OS1 Overview of operating systems	1
OS2 Operating system principles	1, 7
OS3 Concurrency	2, 4
OS4 Scheduling and dispatch	3
OS5 Memory management	6
OS7 Security and protection	7, 11
OS8 File systems	8
NC1 Introduction to net-centric computing	9
NC2 Communication and networking (partial coverage)	9
NC3 Network security	9
NC4 The web as an example of … (partial coverage)	9
NC5 Building web applications (partial coverage)	10
IM7 Transaction processing	5

Your Feedback is Welcome

Comments, suggestions, and bug reports are welcome; please send email to `max@gustavus.edu`. Bug reports in particular can earn you a bounty of $2.56 apiece as a token of gratitude. (The great computer scientist Donald Knuth started this tradition. Given how close to bug-free his publications have become, it seems to work.) For purposes of this reward, the definition of a bug is simple: if as a result of your email the author chooses to make a change, then you have pointed out a bug. The change need not be the one you suggested, and the bug need not be technical in nature. Unclear writing qualifies, for example.

Features of the Text

Each chapter concludes with five standard elements. The last numbered section within the chapter is always devoted to security matters related to the chapter's topic. Next comes three different lists of opportunities for active participation by the student: exercises, programming projects, and exploration projects. Finally, the chapter ends with historical and bibliographic notes.

The distinction between exercises, programming projects, and exploration projects needs explanation. An exercise can be completed with no outside resources beyond paper and pencil: you need just this textbook and your mind. That does not mean all the exercises are cut and dried, however. Some may call upon you to think creatively; for these, no one answer is correct. Programming projects require a nontrivial amount of programming; that is, they require more than making a small, easily identified change in an existing program. However, a programming project may involve other activities beyond programming. Several of them involve scientific measurement of performance effects, for example; these exploratory aspects may even dominate over the programming aspects. An exploration project, on the other hand, can be an experiment that can be performed with no real programming; at most you might change a designated line within an existing program. The category of exploration projects does not just include experimental work, however. It also includes projects that require you to do research on the Internet or using other library resources.

Supplemental Resources

The author of this text is making supplemental resources available on his own web site. Additionally, the publisher has commissioned additional resources from independent supplement authors and is making them available through the Thomson Course Technology web site.

Author's Supplements

The author's web site, *http://www.gustavus.edu/+max/os-book/*, will contain at least the following materials:

- Source code in Java, C, or C++ for all programs that are shown in the text
- Artwork files for all figures in the text
- An errata list that will be updated on an ongoing basis

Publisher's Supplements

The publisher's web site, *www.course.com*, will contain the same Java, C, and C++ program files that are available on the author's site and printed in the text. The publisher will provide other supplements as well; the author of each independently created supplement will be listed in the preface of the Instructor's Manual. The following descriptions were provided by the publisher:

Electronic Instructor's Manual The Instructor's Manual that accompanies this textbook includes additional instructional material to assist in class preparation, including Sample Syllabi, Chapter Outlines, Technical Notes, Lecture Notes, Quick Quizzes, Teaching Tips, Discussion Topics, and Key Terms.

ExamView® This objective-based test generator lets the instructor create paper, LAN, or Web-based tests from testbanks designed specifically for this Thomson Course Technology text. Instructors can use the QuickTest Wizard to create tests in fewer than five minutes by taking advantage of Thomson Course Technology's question banks, or they can create customized exams.

PowerPoint Presentations Microsoft PowerPoint slides are included for each chapter. Instructors might use the slides in a variety of ways, including as teaching aids during classroom presentations or as printed handouts for classroom distribution. Instructors can modify the slides provided or include slides of their own for additional topics introduced to the class.

Solutions Solutions to Exercises and Projects are provided on the Teaching Tools CD-ROM and may also be found on the Thomson Course Technology Web site at *www.course.com*. The solutions are password protected.

Figure Files Electronic figure files for all art in the text are available on the Teaching Tools CD-ROM.

Distance Learning Thomson Course Technology is proud to present online test banks in WebCT and Blackboard to provide the most complete and dynamic learning experience possible. For more information on how to access the online test bank, contact your local Thomson Course Technology sales representative.

Acknowledgments

This book was made possible by financial and logistical support from my employer, Gustavus Adolphus College, and moral support from my family. I would like to acknowledge the contributions of the publishing team, especially developmental editor Jill Batistick and Product Manager Alyssa Pratt. I am also grateful to my students for doing their own fair share of teaching. I particularly appreciate the often extensive comments I received from the following individuals, each of whom reviewed one or more chapters: Dan Cosley, University of Minnesota, Twin Cities; Allen Downey, Franklin W. Olin College of Engineering; Michael Goldweber, Xavier University; Ramesh Karne, Towson University; G. Manimaran, Iowa State University; Alexander Manov, Illinois Institute of Technology; Peter Reiher, University of California, Los Angeles; Rich Salz, DataPower Technology; Dave Schulz, Wisconsin Lutheran College; Sanjeev Setia, George Mason University; and Jon Weissman, University of Minnesota, Twin Cities. Although I did not adopt all their suggestions, I did not ignore any of them, and I appreciate them all.

1

Introduction

1.1 Chapter Overview

This book covers a lot of ground. In it, I will explain to you the basic principles that underlie a broad range of systems and also give you concrete examples of how those principles play out in several specific systems. You will see not only some of the internal workings of low-level infrastructure, but also how to build higher-level applications on top of that infrastructure to make use of its services. Moreover, this book will draw on material you may have encountered in other branches of computer science and engineering and engage you in activities ranging from mathematical proofs to the experimental measurement of real-world performance and the consideration of how systems are used and abused in social context.

Because the book as a whole covers so much ground, this chapter is designed to give you a quick view of the whole terrain, so that you know what you are getting into. This overview is especially important because several of the topics I cover are interrelated, so that even though I carefully designed the order of presentation, I am still going to confront you with occasional forward references. You will find, however, that this introductory chapter gives you a sufficient overview of all the topics so that you won't be mystified when a chapter on one makes some reference to another.

In Section 1.2, I will explain what an operating system is, and in Section 1.3, I will do the same for middleware. After these two sections, you will know what general topic you are studying. Section 1.4 gives you some reasons for studying that topic, by explaining several roles that I hope this book will serve for you.

After the very broad overview provided by these initial sections, the remaining sections of this chapter are somewhat more focused. Each corresponds to one or more of the later chapters and explains one important category of service provided by operating systems and middleware. Section 1.5 explains how a single computer can run several computations concurrently, a topic addressed in more depth by Chapters 2 and 3. Section 1.6 explains how interactions between those concurrent computations can be kept under control, the topic of Chapters 4 through 7. Sections 1.7 and 1.8 extend the range of interacting computations across time and space, respectively, through mechanisms such as file systems and networking. They preview Chapter 8 and Chapters 9 and 10. Finally, Section 1.9 introduces the topic of security, a topic I revisit at the end of each chapter and then focus on in Chapter 11.

1.2 What Is an Operating System?

An *operating system* is software that uses the hardware resources of a computer system to provide support for the execution of other software. Specifically, an operating system provides the following services:

- The operating system allows multiple computations to take place concurrently on a single computer system. It divides the hardware's time between the computations and handles the shifts of focus between the computations, keeping track of where each one leaves off so that it can later correctly resume.

- The operating system controls the interactions between the concurrent computations. It can enforce rules, such as forbidding computations from modifying data structures while other computations are accessing those structures. It can also provide isolated areas of memory for private use by the different computations.

- The operating system can provide support for controlled interaction of computations even when they do not run concurrently. In particular, general-purpose operating systems provide file systems, which allow computations to read data from files written by earlier computations. This feature is optional because an embedded system, such as the computer controlling a washing machine, might in some cases run an operating system, but not provide a file system or other long-term storage.

- The operating system can provide support for controlled interaction of computations spread among different computer systems by using networking. This is another standard feature of general-purpose operating systems.

These services are illustrated in Figure 1.1.

If you have programmed only general-purpose computers, such as PCs, workstations, and servers, you have probably never encountered a computer system that was not running an operating system or that did not allow multiple computations to be ongoing. For example, when you boot up your own computer, chances are that it runs Linux, Microsoft Windows, or Mac OS X and that you can run multiple application programs in individual windows on the display screen. These three operating systems will serve as my primary examples throughout the book.

To illustrate that a computer can run a single program without an operating system, consider embedded systems. A typical embedded system might have neither keyboard nor display screen. Instead, it might have temperature and pressure sensors and an output that controls the fuel injectors of your car. Alternatively, it might have a primitive keyboard and display, as on a microwave oven, but still be dedicated to running a single program.

Some of the most sophisticated embedded systems run multiple cooperating programs and use operating systems. However, more mundane embedded systems take a simpler form. A single program is directly executed by the embedded processor. That program contains instructions to read from input sensors, carry out appropriate computations, and write to the output devices. This sort of embedded system illustrates what is possible without an operating system. It will also serve as a point

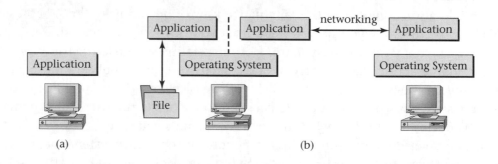

Figure 1.1   Without an operating system, a computer can directly execute a single program, as shown in part (a). Part (b) shows that with an operating system, the computer can support concurrent computations, control the interactions between them (suggested by the dashed line), and allow communication across time and space by way of files and networking.

of reference as I contrast my definition of an operating system with an alternative definition.

One popular alternative definition of an operating system is that it provides application programmers with an abstract view of the underlying hardware resources, taking care of the low-level details so that the applications can be programmed more simply. For example, the programmer can write a simple statement to output a string without concern for the details of making each character appear on the display screen.

I would counter by remarking that abstraction can be provided without an operating system, by linking application programs with separately written libraries of supporting procedures. For example, a program could output a string using the standard mechanism of a programming language, such as C++ or Java. The application programmer would not need to know anything about hardware. However, rather than running on an operating system, the program could be linked with a library that performed the output by appropriately manipulating a microwave oven's display panel. Once running on the oven's embedded processor, the library and the application code would be a single program, nothing more than a sequence of instructions to directly execute. However, from the application programmer's standpoint, the low-level details would have been successfully hidden.

To summarize this argument, a library of input/output routines is not the same as an operating system, because it satisfies only the first part of my definition. It does use underlying hardware to support the execution of other software. However, it does not provide support for controlled interaction between computations. In fairness to the alternative viewpoint, it is the more historically grounded one. Originally, a piece of software could be called an operating system without supporting controlled interaction. However, the language has evolved such that my definition more closely reflects current usage.

I should also address one other alternative view of operating systems, because it is likely to be the view you have formed from your own experience using general-purpose computers. You are likely to think of an operating system as the software with which you interact in order to carry out tasks such as running application programs. Depending on the user interface to which you are accustomed, you might think the operating system is what allows you to click program icons to run them, or you might think the operating system is what interprets commands you type.

There is an element of truth to this perception. The operating system does provide the service of executing a selected application program. However, the operating system provides this service not to human users clicking icons or typing commands, but to other programs already running on the computer, including the one that handles icon clicks or command entries. The operating system allows one program that is running to start another program running. This is just one of the many services the operating system provides to running programs. Another example is writing output into a file. The sum total of features the operating system makes available for application programmers to use in their programs is called the *Application Programming Interface* (*API*). One element of the API is the ability to run other programs.

The reason why you can click a program icon or type in a command to run a program is that general-purpose operating systems come bundled with a user-interface program, which uses the operating system API to run other programs in response to mouse or keyboard input. At a marketing level, this user-interface program may be treated as a part of the operating system; it may not be given a prominent name of its own and may not be available for separate purchase.

For example, Microsoft Windows comes with a user interface known as Explorer, which provides features such as the Start menu and the ability to click icons. (This program is distinct from the similarly named web browser, Internet Explorer.) However, even if you are an experienced Windows user, you may never have heard of Explorer; Microsoft has chosen to give it a very low profile, treating it as an integral part of the Microsoft Windows environment. At a technical level, however, it is distinct from the operating system proper. In order to make the distinction explicit, the true operating system is often called the *kernel*. The kernel is the fundamental portion of Microsoft Windows that provides an API supporting computations with controlled interactions.

A similar distinction between the kernel and the user interface applies to Linux. The Linux kernel provides the basic operating system services through an API, whereas *shells* are the programs (such as bash and tcsh) that interpret typed commands, and *desktop environments* are the programs, such as KDE (K Desktop Environment) and GNOME, that handle graphical interaction.

In this book, I will explain the workings of operating system kernels, the true operating systems themselves, as opposed to the user-interface programs. One reason is because user-interface programs are not constructed in any fundamentally different way than normal application programs. The other reason is because an operating system need not have this sort of user interface at all. Consider again the case of an embedded system that controls automotive fuel injection. If the system is sufficiently sophisticated, it may include an operating system. The main control program may run other, more specialized programs. However, there is no ability for the user to start an arbitrary program running through a shell or desktop environment. In this book, I will draw my examples from general-purpose systems with which you might be familiar, but will emphasize the principles that could apply in other contexts as well.

1.3 What Is Middleware?

Now that you know what an operating system is, I can turn to the other category of software covered by this book: *middleware*. Middleware is software occupying a middle position between application programs and operating systems, as I will explain in this section.

Operating systems and middleware have much in common. Both are software used to support other software, such as the application programs you run. Both provide a similar range of services centered around controlled interaction. Like an operating system, middleware may enforce rules designed to keep the computations from interfering with one another. An example is the rule that only one computation may modify a shared data structure at a time. Like an operating system, middleware may bring computations at different times into contact through persistent storage and may support interaction between computations on different computers by providing network communication services.

Operating systems and middleware are not the same, however. They rely upon different underlying providers of lower-level services. An operating system provides the services in its API by making use of the features supported by the hardware. For example, it might provide API services of reading and writing named, variable-length files by making use of a disk drive's ability to read and write numbered, fixed-length blocks of data. Middleware, on the other hand, provides the services in its API by making use of the features supported by an underlying operating system. For example, the middleware might provide API services for updating relational database tables by making use of an operating system's ability to read and write files that contain the database.

This layering of middleware on top of an operating system, as illustrated in Figure 1.2, explains the name; middleware is in the middle of the vertical stack, between

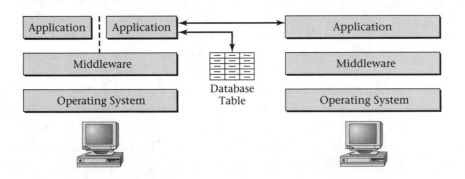

Figure 1.2   Middleware uses services from an operating system and in turn provides services to application programs to support controlled interaction.

the application programs and the operating system. Viewed horizontally rather than vertically, middleware is also in the middle of interactions between different application programs (possibly even running on different computer systems), because it provides mechanisms to support controlled interaction through coordination, persistent storage, naming, and communication.

I already mentioned relational database systems as one example of middleware. Such systems provide a more sophisticated form of persistent storage than the files supported by most operating systems. I use Oracle as my primary source of examples regarding relational database systems. Other middleware I will use for examples in the book includes the Java 2 Platform, Enterprise Edition (J2EE) and IBM's WebSphere MQ. These systems provide support for keeping computations largely isolated from undesirable interactions, while allowing them to communicate with one another even if running on different computers.

The marketing definition of middleware doesn't always correspond exactly with my technical definition. In particular, some middleware is of such fundamental importance that it is distributed as part of the operating system bundle, rather than as a separate middleware product. As an example, general-purpose operating systems all come equipped with some mechanism for translating Internet hostnames, such as *www.gustavus.edu,* into numerical addresses. These mechanisms are typically outside the operating system kernel, but provide a general supporting service to application programs. Therefore, by my definition, they are middleware, even if not normally labeled as such.

1.4 Objectives for the Book

If you work your way through this book, you will gain both knowledge and skills. Notice that I did not say anything about *reading* the book, but rather about *working your way through* the book. Each chapter in this book concludes with exercises, programming projects, exploration projects, and some bibliographic or historical notes. To achieve the objectives of the book, you need to work exercises, carry out projects, and occasionally venture down one of the side trails pointed out by the end-of-chapter notes. Some of the exploration projects will specifically direct you to do research in outside sources, such as on the Internet or in a library. Others will call upon you to do experimental work, such as measuring the performance consequences of a particular design choice. If you are going to invest that kind of time and effort, you deserve some idea of what you stand to gain from it. Therefore, I will explain in the following paragraphs how you will be more knowledgeable and skilled after finishing the book.

First, you will gain a general knowledge of how contemporary operating systems and middleware work and some idea why they work that way. That knowledge may be interesting in its own right, but it also has practical applications. Recall that these systems provide supporting APIs for application programmers to use. Therefore, one payoff will be that if you program applications, you will be positioned to make more effective use of the supporting APIs. This is true even though you won't be an expert at any particular API; instead, you'll see the big picture of what services those APIs provide.

Another payoff will be if you are in a role where you need to alter the configuration of an operating system or middleware product in order to tune its performance or to make it best serve a particular context. Again, this one book alone won't give you all the specific knowledge you need about any particular system, but it will give you the general background to make sense out of more specialized references.

Perhaps the most significant payoff for learning the details of today's systems in the context of the reasons behind their designs is that you will be in a better position to learn tomorrow's systems. You will be able to see in what ways they are different and in what ways they are fundamentally still the same. You will be able to put new features into context, often as a new solution to an old problem, or even just as a variant on an existing solution. If you really get excited by what you learn from this book, you could even use your knowledge as the foundation for more advanced study and become one of the people who develops tomorrow's systems.

Second, in addition to knowledge about systems, you will learn some skills that are applicable even outside the context of operating systems and middleware. Some of the most important skills come from the exploration projects. For example, if you take those projects seriously, you'll practice not only conducting experiments, but also writing reports describing the experiments and their results. That will serve you well in many contexts.

I have also provided you with some opportunities to develop proficiency in using the professional literature, such as documentation and the papers published in conference proceedings. Those sources go into more depth than this book can, and they will always be more up-to-date.

From the programming projects, you'll gain some skill at writing programs that have several interacting components operating concurrently with one another and that keep their interactions under control. You'll also develop some skill at writing programs that interact over the Internet. In neither case will you become a master programmer. However, in both cases, you will be laying a foundation of skills that are relevant to a range of development projects and environments.

Another example of a skill you can acquire is the ability to look at the security ramifications of design decisions. I have a security section in each chapter, rather than a security chapter only at the end of the book, because I want you to develop the habit of asking, "What are the security issues here?" That question is relevant even outside the realm of operating systems and middleware.

As I hope you can see, studying operating systems and middleware can provide a wide range of benefits, particularly if you engage yourself in it as an active participant, rather than as a spectator. With that for motivation, I will now take you on another tour of the services that operating systems and middleware provide. This tour is more detailed than Sections 1.2 and 1.3, but not as detailed as Chapters 2 through 11.

1.5 Multiple Computations on One Computer

The single most fundamental service an operating system provides is to allow multiple computations to be going on at the same time, rather than forcing each to wait until the previous one has run to completion. This allows desktop computers to juggle multiple tasks for the busy humans seated in front of their screens, and it allows server computers to be responsive to requests originating from many different client computers on the Internet. Beyond these responsiveness concerns, concurrent computations can also make more efficient use of a computer's resources. For example, while one computation is stalled waiting for input to arrive, another computation can be making productive use of the processor.

A variety of words can be used to refer to the computations underway on a computer; they may be called threads, processes, tasks, or jobs. In this book, I will use both the word "thread" and the word "process," and it is important that I explain now the difference between them.

A *thread* is the fundamental unit of concurrency. Any one sequence of programmed actions is a thread. Executing a program might create multiple threads, if the program calls for several independent sequences of actions run concurrently with one another. Even if each execution of a program creates only a single thread, which is the more normal case, a typical system will be running several threads: one for each ongoing program execution, as well as some that are internal parts of the operating system itself.

When you start a program running, you are always creating one or more threads. However, you are also creating a *process*. The process is a container that holds the thread or threads that you started running and protects them from unwanted interactions with other unrelated threads running on the same computer. For example, a thread running in one process cannot accidentally overwrite memory in use by a different process.

Because human users normally start a new process running every time they want to make a new computation happen, it is tempting to think of processes as the unit of concurrent execution. This temptation is amplified by the fact that older operating systems required each process to have exactly one thread, so that the two kinds of objects were in one-to-one correspondence, and it was not important to distinguish them. However, in this book, I will consistently make the distinction. When I am referring to the ability to set an independent sequence of programmed actions in motion, I will write about creating threads. Only when I am referring to the ability to protect threads will I write about creating processes.

In order to support threads, operating system APIs include features such as the ability to create a new thread and to kill off an existing thread. Inside the operating system, there must be some mechanism for switching the computer's attention between the various threads. When the operating system suspends execution of one thread in order to give another thread a chance to make progress, the operating system must store enough information about the first thread to be able to successfully resume its execution later. Chapter 2 addresses these issues.

Some threads may not be runnable at any particular time, because they are waiting for some event, such as the arrival of input. However, in general, an operating system will be confronted with multiple runnable threads and will have to choose which one to run at each moment. This problem of scheduling threads' execution has many solutions, which are surveyed in Chapter 3. The scheduling problem is interesting, and has generated so many solutions, because it involves the balancing of system users' competing interests and values. No individual scheduling approach will make everyone happy all the time. My focus is on explaining how the different scheduling approaches fit different contexts of system usage and achieve differing goals. In addition I explain how APIs allow programmers to exert control over scheduling, for example, by indicating that some threads should have higher priority than others.

1.6 Controlling Interactions Between Computations

Running multiple threads at once becomes more interesting if the threads need to interact, rather than execute completely independently of one another. For example, one thread might be producing data that another thread consumes. If one thread is writing data into memory and another is reading the data out, you don't want the reader to get ahead of the writer and start reading from locations that have yet to be written. This illustrates one broad family of control for interaction: control over the relative timing of the threads' execution. Here, a reading step must take place after the corresponding writing step. The general name for control over threads' timing is *synchronization*.

Chapter 4 explains several common synchronization patterns, including keeping a consumer from outstripping the corresponding producer. It also explains the mechanisms that are commonly used to provide synchronization, some of which are supported directly by operating systems, while others require some modest amount of middleware, such as the Java runtime environment.

That same chapter also explains a particularly important difficulty that can arise from the use of synchronization. Synchronization can force one thread to wait for another. What if the second thread happens to be waiting for the first? This sort of cyclic waiting is known as a *deadlock*. My discussion of ways to cope with deadlock also introduces some significant middleware, because database systems provide an interesting example of deadlock handling.

In Chapter 5, I expand on the themes of synchronization and middleware by explaining transactions, which are commonly supported by middleware. A *transaction* is a unit of computational work for which no intermediate state from the middle of the computation is ever visible. Concurrent transactions are isolated from seeing each other's intermediate storage. Additionally, if a transaction should fail, the storage will be left as it was before the transaction started. Even if the computer system should catastrophically crash in the middle of a transaction's execution, the storage after rebooting will not reflect the partial transaction. This prevents results of a half-completed transaction from becoming visible. Transactions are incredibly useful in designing reliable information systems and have widespread commercial deployment. They also provide a good example of how mathematical reasoning can be used to help design practical systems; this will be the chapter where I most prominently expect you to understand a proof.

Even threads that have no reason to interact may accidentally interact, if they are running on the same computer and sharing the same memory. For example, one thread might accidentally write into memory being used by the other. This is one of several reasons why operating systems provide *virtual memory*, the topic of Chapter 6. Virtual memory refers to the technique of modifying addresses on their way from the processor to the memory, so that the addresses actually used for storing values in memory may be different from those appearing in the processor's load and store instructions. This is a general mechanism provided through a combination of hardware and operating system software. I explain several different goals this mechanism can serve, but the most simple is isolating threads in one process from those in another by directing their memory accesses to different regions of memory.

Having broached the topic of providing processes with isolated virtual memory, I devote Chapter 7 to processes. This chapter explains an API for creating processes. However, I also focus on protection mechanisms, not only by building on Chapter 6's introduction of virtual memory, but also by explaining other forms of protection that are used to protect processes from one another and to protect the operating system itself from the processes. Some of these protection mechanisms can be used to protect not just the storage of values in memory, but also longer-term data storage, such as files, and even network communication channels. Therefore, Chapter 7 lays some groundwork for the later treatment of these topics.

Chapter 7 also provides me an opportunity to clarify one point about threads left open by Chapter 2. By showing how operating systems provide a protective boundary between themselves and the running application processes, I can explain where threads fall relative to this boundary. In particular, there are threads that are contained entirely within the operating system kernel, others that are contained entirely within an application process, and yet others that cross the boundary, providing support from within the kernel for concurrent activities within the application process. Although it might seem natural to discuss these categories of threads in Chapter 2, the chapter on threads, I really need to wait for Chapter 7 in order to make any more sense out of the distinctions than I've managed in this introductory paragraph.

When two computations run concurrently on a single computer, the hard part of supporting controlled interaction is to keep the interaction under control. For example, in my earlier example of a pair of threads, one produces some data and the other consumes it. In such a situation, there is no great mystery to how the data can flow from one to the other, because both are using the same computer's memory. The hard part is regulating the use of that shared memory. This stands in contrast to the interactions across time and space, which I will address in Sections 1.7 and 1.8. If the producer and consumer run at different times, or on different computers, the operating system and middleware will need to take pains to convey the data from one to the other.

1.7 Supporting Interaction Across Time

General-purpose operating systems all support some mechanism for computations to leave results in long-term storage, from which they can be retrieved by later computations. Because this storage persists even when the system is shut down and started back up, it is known as *persistent storage*. Normally, operating systems provide persistent storage in the form of named files, which are organized into a hierarchy of directories or folders. Other forms of persistent storage, such as relational database tables and application-defined persistent objects, are generally supported by middleware. In Chapter 8, I focus on file systems, though I also explain some of the connections with middleware. For example, I compare the storage of file directories with that of database indexes. This comparison is particularly important as these areas are converging.

Already the underlying mechanisms are very similar, and file systems are starting to support indexing services like those provided by database systems.

There are two general categories of file APIs, both of which I cover in Chapter 8. The files can be made a part of the process's virtual memory space, accessible with normal load and store instructions, or they can be treated separately, as external entities to read and write with explicit operations.

Either kind of file API provides a relatively simple interface to some quite significant mechanisms hidden within the operating system. Chapter 8 also provides a survey of some of these mechanisms.

As an example of a simple interface to a sophisticated mechanism, an application programmer can make a file larger simply by writing additional data to the end of the file. The operating system, on the other hand, has to choose the location on disk where the new data will be stored. This disk space allocation has a strong influence on performance, because of the physical realities of how disk drives operate.

Another job for the file system is to keep track of where the data for each file is located. It also keeps track of other file-specific information, such as access permissions. Thus, the file system not only stores the files' data, but also stores *metadata*, which is data describing the data.

All these mechanisms are similar to those used by middleware for purposes such as allocating space to hold database tables. Operating systems and middleware also store information, such as file directories and database indexes, used to locate data. The data structures used for these naming and indexing purposes are designed for efficient access, just like those used to track the allocation of disk space to stored objects.

To make the job of operating systems and middleware even more challenging, persistent storage structures are expected to survive system crashes without significant loss of integrity. For example, it is not acceptable after a crash for specific disk space to be listed as available for allocation and also to be listed as allocated to a file. Such a confused state must not occur even if the crash happened just as the file was being created or deleted. Thus, Chapter 8 builds on Chapter 5's explanation of atomic transactions, while also outlining some other mechanisms that can be used to protect the integrity of metadata, directories, and indexes.

Persistent storage is crucially important, perhaps even more so in the Internet age than in prior times, because servers now hold huge amounts of data for use by clients all over the world. Nonetheless, persistent storage no longer plays as unique a role as it once did. Once upon a time, there were many computer systems in which the only way processes communicated was through persistent storage. Today, that is almost unthinkable, because communication often spans the Internet. Therefore, as I explain in Section 1.8, operating systems provide support for networking, and middleware provides further support for the construction of distributed systems.

1.8 Supporting Interaction Across Space

In order to build coherent software systems with components operating on differing computers, programmers need to solve lots of problems. Consider two examples: data flowing in a stream must be delivered in order, even if sent by varying routes through interconnected networks, and message delivery must be incorporated into the all-or-nothing guarantees provided by transactions. Luckily, application programmers don't need to solve most of these problems, because appropriate supporting services are provided by operating systems and middleware.

I divide my coverage of these services into two chapters. Chapter 9 provides a foundation regarding networking, so that this book will stand on its own if you have not previously studied networking. That chapter also covers services commonly provided by operating systems, or in close conjunction with operating systems, such as distributed file systems. Chapter 10, in contrast, explains the higher-level services that middleware provides for application-to-application communication, in such forms as messaging and web services. Each chapter introduces example APIs that you can use as an application programmer, as well as the more general principles behind those specific APIs.

Networking systems, as I explain in Chapter 9, are generally partitioned into layers, where each layer makes use of the services provided by the layer under it in order to provide additional services to the layer above it. At the bottom of the stack is the *physical layer*, concerned with such matters as copper, fiber optics, radio waves, voltages, and wavelengths. Above that is the *link layer*, which provides the service of transmitting a chunk of data to another computer on the same local network. This is the point where the operating system becomes involved. Building on the link-layer foundation, the operating system provides the services of the *network layer* and the *transport layer*. The network layer arranges for data to be relayed through interconnected networks so as to arrive at a computer that may be elsewhere in the world. The transport layer builds on top of this basic computer-to-computer data transmission to provide more useful application-to-application communication channels. For example, the transport layer typically uses sequence numbering and retransmission to provide applications the service of in-order, loss-free delivery of streams of data. This is the level of the most common operating system API, which provides *sockets*, that is, endpoints for these transport-layer connections.

The next layer up is the *application layer*. A few specialized application-layer services, such as distributed file systems, are integrated with operating systems. However, most application-layer software, such as web browsers and email programs, is written by application programmers. These applications can be built directly on an operating system's socket API and exchange streams of bytes that comply with standardized protocols. In Chapter 9, I illustrate this possibility by showing how web browsers and web servers communicate.

Alternatively, programmers of distributed applications can make use of middleware to work at a higher level than sending bytes over sockets. I show two basic approaches to this in Chapter 10: messaging and Remote Procedure Calls (RPCs). Web services are a particular approach to standardizing these kinds of higher-level application communication, and have been primarily used with RPCs: I show how to use them in this way.

In a *messaging* system, an application program requests the delivery of a message. The messaging system not only delivers the message, which lower-level networking could accomplish, but also provides additional services. For example, the messaging is often integrated with transaction processing. A successful transaction may retrieve a message from an incoming message queue, update a database in response to that message, and send a response message to an outgoing queue. If the transaction fails, none of these three changes will happen; the request message will remain in the incoming queue, the database will remain unchanged, and the response message will not be queued for further delivery. Another common service provided by messaging systems is to deliver a message to any number of recipients who have subscribed to receive messages of a particular kind; the sender need not be aware of who the actual receivers are.

Middleware can also provide a mechanism for *Remote Procedure Call* (*RPC*), in which communication between a client and a server is made to look like an ordinary programming language procedure call, such as invoking a method on an object. The only difference is that the object in question is located on a different computer, and so the call and return involve network communication. The middleware hides this complexity, so that the application programmer can work largely as though all the objects were local. In Chapter 10, I explain this concept more fully, and then go on to show how it plays out in the form of web services. A *web service* is an application-layer entity that programs can communicate with using standardized protocols similar to those that humans use to browse the web.

1.9 Security

Operating systems and middleware are often the targets of attacks by adversaries trying to defeat system security. Even attacks aimed at application programs often relate to operating systems and middleware. In particular, easily misused features of operating systems and middleware can be the root cause of an application-level vulnerability. On the other hand, operating systems and middleware provide many features that can be very helpful in constructing secure systems.

A system is secure if it provides an acceptably low risk that an adversary will prevent the system from achieving its owner's objectives. In Chapter 11, I explain in more detail how to think about risk and about the conflicting objectives of system owners and adversaries. In particular, I explain that some of the most common objectives for owners fall into four categories: confidentiality, integrity, availability, and accountability. A system provides *confidentiality* if it prevents inappropriate disclosure of information, *integrity* if it prevents inappropriate modification or destruction of information, and *availability* if it prevents inappropriate interference with legitimate usage. A system provides *accountability* if it provides ways to check how authorized users have exercised their authority. All of these rely on *authentication*, the ability of a system to verify the identity of a user.

Many people have a narrow view of system security. They think of those features that would not even exist, were it not for security issues. Clearly, logging in with a password (or some other, better form of authentication) is a component of system security. Equally clearly, having permission to read some files, but not others, is a component of system security, as are cryptographic protocols used to protect network communication from interception. However, this view of security is dangerously incomplete.

You need to keep in mind that the design of any component of the operating system can have security consequences. Even those parts whose design is dominated by other considerations must also reflect some proactive consideration of security consequences, or the overall system will be insecure. In fact, this is an important principle that extends beyond the operating system to include application software and the humans who operate it.

Therefore, I will make a habit of addressing security issues in every chapter, rather than only at the end of the book. Specifically, each chapter concludes with a section pointing out some of the key security issues associated with that chapter's topic. I also provide a more coherent treatment of security by concluding the book as a whole with Chapter 11, which is devoted exclusively to security. That chapter takes a holistic approach to security, in which human factors play as important a role as technical ones.

Exercises

1.1 What is the difference between an operating system and middleware?

1.2 What do operating systems and middleware have in common?

1.3 What is the relationship between threads and processes?

1.4 What is one way an operating system might isolate threads from unwanted interactions, and what is one way that middleware might do so?

1.5 What is one way an operating system might provide persistent storage, and what is one way middleware might do so?

1.6 What is one way an operating system might support network communication, and what is one way middleware might do so?

1.7 Of all the topics previewed in this chapter, which one are you most looking forward to learning more about? Why?

▣ Programming Project

1.1 Write, test, and debug a program in the language of your choice to carry out any task you choose. Then write a list of all the services you suspect the operating system is providing in order to support the execution of your sample program. If you think the program is also relying on any middleware services, list those as well.

○ Exploration Projects

1.1 Look through the titles of the papers presented at several recent conferences hosted by the USENIX Association (The Advanced Computing Systems Association); you can find the conference proceedings at *www.usenix.org*. To get a better idea of what an individual paper is about, click the title to show the abstract, which is a short summary of the paper. Based on titles and abstracts, pick out a few papers that you think would make interesting supplementary reading as you work your way through this book. Write down a list showing the bibliographic information for the papers you selected and, as near as you can estimate, where in this book's table of contents they would be appropriate to read.

1.2 Conduct a simple experiment in which you take some action on a computer system and observe what the response is. You can choose any action you wish and any computer system for which you have appropriate access. You can either observe a quantitative result, such as how long the response takes or how much output is produced, or a qualitative result, such as in what form the response arrives. Now, try replicating the experiment. Do you always get the same result? Similar ones? Are there any factors that need to be controlled in order to get results that are at least approximately repeatable? For example, to get consistent times, do you need to reboot the system between each trial and prevent other people from using the system? To get consistent output, do you need to make sure input files are kept unchanged? If your action involves a physical device, such as a printer, do you have to control variables such as whether the printer is stocked with paper? Finally, write up a careful report, in which you explain both what experiment you tried and what results you observed. You should explain how repeatable the results proved to be and what limits there were on the repeatability. You should describe the hardware and software configuration in enough detail that someone else could replicate your experiment and would be likely to get similar results.

Notes

The idea that an operating system should isolate computations from unwanted interactions, and yet support desirable interactions, has a long heritage. A 1962 paper [34] by Corbató, Daggett, and Daley points out that "different user programs if simultaneously in core memory may interfere with each other or the supervisor program so some form of memory protection mode should be available when operating user programs." However, that same paper goes on to say that although "great care went into making each user independent of the other users . . . it would be a useful extension of the system if this were not always the case," so that the computer system could support group work, such as war games.

Middleware is not as well-known to the general public as operating systems are, though commercial information-system developers would be lost without it. One attempt to introduce middleware to a somewhat broader audience was Bernstein's 1996 survey article [16].

The USENIX Association, mentioned in Exploration Project 1.1, is only one of several very fine professional societies holding conferences related to the subject matter of this book. The reason why I specifically recommended looking through their proceedings is that they tend to be particularly accessible to students. In part this is because USENIX focuses on bringing practitioners and academics together; thus, the papers generally are pragmatic without being superficial. For recent papers, the full text is not available on their web site. However, any college or university can get free access to the papers, as well as other significant benefits for students.

2

Threads

2.1 Introduction

Computer programs consist of instructions, and computers carry out sequences of computational steps specified by those instructions. We call each sequence of computational steps that are strung together one after another a *thread*. The simplest programs to write are single-threaded, with instructions that should be executed one after another in a single sequence. However, in Section 2.2, you will learn how to write programs that produce more than one thread of execution, each an independent sequence of computational steps, with few if any ordering constraints between the steps in one thread and those in another. Multiple threads can also come into existence by running multiple programs, or by running the same program more than once.

Note the distinction between a program and a thread; the program contains instructions, whereas the thread consists of the execution of those instructions. Even for single-threaded programs, this distinction matters. If a program contains a loop, then a very short program could give rise to a very long thread of execution. Also, running the same program ten times will give rise to ten threads, all executing one program. Figure 2.1 summarizes how threads arise from programs.

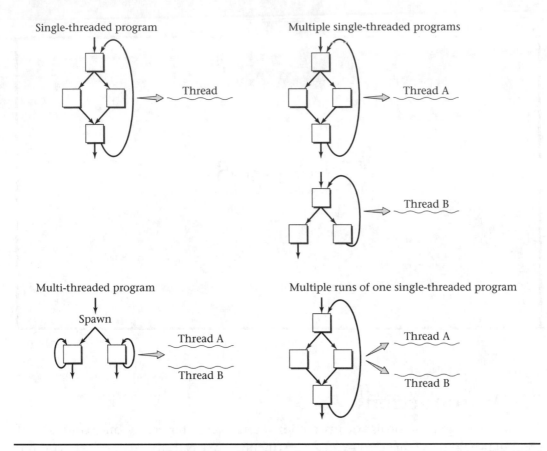

Figure 2.1 Programs give rise to threads

Each thread has a lifetime, extending from the time its first instruction execution occurs until the time of its last instruction execution. If two threads have overlapping lifetimes, as illustrated in Figure 2.2, we say they are *concurrent*. One of the most fundamental goals of an operating system is to allow multiple threads to run concurrently on the same computer. That is, rather than waiting until the first thread has completed before a second thread can run, it should be possible to divide the computer's attention between them. If the computer hardware includes multiple processors, then it will naturally be possible to run threads concurrently, one per processor. However, the operating system's users will often want to run more concurrent threads than the hardware has processors, for reasons described in Section 2.3. Therefore, the operating system will need to divide each processor's attention between multiple threads. In this introductory textbook I will mostly limit myself to the case of all the threads needing

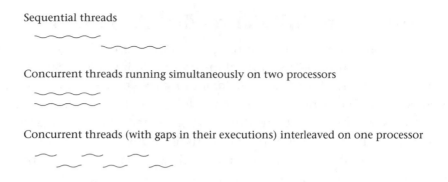

Figure 2.2   Sequential and concurrent threads

to be run on a single processor. I will explicitly indicate those places where I do address the more general multi-processor case.

In order to make the concept of concurrent threads concrete, Section 2.2 shows how to write a program that spawns multiple threads each time the program is run. Once you know how to create threads, I will explain in Section 2.3 some of the reasons why it is desirable to run multiple threads concurrently and will offer some typical examples of the uses to which threads are put.

These first two sections explain the application programmer's view of threads: how and why the programmer would use concurrent threads. This sets us up for the next question: how does the operating system support the application programmer's desire for concurrently executing threads? In Sections 2.4 and 2.5, we will examine how the system does so. In this chapter, we will consider only the fundamentals of how the processor's attention is switched from one thread to another. Some of the related issues I address in other chapters include deciding which thread to run at each point (Chapter 3) and controlling interaction among the threads (Chapters 4, 5, 6, and 7). Also, as explained in Chapter 1, I will wait until Chapter 7 to explain the protection boundary surrounding the operating system. Thus, I will need to wait until that chapter to distinguish threads that reside entirely within that boundary, threads provided from inside the boundary for use outside of it, and threads residing entirely outside the boundary (known as *user-level threads* or, in Microsoft Windows, *fibers*).

Finally, the chapter concludes with the standard features of this book: a brief discussion of security issues, followed by exercises, programming and exploration projects, and notes.

2.2 Example of Multi-Threaded Programs

Whenever a program initially starts running, the computer carries out the program's instructions in a single thread. Therefore, if the program is intended to run in multiple threads, the original thread needs at some point to spawn off a child thread that does some actions, while the parent thread continues to do others. (For more than two threads, the program can repeat the thread-creation step.) Most programming languages have an application programming interface (or API) for threads that includes a way to create a child thread. In this section, I will use the Java API and the API for C that is called *pthreads*, for *POSIX threads*. (As you will see throughout the book, POSIX is a comprehensive specification for UNIX-like systems, including many APIs beyond just thread creation.)

Realistic multi-threaded programming requires the control of thread interactions, using techniques I show in Chapter 4. Therefore, my examples in this chapter are quite simple, just enough to show the spawning of threads.

To demonstrate the independence of the two threads, I will have both the parent and the child thread respond to a timer. One will sleep three seconds and then print out a message. The other will sleep five seconds and then print out a message. Because the threads execute concurrently, the second message will appear approximately two seconds after the first. (In Programming Projects 2.1, 2.2, and 2.3, you can write a somewhat more realistic program, where one thread responds to user input and the other to the timer.)

Figure 2.3 shows the Java version of this program. The **main** program first creates a **Thread** object called **childThread**. The **Runnable** object associated with the child thread has a **run** method that sleeps three seconds (expressed as 3000 milliseconds) and then prints a message. This **run** method starts running when the main procedure invokes **childThread.start()**. Because the **run** method is in a separate thread, the main thread can continue on to the subsequent steps, sleeping five seconds (5000 milliseconds) and printing its own message.

Figure 2.4 is the equivalent program in C, using the pthreads API. The **child** procedure sleeps three seconds and prints a message. The **main** procedure creates a **child_thread** running the **child** procedure, and then itself sleeps five seconds and prints a message. The most significant difference from the Java API is that **pthread_create** both creates the child thread and starts it running, whereas in Java those are two separate steps.

In addition to portable APIs, such as the Java and pthreads APIs, many systems provide their own non-portable APIs. For example, Microsoft Windows has the Win32 API, with procedures such as **CreateThread** and **Sleep**. In Programming Project 2.4, you can modify the program from Figure 2.4 to use this API.

```java
public class Simple2Threads {
  public static void main(String args[]){
    Thread childThread = new Thread(new Runnable(){
        public void run(){
          sleep(3000);
          System.out.println("Child is done sleeping 3 seconds.");
        }
      });
    childThread.start();
    sleep(5000);
    System.out.println("Parent is done sleeping 5 seconds.");
  }

  private static void sleep(int milliseconds){
    try{
      Thread.sleep(milliseconds);
    } catch(InterruptedException e){
      // ignore this exception; it won't happen anyhow
    }
  }
}
```

Figure 2.3   A simple multi-threaded program in Java

```c
#include <pthread.h>
#include <signal.h>
#include <stdio.h>

static void *child(void *ignored){
  sleep(3);
  printf("Child is done sleeping 3 seconds.\n");
  return NULL;
}

int main(int argc, char *argv[]){
  pthread_t child_thread;
  int code;

  code = pthread_create(&child_thread, NULL, child, NULL);
  if(code){
    fprintf(stderr, "pthread_create failed with code %d\n", code);
  }
  sleep(5);
  printf("Parent is done sleeping 5 seconds.\n");
  return 0;
}
```

Figure 2.4   A simple multi-threaded program in C

2.3 Reasons for Using Concurrent Threads

You have now seen how a single execution of one program can result in more than one thread. Presumably, you were already at least somewhat familiar with generating multiple threads by running multiple programs, or by running the same program multiple times. Regardless of how the threads come into being, we are faced with a question. Why is it desirable for the computer to execute multiple threads concurrently, rather than waiting for one to finish before starting another? Fundamentally, most uses for concurrent threads serve one of two goals:

Responsiveness: allowing the computer system to respond quickly to something external to the system, such as a human user or another computer system. Even if one thread is in the midst of a long computation, another thread can respond to the external agent. Our example programs in Section 2.2 illustrated responsiveness: both the parent and the child thread responded to a timer.

Resource utilization: keeping most of the hardware resources busy most of the time. Even if one thread has no need for a particular piece of hardware, another may be able to make productive use of it.

Each of these two general themes has many variations, some of which we explore in the remainder of this section. A third reason why programmers sometimes use concurrent threads is as a tool for modularization. With this, a complex system may be decomposed into a group of interacting threads.

Let's start by considering the responsiveness of a web server, which provides many client computers with the specific web pages they request over the Internet. Whenever a client computer makes a network connection to the server, it sends a sequence of bytes that contain the name of the desired web page. Therefore, before the server program can respond, it needs to read in those bytes, typically using a loop that continues reading in bytes from the network connection until it sees the end of the request. Suppose one of the clients is connecting using a very slow network connection, perhaps via a dial-up modem. The server may read the first part of the request and then have to wait a considerable length of time before the rest of the request arrives over the network. What happens to other clients in the meantime? It would be unacceptable for a whole web site to grind to a halt, unable to serve any clients, just waiting for one slow client to finish issuing its request. One way some web servers avoid this unacceptable situation is by using multiple threads, one for each client connection, so that even if one thread is waiting for data from one client, other threads can continue interacting with the other clients. Figure 2.5 illustrates the unacceptable single-threaded web server and the more realistic multi-threaded one.

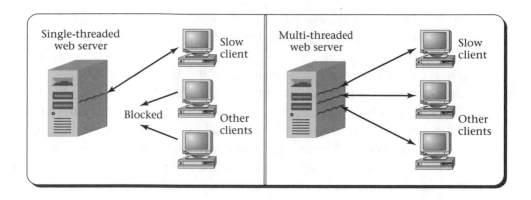

Figure 2.5   Single-threaded and multi-threaded web servers

On the client side, a web browser may also illustrate the need for responsiveness. Suppose you start loading in a very large web page, which takes considerable time to download. Would you be happy if the computer froze up until the download finished? Probably not. You expect to be able to work on a spreadsheet in a different window, or scroll through the first part of the web page to read as much as has already downloaded, or at least click on the Stop button to give up on the time-consuming download. Each of these can be handled by having one thread tied up loading the web page over the network, while another thread is responsive to your actions at the keyboard and mouse.

This web browser scenario also lets me foreshadow later portions of the textbook concerning the controlled interaction between threads. Note that I sketched several different things you might want to do while the web page downloaded. In the first case, when you work on a spreadsheet, the two concurrent threads have almost nothing to do with one another, and the operating system's job, beyond allowing them to run concurrently, will mostly consist of isolating each from the other, so that a bug in the web browser doesn't overwrite part of your spreadsheet, for example. This is generally done by encapsulating the threads in separate protection environments known as *processes*, as we will discuss in Chapters 6 and 7. (Some systems call processes *tasks*, while others use *task* as a synonym for *thread*.) If, on the other hand, you continue using the browser's user interface while the download continues, the concurrent threads are closely related parts of a single application, and the operating system need not isolate the threads from one another. However, it may still need to provide mechanisms for regulating their interaction. For example, some coordination between the downloading thread and the user-interface thread is needed to ensure that you can scroll through as much of the page as has been downloaded, but no further. This coordination between threads is known as *synchronization* and is the topic of Chapters 4 and 5.

Turning to the utilization of hardware resources, the most obvious scenario is when you have a dual-processor computer. In this case, if the system ran only one thread at a time, only half the processing capacity would ever be used. Even if the human user of the computer system doesn't have more than one task to carry out, there may be useful housekeeping work to keep the second processor busy. For example, most operating systems, if asked to allocate memory for an application program's use, will store all zeros into the memory first. Rather than holding up each memory allocation while the zeroing is done, the operating system can have a thread that proactively zeros out unused memory, so that when needed, it will be all ready. If this housekeeping work (zeroing of memory) were done on demand, it would slow down the system's real work; by using a concurrent thread to utilize the available hardware more fully, the performance is improved. This example also illustrates that not all threads need to come from user programs. A thread can be part of the operating system itself, as in the example of the thread zeroing out unused memory.

Even in a single-processor system, resource utilization considerations may justify using concurrent threads. Remember that a computer system contains hardware resources, such as disk drives, other than the processor. Suppose you have two tasks to complete on your PC: you want to scan all the files on disk for viruses, and you want to do a complicated photo-realistic rendering of a three-dimensional scene including not only solid objects, but also shadows cast on partially transparent smoke clouds. From experience, you know that each of these will take about an hour. If you do one and then the other, it will take two hours. If instead you do the two concurrently—running the virus scanner in one window while you run the graphics rendering program in another window—you may be pleasantly surprised to find both jobs done in only an hour and a half.

The explanation for the half-hour savings in elapsed time is that the virus scanning program spends most of its time using the disk drive to read files, with only modest bursts of processor activity each time the disk completes a read request, whereas the rendering program spends most of its time doing processing, with very little disk activity. As illustrated in Figure 2.6, running them in sequence leaves one part of the computer's hardware idle much of the time, whereas running the two concurrently keeps the processor and disk drive both busy, improving the overall system efficiency. Of course, this assumes the operating system's scheduler is smart enough to let the virus scanner have the processor's attention (briefly) whenever a disk request completes, rather than making it wait for the rendering program. I will address this issue in Chapter 3.

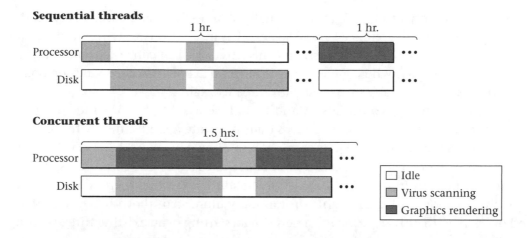

Figure 2.6 Overlapping processor-intensive and disk-intensive activities

As you have now seen, threads can come from multiple sources and serve multiple roles. They can be internal portions of the operating system, as in the example of zeroing out memory, or part of the user's application software. In the latter case, they can either be dividing up the work within a multi-threaded process, such as the web server and web browser examples, or can come from multiple independent processes, as when a web browser runs in one window and a spreadsheet in another. Regardless of these variations, the typical reasons for running the threads concurrently remain unchanged: either to provide increased responsiveness or to improve system efficiency by more fully utilizing the hardware. Moreover, the basic mechanism used to divide the processor's attention among multiple threads remains the same in these different cases as well; I describe that mechanism in Sections 2.4 and 2.5. Of course, some cases require the additional protection mechanisms provided by processes, which we discuss in Chapters 6 and 7. However, even then, it is still necessary to leave off work on one thread and pick up work on another.

2.4 Switching Between Threads

In order for the operating system to have more than one thread underway on a processor, the system needs to have some mechanism for switching attention between threads. In particular, there needs to be some way to leave off from in the middle of a thread's sequence of instructions, work for a while on other threads, and then pick back up in the original thread right where it left off. In order to explain thread switching as simply as possible, I will initially assume that each thread is executing code that contains, every once in a while, explicit instructions to temporarily switch to another thread. Once you understand this mechanism, I can then build on it for the more realistic case where the thread contains no explicit thread-switching points, but rather is automatically interrupted for thread switches.

Suppose we have two threads, A and B, and we use A1, A2, A3, and so forth as names for the instruction execution steps that constitute A, and similarly for B. In this case, one possible execution sequence might be as shown in Figure 2.7. As I will explain subsequently, when thread A executes `switchFromTo(A,B)` the computer starts executing instructions from thread B. In a more realistic example, there might be more than two threads, and each might run for many more steps (both between switches and overall), with only occasionally a new thread starting or an existing thread exiting.

thread A	thread B
A1	
A2	
A3	
`switchFromTo(A,B)`	
	B1
	B2
	B3
	`switchFromTo(B,A)`
A4	
A5	
`switchFromTo(A,B)`	
	B4
	B5
	B6
	B7
	`switchFromTo(B,A)`
A6	
A7	
A8	
`switchFromTo(A,B)`	
	B8
	B9

Figure 2.7 Switching between threads

Our goal is that the steps of each thread form a coherent execution sequence. That is, from the perspective of thread A, its execution should not be much different from one in which A1 through A8 occurred consecutively, without interruption, and similarly for thread B's steps B1 through B9. Suppose, for example, steps A1 and A2 load two values from memory into registers, A3 adds them, placing the sum in a register, and A4 doubles that register's contents, so as to get twice the sum. In this case, we want to make sure that A4 really does double the sum computed by A1 through A3, rather than doubling some other value that thread B's steps B1 through B3 happen to store in the same register. Thus, we can see that switching threads cannot simply be a matter of a jump instruction transferring control to the appropriate instruction in the other thread. At a minimum, we will also have to save registers into memory and restore them from there, so that when a thread resumes execution, its own values will be back in the registers.

In order to focus on the essentials, let's put aside the issue of how threads start and exit. Instead, let's focus just on the normal case where one thread in progress puts itself on hold and switches to another thread where that other thread last left off, such as the switch from A5 to B4 in the preceding example. To support switching threads, the operating system will need to keep information about each thread, such as at what point that thread should resume execution. If this information is stored in a block of memory for each thread, then we can use the addresses of those memory areas to refer to the threads. The block of memory containing information about a thread is called a *thread control block* or *task control block (TCB)*. Thus, another way of saying that we use the addresses of these blocks is to say that we use pointers to thread control blocks to refer to threads.

Our fundamental thread-switching mechanism will be the `switchFromTo` procedure, which takes two of these thread control block pointers as parameters: one specifying the thread that is being switched out of, and one specifying the next thread, which is being switched into. In our running example, `A` and `B` are pointer variables pointing to the two threads' control blocks, which we use alternately in the roles of outgoing thread and next thread. For example, the program for thread A contains code after instruction A5 to switch from `A` to `B`, and the program for thread B contains code after instruction B3 to switch from `B` to `A`. Of course, this assumes that each thread knows both its own identity and the identity of the thread to switch to. Later, we will see how this unrealistic assumption can be eliminated. For now, though, let's see how we could write the `switchFromTo` procedure so that `switchFromTo(A,B)` would save the current execution status information into the structure pointed to by `A`, read back previously saved information from the structure pointed to by `B`, and resume where thread B left off.

We already saw that the execution status information to save includes not only a position in the program, often called the *program counter (PC)* or *instruction pointer (IP)*, but also the contents of registers. Another critical part of the execution status for programs compiled with most higher level language compilers is a portion of the memory used to store a stack, along with a stack pointer register that indicates the position in memory of the current top of the stack. You likely have encountered this form of storage in some prior course—computer organization, programing language principles, or even introduction to computer science. If not, Appendix A provides the information you will need before proceeding with the remainder of this chapter.

When a thread resumes execution, it must find the stack the way it left it. For example, suppose thread A pushes two items on the stack and then is put on hold for a while, during which thread B executes. When thread A resumes execution, it should find the two items it pushed at the top of the stack—even if thread B did some pushing of its own and has not yet gotten around to popping. We can arrange for this by giving each thread its own stack, setting aside a separate portion of memory for each of them. When thread A is executing, the *stack pointer* (or SP register) will be pointing somewhere within thread A's stack area, indicating how much of that area is occupied at that time. Upon switching to thread B, we need to save away A's stack pointer, just like other registers, and load in thread B's stack pointer. That way, while thread B is executing, the stack pointer will move up and down within B's stack area, in accordance with B's own pushes and pops.

Having discovered this need to have separate stacks and switch stack pointers, we can simplify the saving of all other registers by pushing them onto the stack before switching and popping them off the stack after switching, as shown in Figure 2.8. We can use this approach to outline the code for switching from the outgoing thread to the next thread, using **outgoing** and **next** as the two pointers to thread control blocks. (When switching from **A** to **B**, **outgoing** will be **A** and **next** will be **B**. Later, when switching back from **B** to **A**, **outgoing** will be **B** and **next** will be **A**.) We will use **outgoing->SP** and **outgoing->IP** to refer to two slots within the structure pointed to by **outgoing**, the slot used to save the stack pointer and the one used to save the instruction pointer. With these assumptions, our code has the following general form:

```
    push each register on the (outgoing thread's) stack
    store the stack pointer into outgoing->SP
    load the stack pointer from next->SP
    store label L's address into outgoing->IP
    load in next->IP and jump to that address
L:
    pop each register from the (resumed outgoing thread's) stack
```

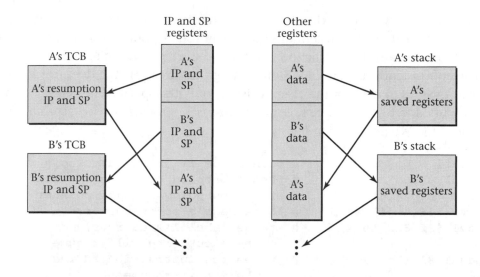

Figure 2.8   Saving registers in thread control blocks and per-thread stacks

Note that the code before the label (L) is done at the time of switching away from the outgoing thread, whereas the code after that label is done later, upon resuming execution when some other thread switches back to the original one.

This code not only stores the outgoing thread's stack pointer away, but also restores the next thread's stack pointer. Later, the same code will be used to switch back. Therefore, we can count on the original thread's stack pointer to have been restored when control jumps to label L. Thus, when the registers are popped, they will be popped from the original thread's stack, matching the pushes at the beginning of the code.

We can see how this general pattern plays out in a real system, by looking at the thread-switching code from the Linux operating system for the i386 architecture. (The i386 architecture is also known as the x86 or IA-32; it is a popular processor architecture used in standard personal computer processors such as the Pentium 4 and the Athlon.) If you don't want to see real code, you can skip ahead to the paragraph after the block of assembly code. However, even if you aren't familiar with i386 assembly language, you ought to be able to see how this code matches the preceding pattern.

This is real code extracted from the Linux kernel, though with some peripheral complications left out. The stack pointer register is named **%esp**, and when this code starts running, the registers known as **%ebx** and **%esi** contain the **outgoing** and **next** pointers, respectively. Each of those pointers is the address of a thread control block.

The location at offset 812 within the TCB contains the thread's instruction pointer, and the location at offset 816 contains the thread's stack pointer. (That is, these memory locations contain the instruction pointer and stack pointer to use when resuming that thread's execution.) The code surrounding the thread switch does not keep any important values in most of the other registers; only the special flags register and the register named %ebp need to be saved and restored. With that as background, here is the code, with explanatory comments:

```
        pushfl                  # pushes the flags on outgoing's stack
        pushl %ebp              # pushes %ebp on outgoing's stack
        movl %esp,816(%ebx)     # stores outgoing's stack pointer
        movl 816(%esi),%esp     # loads next's stack pointer
        movl $1f,812(%ebx)      # stores label 1's address,
                                #     where outgoing will resume
        pushl 812(%esi)         # pushes the instruction address
                                #     where next resumes
        ret                     # pops and jumps to that address
1:      popl %ebp               # upon later resuming outgoing,
                                #     restores %ebp
        popfl                   # restores the flags
```

Having seen the core idea of how a processor is switched from running one thread to running another, we can now eliminate the assumption that each thread switch contains the explicit names of the outgoing and next threads. That is, we want to get away from having to name threads A and B in switchFromTo(A,B). It is easy enough to know which thread is being switched away from, if we just keep track at all times of the currently running thread, for example, by storing a pointer to its control block in a global variable called current. That leaves the question of which thread is being selected to run next. What we will do is have the operating system keep track of all the threads in some sort of data structure, such as a list. There will be a procedure, chooseNextThread(), which consults that data structure and, using some scheduling policy, decides which thread to run next. In Chapter 3, I will explain how this scheduling is done; for now, take it as a black box. Using this tool, one can write a procedure, yield(), which performs the following four steps:

```
outgoing = current;
next = chooseNextThread();
current = next;    // so the global variable will be right
switchFromTo(outgoing, next);
```

Now, every time a thread decides it wants to take a break and let other threads run for a while, it can just invoke yield(). This is essentially the approach taken by real systems, such as Linux. One complication in a multiprocessor system is that the `current` thread needs to be recorded on a per-processor basis.

Thread switching is often called *context switching*, because it switches from the execution context of one thread to that of another thread. Many authors, however, use the phrase *context switching* differently, to refer to switching processes with their protection contexts—a topic we will discuss in Chapter 7. If the distinction matters, the clearest choice is to avoid the ambiguous term *context switching* and use the more specific *thread switching* or *process switching*.

Thread switching is the most common form of *dispatching* a thread, that is, of causing a processor to execute it. The only way a thread can be dispatched without a thread switch is if a processor is idle.

2.5 Preemptive Multitasking

At this point, I have explained thread switching well enough for systems that employ *cooperative multitasking*, that is, where each thread's program contains explicit code at each point where a thread switch should occur. However, more realistic operating systems use what is called *preemptive multitasking*, in which the program's code need not contain any thread switches, yet thread switches will nonetheless automatically be performed from time to time.

One reason to prefer preemptive multitasking is because it means that buggy code in one thread cannot hold all others up. Consider, for example, a loop that is expected to iterate only a few times; it would seem safe, in a cooperative multitasking system, to put thread switches only before and after it, rather than also in the loop body. However, a bug could easily turn the loop into an infinite one, which would hog the processor forever. With preemptive multitasking, the thread may still run forever, but at least from time to time it will be put on hold and other threads will be allowed to progress.

Another reason to prefer preemptive multitasking is that it allows thread switches to be performed when they best achieve the goals of responsiveness and resource utilization. For example, the operating system can preempt a thread when input becomes available for a waiting thread or when a hardware device falls idle.

Even with preemptive multitasking, it may occasionally be useful for a thread to voluntarily give way to the other threads, rather than to run as long as it is allowed. Therefore, even preemptive systems normally provide `yield()`. The name varies depending on the API, but often has `yield` in it; for example, the pthreads API uses the name `sched_yield()`. One exception to this naming pattern is the Win32 API of Microsoft Windows, which uses the name `SwitchToThread()` for the equivalent of `yield()`.

Preemptive multitasking does not need any fundamentally different thread switching mechanism; it simply needs the addition of a hardware interrupt mechanism. In case you are not familiar with how interrupts work, I will first take a moment to review this aspect of hardware organization.

Normally a processor will execute consecutive instructions one after another, deviating from sequential flow only when directed by an explicit jump instruction or by some variant such as the `ret` instruction used in the Linux code for thread switching. However, there is always some mechanism by which external hardware (such as a disk drive or a network interface) can signal that it needs attention. A hardware timer can also be set to demand attention periodically, such as every millisecond. When an I/O device or timer needs attention, an *interrupt* occurs, which is almost as though a procedure call instruction were forcibly inserted between the currently executing instruction and the next one. Thus, rather than moving on to the program's next instruction, the processor jumps off to a special procedure called the *interrupt handler*. The interrupt handler, which is part of the operating system, deals with the hardware device and then executes a *return from interrupt* instruction, which jumps back to the instruction that had been about to execute when the interrupt occurred. Of course, in order for the program's execution to continue as expected, the interrupt handler needs to be careful to save all the registers at the start and restore them before returning.

Using this interrupt mechanism, an operating system can provide preemptive multitasking. When an interrupt occurs, the interrupt handler first takes care of the immediate needs, such as accepting data from a network interface controller or updating the system's idea of the current time by one millisecond. Then, rather than simply restoring the registers and executing a return from interrupt instruction, the interrupt handler checks whether it would be a good time to preempt the current thread and switch to another. For example, if the interrupt signaled the arrival of data for which a thread had long been waiting, it might make sense to switch to that thread. Or, if the interrupt was from the timer and the current thread had been executing for a long time, it may make sense to give another thread a chance. These policy decisions are related to scheduling, the topic of Chapter 3. In any case, if the operating system decides to preempt the current thread, the interrupt handler switches threads using a mechanism such as the `switchFromTo` procedure.

2.6 Security and Threads

One premise of this book is that every topic raises its own security issues. Multi-threading is no exception. However, this section will be quite brief, because with the material covered in this chapter, I can present only the security problems connected with multi-threading, not the solutions. So that I do not divide problems from their solutions, this section provides only a thumbnail sketch, leaving serious consideration of the problems and their solutions to the chapters that introduce the necessary tools.

Security issues arise when some threads are unable to execute because others are hogging the computer's attention. Security issues also arise because of unwanted interactions between threads. Unwanted interactions include a thread writing into storage that another thread is trying to use or reading from storage that another thread considers confidential. These problems are most likely to arise if the programmer has a difficult time understanding how the threads may interact with one another.

The security section in Chapter 3 addresses the problem of some threads monopolizing the computer. The security sections in Chapters 4, 5, and 7 address the problem of controlling threads' interaction. Each of these chapters also has a strong emphasis on design approaches that make interactions easy to understand, thereby minimizing the risks that arise from incomplete understanding.

Exercises

2.1 Based on the examples in Section 2.2, name at least one difference between the **sleep** procedure in the POSIX API and the **Thread.sleep** method in the Java API.

2.2 Give at least three more examples, beyond those given in the text, where it would be useful to run more concurrent threads on a computer than that computer's number of processors. Indicate how your examples fit the general reasons to use concurrency listed in the text.

2.3 Suppose thread A goes through a loop 100 times, each time performing one disk I/O operation, taking 10 milliseconds, and then some computation, taking 1 millisecond. While each 10-millisecond disk operation is in progress, thread A cannot make any use of the processor. Thread B runs for 1 second, purely in the processor, with no I/O. One millisecond of processor time is spent each time the processor switches threads; other than this switching cost, there is no problem with the processor working on thread B during one of thread A's I/O operations. (The processor and disk drive do not contend for memory access bandwidth, for example.)

    (a) Suppose the processor and disk work purely on thread A until its completion, and then the processor switches to thread B and runs all of that thread. What will the total elapsed time be?

    (b) Suppose the processor starts out working on thread A, but every time thread A performs a disk operation, the processor switches to B during the operation and then back to A upon the disk operation's completion. What will the total elapsed time be?

2.4 Consider a uniprocessor system where each arrival of input from an external source triggers the creation and execution of a new thread, which at its completion produces some output. We are interested in the response time from triggering input to resulting output.

(a) Input arrives at time 0 and again after 1 second, 2 seconds, and so forth. Each arrival triggers a thread that takes 600 milliseconds to run. Before the thread can run, it must be created and dispatched, which takes 10 milliseconds. What is the average response time for these inputs?

(b) Now a second source of input is added, with input arriving at times 0.1 seconds, 1.1 seconds, 2.1 seconds, and so forth. These inputs trigger threads that take only 100 milliseconds to run, but they still need 10 milliseconds to create and dispatch. When an input arrives, the resulting new thread is not created or dispatched until the processor is idle. What is the average response time for this second class of inputs? What is the combined average response time for the two classes?

(c) Suppose we change the way the second class of input is handled. When the input arrives, the new thread is immediately created and dispatched, even if that preempts an already running thread. When the new thread completes, the preempted thread resumes execution after a 1-millisecond thread-switching delay. What is the average response time for each class of inputs? What is the combined average for the two together?

2.5 When control switches away from a thread and later switches back to that thread, the thread resumes execution where it left off. Similarly, when a procedure calls a subroutine and later the subroutine returns, execution picks back up where it left off in the calling procedure. Given this similarity, what is the essential difference between thread switching and subroutine call/return? You saw that each thread has a separate stack, each in its own area of memory. Why is this not necessary for subroutine invocations?

▣ Programming Projects

2.1 If you program in C, read the documentation for **pthread_kill**. Using this information and the model provided in Figure 2.4 on page 23, write a program where the initial (main) thread creates a second thread. The main thread should read input from the keyboard, waiting until the user presses the Enter key. At that point, it should kill off the second thread and print out a message reporting that it has done so. Meanwhile, the second thread should be in an infinite loop, each time around sleeping five seconds and then printing out a message. Try running your program. Can the sleeping thread print its periodic messages while the main thread is waiting for keyboard input? Can the main thread read input, kill the sleeping thread, and print a message while the sleeping thread is in the early part of one of its five-second sleeps?

2.2 If you program in Java, read the documentation for the **stop** method in the **Thread** class. (Ignore the information about it being deprecated. That will make sense only after you read Chapter 4 of this book.) Write the program described in Programming Project 2.1, except do so in Java. You can use the program shown in Figure 2.3 on page 23 as a model.

2.3 Read the API documentation for some programming language other than C, C++, or Java to find out how to spawn off a thread and how to sleep. Write a program in this language equivalent to the Java and C example programs in Figures 2.3 and 2.4 on page 23. Then do the equivalent of Programming Projects 2.1 and 2.2 using the language you have chosen.

2.4 If you program in C under Microsoft Windows, you can use the native Win32 API instead of the portable pthreads API. Read the documentation of **CreateThread** and **Sleep** and modify the program of Figure 2.4 on page 23 to use these procedures.

Exploration Projects

2.1 Try the experiment of running a disk-intensive process and a processor-intensive process concurrently. Write a report carefully explaining what you did and in which hardware and software system context you did it, so that someone else could replicate your results. Your report should show how the elapsed time for the concurrent execution compared with the times from sequential execution. Be sure to do multiple trials and to reboot the system before each run to eliminate effects that come from keeping disk data in memory for re-use. If you can find documentation for any performance-monitoring tools on your system, which would provide information such as the percentage of CPU time used or the number of disk I/O operations per second, you can include this information in your report as well.

2.2 Early versions of Microsoft Windows and Mac OS used cooperative multitasking. Use the web, or other sources of information, to find out when each switched to preemptive multitasking. Can you find and summarize any examples of what was written about this change at the time?

2.3 How frequently does a system switch threads? You can find this out on a Linux system by using the vmstat program. Read the man page for **vmstat**, and then run it to find the number of context switches per second. Write a report in which you carefully explain what you did and the hardware and software system context in which you did it, so that someone else could replicate your results.

Notes

The idea of executing multiple threads concurrently seems to have occurred to several people (more or less concurrently) in the late 1950s. They did not use the word *thread*, however. For example, a 1959 article by E. F. Codd et al. [30] stated that "the second form of parallelism, which we shall call *nonlocal*, provides for concurrent execution of instructions which need not be neighbors in an instruction stream, but which may belong, if you please, to entirely separate and unrelated programs." From the beginning, authors were aware of both reasons for using concurrency that I have emphasized (resource utilization and responsiveness). The same article by Codd et al., for example, reports that "one object of concurrently running tasks which belong to different (perhaps totally unrelated) programs is to achieve a more balanced loading of the facilities than would be possible if all the tasks belonged to a single program. Another object is to achieve a specified real-time response in a situation in which messages, transactions, etc., are to be processed on-line."

I mentioned that an operating system may dedicate a thread to preemptively zeroing out memory. One example of this is the *zero page thread* in Microsoft Windows. See Russinovich and Solomon's book [109] for details.

I extracted the Linux thread switching code from version 2.6.0-test1 of the kernel. Details (such as the offsets 812 and 816) may differ in other versions. The kernel source code is written in a combination of assembly language and C, contained in **include/asm-i386/system.h** as included into **kernel/sched.c**. To obtain pure assembly code, I fed the source through the **gcc** compiler. Also, the **ret** instruction is a simplification; the actual kernel at that point jumps to a block of code that ends with the **ret** instruction.

My brief descriptions of the POSIX and Java APIs are intended only as concrete illustrations of broader concepts, not as a replacement for documentation of those APIs. You can find the official documentation on the web at *http://www.opengroup.org* and *http://java.sun.com*, respectively.

3

Scheduling

3.1 Introduction

In Chapter 2, you saw that operating systems support the concurrent execution of multiple threads by repeatedly switching each processor's attention from one thread to another. This switching implies that some mechanism, known as a *scheduler*, is needed to choose which thread to run at each time. Other system resources may need scheduling as well; for example, if several threads read from the same disk drive, a disk scheduler may place them in order. For simplicity, I will consider only processor scheduling. Normally, when people speak of *scheduling*, they mean processor scheduling; similarly, the *scheduler* is understood to mean the processor scheduler.

A scheduler should make decisions in a way that keeps the computer system's users happy. For example, picking the same thread all the time and completely ignoring the others would generally not be a good scheduling policy. Unfortunately, there is no one policy that will make all users happy all the time. Sometimes the reason is as simple as different users having conflicting desires: for example, user A wants task A completed quickly, while user B wants task B completed quickly. Other times, though, the relative merits of different scheduling policies will depend not on whom you ask, but rather on the context in which you ask. As a simple example, a student enrolled in several courses is unlikely to decide which assignment to work on without considering when the assignments are due.

Because scheduling policies need to respond to context, operating systems provide scheduling mechanisms that leave the user in charge of more subtle policy choices. For example, an operating system may provide a mechanism for running whichever thread has the highest numerical priority, while leaving the user the job of assigning priorities to the threads. Even so, no one mechanism (or general family of policies) will suit all goals. Therefore, I spend much of this chapter describing the different goals that users have for schedulers and the mechanisms that can be used to achieve those goals, at least approximately. Particularly since users may wish to achieve several conflicting goals, they will generally have to be satisfied with "good enough."

Before I get into the heavily values-laden scheduling issues, though, I will present one goal everyone can agree upon: a thread that can make productive use of a processor should always be preferred over one that is waiting for something, such as the completion of a time delay or the arrival of input. In Section 3.2, you will see how schedulers arrange for this by keeping track of each thread's state and scheduling only those threads that can run usefully.

Following the section on thread states, I devote Section 3.3 entirely to the question of users' goals, independent of how they are realized. Then I spend one section apiece on three broad families of schedulers, examining for each not only how it works but also how it can serve users' goals. These three families of schedulers are those based on fixed thread priorities (Section 3.4), those based on dynamically adjusted thread priorities (Section 3.5), and those based less on priorities than on controlling each thread's proportional share of processing time (Section 3.6). This three-way division is not the only possible taxonomy of schedulers, but it will serve to help me introduce several operating systems' schedulers and explain the principles behind them while keeping in mind the context of users' goals. After presenting the three families of schedulers, I will briefly remark in Section 3.7 on the role scheduling plays in system security. The chapter concludes with exercises, programming and exploration projects, and notes.

3.2 Thread States

A typical thread will have times when it is waiting for some event, unable to execute any useful instructions until the event occurs. Consider a web server that reads a client's request from the network, reads the requested web page from disk, and then sends the page over the network to the client. Initially the server thread is waiting for the network interface to have some data available. If the server thread were scheduled on a processor while it was waiting, the best it could do would be to execute a loop that checked over and over whether any data has arrived—hardly a productive use of the processor's time. Once data is available from the network, the server thread can execute some useful instructions to read the bytes in and check whether the request is complete. If not, the server needs to go back to waiting for more data to arrive. Once the request is complete, the server will know what page to load from disk and can issue the appropriate request to the disk drive. At that point, the thread once again needs to wait until such time as the disk has completed the requisite physical movements to locate the page. To take a different example, a video display program may display one frame of video and then wait some fraction of a second before displaying the next so that the movie doesn't play too fast. All the thread could do between frames would be to keep checking the computer's real-time clock to see whether enough time had elapsed—again, not a productive use of the processor.

In a single-thread system, it is plausible to wait by executing a loop that continually checks for the event in question. This approach is known as *busy waiting*. However, a modern general-purpose operating system will have multiple threads competing for the processor. In this case, busy waiting is a bad idea because any time that the scheduler allocates to the busy-waiting thread is lost to the other threads without achieving any added value for the thread that is waiting.

Therefore, operating systems provide an alternative way for threads to wait. The operating system keeps track of which threads can usefully run and which are waiting. The system does this by storing runnable threads in a data structure called the *run queue* and waiting threads in *wait queues*, one per reason for waiting. Although these structures are conventionally called queues, they may not be used in the first-in, first-out style of true queues. For example, there may be a list of threads waiting for time to elapse, kept in order of the desired time. Another example of a wait queue would be a set of threads waiting for the availability of data on a particular network communication channel.

Rather than executing a busy-waiting loop, a thread that wants to wait for some event notifies the operating system of this intention. The operating system removes the thread from the run queue and inserts the thread into the appropriate wait queue, as shown in Figure 3.1. Because the scheduler considers only threads in the run queue for execution, it will never select the waiting thread to run. The scheduler will be choosing only from those threads that can make progress if given a processor on which to run.

In Chapter 2, I mentioned that the arrival of a hardware interrupt can cause the processor to temporarily stop executing instructions from the current thread and to start executing instructions from the operating system's interrupt handler. One of the services this interrupt handler can perform is determining that a waiting thread doesn't need to wait any longer. For example, the computer's real-time clock may be

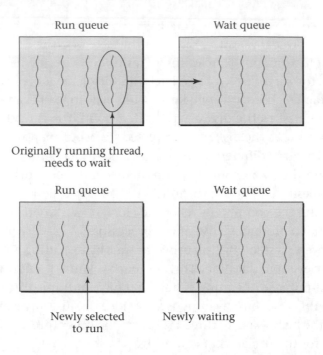

Figure 3.1 When a thread needs to wait, the operating system moves it from the run queue to a wait queue. The scheduler selects one of the threads remaining in the run queue to dispatch, so it starts running.

configured to interrupt the processor every one-hundredth of a second. The interrupt handler could check the first thread in the wait queue of threads that are waiting for specific times to elapse. If the time this thread was waiting for has not yet arrived, no further threads need to be checked because the threads are kept in time order. If, on the other hand, the thread has slept as long as it requested, then the operating system can move it out of the list of sleeping threads and into the run queue, where the thread is available for scheduling. In this case, the operating system should check the next thread similarly, as illustrated in Figure 3.2.

Putting together the preceding information, there are at least three distinct states a thread can be in:

- *Runnable* (but not running), awaiting dispatch by the scheduler
- *Running* on a processor
- *Waiting* for some event

Some operating systems may add a few more states in order to make finer distinctions (waiting for one kind of event versus waiting for another kind) or to handle special circumstances (for example, a thread that has finished running, but that needs to be kept

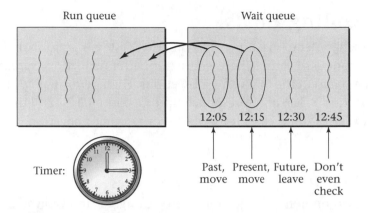

Figure 3.2 When the operating system handles a timer interrupt, all threads waiting for times that have now past are moved to the run queue. Because the wait queue is kept in time order, the scheduler need only check threads until it finds one waiting for a time still in the future. In this figure, times are shown on a human scale for ease of understanding.

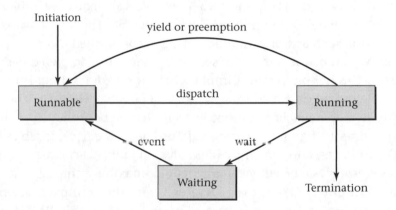

Figure 3.3 Threads change states as shown here. When a thread is initially created, it is runnable, but is not actually running on a processor until dispatched by the scheduler. A running thread can voluntarily yield the processor or can be preempted by the scheduler in order to run another thread. In either case, the formerly running thread returns to the runnable state. Alternatively, a running thread may wait for an external event before becoming runnable again. A running thread may also terminate.

around until another thread is notified). For simplicity, I will stick to the three basic states in the foregoing list. At critical moments in the thread's lifetime, the operating system will change the thread's state. These thread state changes are indicated in Figure 3.3. Again, a real operating system may add a few additional transitions; for example, it may be possible to forcibly terminate a thread, even while it is in a waiting state, rather than having it terminate only of its own accord while running.

3.3 Scheduling Goals

Users expect a scheduler to maximize the computer system's performance and to allow them to exert control. Each of these goals can be refined into several more precise goals, which I explain in the following subsections. High performance may mean high throughput (Section 3.3.1) or fast response time (Section 3.3.2), and user control may be expressed in terms of urgency, importance, or resource allocation (Section 3.3.3).

3.3.1 Throughput

Many personal computers have far more processing capability available than work to do, and they largely sit idle, patiently waiting for the next keystroke from a user. However, if you look behind the scenes at a large Internet service, such as Google, you'll see a very different situation. Large rooms filled with rack after rack of computers are necessary in order to keep up with the pace of incoming requests; any one computer can cope only with a small fraction of the traffic. For economic reasons, the service provider wants to keep the cluster of servers as small as possible. Therefore, the throughput of each server must be as high as possible. The *throughput* is the rate at which useful work, such as search transactions, is accomplished. An example measure of throughput would be the number of search transactions completed per second.

Maximizing throughput certainly implies that the scheduler should give each processor a runnable thread on which to work, if at all possible. However, there are some other, slightly less obvious, implications as well. Remember that a computer system has more components than just processors. It also has I/O devices (such as disk drives and network interfaces) and a memory hierarchy, including cache memories. Only by using all these resources efficiently can a scheduler maximize throughput.

I already mentioned I/O devices in Chapter 2, with the example of a computationally intensive graphics rendering program running concurrently with a disk-intensive virus scanner. I will return to this example later in the current chapter to see one way in which the two threads can be efficiently interleaved. In a nutshell, the goal is to keep both the processor and the disk drive busy all the time. If you have ever had an assistant for a project, you may have some appreciation for what this entails: whenever your assistant was in danger of falling idle, you had to set your own work aside long enough to explain the next assignment. Similarly, the processor must switch threads when necessary to give the disk more work to do.

Cache memories impact throughput-oriented scheduling in two ways, though one arises only in multiprocessor systems. In any system, switching between different threads more often than necessary will reduce throughput because processor time will be wasted on the overhead of context switching, rather than be available for useful work. The main source of this context-switching overhead is not the direct cost of the switch itself, which entails saving a few registers out and loading them with the other thread's values. Instead, the big cost is in reduced cache memory performance, for reasons I will explain in a moment. On multiprocessor systems, a second issue arises: a thread is likely to run faster when scheduled on the same processor as it last ran on. Again, this results from cache memory effects. To maximize throughput, schedulers therefore try to maintain a specific *processor affinity* for each thread, that is, to consistently schedule the thread on the same processor unless there are other countervailing considerations.

You probably learned in a computer organization course that *cache memories* provide fast storage for those addresses that have been recently accessed or that are near to recently accessed locations. Because programs frequently access the same locations again (that is, exhibit *temporal locality*) or access nearby locations (that is, exhibit *spatial locality*), the processor will often be able to get its data from the cache rather than from the slower main memory. Now suppose the processor switches threads. The new thread will have its own favorite memory locations, which are likely to be quite different. The cache memory will initially suffer many misses, slowing the processor to the speed of the main memory, as shown in Figure 3.4. Over time, however, the new thread's data will displace the data from the old thread, and the perfomance will improve. Suppose that just at the point where the cache has adapted to the second thread, the

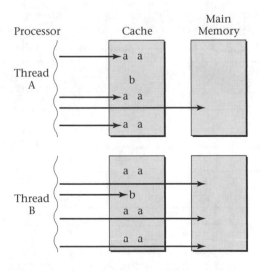

Figure 3.4 When a processor has been executing thread A for a while, the cache will mostly hold thread A's values, and the cache hit rate may be high. If the processor then switches to thread B, most memory accesses will miss in the cache and go to the slower main memory.

scheduler were to decide to switch back. Clearly this is not a recipe for high-throughput computing.

On a multiprocessor system, processor affinity improves throughput in a similar manner by reducing the number of cycles the processor stalls waiting for data from slower parts of the memory hierarchy. Each processor has its own local cache memory. If a thread resumes running on the same processor on which it previously ran, there is some hope it will find its data still in the cache. At worst, the thread will incur cache misses and need to fetch the data from main memory. The phrase "at worst" may seem odd in the context of needing to go all the way to main memory, but in a multiprocessor system, fetching from main memory is not the highest cost situation.

Memory accesses are even more expensive if they refer to data held in another processor's cache. That situation can easily arise if the thread is dispatched on a different processor than it previously ran on, as shown in Figure 3.5. In this circumstance, the multiprocessor system's *cache coherence* protocol comes into play. Typically, this means first transferring the data from the old cache to the main memory and then transferring it from the main memory to the new cache. This excess coherence traffic (beyond what is needed for blocks shared by multiple threads) reduces throughput if the scheduler has not arranged for processor affinity.

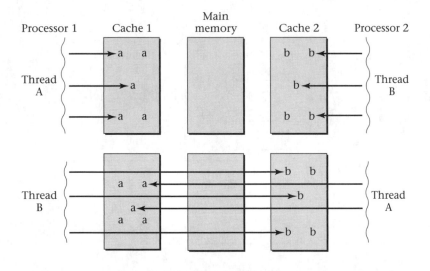

Figure 3.5 If processor 1 executes thread A and processor 2 executes thread B, after a while each cache will hold the corresponding thread's values. If the scheduler later schedules each thread on the opposite processor, most memory accesses will miss in the local cache and need to use the cache coherence protocol to retrieve data from the other cache.

3.3.2 Response Time

Other than throughput, the principle measure of a computer system's performance is *response time:* the elapsed time from a triggering event (such as a keystroke or a network packet's arrival) to the completed response (such as an updated display or the transmission of a reply packet). Notice that a high-performance system in one sense may be low-performance in the other. For example, frequent context switches, which are bad for throughput, may be necessary to optimize response time. Systems intended for direct interaction with a single user tend to be optimized for response time, even at the expense of throughput, whereas centralized servers are usually designed for high throughput as long as the response time is kept tolerable.

If an operating system is trying to schedule more than one runnable thread per processor and if each thread is necessary in order to respond to some event, then response time inevitably involves tradeoffs. Responding more quickly to one event by running the corresponding thread means responding more slowly to some other event by leaving its thread in the runnable state, awaiting later dispatch. One way to resolve this trade-off is by using user-specified information on the relative urgency or importance of the threads, as I describe in Section 3.3.3. However, even without that information, the operating system may be able to do better than just shrug its virtual shoulders.

Consider a real-world situation. You get an email from a long-lost friend, reporting what has transpired in her life and asking for a corresponding update on what you have been doing for the last several years. You have barely started writing what will inevitably be a long reply when a second email message arrives, from a close friend, asking whether you want to go out tonight. You have two choices. One is to finish writing the long letter and then reply "sure" to the second email. The other choice is to temporarily put your long letter aside, send off the one-word reply regarding tonight, and then go back to telling the story of your life. Either choice extends your response time for one email in order to keep your response time for the other email as short as possible. However, that symmetry doesn't mean there is no logical basis for choice. Prioritizing the one-word reply provides much more benefit to its response time than it inflicts harm on the other, more time-consuming task.

If an operating system knows how much processor time each thread will need in order to respond, it can use the same logic as in the email example to guide its choices. The policy of *Shortest Job First* (*SJF*) scheduling minimizes the average response time, as you can demonstrate in Exercise 3.5. This policy dates back to *batch processing* systems, which processed a single large *job* of work at a time, such as a company's payroll or accounts payable. System operators could minimize the average *turnaround time* from when a job was submitted until it was completed by processing the shortest one first.

The operators usually had a pretty good idea how long each job would take, because the same jobs were run on a regular basis. However, the reason why you should be interested in SJF is not for scheduling batch jobs (which you are unlikely to encounter), but as background for understanding how a modern operating system can improve the responsiveness of threads.

Normally, an operating system won't know how much processor time each thread will need in order to respond. One solution is to guess, based on past behavior. The system can prioritize those threads that have not consumed large bursts of processor time in the past, where a *burst* is the amount of processing done between waits for external events. Another solution is for the operating system to hedge its bets, so that even if it doesn't know which thread needs to run only briefly, it won't sink too much time into the wrong thread. By switching frequently between the runnable threads, if any one of them needs only a little processing time, it will get that time relatively soon even if the other threads involve long computations.

The successfulness of this hedge depends not only on the duration of the *time slices* given to the threads, but also on the number of runnable threads competing for the processor. On a lightly loaded system, frequent switches may suffice to ensure responsiveness. By contrast, consider a system that is heavily loaded with many long-running computations, but that also occasionally has an interactive thread that needs just a little processor time. The operating system can ensure responsiveness only by identifying and prioritizing the interactive thread, so that it doesn't have to wait in line behind all the other threads' time slices. However brief each of those time slices is, if there are many of them, they will add up to a substantial delay.

3.3.3 Urgency, Importance, and Resource Allocation

The goals of high throughput and quick response time do not inherently involve user control over the scheduler; a sufficiently smart scheduler might make all the right decisions on its own. On the other hand, there are user goals that revolve precisely around the desire to be able to say the following: "*This* thread is a high priority; work on it." I will explain three different notions that often get confusingly lumped under the heading of priority. To disentangle the confusion, I will use different names for each of them: *urgency*, *importance*, and *resource allocation*. I will reserve the word *priority* for my later descriptions of specific scheduling mechanisms, where it may be used to help achieve any scheduling goal: throughput, responsiveness, or the control of urgency, importance, or resource allocation.

A task is urgent if it needs to be done soon. For example, if you have a small homework assignment due tomorrow and a massive term paper to write within the next two days, the homework is more urgent. That doesn't necessarily mean it would be smart for you to prioritize the homework; you might make a decision to take a zero on the homework in order to free up more time for the term paper. If so, you are basing your decision not only on the two tasks' urgency, but also on their importance; the term paper is more important. In other words, importance indicates how much is at stake in accomplishing a task in a timely fashion.

Importance alone is not enough to make good scheduling decisions either. Suppose the term paper wasn't due until a week from now. In that case, you might decide to work on the homework today, knowing that you would have time to write the paper starting tomorrow. Or, to take a third example, suppose the term paper (which you have yet to even start researching) was due in an hour, with absolutely no late papers accepted. In that case, you might realize it was hopeless to even start the term paper, and so decide to put your time into the homework instead.

Although urgency and importance are quite different matters, the precision with which a user specifies urgency will determine how that user can control scheduling to reflect importance. If tasks have hard deadlines, then importance can be dealt with as in the homework example—through a process of ruthless triage. Here, importance measures the cost of dropping a task entirely. On the other hand, the deadlines may be "soft," with the importance measuring how bad it is for each task to be late. At the other extreme, the user might provide no information at all about urgency, instead demanding all results "as soon as possible." In this case, a high importance task might be one to work on whenever possible, and a low importance task might be one to fill in the idle moments, when there is nothing more important to do.

Other than urgency and importance, another way in which users may wish to express the relationship between different threads is by controlling what fraction of the available processing resources they are allocated. Sometimes, this is a matter of fairness. For example, if two users are sharing a computer, it might be fair to devote half of the processing time to one user's threads and the other half of the processing time to the other user's threads. In other situations, a specific degree of inequity may be desired. For example, a web hosting company may sell shares of a large server to small companies for their web sites. A company that wants to provide good service to a growing customer base might choose to buy two shares of the web server, expecting to get twice as much of the server's processing time in return for a larger monthly fee.

When it was common for thousands of users, such as university students, to share a single computer, considerable attention was devoted to so-called *fair-share scheduling*, in which users' consumption of the shared processor's time was balanced out over relatively long time periods, such as a week. That is, a user who did a lot of computing early in the week might find his threads allocated only a very small portion of the processor's time later in the week, so that the other users would have a chance to catch up. A fair share didn't have to mean an equal share; the system administrator could grant differing allocations to different users. For example, students taking an advanced course might receive more computing time than introductory students.

With the advent of personal computers, fair-share scheduling has fallen out of favor, but another resource-allocation approach, *proportional-share scheduling*, is still very much alive. (For example, you will see that the Linux scheduler is largely based on the proportional-share scheduling idea.) The main reason why I mention fair-share scheduling is to distinguish it from proportional-share scheduling, because the two concepts have names that are so confusingly close.

Proportional-share scheduling balances the processing time given to threads over a much shorter time scale, such as a second. The idea is to focus only on those threads that are runnable and to allocate processor time to them in proportion with the shares the user has specified. For example, suppose that I have a big server on which three companies have purchased time. Company A pays more per month than companies B and C, so I have given two shares to company A and only one share each to companies B and C. Suppose, for simplicity, that each company runs just one thread, which I will call thread A, B, or C, correspondingly. If thread A waits an hour for some input to arrive over the network while threads B and C are runnable, I will give half the processing time to each of B and C, because they each have one share. When thread A's input finally arrives and the thread becomes runnable, it won't be given an hour-long block of processing time to "catch up" with the other two threads. Instead, it will get half the processor's time, and threads B and C will each get one-quarter, reflecting the 2:1:1 ratio of their shares.

The simplest sort of proportional-share scheduling (such as Linux supports) allows shares to be specified only for individual threads, such as threads A, B, and C in the preceding example. A more sophisticated version allows shares to be specified collectively for all the threads run by a particular user or otherwise belonging to a logical group. For example, each user might get an equal share of the processor's time, independent of how many runnable threads the user has. Users who run multiple threads simply subdivide their shares of the processing time. Similarly, in the example where a big server is contracted out to multiple companies, I would probably want to allow each company to run multiple threads while still controlling the overall resource allocation among the companies, not just among the individual threads.

Having learned about urgency, importance, and resource allocation, one important lesson is that without further clarification, you cannot understand what a user means by a sentence such as "thread A is higher priority than thread B." The user may want you to devote twice as much processing time to A as to B, because A has higher priority in the sense of meriting a larger proportion of resources. Then again, the user may want you to devote almost all processing time to A, running B only in the spare moments when A goes into a waiting state, because A is higher priority in the sense of greater importance, greater urgency, or both.

Unfortunately, many operating systems have traditionally not given the user a rich enough vocabulary to directly express more than one of these goals. For example, the UNIX family of operating systems (including Mac OS X and Linux) provides a way for the user to specify the *niceness* of a thread. The word *nice* should be understood in the sense that a very nice thread is one that is prone to saying, "Oh no, that's all right, you go ahead of me, I can wait." In other words, a high niceness is akin to a low priority. However, different members of this operating system family interpret this single parameter, niceness, differently.

The original tradition, to which Mac OS X still adheres, is that niceness is an expression of importance; a very nice thread should normally only run when there is spare processor time. Some newer UNIX-family schedulers, as in Linux, instead interpret the same niceness number as an expression of resource allocation proportion, with nicer threads getting proportionately less processor time. It is pointless arguing which of these interpretations of niceness is the right one; the problem is that users have two different things they may want to tell the scheduler, and they will never be able to do so with only one control knob.

Luckily, some operating systems have provided somewhat more expressive vocabularies for user control. For example, Mac OS X allows the user to either express the urgency of a thread (through a deadline and related information) or its importance (through a niceness). These different classes of threads are placed in a hierarchical relationship; the assumption is that all threads with explicit urgency information are more important than any of the others. Similarly, some proportional-share schedulers, akin to Linux's, use niceness for proportion control, but also allow threads to be explicitly flagged as low-importance threads to be run only during otherwise idle time.

As a summary of this section, Figure 3.6 shows a taxonomy of the scheduling goals I have described. Figure 3.7 previews the scheduling mechanisms I describe in

Figure 3.6 A user may want the scheduler to improve system performance or to allow user control. Two different performance goals are high throughput and fast response time. Three different ways in which a user may exert control are by specifying threads' urgency, importance, or resource share.

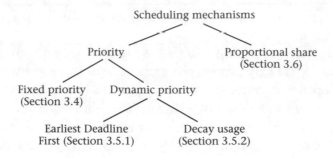

Figure 3.7 A scheduling mechanism may be based on always running the highest priority thread, or on pacing the threads to each receive a proportional share of processor time. Priorities may be fixed, or they may be adjusted to reflect either the deadline by which a thread must finish or the thread's amount of processor usage.

Mechanism	Goals
fixed priority	urgency, importance
Earliest Deadline First	urgency
decay usage	importance, throughput, response time
proportional share	resource allocation

Figure 3.8 For each scheduling mechanism I present, I explain how it can satisfy one or more of the scheduling goals.

the next three sections, and Figure 3.8 shows which goals each of them is designed to satisfy.

3.4 Fixed-Priority Scheduling

Many schedulers use a numerical *priority* for each thread; this controls which threads are selected for execution. The threads with higher priority are selected in preference to those with lower priority. No thread will ever be running if another thread with higher priority is not running, but is in the runnable state. The simplest way the priorities can be assigned is for the user to manually specify the priority of each thread, generally with some default value if none is explicitly specified. Although there may be some way for the user to manually change a thread's priority, one speaks of *fixed-priority scheduling* as long as the operating system never automatically adjusts a thread's priority.

Fixed-priority scheduling suffices to achieve user goals only under limited circumstances. However, it is simple, so many real systems offer it, at least as one option. For example, both Linux and Microsoft Windows allow fixed-priority scheduling to be selected for specific threads. Those threads take precedence over any others, which are scheduled using other means I discuss in Sections 3.5.2 and 3.6. In fact, fixed-priority scheduling is included as a part of the international standard known as POSIX, which many operating systems attempt to follow.

As an aside about priorities, whether fixed or otherwise, it is important to note that some real systems use smaller priority numbers to indicate more prefered threads and larger priority numbers to indicate those that are less prefered. Thus, a "higher priority" thread may actually be indicated by a lower priority number. In this book, I will consistently use "higher priority" and "lower priority" to mean more and less preferred, independent of how those are encoded as numbers by a particular system.

In a fixed-priority scheduler, the run queue can be kept in a data structure ordered by priority. If you have studied algorithms and data structures, you know that in theory this could be efficiently done using a clever representation of a priority queue, such as a binary heap. However, in practice, most operating systems use a much simpler structure, because they use only a small range of integers for the priorities. Thus, it suffices to keep an array with one entry per possible priority. The first entry contains a list of threads with the highest priority, the second entry contains a list of threads with the next highest priority, and so forth.

Whenever a processor becomes idle because a thread has terminated or entered a waiting state, the scheduler dispatches a runnable thread of highest available priority. The scheduler also compares priorities when a thread becomes runnable because it is newly initiated or because it is done waiting. If the newly runnable thread has higher priority than a running thread, the scheduler preempts the running thread of lower priority; that is, the lower-priority thread ceases to run and returns to the run queue. In its place, the scheduler dispatches the newly runnable thread of higher priority.

Two possible strategies exist for dealing with ties, in which two or more runnable threads have equally high priority. (Assume there is only one processor on which to run them, and that no thread has higher priority than they do.) One possibility is to run the thread that became runnable first until it waits for some event or chooses to voluntarily yield the processor. Only then is the second, equally high-priority thread dispatched. The other possibility is to share the processor's attention between those threads that are tied for highest priority by alternating among them in a *round-robin* fashion. That is, each thread runs for some small interval of time (typically tens or hundreds of milliseconds), and then it is preempted from the clock interrupt handler and the next thread of equal priority is dispatched, cycling eventually back to the first of the threads. The POSIX standard provides for both of these options; the user can select either a first-in, first-out (FIFO) policy or a round-robin (RR) policy.

Fixed-priority scheduling is not viable in an open, general-purpose environment where a user might accidentally or otherwise create a high-priority thread that runs for a long time. However, in an environment where all the threads are part of a carefully quality-controlled system design, fixed-priority scheduling may be a reasonable choice. In particular, it is frequently used for so-called *hard-real-time systems*, such as those that control the flaps on an airplane's wings.

Threads in these hard-real-time systems normally perform periodic tasks. For example, one thread may wake up every second to make a particular adjustment in the flaps and then go back to sleep for the remainder of the second. Each of these tasks has a deadline by which it must complete; if the deadline is missed, the program has failed to meet its specification. (That is what is meant by "hard real time.") In the simplest case, the deadline is the same as the period; for example, each second's adjustment must be done before the second is up. The designers of a system like this know all the threads that will be running and carefully analyze the ensemble to make sure no deadlines will ever be missed. In order to do this, the designers need to have a worst-case estimate of how long each thread will run, per period.

I can illustrate the analysis of a fixed-priority schedule for a hard-real-time system with some simple examples, which assume that the threads are all periodic, with deadlines equal to their periods, and with no interactions among them other than the competition for a single processor. To see how the same general ideas can be extended to cases where these assumptions don't hold, you could read a book devoted specifically to real-time systems.

Two key theorems, proved by Liu and Layland in a 1973 article, make it easy to analyze such a periodic hard-real-time system under fixed-priority scheduling:

- If the threads will meet their deadlines under any fixed priority assignment, then they will do so under a *rate-monotonic* assignment. That is, the more rapid a thread's period, the higher its priority should be.

- To check that deadlines are met, it suffices to consider the worst-case situation, which is that all the threads' periods start at the same moment.

Therefore, to test whether any fixed-priority schedule is feasible, assign priorities in the rate-monotonic fashion. Assume all the threads are newly runnable at time 0 and plot out what happens after that, seeing whether any deadline is missed.

To test the feasibilty of a real-time schedule, it is conventional to use a *Gantt chart*. This can be used to see whether a rate-monotonic fixed-priority schedule will work for a given set of threads. If not, some scheduling approach other than fixed priorities may work, or it may be necessary to redesign using less demanding threads or hardware with more processing power.

A Gantt chart is a bar, representing the passage of time, divided into regions labeled to show what thread is running during the corresponding time interval. For example, the Gantt chart

T1	T2	T1
0 5	15	20

shows thread T1 as running from time 0 to time 5 and again from time 15 to time 20; thread T2 runs from time 5 to time 15.

Consider an example with two periodically executing threads. One, T1, has a period and deadline of four seconds and a worst-case execution time per period of two seconds. The other, T2, has a period and deadline of six seconds and a worst-case execution time per period of three seconds. On the surface, this looks like it might just barely be feasible on a single processor: T1 has an average demand of half a processor (two seconds per four) and T2 also has an average demand of half a processor (three seconds per six), totalling to one fully utilized, but not oversubscribed, processor. Assume that all overheads, such as the time to do context switching between the threads, have been accounted for by including them in the threads' worst-case execution times.

However, to see whether this will really work without any missed deadlines, I need to draw a Gantt chart to determine whether the threads can get the processor when they need it. Because T1 has the shorter period, I assign it the higher priority. By Liu and Layland's other theorem, I assume both T1 and T2 are ready to start a period at time 0. The first six seconds of the resulting Gantt chart looks like this:

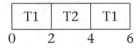

Note that T1 runs initially, when both threads are runnable, because it has the higher priority. Thus, it has no difficulty making its deadline. When T1 goes into a waiting state at time 2, T2 is able to start running. Unfortunately, it can get only two seconds of running done by the time T1 becomes runnable again, at the start of its second period, which is time 4. At that moment, T2 is preempted by the higher-priority thread T1, which occupies the processor until time 6. Thus, T2 misses its deadline: by time 6, it has run for only two seconds, rather than three.

If you accept Liu and Layland's theorem, you will know that switching to the other fixed-priority assignment (with T2 higher priority than T1) won't solve this problem. However, rather than taking this theorem at face value, you can draw the Gantt chart for this alternative priority assignment in Exercise 3.3 and see that again one of the threads misses its deadline.

In Section 3.5, I will present a scheduling mechanism that can handle the preceding scenario successfully. First, though, I will show one more example—this time one for which fixed-priority scheduling suffices. Suppose T2's worst-case execution time were only two seconds per six second period, with all other details the same as before. In this case, a Gantt chart for the first twelve seconds would look as follows:

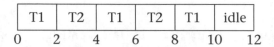

Notice that T1 has managed to execute for two seconds during each of its three periods (0–4, 4–8, and 8–12), and that T2 has managed to execute for two seconds during each of its two periods (0–6 and 6–12). Thus, neither missed any deadlines. Also, you should be able to convince yourself that you don't need to look any further down the timeline, because the pattern of the first 12 seconds will repeat itself during each subsequent 12 seconds.

3.5 Dynamic-Priority Scheduling

Priority-based scheduling can be made more flexible by allowing the operating system to automatically adjust threads' priorities to reflect changing circumstances. The relevant circumstances, and the appropriate adjustments to make, depend on what user goals the system is trying to achieve. In this section, I will present a couple of different variations on the theme of dynamically adjusted priorites. First, for continuity with Section 3.4, Section 3.5.1 shows how priorities can be dynamically adjusted for periodic hard-real-time threads using a technique known as Earliest Deadline First scheduling. Then Section 3.5.2 explains decay usage scheduling, a dynamic adjustment policy commonly used in general-purpose computing environments.

3.5.1 Earliest Deadline First Scheduling

You saw in Section 3.4 that rate-monotonic scheduling is the optimal fixed-priority scheduling method, but that even it couldn't schedule two threads, one of which needed two seconds every four and the other of which needed three seconds every six. That goal is achievable with an optimal method for dynamically assigning priorities to threads. This method is known as *Earliest Deadline First* (*EDF*). In EDF scheduling, each time a thread becomes runnable you re-assign priorities according to the following rule: the sooner a thread's next deadline, the higher its priority. The optimality of EDF is another of Liu and Layland's theorems.

Consider again the example with T1 needing two seconds per four and T2 needing three seconds per six. Using EDF scheduling, the Gantt chart for the first twelve seconds of execution would be as follows:

T1	T2	T1	T2	T1
0	2	5	7	10 12

There is no need to continue the Gantt chart any further because it will start repeating. Notice that neither thread misses any deadlines: T1 receives two seconds of processor time in each period (0–4, 4–8, and 8–12), while T2 receives three seconds of processing in each of its periods (0–6 and 6–12). This works better than rate-monotonic scheduling because the threads are prioritized differently at different times. At time 0, T1 is prioritized over T2 because its deadline is sooner (time 4 versus 6). However, when T1 becomes runnable a second time, at time 4, it gets lower priority than T2 because now it has a later deadline (time 8 versus 6). Thus, the processor finishes work on the first period of T2's work, rather than starting in on the second period of T1's work.

In this example, there is a tie in priorities at time 8, when T1 becomes runnable for the third time. Its deadline of 12 is the same as T2's. If you break the priority tie in favor of the already-running thread, T2, you obtain the preceding Gantt chart. In practice, this is the correct way to break the tie, because it will result in fewer context switches. However, in a theoretical sense, any tie-breaking strategy will work equally well. In Exercise 3.4, you can redraw the Gantt chart on the assumption that T2 is preempted in order to run T1.

3.5.2 Decay Usage Scheduling

Although we all benefit from real-time control systems, such as those keeping airplanes in which we ride from crashing, they aren't the most prominent computers in our lives. Instead, we mostly notice the workstation computers that we use for daily chores, like typing this book. These computers may execute a few real-time threads for tasks such as keeping an MP3 file of music decoding and playing at its natural rate. However, typically, most of the computer user's goals are not expressed in terms of deadlines, but rather in terms of a desire for quick response to interaction and efficient (high throughput) processing of major, long-running computations. Dynamic priority adjustment can help with these goals too, in operating systems such as Mac OS X or Microsoft Windows.

Occasionally, users of general-purpose workstation computers want to express an opinion about the priority of certain threads in order to achieve goals related to urgency, importance, or resource allocation. This works especially well for importance; for example, a search for signs of extra-terrestrial intelligence might be rated a low priority based on its small chance of success. These user-specified priorities can serve as *base priorities*, which the operating system will use as a starting point for its automatic adjustments. Most of the time, users will accept the default base priority for all their threads, and so the only reason threads will differ in priority is because of the automatic adjustments. For simplicity, in the subsequent discussion, I will assume that all threads have the same base priority.

In this kind of system, threads that tie for top priority after incorporating the automatic adjustments are processed in a round-robin fashion, as discussed earlier. That is, each gets to run for one *time slice*, and then the scheduler switches to the next of the threads. The length of time each thread is allowed to run before switching may also be called a *quantum*, rather than a time slice. The thread need not run for its full time slice; it could, for example, make an I/O request and go into a waiting state long before the time slice is up. In this case, the scheduler would immediately switch to the next thread.

One reason for the operating system to adjust priorities is to maximize throughput in a situation in which one thread is processor-bound and another is disk-bound. For example, in Chapter 2, I introduced a scenario where the user is running a processor-intensive graphics rendering program in one window, while running a disk-intensive virus scanning program in another window. As I indicated there, the operating system can keep both the processor and the disk busy, resulting in improved throughput relative to using only one part of the computer system at a time. While the disk is working on a read request from the virus scanner, the processor can be doing some of the graphics rendering. As soon as the disk transaction is complete, the scheduler should switch the processor's attention to the virus scanner. That way, the virus scanner can quickly look at the data that was read in and issue its next read request, so that the disk drive can get back to work without much delay. The graphics program will have time enough to run again once the virus scanning thread is back to waiting for the disk. In order to achieve this high-throughput interleaving of threads, the operating system needs to assign the disk-intensive thread a higher priority than the processor-intensive one.

Another reason for the operating system to adjust priorities is to minimize response time in a situation where an interactive thread is competing with a long-running computationally intensive thread. For example, suppose that you are running a program in one window that is trying to set a new world record for computing digits of π, while in another window you are typing a term paper. During the long pauses while you rummage through your notes and try to think of what to write next, you don't mind the processor giving its attention to computing π. But the moment you have an inspiration and start typing, you want the word processing program to take precedence, so that it can respond quickly to your keystrokes. Therefore, the operating system must have given this word processing thread a higher priority.

Notice that in both these situations, a computationally intensive thread is competing with a thread that has been unable to use the processor for a while, either because it was waiting for a disk transaction to complete or because it was waiting for the user to press another key. Therefore, the operating system should adjust upward the priority of threads that are in the waiting state and adjust downward the priority of threads that are in the running state. In a nutshell, that is what *decay usage schedulers*, such as the one in Mac OS X, do. The scheduler in Microsoft Windows also fits the same general pattern, although it is not strictly a decay usage scheduler. I will discuss both these schedulers in more detail in the remainder of this section.

A decay usage scheduler, such as in Mac OS X, adjusts each thread's priority downward from the base priority by an amount that reflects recent processor usage by that thread. (However, there is some cap on this adjustment; no matter how much the thread has run, its priority will not sink below some minimum value.) If the thread has recently been running a lot, it will have a priority substantially lower than its base priority. If the thread has not run for a long time (because it has been waiting for the user, for example), then its priority will equal the base priority. That way, a thread that wakes up after a long waiting period will take priority over a thread that has been able to run.

The thread's recent processor usage increases when the thread runs and *decays* when the thread waits, as shown in Figure 3.9. When the thread has been running, its usage increases by adding in the amount of time that it ran. When the thread has been waiting, its usage decreases by being multiplied by some constant every so often; for example, Mac OS X multiplies the usage by 5/8, eight times per second. Rather than continuously updating the usage of every thread, the system can calculate most of the updates to a particular thread's usage just when its state changes, as I describe in the next two paragraphs.

The currently running thread has its usage updated whenever it voluntarily yields the processor, has its time slice end, or faces potential preemption because another thread comes out of the waiting state. At these points, the amount of time the thread has been running is added to its usage, and its priority is correspondingly lowered. In Mac OS X, the time spent in the running state is scaled by the current overall load on the system before it is added to the thread's usage. That way, a thread that runs during a time of high load will have its priority drop more quickly to give the numerous other contending threads their chances to run.

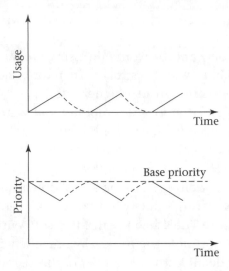

Figure 3.9 In a decay usage scheduler, such as Mac OS X uses, a thread's usage increases while it runs and decays exponentially while it waits. This causes the priority to decrease while running and increase while waiting.

When a thread is done spending time in the waiting state, its usage is adjusted downward to reflect the number of decay periods that have elapsed. For example, in Mac OS X, the usage is multiplied by $(5/8)^n$, where n is the number of eighths of a second that have elapsed. Because this is an exponential decay, even a fraction of a second of waiting is enough to bring the priority much of the way back to the base, and after a few seconds of waiting, even a thread that previously ran a great deal will be back to base priority. In fact, Mac OS X approximates $(5/8)^n$ as 0 for $n \geq 30$, so any thread that has been waiting for at least 3.75 seconds will be exactly at base priority.

Microsoft Windows uses a variation on this theme. Recall that a decay usage scheduler adjusts the priority downward from the base to reflect recent running and restores the priority back up toward the base when the thread waits. Windows does the reverse: when a thread comes out of a wait state, it is given an elevated priority, which then sinks back down toward the base priority as the thread runs. The net effect is the same: a thread that has been waiting gets a higher priority than one that has been running. The other difference is in how the specific numerical size of the change is calculated. When the thread runs, Windows decreases its priority down to the base in a linear fashion, as with decay usage scheduling. However, Windows does not use exponential decay to boost waiting threads. Instead, a thread that has been waiting is given a priority boost that depends on what it was waiting for: a small boost after waiting for a disk drive, a larger boost after waiting for input from the keyboard, and so forth. Because the larger boosts are associated with the kinds of waiting that usually take longer, the net effect is broadly similar to what exponential decay of a usage estimate achieves.

As described in Section 3.4, a scheduler can store the run queue as an array of thread lists, one per priority level. In this case, it can implement priority adjustments by moving threads from one level to another. Therefore, the Mac OS X and Microsoft Windows schedulers are both considered examples of the broader class of *multilevel feedback queue schedulers*. The original multilevel scheduler placed threads into levels primarily based on the amount of main memory they used. It also used longer time slices for the lower priority levels. Today, the most important multilevel feedback queue schedulers are those approximating decay-usage scheduling.

One advantage to decreasing the priority of running processes below the base, as in Mac OS X, rather than only down to the base, as in Microsoft Windows, is that doing so will normally prevent any runnable thread from being permanently ignored, even if a long-running thread has a higher base priority. Of course, a Windows partisan could reply that if base priorities indicate importance, the less important thread arguably should be ignored. However, in practice, totally shutting out any thread is a bad idea; one reason is the phenomenon of *priority inversion*, which I will explain in Chapter 4. Therefore, Windows has a small escape hatch: every few seconds, it temporarily boosts the priority of any thread that is otherwise unable to get dispatched.

One thing you may notice from the foregoing examples is the tendency of magic numbers to crop up in these schedulers. Why is the usage decayed by a factor of 5/8, eight times a second, rather than a factor of 1/2, four times a second? Why is the time quantum for round-robin execution 10 milliseconds under one system and 30 milliseconds under another? Why does Microsoft Windows boost a thread's priority by six after waiting for keyboard input, rather than by five or seven?

The answer to all these questions is that system designers have tuned the numerical parameters in each system's scheduler by trial and error. They have done experiments using workloads similar to those they expect their system to encounter in real use. Keeping the workload fixed, the experimenter varies the scheduler parameters and measures such performance indicators as response time and throughput. No one set of parameters will optimize all measures of performance for all workloads. However, by careful, systematic experimentation, parameters can be found that are likely to keep most users happy most of the time. Sometimes system administrators can adjust one or more of the parameters to suit the particular needs of their own installations, as well.

Before leaving decay usage schedulers, it is worth pointing out one kind of user goal that these schedulers are not very good at achieving. Suppose you have two processing-intensive threads and have decided you would like to devote two-thirds of your processor's attention to one and one-third to the other. If other threads start running, they can get some of the processor's time, but you still want your first thread to get twice as much processing as any of the other threads. In principle, you might be able to achieve this resource allocation goal under a decay usage scheduler by appropriately fiddling with the base priorities of the threads. However, in practice it is very difficult to come up with appropriate base priorities to achieve desired processor proportions. Therefore, if this kind of goal is important to a system's users, a different form of scheduler should be used, such as I discuss in Section 3.6.

3.6 Proportional-Share Scheduling

When resource allocation is a primary user goal, the scheduler needs to take a somewhat longer-term perspective than the approaches I have discussed thus far. Rather than focusing just on which thread is most important to run at the moment, the scheduler needs to be pacing the threads, doling out processor time to them at controlled rates.

Researchers have proposed three basic mechanisms for controlling the rate at which threads are granted processor time:

- Each thread can be granted the use of the processor equally often, just as in a simple round-robin. However, those that have larger allocations are granted a longer time slice each time around than those with smaller allocations.

- A uniform time slice can be used for all threads. However, those that have larger allocations can run more often, because the threads with smaller allocations "sit out" some of the rotations through the list of runnable threads.

- A uniform time slice can be used for all threads. However, those with larger allocations are chosen to run more often (on the average), because the threads are selected by a lottery with weighted odds, rather than in any sort of rotation.

The last of these three (*lottery scheduling*) is not terribly practical, because although each thread will get its appropriate share of processing time over the long run, there may be significant deviations over the short run. Consider, for example, a system with two threads, each of which should get half the processing time. If the time-slice duration is one-twentieth of a second, each thread should run ten times per second. Yet one thread might get shut out for a whole second, risking a major loss of responsiveness, just by having a string of bad luck. A coin flipped twenty times per second all day long may well come up heads twenty times in a row at some point. In Programming Project 3.2, you will calculate the probability and discover that over the course of a day the chance of one thread or the other going a whole second without running is actually quite high. Despite this shortcoming, lottery scheduling has received considerable attention in the research literature.

Turning to the two non-lottery approaches, I can illustrate the difference between them with an example. Suppose three threads (T1, T2, and T3) are to be allocated resources in the proportions 3:2:1. Thus, T1 should get half the processor's time, T2 one-third, and T3 one-sixth. If I follow the approach of a round-robin with variable-size time slices, I might get the following Gantt chart (the times are intended to be realistic values if interpreted in milliseconds):

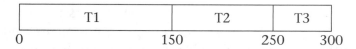

Taking the other approach, I could use a fixed time slice of 50 milliseconds, but with T2 sitting out one round in every three, and T3 sitting out two rounds out of three. The Gantt chart for the first three scheduling rounds would look as follows (thereafter, the pattern would repeat):

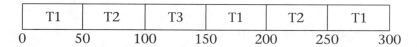

Both of these alternatives come into play in the Linux scheduler. In Linux, the user-specified *niceness* of a thread controls the proportion of processor time that the thread will receive. Primarily, this is done by allocating variable-sized time slices, as in the first Gantt chart. However, the scheduler will under some circumstances subdivide large time slices into several smaller ones, in order to make poor interactive responsiveness less likely. This results in a picture more nearly like the second Gantt chart. Regardless of how the time slices are subdivided (or not), each normal niceness thread receives approximately 100 milliseconds per round, whereas an extremely nice thread can receive as little as 5 milliseconds, and a particularly nasty thread (one with negative niceness) can get as much as 800 milliseconds.

The proportional-sharing approach I have discussed thus far provides the core of Linux's scheduler and is all that matters when the workload consists exclusively of processor-intensive threads. However, in order to better accomodate threads that also do I/O, the Linux scheduler includes some elements of a dynamically adjusted priority scheme as well. Unlike a traditional priority-based scheme, the priorities do not indirectly control how much processor time each thread gets; that remains directly controlled by the allocation of time slices. Instead, the priorities control only how soon the threads receive their allotted processor time, particularly upon switching from the waiting state to the runnable state.

The scheduler keeps track of each thread's niceness and two other numbers derived from it: the time slice and the priority. The time slice is controlled exclusively by the niceness, as described earlier. The priority, on the other hand, starts with a base priority derived from the niceness, but also incorporates a dynamic adjustment to reflect the thread's past behavior. The current version of the Linux scheduler uses a particularly complicated process to calculate the dynamic priority adjustment, but the basic principle is staightforward: waiting causes the priority to rise, while running causes the priority to sink—the same basic principle as in decay usage scheduling or the Microsoft Windows scheduler.

The 40-point niceness control range available to users translates directly into a 40-point base priority range, whereas the dynamic adjustments are at most plus or minus five points, and may be restricted to even less than that, because the adjusted priority is limited to stay within the 40-point range. Thus, no matter how much sleeping or running threads do, if two differ by more than 10 niceness points, the nicer thread will always be lower priority than the less nice thread. In the common case that the user runs all threads at the default niceness, however, their priority ordering will be determined by their behavior, with interactive threads taking priority over disk-bound threads, which in turn take priority over processor-bound threads.

The Linux scheduler stores the runnable threads in a run queue that contains two arrays, each with one slot per possible priority value. Each array element is a list of threads that share that priority value. In other words, each of the two arrays is organized just like the run queue of a normal priority scheduler. The reason why two arrays are used is to handle the proportional-share allocation of time slices. One array, the active array, holds the threads that still have some of their current allocation remaining. The other array, the expired array, holds those threads that have used their entire current allocation and cannot be run again until new allocations take effect.

Under normal operation, the scheduler runs a thread from the active array, choosing the one at the head of the highest priority list that isn't empty. If the thread completes its full time slice, it is placed into the expired array. When the active array is completely empty, the two arrays are swapped with the expired array now becoming the active array, so that all the threads can run again. In order that the threads have a new allocation of time, each thread's time slice is "charged back up" at the time it is moved to the expired array. That way, all the threads in the expired array will be ready to run when that array becomes active.

For compute-bound threads that stay runnable, the priority ordering is irrelevant; each will run once per time the arrays are swapped. However, for interactive or I/O-bound threads, priority matters. When a thread in the waiting state becomes runnable, it is inserted into the active array in the position corresponding to its priority. If the newly runnable thread's priority is higher than that of the currently running thread, the currently running thread is preempted, so that the new higher-priority thread can run immediately instead. Thus, threads that have high priority will receive fast response time, whether the high priority is because the user gave them a low niceness, or because the scheduler noticed they waited more than they ran.

If the scheduler preempts a thread before it has consumed its time slice, the thread remains in the active array, so that it can finish the time slice up without waiting for the next array swap.

One final complication in the Linux scheduler is worth pointing out, although it doesn't change the overall picture. Recall that normally when a thread consumes its full time slice, it is charged back up with a new time slice and placed in the expired array to await the next swap. However, under limited circumstances, the scheduler returns the recharged thread to the active array, rather than placing it in the expired array. Thus, the thread will be granted another full time slice, while the threads in the expired array continue to wait for their next time slice.

Clearly this exceptional treatment confounds the basic proportional sharing idea; threads that receive extra time slices will be able to use more of the processor than their niceness would normally allow. Also, if threads were repeatedly returned to the active array, the threads in the expired array would receive very poor response time; in the worst case, they might suffer complete *starvation*, never receiving any processor time.

To mitigate these problems, the Linux scheduler returns recharged threads to the active array only if they have a sufficient combination of interactive behavior (waiting more than running) and low niceness. Those threads may need just a bit more processor time to get back to waiting and may have an impatient user. Moreover, to prevent starvation, if enough time elapses without the expired array getting a chance to become active, the exception is suppressed entirely.

3.7 Security and Scheduling

The kind of attack most relevant to scheduling is the *denial of service (DoS)* attack, that is, an attack with the goal of preventing legitimate users of a system from being able to use it. Denial of service attacks are frequently nuisances motivated by little more than the immaturity of the perpetrators. However, they can be part of a more sophisticated scheme. For example, consider the consequences if a system used for coordinating a military force were vulnerable to a denial of service attack.

The most straightforward way an attacker could misuse a scheduler in order to mount a denial of service attack would be to usurp the mechanisms provided for administrative control. Recall that schedulers typically provide some control parameter for each thread, such as a deadline, a priority, a base priority, or a resource share. An authorized system administrator needs to be able to say "This thread is a really low priority" or the analogous statement about one of the other parameters. If an attacker could exercise that same control, a denial of service attack could be as simple as giving a low priority to a critical thread.

Therefore, real operating systems guard the thread-control interfaces. Typically, only a user who has been authenticated as the "owner" of a particular thread or as a bona fide system administrator can control that thread's scheduling parameters. Naturally, this relies upon other aspects of the system's security that I will consider in later chapters: the system must be protected from tampering, must be able to authenticate the identity of its users, and must be programmed in a sufficiently error-free fashion that its checks cannot be evaded.

Because real systems guard against an unauthorized user de-prioritizing a thread, attackers use a slightly more sophisticated strategy. Rather than de-prioritizing the targeted thread, they compete with it. That is, the attackers create other threads that attempt to siphon off enough of a scarce resource, such as processor time, so that little or none will be left for the targeted thread.

One response of system designers has been to arrange that any denial of service attack will be sufficiently cumbersome that it can be easily distinguished from normal behavior and hence interdicted. For example, recall that a single thread at a high fixed priority could completely starve all the normal threads. Therefore, most systems prohibit normal users from running such threads, reserving that privilege to authorized system administrators. In fact, typical systems place off-limits all fixed priorities and all higher-than-normal priorities, even if subject to decay-usage adjustment. The result is that an attacker must run many concurrent threads in order to drain off a significant fraction of the processor's time. Because legitimate users generally won't have any reason to do that, denial of service attacks can be distinguished from ordinary behavior. A limit on the number of threads per user will constrain denial of service attacks without causing most users much hardship. However, there will inevitably be a trade-off between the degree to which denial of service attacks are mitigated and the degree to which normal users retain flexibility to create threads.

Alternatively, a scheduling policy can be used that is intrinsically more resistant to denial of service attacks. In particular, proportional-share schedulers have considerable promise in this regard. The simple version that Linux includes is still vulnerable to attack using a large number of threads. However, as I mentioned earlier, a more sophisticated version can assign resource shares to users or other larger groups, with those shares subject to hierarchical subdivision. This was originally proposed by Waldspurger as part of lottery scheduling, which I observed is disfavored because of its susceptibility to short-term unfairness in the distribution of processing time. However, Waldspurger later showed how the same hierarchical approach could be used with *stride scheduling*, a deterministic proportional-share scheduler.

Long-running server threads, which over their lifetimes may process requests originating from many different users, present an additional complication. If resources are allocated per user, which user should be funding the server thread's resource consumption? The simplest approach is to have a special user just for the purpose with a large enough resource allocation to provide for all the work the server thread does on behalf of all the users. Unfortunately, that is too coarse-grained to prevent denial of service attacks. If a user submits many requests to the server thread, he or she may use up its entire processor time allocation. This would deny service to other users' requests made to the same server thread. Admittedly, threads not using the service will be isolated from the problem, but that may be small solace if the server thread in question is a critical one.

To address this issue, recent research has suggested that threads should be able to switch from one user's resource allocation to another, as the threads handle different requests. The idea is to allocate resources not directly to threads, but to independent *resource containers* instead. At any one time, each thread draws resources from one resource container. However, it can switch to drawing from a different resource container. This solves the problem of fairly accounting for server threads' usage. Because multiple threads can be made to draw out of a single resource container, the same proposal also can prevent users from receiving more processor time by running more threads.

Finally, keep in mind that no approach to processor scheduling taken alone will prevent denial of service attacks. An attacker will simply overwhelm some other resource than processor time. For example, in the 1990s, attackers frequently targeted systems' limited ability to establish new network connections. Nonetheless, a comprehensive approach to security needs to include processor scheduling, as well as networking and other components.

Exercises

3.1 Gantt charts, which I introduced in the context of hard-real-time scheduling, can also be used to illustrate other scheduling concepts, such as those concerning response time. Suppose thread T1 is triggered by an event at time 0 and needs to run for 1.5 seconds before it can respond. Suppose thread T2 is triggered by an event occuring 0.3 seconds later than T1's trigger, and that T2 needs to run

0.2 seconds before it can respond. Draw a Gantt chart for each of the following three cases, and for each indicate the response time of T1, the response time of T2, and the average response time:

(a) T1 is allowed to run to completion before T2 is run.

(b) T1 is preempted when T2 is triggered; only after T2 has completed does T1 resume.

(c) T1 is preempted when T2 is triggered; the two threads are then executed in a round-robin fashion (starting with T2), until one of them completes. The time slice (or quantum) is .05 seconds.

3.2 Suppose a Linux system is running three threads, each of which runs an infinite loop with nothing in the body, so that it just chews up as much processor time as it is given. One thread is run by one user, whereas the other two threads are run by a second user (perhaps logged in over the network or in a second virtual console). Does the scheduler give each user a fair share (one-half) of the processor's time, or does it give each thread a fair share (one-third)? You can answer this question from the text of this chapter, but see also Exploration Project 3.1. Also, which behavior would you prefer? Explain why.

3.3 Draw a Gantt chart for two threads, T1 and T2, scheduled in accordance to fixed priorities with T2 at a higher priority than T1. Both threads run periodically. One, T1, has a period and deadline of four seconds and an execution time per period of two seconds. The other, T2, has a period and deadline of six seconds and an execution time per period of three seconds. Assume both threads start a period at time 0. Draw the Gantt chart far enough to show one of the threads missing a deadline.

3.4 Draw a Gantt chart for two threads, T1 and T2, scheduled in accordance with the Earliest Deadline First policy. If the threads are tied for earliest deadline, preempt the already-running thread in favor of the newly runnable thread. Both threads run periodically. One, T1, has a period and deadline of four seconds and an execution time per period of two seconds. The other, T2, has a period and deadline of six seconds and an execution time per period of three seconds. Assume both threads start a period at time 0. Draw the Gantt chart to the point where it would start to repeat. Are the deadlines met?

3.5 Suppose a system has three threads (T1, T2, and T3) that are all available to run at time 0 and need one, two, and three seconds of processing, respectively. Suppose that each thread is run to completion before starting another. Draw six different Gantt charts, one for each possible order the threads can be run in. For each chart, compute the turnaround time of each thread; that is, the time elapsed from when it was ready (time 0) until it is complete. Also, compute the average turnaround time for each order. Which order has the shortest average turnaround time? What is the name for the scheduling policy that produces this order?

▣ Programming Projects

3.1 On a system where you can install modified Linux kernels, test the effect of eliminating dynamic priority adjustments. (You will find the relevant code in the file `kernel/sched.c`.) You should be able to demonstrate that there is no change in how compute-bound processes share the processor in accordance with their niceness. You should also be able to demonstrate that the responsiveness of interactive processes is degraded when there are lots of compute-bound processes running as well. Rather than testing response time with a process that reads input from the user, you can more easily get quantitative results with a process that repeatedly sleeps and measures how much longer each sleeping period actually is than was requested. Write a report in which you explain what you did, and the hardware and software system context in which you did it, carefully enough that someone could replicate your results.

3.2 Consider a coin that is weighted so that it comes up heads with probability p and tails with probability $1 - p$, for some value of p between 0 and 1. Let $f(n, k, p)$ be the probability that in a sequence of n tosses of this coin there is a run of a least k consecutive heads.

   (a) Prove that $f(n, k, p)$ can be defined by the following recurrence. If $n < k$, $f(n, k, p) = 0$. If $n = k$, $f(n, k, p) = p^k$. If $n > k$,

$$f(n, k, p) = f(n - 1, k, p) + p^k(1 - p)(1 - f(n - k - 1, k, p)).$$

   (b) Write a program to calculate $f(n, k, p)$ using the above recurrence. To make your program reasonably efficient, you will need to use the algorithm design technique known as dynamic programing. That is, you should create an $n + 1$ element array, and then for i from 0 to n, fill in element i of the array with $f(i, k, p)$. Whenever the calculation of one of these values of f requires another value of f, retrieve the required value from the array, rather than using a recursive call. At the end, return element n of the array.

   (c) If threads A and B each are selected with probability $1/2$ and the time slice is $1/20$ of a second, the probability that sometime during a day thread A will go a full second without running is $f(20 \cdot 60 \cdot 60 \cdot 24, 20, 1/2)$. Calculate this value using your program.

   (d) The system's performance is no better if thread B goes a long time without running than if thread A does. This leads one to consider the probability that in *n* tosses of a fair coin there are at least *k* consecutive heads or *k* consecutive tails. Show that this probability is $f(n-1, k\ 1, 1/2)$. Use this to calculate the probability that one or the other of threads A and B goes a second without processor time in the course of a day.

Exploration Projects

3.1 Experimentally verify your answer to Exercise 3.2 with the help of another user. The `top` command will show you what fraction of the processor each thread gets.

3.2 Experimentally measure the impact of niceness on the amount of processor time given to compute-bound threads under as many UNIX-like uniprocessor systems as you have access to. This will be most interesting if you can compare a system with a proportional-share scheduler (such as Linux) with a system that uses a decay usage scheduler (such as Mac OS X or most older versions of UNIX). Be sure to experiment on a system that is otherwise idle. Write a simple test program that just loops. Run one copy normally (niceness 0) and another using the `nice` command at elevated niceness. Use the `top` command to observe what fraction of the processor each thread gets. Repeat the test using different degrees of elevated niceness, from 1 to 19. Also, repeat the test in situations other than one thread of each niceness; for example, what if there are four normal niceness threads and only one elevated niceness thread? Write a report in which you explain what you did, and the hardware and software system context in which you did it, carefully enough that someone could replicate your results. Try to draw some conclusions about the suitability of niceness as a resource allocation tool on the systems you studied.

Notes

I introduced the notion of thread states by explaining the inefficiency of busy waiting and indicated that the alternative is for a thread that wants to wait to notify the operating system. This issue was recognized early in the history of operating systems. For example, the same 1959 paper [30] by Codd et al. that I quoted in Chapter 2 remarks, "For the sake of efficient use of the machine, one further demand is made of the programmer or compiler. When a point is reached in a problem program beyond which activity on the central processing unit cannot proceed until one or more input-output operations are completed, the control must be passed to the supervisory program so that other problem programs may be serviced." (The "supervisory program" is what today is called an operating system.)

I remarked that the main cost of thread switching is lost cache performance. This observation has been quantified in various measurement studies, such as one by Regehr [103].

I use the terms *quantum* and *time slice* interchangeably, in keeping with contemporary usage. Early operating systems used these words differently: *quanta* were finer subdivisions of coarser time slices. A subset of the runnable threads would get brief quanta in a round-robin. When a thread had received enough quanta to use up its whole time slice, it would be moved out of the round-robin for a while, and another thread would move in to take its place.

I mentioned fair-share, multilevel feedback queue, lottery, and stride scheduling only in passing. Early references for them are numbers [77], [34], [132], and [133], respectively.

Liu and Layland wrote a seminal 1973 article on hard-real-time scheduling [91]. For a survey of how rate-monotonic scheduling has been generalized to more realistic circumstances, see the article by Sha, Rajkumar, and Sathaye [115].

I drew examples from three real systems' schedulers: Mac OS X, Microsoft Windows, and Linux. For two of these (Mac OS X and Linux), the only reliable way to find the information is by reading the kernel source code, as I did (versions Darwin 6.6 and Linux 2.6.11). For Microsoft Windows, the source code is not publicly available, but conversely, one doesn't need to dig through it to find a more detailed description than mine: there is a very careful one in Russinovich and Solomon's book [109].

My segue from decay usage scheduling to proportional-share scheduling was the remark that one could, in principle, achieve proportional shares by suitably setting the base priorities of a decay usage scheduler, but that in practice, it was difficult to map proportions to base priorities. The mathematical modeling study by Hellerstein [66] provides evidence for both aspects of this claim. Hellerstein explicitly shows that one can, in principle, achieve what he terms "service rate objectives." However, less explicitly, he also shows this is not practical; reading his graphs carefully, one can see that there are two choices. Either the service rates are so insensitive to the base priorities as to render most proportions out of reach, or there is a region of such extreme sensitivity that one jumps over many potential proportions in stepping from one base priority difference to the next.

Resource containers are described by Banga, Druschel, and Mogul [9].

Synchronization and Deadlocks

4.1 Introduction

In Chapters 2 and 3, you have seen how an operating system can support concurrent threads of execution. Now the time has come to consider how the system supports controlled interaction between those threads. Because threads running at the same time on the same computer can inherently interact by reading and writing a common set of memory locations, the hard part is providing control. In particular, this chapter will examine control over the relative timing of execution steps that take place in differing threads.

Recall that the scheduler is granted considerable authority to temporarily preempt the execution of a thread and dispatch another thread. The scheduler may do so in response to unpredictable external events, such as how long an I/O request takes to complete. Therefore, the computational steps taken by two (or more) threads will be interleaved in a quite unpredictable manner, unless the programmer has taken explicit measures to control the order of events. Those control measures are known as *synchronization*. Synchronization causes one thread to wait for another.

In Section 4.2, I will provide a more detailed case for why synchronization is needed by describing the problems that can occur when interacting threads are not properly synchronized. The uncontrolled interactions are called races. By examining some typical races, I will illustrate the need for one particular form of synchronization, mutual exclusion. Mutual exclusion ensures that only one thread at a time can operate on a shared data structure or other resource. Section 4.3 presents two closely related ways mutual exclusion can be obtained. They are known as mutexes and monitors.

After covering mutual exclusion, I will turn to other, more general synchronization challenges and to mechanisms that can address those challenges. To take one example, you may want to ensure that some memory locations are read after they have been filled with useful values, rather than before. I devote Section 4.4 to enumerating several of the most common synchronization patterns other than mutual exclusion. Afterward, I devote Sections 4.5 and 4.6 to two popular mechanisms used to handle these situations. One, condition variables, is an important extension to monitors; the combination of monitors with condition variables allows many situations to be cleanly handled. The other, semaphores, is an old favorite because it provides a single, simple mechanism that in principle suffices for all synchronization problems. However, semaphores can be hard to understand and use correctly.

Synchronization solves the problem of races, but it creates a new problem of its own: deadlock. Recall that synchronization typically involves making threads wait; for example, in mutual exclusion, a thread may need to wait its turn in order to enforce the rule of one at a time. Deadlock results when a cycle of waiting threads forms; for example, thread A waits for thread B, which happens to be waiting for thread A, as shown in Figure 4.1. Because this pathology results from synchronization, I will address it and three of the most practical cures in Section 4.7, after completing the study of synchronization itself.

Synchronization interacts with scheduling (the topic of Chapter 3) in some interesting ways. In particular, unless special precautions are taken, synchronization mechanisms can subvert priority scheduling, allowing a low-priority thread to run while a high-priority thread waits. Therefore, in Section 4.8, I will briefly consider the interactions between synchronization and scheduling, as well as what can be done to tame them.

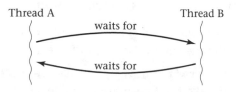

Figure 4.1   Deadlock results when threads wait for one another in a complete cycle. In this simple example, thread A is waiting for thread B, which is waiting for thread A.

Finally, I conclude the chapter in Section 4.9 by looking at security issues related to synchronization. In particular, I show how subtle synchronization bugs, which may nearly never cause a malfunction unless provoked, can be exploited by an attacker in order to circumvent the system's normal security policies. After this concluding section, I provide exercises, programming and exploration projects, and notes.

Despite the wide range of synchronization-related topics I cover in this chapter, there are two I leave for later chapters. Atomic transactions are a particularly sophisticated and important synchronization pattern, commonly encountered in middleware; therefore, I devote Chapter 5 entirely to them. Also, explicitly passing a message between threads (for example, via a network) provides synchronization as well as communication, because the message cannot be received until after it has been transmitted. Despite this synchronization role, I chose to address various forms of message passing in Chapters 9 and 10, the chapters related to communication.

4.2 Races and the Need for Mutual Exclusion

When two or more threads operate on a shared data structure, some very strange malfunctions can occur if the timing of the threads turns out precisely so that they interfere with one another. For example, consider the following code that might appear in a `sellTicket` procedure (for an event without assigned seats):

```
if(seatsRemaining > 0){
  dispenseTicket();
  seatsRemaining = seatsRemaining - 1;
} else
  displaySorrySoldOut();
```

On the surface, this code looks like it should never sell more tickets than seats are available. However, what happens if multiple threads (perhaps controlling different points of sale) are executing the same code? Most of the time, all will be well. Even if two people try to buy tickets at what humans perceive as the same moment, on the time scale of the computer, probably one will happen first and the other second, as shown in Figure 4.2. In that case, all is well. However, once in a blue moon, the timing may be exactly wrong, and the following scenario results, as shown in Figure 4.3.

1. Thread A checks `seatsRemaining > 0`. Because `seatsRemaining` is 1, the test succeeds. Thread A will take the first branch of the `if`.

2. Thread B checks `seatsRemaining > 0`. Because `seatsRemaining` is 1, the test succeeds. Thread B will take the first branch of the `if`.

3. Thread A dispenses a ticket and decreases `seatsRemaining` to 0.

4. Thread B dispenses a ticket and decreases `seatsRemaining` to −1.

5. One customer winds up sitting on the lap of another.

Thread A	Thread B

`if(seatsRemaining > 0)`
`dispenseTicket();`
`seatsRemaining=seatsRemaining-1;`	

	`if(seatsRemaining > 0)...else` `displaySorrySoldOut();`

Figure 4.2   Even if two humans think they are trying to buy the last ticket at the same time, chances are good that one's thread (thread A in this example) will run before the other's. Thread B will then correctly discover that no seats remain.

Thread A	Thread B
`if(seatsRemaining > 0)`	
	`if(seatsRemaining > 0)`
`dispenseTicket();`	
	`dispenseTicket();`
`seatsRemaining=seatsRemaining-1;`	
	`seatsRemaining=seatsRemaining-1;`

Figure 4.3   If threads A and B are interleaved, both can act as though there were a ticket left to sell, even though only one really exists for the two of them.

Of course, there are plenty of other equally unlikely scenarios that result in misbehavior. In Exercise 4.1, you can come up with a scenario where, starting with **seatsRemaining** being 2, two threads each dispense a ticket, but **seatsRemaining** is left as 1 rather than 0.

These scenarios are examples of *races*. In a race, two threads use the same data structure, without any mechanism to ensure only one thread uses the data structure at a time. If either thread precedes the other, all is well. However, if the two are interleaved, the program malfunctions. Generally, the malfunction can be expressed as some invariant property being violated. In the ticket-sales example, the invariant is that the value of **seatsRemaining** should be nonnegative and when added to the number of tickets dispensed should equal the total number of seats. (This invariant assumes that **seatsRemaining** was initialized to the total number of seats.)

When an invariant involves more than one variable, a race can result even if one of the threads only reads the variables, without modifying them. For example, suppose there are two variables, one recording how many tickets have been sold and the other recording the amount of cash in the money drawer. There should be an invariant relation between these: the number of tickets sold times the price per ticket, plus the amount of starting cash, should equal the cash on hand. Suppose one thread is in the midst of selling a ticket. It has updated one of the variables, but not yet the other. If at exactly that moment another thread chooses to run an audit function, which inspects the values of the two variables, it will find them in an inconsistent state.

That inconsistency may not sound so terrible, but what if a similar inconsistency occurred in a medical setting, and one variable recorded the drug to administer, while the other recorded the dose? Can you see how dangerous an inconsistency could be? Something very much like that happened in a radiation therapy machine, the Therac-25, with occasionally lethal consequences. (Worse, some patients suffered terrible but not immediately lethal injuries and lingered for some time in excruciating, intractable pain.)

From the ticket-sales example, you can see that having two threads carrying out operations on the same data structure is harmless, as long as there never are two operations under way at the same time. In other words, the interleaving of the threads' execution needs to be at the granularity of complete operations, such as selling a ticket or auditing the cash drawer. The two threads can take turns selling tickets in any arbitrary fashion, not just in strict alternation. However, each sale should be completed without interruption.

The reason why any interleaving of complete operations is safe is because each is designed to both rely on the invariant and preserve it. Provided that you initially construct the data structure in a state where the invariant holds, any sequence whatsoever of invariant-preserving operations will leave the invariant intact.

What is needed, then, is a synchronization mechanism that allows one thread to lock the data structure before it begins work, thereby excluding all other threads from operating on that structure. When the thread that locked the structure is done, it unlocks, allowing another thread to take its turn. Because any thread in the midst of one of the operations temporarily excludes all the others, this arrangement is called *mutual exclusion*. Mutual exclusion establishes the granularity at which threads may be interleaved by the scheduler.

4.3 Mutexes and Monitors

As you saw in Section 4.2, threads that share data structures need to have a mechanism for obtaining exclusive access to those structures. A programmer can arrange for this exclusive access by creating a special lock object associated with each shared data structure. The lock can be held by only one thread at a time. If the threads operate on (or even examine) the data structure only when holding the corresponding lock, this discipline will prevent races.

To support this form of race prevention, operating systems and middleware generally provide mutual exclusion locks. Because the name *mutual exclusion lock* is rather ungainly, something shorter is generally used. Some programmers simply talk of *locks*, but that can lead to confusion because other synchronization mechanisms are also called locks. (For example, I introduce readers/writers locks in Section 4.4.2.) Therefore, the name *mutex* has become popular as a shortened form of *mutual exclusion lock*. In particular, the POSIX standard refers to mutexes. Therefore, I will use that name in this book as well.

Section 4.3.1 presents the POSIX application programming interface (API) for mutexes. Section 4.3.2 discusses an alternative, more structured interface to mutexes, known as monitors. Finally, Section 4.3.3 shows what lies behind both of those interfaces by explaining the mechanisms typically used to implement mutexes.

4.3.1 The Mutex Application Programming Interface

A mutex can be in either of two states: locked (that is, held by some thread), or unlocked (that is, not held by any thread). Any implementation of mutexes must have some way to create a mutex and initialize its state. Conventionally, mutexes are initialized to the unlocked state. As a minimum, there must be two other operations: one to lock a mutex, and one to unlock it.

The lock and unlock operations are much less symmetrical than they sound. The unlock operation can be applied only when the mutex is locked; this operation does its job and returns, without making the calling thread wait. The lock operation, on the other hand, can be invoked even when the lock is already locked. For this reason, the calling thread may need to wait, as shown in Figure 4.4. When a thread invokes the lock operation on a mutex, and that mutex is already in the locked state, the thread is

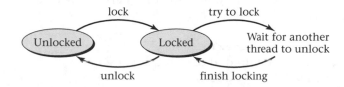

Figure 4.4 Locking an unlocked mutex and unlocking a locked one change the mutex's state. However, a thread can also try to lock an already-locked mutex. In this case, the thread waits and acquires the mutex lock when another thread unlocks it.

made to wait until another thread has unlocked the mutex. At that point, the thread that wanted to lock the mutex can resume execution, find the mutex unlocked, lock it, and proceed.

If more than one thread is trying to lock the same mutex, only one of them will switch the mutex from unlocked to locked; that thread will be allowed to proceed. The others will wait until the mutex is again unlocked. This behavior of the lock operation provides mutual exclusion. For a thread to proceed past the point where it invokes the lock operation, it must be the single thread that succeeds in switching the mutex from unlocked to locked. Until the thread unlocks the mutex, one can say it *holds* the mutex (that is, has exclusive rights) and can safely operate on the associated data structure in a race-free fashion.

This freedom from races exists regardless of which one of the waiting threads is chosen as the one to lock the mutex. However, the question of which thread goes first may matter for other reasons; I return to it in Section 4.8.2.

Besides the basic operations to initialize a mutex, lock it, and unlock it, there may be other, less essential, operations as well. For example, there may be one to test whether a mutex is immediately lockable without waiting, and then to lock it if it is so. For systems that rely on manual reclamation of memory, there may also be an operation to destroy a mutex when it will no longer be used.

Individual operating systems and middleware systems provide mutex APIs that fit the general pattern I described, with varying details. In order to see one concrete example of an API, I will present the mutex operations included in the POSIX standard. Because this is a standard, many different operating systems provide this API, as well as perhaps other system-specific APIs.

In the POSIX API, you can declare `my_mutex` to be a mutex and initialize it with the default attributes as follows:

```
pthread_mutex_t my_mutex;
pthread_mutex_init(&my_mutex, 0);
```

A thread that wants to lock the mutex, operate on the associated data structure, and then unlock the mutex would do the following (perhaps with some error-checking added):

```
pthread_mutex_lock(&my_mutex);
// operate on the protected data structure
pthread_mutex_unlock(&my_mutex);
```

As an example, Figure 4.5 shows the key procedures from the ticket-sales example, written in C using the POSIX API. When all threads are done using the mutex (leaving

```
void sellTicket(){
  pthread_mutex_lock(&my_mutex);
  if(seatsRemaining > 0){
    dispenseTicket();
    seatsRemaining = seatsRemaining - 1;
    cashOnHand = cashOnHand + PRICE;
  } else
    displaySorrySoldOut();
  pthread_mutex_unlock(&my_mutex);
}

void audit(){
  pthread_mutex_lock(&my_mutex);
  int revenue = (TOTAL_SEATS - seatsRemaining) * PRICE;
  if(cashOnHand != revenue + STARTING_CASH){
    printf("Cash fails to match.\n");
    exit(1);
  }
  pthread_mutex_unlock(&my_mutex);
}
```

Figure 4.5 Each of these procedures begins by locking **my_mutex** and ends by unlocking it. Therefore, they will never race, even if called from concurrent threads. Additional code not shown here (perhaps in the main procedure) would first initialize **my_mutex**.

it in the unlocked state), the programmer is expected to destroy it, so that any underlying memory can be reclaimed. This is done by executing the following procedure call:

```
pthread_mutex_destroy(&my_mutex);
```

POSIX also provides a couple of variants on **pthread_mutex_lock** that are useful under more limited circumstances. One, **pthread_mutex_trylock**, differs in that it will never wait to acquire a mutex. Instead, it returns an error code if unable to immediately acquire the lock. The other, **pthread_mutex_timedlock**, allows the programmer to specify a maximum amount of time to wait. If the mutex cannot be acquired within that time, **pthread_mutex_timedlock** returns an error code.

Beyond their wide availability, another reason why POSIX mutexes are worth studying is that the programmer is allowed to choose among several variants, which provide different answers to two questions about exceptional circumstances. Other mutex APIs might include one specific answer to these questions, rather than exposing the full range of possibilities. The questions at issue are as follows:

- What happens if a thread tries to unlock a mutex that is unlocked, or that was locked by a different thread?
- What happens if a thread tries to lock a mutex that it already holds? (Note that if the thread were to wait for itself to unlock the mutex, this situation would constitute the simplest possible case of a deadlock. The cycle of waiting threads would consist of a single thread, waiting for itself.)

The POSIX standard allows the programmer to select from four different types of mutexes, each of which answers these two questions in a different way:

PTHREAD_MUTEX_DEFAULT If a thread tries to lock a mutex it already holds or unlock one it doesn't hold, all bets are off as to what will happen. The programmer has a responsibility never to make either of these attempts. Different POSIX-compliant systems may behave differently.

PTHREAD_MUTEX_ERROR_CHECK If a thread tries to lock a mutex that it already holds, or unlock a mutex that it doesn't hold, the operation returns an error code.

PTHREAD_MUTEX_NORMAL If a thread tries to lock a mutex that it already holds, it goes into a deadlock situation, waiting for itself to unlock the mutex, just as it would wait for any other thread. If a thread tries to unlock a mutex that it doesn't hold, all bets are off; each POSIX-compliant system is free to respond however it likes.

PTHREAD_MUTEX_RECURSIVE If a thread tries to unlock a mutex that it doesn't hold, the operation returns an error code. If a thread tries to lock a mutex that it already holds, the system simply increments a count of how many times the thread has locked the mutex and allows the thread to proceed. When the thread invokes the unlock operation, the counter is decremented, and only when it reaches 0 is the mutex really unlocked.

If you want to provoke a debate among experts on concurrent programming, ask their opinion of *recursive locking*, that is, of the mutex behavior specified by the POSIX option **PTHREAD_MUTEX_RECURSIVE**. On the one hand, recursive locking gets rid of one especially silly class of deadlocks, in which a thread waits for a mutex it already holds. On the other hand, a programmer with recursive locking available may not follow as disciplined a development approach. In particular, the programmer may not keep track of exactly which locks are held at each point in the program's execution.

4.3.2 Monitors: A More Structured Interface to Mutexes

Object-oriented programming involves packaging together data structures with the procedures that operate on them. In this context, mutexes can be used in a very rigidly structured way:

- All state within an object should be kept private, accessible only to code associated with that object.

- Every object (that might be shared between threads) should contain a mutex as an additional field, beyond those fields containing the object's state.

- Every method of an object (except private ones used internally) should start by locking that object's mutex and end by unlocking the mutex immediately before returning.

If these three rules are followed, then it will be impossible for two threads to race on the state of an object, because all access to the object's state will be protected by the object's mutex.

Programmers can follow these rules manually, or the programming language can provide automatic support for the rules. Automation ensures that the rules are consistently followed. It also means the source program will not be cluttered with mutex clichés, and hence will be more readable.

An object that automatically follows the mutex rules is called a *monitor*. Monitors are found in some programming languages, such as Concurrent Pascal, that have been used in research settings without becoming commercially popular. In these languages, using monitors can be as simple as using the keyword **monitor** at the beginning of a declaration for a class of objects. All public methods will then automatically lock and unlock an automatically supplied mutex. (Monitor languages also support another synchronization feature, condition variables, which I discuss in Section 4.5.)

Although true monitors have not become popular, the Java programming language provides a close approximation. To achieve monitor-style synchronization, the Java programmer needs to exercise some self-discipline, but less than with raw mutexes. More importantly, the resulting Java program is essentially as uncluttered as a true monitor program would be; all that is added is one keyword, **synchronized**, at the declaration of each nonprivate method.

Each Java object automatically has a mutex associated with it, of the recursively lockable kind. The programmer can choose to lock any object's mutex for the duration of any block of code by using a **synchronized** statement:

```
synchronized(someObject){
  // the code to do while holding someObject's mutex
}
```

Note that in this case, the code need not be operating on the state of `someObject`; nor does this code need to be in a method associated with that object. In other words, the `synchronized` statement is essentially as flexible as using raw mutexes, with the one key advantage that locking and unlocking are automatically paired. This advantage is important, because it eliminates one big class of programming errors. Programmers often forget to unlock mutexes under exceptional circumstances. For example, a procedure may lock a mutex at the beginning and unlock it at the end. However, in between may come an `if` statement that can return from the procedure with the mutex still locked.

Although the `synchronized` statement is flexible, typical Java programs don't use it much. Instead, programmers add the keyword `synchronized` to the declaration of public methods. For example, a `TicketVendor` class might follow the outline in Figure 4.6. Marking a method `synchronized` is equivalent to wrapping the entire body of that method in a `synchronized` statement:

```
synchronized(this){
  // the body
}
```

In other words, a synchronized method on an object will be executed while holding that object's mutex. For example, the `sellTicket` method is synchronized, so if two different threads invoke it, one will be served while the other waits its turn, because the `sellTicket` method is implicitly locking a mutex upon entry and unlocking it upon return, just like was done explicitly in the POSIX version of Figure 4.5. Similarly, a thread executing the `audit` method will need to wait until no ticket sale is in progress, because this method is also marked synchronized, and so acquires the same mutex.

In order to program in a monitor style in Java, you need to be disciplined in your use of the `private` and `public` keywords (including making all state `private`), and you need to mark all the public methods as `synchronized`.

4.3.3 Underlying Mechanisms for Mutexes

In this subsection, I will show how mutexes typically operate behind the scenes. I start with a version that functions correctly, but is inefficient, and then show how to build a more efficient version on top of it, and then a yet more efficient version on top of that. Keep in mind that I will not throw away my first two versions: they play a critical role in the final version. For simplicity, all three versions will be of the `PTHREAD_MUTEX_NORMAL` kind; that is, they won't do anything special if a thread tries to lock a mutex it already holds, nor if it tries to unlock one it doesn't hold. In Exercise 4.3, you can figure out the changes needed for `PTHREAD_MUTEX_RECURSIVE`.

```java
public class TicketVendor {
  private int seatsRemaining, cashOnHand;
  private static final int PRICE = 1000;

  public synchronized void sellTicket(){
    if(seatsRemaining > 0){
      dispenseTicket();
      seatsRemaining = seatsRemaining - 1;
      cashOnHand = cashOnHand + PRICE;
    } else
      displaySorrySoldOut();
  }

  public synchronized void audit(){
    // check seatsRemaining, cashOnHand
  }

  private void dispenseTicket(){
    // ...
  }

  private void displaySorrySoldOut(){
    // ...
  }

  public TicketVendor(){
    // ...
  }
}
```

Figure 4.6   Outline of a monitor-style class in Java.

The three versions of mutex are called the basic spinlock, cache-conscious spinlock, and queuing mutex, in increasing order of sophistication. The meaning of these names will become apparent as I explain the functioning of each kind of mutex. I will start with the basic spinlock.

All modern processor architectures have at least one instruction that can be used to both change the contents of a memory location and obtain information about the previous contents of the location. Crucially, these instructions are executed *atomically*, that is, as an indivisible unit that cannot be broken up by the arrival of an interrupt nor interleaved with the execution of an instruction on another processor. The details of these instructions vary; for concreteness, I will use the *exchange* operation, which atomically swaps the contents of a register with the contents of a memory location.

Suppose I represent a basic spinlock as a memory location that contains 1 if the mutex is unlocked and 0 if the mutex is locked. The unlock operation can be trivial: to unlock a mutex, just store 1 into it. The lock operation is a bit trickier and uses the atomic exchange operation; I can express it in pseudocode, as shown in Figure 4.7. The key idea here is to keep looping until the thread succeeds in changing the mutex from 1 to 0. Until then (so long as some other thread holds the lock), the thread keeps swapping one 0 with another 0, which does no harm. This process is illustrated in Figure 4.8.

To understand the motivation behind the cache-conscious spinlock, you need to know a little about cache coherence protocols in multiprocessor systems. Copies of

```
to lock mutex:
  let temp = 0
  repeat
    atomically exchange temp and mutex
  until temp = 1
```

Figure 4.7 The basic spinlock version of a mutex is a memory location storing 1 for unlocked and 0 for locked. Locking the mutex consists of repeatedly exchanging a register containing 0 with the memory location until the location is changed from 1 to 0.

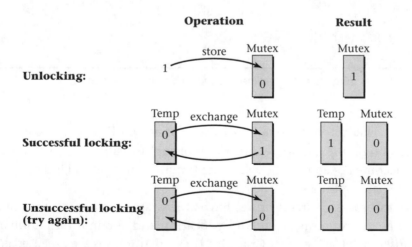

Figure 4.8 Unlocking a basic spinlock consists of storing a 1 into it. Locking it consists of storing a 0 into it using an atomic exchange instruction. The exchange instruction allows the locking thread to verify that the value in memory really was changed from 1 to 0. If not, the thread repeats the attempt.

a given block of memory can reside in several different processors' caches, as long as the processors only read from the memory locations. As soon as one processor wants to write into the cache block, however, some communication between the caches is necessary so that other processors don't read out-of-date values. Most typically, the cache where the writing occurs invalidates all the other caches' copies so that it has exclusive ownership. If one of the other processors now wants to write, the block needs to be flushed out of the first cache and loaded exclusively into the second. If the two processors keep alternately writing into the same block, there will be continual traffic on the memory interconnect as the cache block is transferred back and forth between the two caches.

This is exactly what will happen with the basic spinlock version of mutex locking if two threads (on two processors) are both waiting for the same lock. The atomic exchange instructions on the two processors will both be writing into the cache block containing the spinlock. Contention for a mutex may not happen often. When it does, however, the performance will be sufficiently terrible to motivate an improvement. Cache-conscious spinlocks will use the same simple approach as basic spinlocks when there is no contention, but will get rid of the cache coherence traffic while waiting for a contended mutex.

In order to allow multiple processors to wait for a lock without generating traffic outside their individual caches, they must be waiting while using only reads of the mutex. When they see the mutex become unlocked, they then need to try grabbing it with an atomic exchange. This approach leads to the pseudocode shown in Figure 4.9. Notice that in the common case where the mutex can be acquired immediately, this version acts just like the original. Only if the attempt to acquire the mutex fails is anything done differently. Even then, the mutex will eventually be acquired the same way as before.

```
to lock mutex:
  let temp = 0
  repeat
    atomically exchange temp and mutex
    if temp = 0 then
      while mutex = 0
        do nothing
  until temp = 1
```

Figure 4.9 Cache-conscious spinlocks are represented the same way as basic spinlocks, using a single memory location. However, the lock operation now uses ordinary read instructions in place of most of the atomic exchanges while waiting for the mutex to be unlocked.

The two versions of mutexes that I have presented thus far share one key property, which explains why both are called spinlocks. They both engage in busy waiting if the mutex is not immediately available. Recall from my discussion of scheduling that busy waiting means waiting by continually executing instructions that check for the awaited event. A mutex that uses busy waiting is called a *spinlock*.

The alternative to busy waiting is to notify the operating system that the thread needs to wait. The operating system can then change the thread's state to waiting and move it to a wait queue, where it is not eligible for time on the processor. Instead, the scheduler will use the processor to run other threads. When the mutex is unlocked, the waiting thread can be made runnable again. Because this form of mutex makes use of a wait queue, it is called a queuing mutex.

Spinlocks are inefficient, for the same reason as any busy waiting is inefficient. The thread does not make any more headway, no matter how many times it spins around its loop. Therefore, using the processor for a different thread would benefit that other thread without harming the waiting one.

However, there is one flaw in this argument. There is some overhead cost for notifying the operating system of the desire to wait, changing the thread's state, and doing a context switch, with the attendant loss of cache locality. Thus, in a situation where the spinlock needs to spin only briefly before finding the mutex unlocked, the thread might actually waste less time busy waiting than it would waste getting out of other threads' ways. The relative efficiency of spinlocks and queuing mutexes depends on how long the thread needs to wait before the mutex becomes available.

For this reason, spinlocks are appropriate to use for mutexes that are held only briefly, and hence should be quickly acquirable. As an example, the Linux kernel uses spinlocks to protect many of its internal data structures during the brief operations on them. For example, I mentioned that the scheduler keeps the runnable threads in two arrays, organized by priority. Whenever the scheduler wants to insert a thread into one of these arrays, or otherwise operate on them, it locks a spinlock, does the brief operation, and then unlocks the spinlock.

Queuing mutexes are still needed for those cases where a thread might hold a mutex a long time—long enough that other contenders shouldn't busy wait. These mutexes will be more complex. Rather than being stored in a single memory location (as with spinlocks), each mutex will have three components:

- A memory location used to record the mutex's state, 1 for unlocked or 0 for locked.
- A list of threads waiting to acquire the mutex. This list is what allows the scheduler to place the threads in a waiting state, in place of busy waiting. Using the terminology of Chapter 3, this list is a wait queue.
- A cache-conscious spinlock, used to protect against races in operations on the mutex itself.

```
to lock mutex:
  lock mutex.spinlock (in cache-conscious fashion)
  if mutex.state = 1 then
    let mutex.state = 0
    unlock mutex.spinlock
  else
    add current thread to mutex.waiters
    remove current thread from runnable threads
    unlock mutex.spinlock
    yield to a runnable thread
```

Figure 4.10   An attempt to lock a queuing mutex that is already in the locked state causes the thread to join the wait queue, `mutex.waiters`.

```
to unlock mutex:
  lock mutex.spinlock (in cache-conscious fashion)
  if mutex.waiters is empty then
    let mutex.state = 1
  else
    move one thread from mutex.waiters to runnable
  unlock mutex.spinlock
```

Figure 4.11   If there is any waiting thread, the unlock operation on a queuing mutex causes a thread to become runnable. Note that in this case, the mutex is left in the locked state; effectively, the locked mutex is being passed directly from one thread to another.

In my pseudocode, I will refer to these three components as `mutex.state`, `mutex.waiters`, and `mutex.spinlock`, respectively.

Under these assumptions, the locking and unlocking operations can be performed as shown in the pseudocode of Figures 4.10 and 4.11. Figures 4.12 and 4.13 illustrate the functioning of these operations. One important feature to note in this mutex design concerns what happens when a thread performs the unlock operation on a mutex that has one or more threads in the waiters list. As you can see in Figure 4.11, the mutex's state variable is not changed from the locked state (0) to the unlocked state (1). Instead, the mutex is left locked, and one of the waiting threads is woken up. In other words, the locked mutex is passed directly from one thread to another, without ever really being unlocked. In Section 4.8.2, I will explain how this design is partially responsible for the so-called convoy phenomenon, which I describe there. In that same section, I will also present an alternative design for mutexes that puts the mutex into the unlocked state.

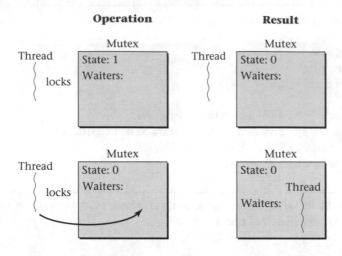

Figure 4.12 Locking a queuing mutex that is unlocked simply changes the mutex's state. Locking an already-locked queuing mutex, on the other hand, puts the thread into the waiters list.

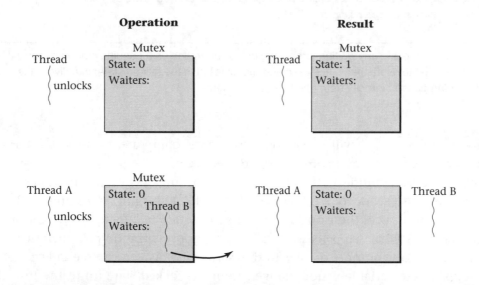

Figure 4.13 Unlocking a queuing mutex with no waiting threads simply changes the mutex's state. Unlocking a queuing mutex with waiting threads, on the other hand, leaves the state set to locked but causes one of the waiting threads to start running again, having acquired the lock.

4.4 Other Synchronization Patterns

Recall that synchronization refers to any form of control over the relative timing of two or more threads. As such, synchronization includes more than just mutual exclusion; a programmer may want to impose some restriction on relative timing other than the rule of one thread at a time. In this section, I present three other patterns of synchronization that crop up over and over again in many applications: bounded buffers, readers/writers locks, and barriers. Sections 4.4.1 through 4.4.3 will describe the desired synchronization; Sections 4.5 and 4.6 show techniques that can be used to achieve the synchronization.

4.4.1 Bounded Buffers

Often, two threads are linked together in a processing *pipeline*. That is, the first thread produces a sequence of values that are consumed by the second thread. For example, the first thread may be extracting all the textual words from a document (by skipping over the formatting codes) and passing those words to a second thread that speaks the words aloud.

One simple way to organize the processing would be by strict alternation between the producing and consuming threads. In the preceding example, the first thread would extract a word, and then wait while the second thread converted it into sound. The second thread would then wait while the first thread extracted the next word. However, this approach doesn't yield any concurrency: only one thread is runnable at a time. This lack of concurrency may result in suboptimal performance if the computer system has two processors, or if one of the threads spends a lot of time waiting for an I/O device.

Instead, consider running the producer and the consumer concurrently. Every time the producer has a new value ready, the producer will store the value into an intermediate storage area, called a *buffer*. Every time the consumer is ready for the next value, it will retrieve the value from the buffer. Under normal circumstances, each can operate at its own pace. However, if the consumer goes to the buffer to retrieve a value and finds the buffer empty, the consumer will need to wait for the producer to catch up. Also, if you want to limit the size of the buffer (that is, to use a *bounded buffer*), you need to make the producer wait if it gets too far ahead of the consumer and fills the buffer. Putting these two synchronization restrictions in place ensures that over the long haul, the rate of the two threads will match up, although over the short term, either may run faster than the other.

You should be familiar with the bounded buffer pattern from businesses in the real world. For example, the cooks at a fast-food restaurant fry burgers concurrently with

Figure 4.14 A cook fries burgers and places them in a bounded buffer, queued up for later sale. A cashier takes burgers from the buffer to sell. If there are none available, the cashier waits. Similarly, if the buffer area is full, the cook takes a break from frying burgers.

the cashiers selling them. In between the two is a bounded buffer of already-cooked burgers. The exact number of burgers in the buffer will grow or shrink somewhat as one group of workers is temporarily a little faster than the other. Only under extreme circumstances does one group of workers have to wait for the other, as illustrated in Figure 4.14.

One easy place to see bounded buffers at work in computer systems is the *pipe* feature built into UNIX-family operating systems, including Linux and Mac OS X. (Microsoft Windows also now has an analogous feature.) Pipes allow the output produced by one process to serve as input for another. For example, on a Mac OS X system, you could open a terminal window with a shell in it and give the following command:

```
ls | say
```

This runs two programs concurrently. The first, `ls`, lists the files in your current directory. The second one, `say`, converts its textual input into speech and plays it over the computer's speakers. In the shell command, the vertical bar character (|) indicates the pipe from the first program to the second. The net result is a spoken listing of your files.

A more mundane version of this example works not only on Mac OS X, but also on other UNIX-family systems such as Linux:

```
ls | tr a-z A-Z
```

Again, this runs two programs concurrently. This time the second one, `tr`, copies characters from its input to its output, with some changes (transliterations) along the way; in this case, replacing lowercase letters `a-z` with the corresponding uppercase letters

A-Z. The net result is an uppercase listing of your files. The file listing may get ahead of the transliteration, as long as it doesn't overflow a buffer the operating system provides for the pipe. Once there is a backlog of listed files in the buffer, the transliteration can run as fast as it wants until it exhausts that backlog.

4.4.2 Readers/Writers Locks

My next example of a synchronization pattern is actually quite similar to mutual exclusion. Recall that in the ticket-sales example, the audit function needed to acquire the mutex, even though auditing is a read-only operation, in order to make sure that the audit read a consistent combination of state variables. That design achieved correctness, but at the cost of needlessly limiting concurrency: it prevented two audits from being under way at the same time, even though two (or more) read-only operations cannot possibly interfere with each other. My goal now is to rectify that problem.

A *readers/writers lock* is much like a mutex, except that when a thread locks the lock, it specifies whether it is planning to do any writing to the protected data structure or only reading from it. Just as with a mutex, the lock operation may not immediately complete; instead, it waits until such time as the lock can be acquired. The difference is that any number of readers can hold the lock at the same time, as shown in Figure 4.15;

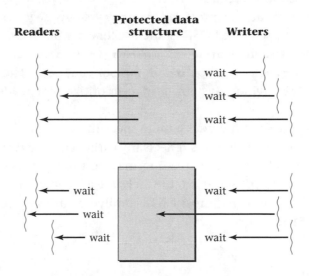

Figure 4.15   A readers/writers lock can be held either by any number of readers or by one writer. When the lock is held by readers, all the reader threads can read the protected data structure concurrently.

they will not wait for each other. A reader will wait, however, if a writer holds the lock. A writer will wait if the lock is held by any other thread, whether by another writer or by one or more readers.

Readers/writers locks are particularly valuable in situations where some of the read-only operations are time-consuming, as when reading a file stored on disk. This is especially true if many readers are expected. The choice between a mutex and a readers/writers lock is a performance trade-off. Because the mutex is simpler, it has lower overhead. However, the readers/writers lock may pay for its overhead by allowing more concurrency.

One interesting design question arises if a readers/writers lock is held by one or more readers and has one or more writers waiting. Suppose a new reader tries to acquire the lock. Should it be allowed to, or should it be forced to wait until after the writers? On the surface, there seems to be no reason for the reader to wait, because it can coexist with the existing readers, thereby achieving greater concurrency. The problem is that an overlapping succession of readers can keep the writers waiting arbitrarily long. The writers could wind up waiting even when the only remaining readers arrived long after the writers did. This is a form of *starvation*, in that a thread is unfairly prevented from running by other threads. To prevent this particular kind of starvation, some versions of readers/writers locks make new readers wait until after the waiting writers.

In Section 4.5, you will learn how you could build readers/writers locks from more primitive synchronization mechanisms. However, because readers/writers locks are so generally useful, they are already provided by many systems, so you may never actually have to build them yourself. The POSIX standard, for example, includes readers/writers locks with procedures such as **pthread_rwlock_init**, **pthread_rwlock_rdlock**, **pthread_rwlock_wrlock**, and **pthread_rwlock_unlock**. The POSIX standard leaves it up to each individual system how to prioritize new readers versus waiting writers.

The POSIX standard also includes a more specialized form of readers/writers locks specifically associated with files. This reflects my earlier comment that readers/writers locking is especially valuable when reading may be time-consuming, as with a file stored on disk. In the POSIX standard, file locks are available only through the complex **fcntl** procedure. However, most UNIX-family operating systems also provide a simpler interface, **flock**.

4.4.3 Barriers

Barrier synchronization is the last common synchronization pattern I will discuss. Barriers are most commonly used in programs that do large-scale numerical calculations for scientific or engineering applications, such as simulating ocean currents. However, they may also crop up in other applications, as long as there is a requirement for all threads in a group to finish one phase of the computation before any of them moves on to the next phase. In scientific computations, the threads are often dividing up the processing of a large matrix. For example, ten threads may each process 200 rows of a 2000-row matrix. The requirement for all threads to finish one phase of processing before starting the next comes from the fact that the overall computation is a sequence of matrix operations; parallel processing occurs only within each matrix operation.

When a barrier is created (initialized), the programmer specifies how many threads will be sharing it. Each of the threads completes the first phase of the computation and then invokes the barrier's wait operation. For most of the threads, the wait operation does not immediately return; therefore, the thread calling it cannot immediately proceed. The one exception is whichever thread is the last to call the wait operation. The barrier can tell which thread is the last one, because the programmer specified how many threads there are. When this last thread invokes the wait operation, the wait operation immediately returns. Moreover, all the other waiting threads finally have their wait operations also return, as illustrated in Figure 4.16. Thus, they can now all proceed on to the second phase of the computation. Typically, the same barrier can then be reused between the second and third phases, and so forth. (In other words, the barrier reinitializes its state once it releases all the waiting threads.)

Just as with readers/writers locks, you will see how barriers can be defined in terms of more general synchronization mechanisms. However, once again there is little reason to do so in practice, because barriers are provided as part of POSIX and other widely available APIs.

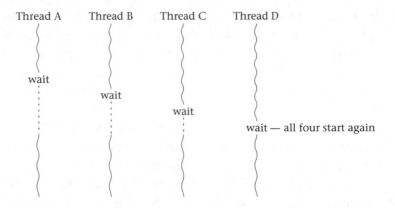

Figure 4.16 A barrier is created for a specific number of threads. In this case, there are four. When the last of those threads invokes the wait operation, all the waiting threads in the group start running again.

4.5 Condition Variables

In order to solve synchronization problems, such as the three described in Section 4.4, you need some mechanism that allows a thread to wait until circumstances are appropriate for it to proceed. A producer may need to wait for buffer space, or a consumer may need to wait for data. A reader may need to wait until a writer has unlocked, or a writer may need to wait for the last reader to unlock. A thread that has reached a barrier may need to wait for all the other threads to do so. Each situation has its own condition for which a thread must wait, and there are many other application-specific conditions besides. (A video playback that has been paused might wait until the user presses the pause button again.)

All these examples can be handled by using *condition variables*, a synchronization mechanism that works in partnership with monitors or with mutexes used in the style of monitors. There are two basic operations on a condition variable: *wait* and *notify*. (Some systems use the name *signal* instead of notify.) A thread that finds circumstances not to its liking executes the wait operation and thereby goes to sleep until such time as another thread invokes the notify operation. For example, in a bounded buffer, the producer might wait on a condition variable if it finds the buffer full. The consumer, upon freeing up some space in the buffer, would invoke the notify operation on that condition variable.

Before delving into all the important details and variants, a concrete example may be helpful. Figure 4.17 shows the Java code for a **BoundedBuffer** class.

Before I explain how this example works, and then return to a more general discussion of condition variables, you should take a moment to consider how you would test such a class. First, it might help to reduce the size of the buffer, so that all qualitatively different situations can be tested more quickly. Second, you need a test program that has multiple threads doing insertions and retrievals, with some way to see the difference between when each operation is started and when it completes. In the case of the retrievals, you will also need to see that the retrieved values are correct. Designing such a test program is surprisingly interesting; you can have this experience in Programming Project 4.5.

In Java, each object has a single condition variable automatically associated with it, just as it has a mutex. The **wait** method waits on the object's condition variable, and the **notifyAll** method wakes up all threads waiting on the object's condition variable. Both of these methods need to be called by a thread that holds the object's mutex. In my **BoundedBuffer** example, I ensured this in a straightforward way by using **wait** and **notifyAll** inside methods that are marked **synchronized**.

Having seen that **wait** and **notifyAll** need to be called with the mutex held, you may spot a problem. If a waiting thread holds the mutex, there will be no way for

```
public class BoundedBuffer {
  private Object[] buffer = new Object[20]; // arbitrary size
  private int numOccupied = 0;
  private int firstOccupied = 0;

  /* invariant: 0 <= numOccupied <= buffer.length
     0 <= firstOccupied < buffer.length
     buffer[(firstOccupied + i) % buffer.length]
     contains the (i+1)th oldest entry,
     for all i such that 0 <= i < numOccupied  */

  public synchronized void insert(Object o)
    throws InterruptedException
  {
    while(numOccupied == buffer.length)
      // wait for space
      wait();
    buffer[(firstOccupied + numOccupied) % buffer.length] = o;
    numOccupied++;
    // in case any retrieves are waiting for data, wake them
    notifyAll();
  }

  public synchronized Object retrieve()
    throws InterruptedException
  {
    while(numOccupied == 0)
      // wait for data
      wait();
    Object retrieved = buffer[firstOccupied];
    buffer[firstOccupied] = null; // may help garbage collector
    firstOccupied = (firstOccupied + 1) % buffer.length;
    numOccupied--;
    // in case any inserts are waiting for space, wake them
    notifyAll();
    return retrieved;
  }
}
```

Figure 4.17   BoundedBuffer class using monitors and condition variables.

any other thread to acquire the mutex, and thus be able to call `notifyAll`. Until you learn the rest of the story, it seems as though any thread that invokes `wait` is doomed to eternal waiting.

The solution to this dilemma is as follows. When a thread invokes the wait operation, it must hold the associated mutex. However, the wait operation releases the mutex before putting the thread into its waiting state. That way, the mutex is available to a potential waker. When the waiting thread is awoken, it reacquires the mutex before the wait operation returns. (In the case of recursive mutexes, as used in Java, the awakening thread reacquires the mutex with the same lock count as before, so that it can still do just as many unlock operations.)

The fact that a waiting thread temporarily releases the mutex helps explain two features of the `BoundedBuffer` example. First, the waiting is done at the very beginning of the methods. This ensures that the invariant is still intact when the mutex is released. (More generally, the waiting could happen later, as long as no state variables have been updated, or even as long as they have been put back into an invariant-respecting state.) Second, the waiting is done in a loop; only when the waited-for condition has been verified to hold does the method move on to its real work. The loop is essential because an awoken thread needs to reacquire the mutex, contending with any other threads that are also trying to acquire the mutex. There is no guarantee that the awoken thread will get the mutex first. As such, there is no guarantee what state it will find; it may need to wait again. Another reason the loop is necessary is because on rare occasion the `wait` procedure may return without `notify` or `notifyAll` having been invoked, a circumstance known as a *spurious wakeup*.

When a waiting thread releases the mutex in order to wait on the condition variable, these two actions are done indivisibly. There is no way another thread can acquire the mutex before the first thread has started waiting on the condition variable. This ensures no other thread will do a notify operation until after the thread that wants to wait is actually waiting.

In addition to waiting for appropriate conditions at the top of each method, I have invoked `notifyAll` at the end of each method. This position is less crucial, because the `notifyAll` method does not release the mutex. The calling thread continues to hold the mutex until it reaches the end of the synchronized method. Because an awoken thread needs to reacquire the mutex, it will not be able to make any headway until the notifying method finishes, regardless of where in that method the notification is done.

One early version of monitors with condition variables (as described by Hoare) used a different approach. The notify operation immediately transferred the mutex to the awoken thread, with no contention from other waiting threads. The thread performing the notify operation then waited until it received the mutex back from the awoken thread. Today, however, the version I described previously seems to be dominant. In particular, it is used not only in Java, but also in the POSIX API.

The `BoundedBuffer` code in Figure 4.17 takes a very aggressive approach to notifying waiting threads: at the end of any operation all waiting threads are woken using `notifyAll`. This is a very safe approach; if the `BoundedBuffer`'s state was changed in a way of interest to any thread, that thread will be sure to notice. Other threads that don't care can simply go back to waiting. However, the program's efficiency may be improved somewhat by reducing the amount of notification done. Remember, though, that correctness should always come first, with optimization later, if at all. Before optimizing, check whether the simple, correct version actually performs inadequately.

There are two approaches to reducing notification. One is to put the `notifyAll` inside an `if` statement, so that it is done only under some circumstances, rather than unconditionally. In particular, producers should be waiting only if the buffer is full, and consumers should be waiting only if the buffer is empty. Therefore, the only times when notification is needed are when inserting into an empty buffer or retrieving from a full buffer. In Programming Project 4.6, you can modify the code to reflect this and test that it still works.

The other approach to reducing notification is to use the `notify` method in place of `notifyAll`. This way, only a single waiting thread is awoken, rather than all waiting threads. Remember that optimization should be considered only if the straightforward version performs inadequately. This cautious attitude is appropriate because programmers find it rather tricky to reason about whether `notify` will suffice. As such, this optimization is quite error prone. In order to verify that the change from `notifyAll` to `notify` is correct, you need to check two conditions:

1. There is no danger of waking too few threads. Either you have some way to know that only one is waiting, or you know that only one would be able to proceed, with the others looping back to waiting.

2. There is no danger of waking the wrong thread. Either you have some way to know that only one is waiting, or you know that all are equally able to proceed. If there is any thread that could proceed if it got the mutex first, then all threads have that property. For example, if all the waiting threads are executing the identical while loop, this condition will be satisfied.

In Exercise 4.4, you can show that these two conditions do not hold for the `BoundedBuffer` example: replacing `notifyAll` with `notify` would not be safe in this case. This is true even if the notification operation is done unconditionally, rather than inside an `if` statement.

One limitation of Java is that each object has only a single condition variable. In the **BoundedBuffer** example, any thread waits on that one condition variable, whether it is waiting for space in the **insert** method or for data in the **retrieve** method. In a system which allows multiple condition variables to be associated with the same monitor (or mutex), you could use two different condition variables. That would allow you to specifically notify a thread waiting for space (or one waiting for data).

The POSIX API allows multiple condition variables per mutex. In Programming Project 4.7 you can use this feature to rewrite the **BoundedBuffer** example with two separate condition variables, one used to wait for space and the other used to wait for data.

POSIX condition variables are initialized with **pthread_cond_init** independent of any particular mutex; the mutex is instead passed as an argument to **pthread_cond_wait**, along with the condition variable being waited on. This is a somewhat error-prone arrangement, because all concurrent waiters need to pass in the same mutex. The operations corresponding to **notify** and **notifyAll** are called **pthread_cond_signal** and **pthread_cond_broadcast**.

The same technique I illustrated with **BoundedBuffer** can be applied equally well for readers/writers locks or barriers; I leave these as Programming Projects 4.8 and 4.11. More importantly, the same technique will also work for application-specific synchronization needs. For example, a video player might have a state variable that records whether it is currently paused. The playback thread checks that variable before displaying each frame, and if paused, waits on a condition variable. The user-interface thread sets the variable in response to the user pressing the pause button. When the user interface puts the variable into the unpaused state, it does a notify operation on the condition variable. You can develop an application analogous to this in Programming Project 4.3.

4.6 Semaphores

You have seen that monitors with condition variables are quite general and can be used to synthesize other more special-purpose synchronization mechanisms, such as readers/writers locks. Another synchronization mechanism with the same generality is the semaphore. For most purposes, semaphores are less natural, resulting in more error-prone code. In those applications where they are natural (for example, bounded buffers), they result in very succinct, clear code. That is probably not the main reason for their continued use, however. Instead, they seem to be hanging on largely out of historical inertia, having gotten a seven- to nine-year head start over monitors. (Semaphores date to 1965, as opposed to the early 1970s for monitors.)

A *semaphore* is essentially an unsigned integer variable, that is, a variable that can take on only nonnegative integer values. However, semaphores may not be freely operated on with arbitrary arithmetic. Instead, only three operations are allowed:

- At the time the semaphore is created, it may be initialized to any nonnegative integer of the programmer's choice.

- A semaphore may be increased by 1. The operation to do this is generally called either **up** or **V**. The letter **V** is short for a Dutch word that made sense to Dijkstra, the 1965 originator of semaphores. I will use **up**.

- A semaphore may be decreased by 1. The operation to do this is frequently called either **down** or **P**. Again, **P** is a Dutch abbreviation. I will use **down**. Because the semaphore's value must stay nonnegative, the thread performing a **down** operation waits if the value is 0. Only once another thread has performed an **up** operation to make the value positive does the waiting thread continue with its **down** operation.

One common use for semaphores is as mutexes. If a semaphore is initialized to 1, it can serve as a mutex, with **down** as the locking operation and **up** as the unlocking operation. Assuming that locking and unlocking are properly paired, the semaphore will only ever have the values 0 and 1. When it is locked, the value will be 0, and any further attempt to lock it (using **down**) will be forced to wait. When it is unlocked, the value will be 1, and locking can proceed. Note, however, that semaphores used in this limited way have no advantage over mutexes. Moreover, if a program bug results in an attempt to unlock an already unlocked mutex, a special-purpose mutex could signal the error, whereas a general-purpose semaphore will simply increase to 2, likely causing nasty behavior later when two threads are both allowed to execute **down**.

A better use for semaphores is for keeping track of the available quantity of some resource, such as free spaces or data values in a bounded buffer. Whenever a thread creates a unit of the resource, it increases the semaphore. Whenever a thread wishes to consume a unit of the resource, it first does a **down** operation on the semaphore. This both forces the thread to wait until at least one unit of the resource is available and stakes the thread's claim to that unit.

Following this pattern, the **BoundedBuffer** class can be rewritten to use semaphores, as shown in Figure 4.18. This assumes the availability of a class of semaphores.

```
public class BoundedBuffer {
  private java.util.List buffer =
    java.util.Collections.synchronizedList
    (new java.util.LinkedList());

  private static final int SIZE = 20; // arbitrary

  private Semaphore occupiedSem = new Semaphore(0);
  private Semaphore freeSem = new Semaphore(SIZE);

  /* invariant: occupiedSem + freeSem = SIZE
     buffer.size() = occupiedSem
     buffer contains entries from oldest to youngest */

  public void insert(Object o) throws InterruptedException{
    freeSem.down();
    buffer.add(o);
    occupiedSem.up();
  }

  public Object retrieve() throws InterruptedException{
    occupiedSem.down();
    Object retrieved = buffer.remove(0);
    freeSem.up();
    return retrieved;
  }
}
```

Figure 4.18 Alternative `BoundedBuffer` class, using semaphores.

In Programming Project 4.12, you can write a `Semaphore` class using Java's built-in mutexes and condition variables.

In order to show semaphores in the best possible light, I also moved away from using an array to store the buffer. Instead, I used a `List`, provided by the Java API. If, in Programming Project 4.13, you try rewriting this example to use an array (as in Figure 4.17), you will discover two blemishes. First, you will need the `numOccupied` integer variable, as in Figure 4.17. This duplicates the information contained in `occupiedSem`, simply in a different form. Second, you will need to introduce explicit mutex synchronization with `synchronized` statements around the code that updates the nonsemaphore state variables. With those complications, semaphores lose some of their charm. However, by using a `List`, I hid the extra complexity.

4.7 Deadlock

In Chapter 2, I introduced concurrency as a way to solve problems of responsiveness and throughput. Unfortunately, concurrency created its own problem—races. Therefore, I introduced synchronization to solve the problem of races. The obvious question is, what new problems arise from synchronization? One easy answer is that synchronization has reintroduced the original responsiveness and throughput problems to some lesser degree, because synchronization reduces concurrency. However, as you will see in this section, synchronization also creates an entirely new problem, and one that is potentially more serious. Section 4.7.1 explains this problem, known as deadlock, whereby threads can wind up permanently waiting. Sections 4.7.2 through 4.7.4 explain three different solutions to the problem.

4.7.1 The Deadlock Problem

To illustrate what a deadlock is, and how one can arise, consider a highly simplified system for keeping bank accounts. Suppose each account is an object with two components: a mutex and a current balance. A procedure for transferring money from one account to another might look as follows, in pseudocode:

```
to transfer amount from sourceAccount to destinationAccount:
  lock sourceAccount.mutex
  lock destinationAccount.mutex
  sourceAccount.balance = sourceAccount.balance - amount
  destinationAccount.balance = destinationAccount.balance + amount
  unlock sourceAccount.mutex
  unlock destinationAccount.mutex
```

Suppose I am feeling generous and transfer $100 from `myAccount` to `yourAccount`. Suppose you are feeling even more generous and transfer $250 from `yourAccount` to `myAccount`. With any luck, at the end I should be $150 richer and you should be $150 poorer. If either transfer request is completed before the other starts, this is exactly what happens. However, what if the two execute concurrently?

The mutexes prevent any race condition, so you can be sure that the accounts are not left in an inconsistent state. Note that we have locked both accounts for the entire duration of the transfer, rather than locking each only long enough to update its balance. That way, an auditor can't see an alarming situation where money has disappeared from one account but not yet appeared in the other account.

However, even though there is no race, not even with an auditor, all is not well. Consider the following sequence of events:

1. I lock the source account of my transfer to you. That is, I lock `myAccount.mutex`.

2. You lock the source account of your transfer to me. That is, you lock `yourAccount.mutex`.

3. I try to lock the destination account of my transfer to you. That is, I try to lock `yourAccount.mutex`. Because you already hold this mutex, I am forced to wait.

4. You try to lock the destination account of your transfer to me. That is, you try to lock `myAccount.mutex`. Because I already hold this mutex, you are forced to wait.

At this point, each of us is waiting for the other: we have deadlocked.

More generally, a *deadlock* exists whenever there is a cycle of threads, each waiting for some resource held by the next. In the example, there were two threads and the resources involved were two mutexes. Although deadlocks can involve other resources as well (consider readers/writers locks, for example), I will focus on mutexes for simplicity.

As an example of a deadlock involving more than two threads, consider generalizing the preceding scenario of transferring money between bank accounts. Suppose, for example, that there are five bank accounts, numbered 0 through 4. There are also five threads. Each thread is trying to transfer money from one account to another, as shown in Figure 4.19. As before, each transfer involves locking the source and destination accounts. Once again, the threads can deadlock if each one locks the source account first, and then tries to lock the destination account. This situation is

Thread	Source Account	Destination Account
0	0	1
1	1	2
2	2	3
3	3	4
4	4	0

Figure 4.19   Each of five threads tries to transfer money from a source account to a destination account. If each thread locks its source account, none will be able to proceed by locking its destination account.

Figure 4.20 Five philosophers, numbered 0 through 4, have places around a circular dining table. There is a fork between each pair of adjacent places. When each philosopher tries to pick up two forks, one at a time, deadlock can result.

much more famous when dressed up as the dining philosophers problem, which I describe next.

In 1972, Dijkstra wrote about a group of five philosophers, each of whom had a place at a round dining table, where they ate a particularly difficult kind of spaghetti that required two forks. There were five forks at the table, one between each pair of adjacent plates, as shown in Figure 4.20. Apparently Dijkstra was not concerned with communicable diseases such as mononucleosis, because he thought it was OK for the philosophers seated to the left and right of a particular fork to share it. Instead, he was concerned with the possibility of deadlock. If all five philosophers start by picking up their respective left-hand forks and then wait for their right-hand forks to become available, they wind up deadlocked. In Exploration Project 4.2, you can try out a computer simulation of the dining philosophers. In that same Exploration Project, you can also apply the deadlock prevention approach described in Section 4.7.2 to the dining philosophers problem.

Deadlocks are usually quite rare even if no special attempt is made to prevent them, because most locks are not held very long. Thus, the window of opportunity for deadlocking is quite narrow, and, like races, the timing must be exactly wrong. For a very noncritical system, one might choose to ignore the possibility of deadlocks. Even if the system needs the occasional reboot due to deadlocking, other malfunctions will probably be more common. Nonetheless, you should learn some options for dealing with deadlocks, both because some systems are critical and because ignoring a known problem is unprofessional. In Sections 4.7.2 through 4.7.4, I explain three of the most practical ways to address the threat of deadlocks.

4.7.2 Deadlock Prevention Through Resource Ordering

The ideal way to cope with deadlocks is to prevent them from happening. One very practical technique for deadlock prevention can be illustrated through the example of transferring money between two bank accounts. Each of the two accounts is stored somewhere in the computer's memory, which can be specified through a numerical address. I will use the notation `min(account1, account2)` to mean whichever of the two account objects occurs at the lower address (earlier in memory). Similarly, I will use `max(account1, account2)` to mean whichever occurs at the higher address. I can use this ordering on the accounts (or any other ordering, such as by account number) to make a deadlock-free transfer procedure:

```
to transfer amount from sourceAccount to destinationAccount:
  lock min(sourceAccount, destinationAccount).mutex
  lock max(sourceAccount, destinationAccount).mutex
  sourceAccount.balance = sourceAccount.balance - amount
  destinationAccount.balance = destinationAccount.balance + amount
  unlock sourceAccount.mutex
  unlock destinationAccount.mutex
```

Now if I try transferring money to you, and you try transferring money to me, we will both lock the two accounts' mutexes in the same order. No deadlock is possible; one transfer will run to completion, and then the other.

The same technique can be used whenever all the mutexes (or other resources) to be acquired are known in advance. Each thread should acquire the resources it needs in an agreed-upon order, such as by increasing memory address. No matter how many threads and resources are involved, no deadlock can occur.

As one further example of this technique, you can look at some code from the Linux kernel. Recall from Chapter 3 that the scheduler keeps the run queue, which holds runnable threads, in a pair of arrays organized by priority. In the kernel source code, this structure is known as a runqueue. Each processor in a multiprocessor system has its own runqueue. When the scheduler moves a thread from one processor's runqueue to another's, it needs to lock both runqueues. Figure 4.21 shows the code to do this. Note that this procedure uses the deadlock prevention technique with one refinement: it also tests for the special case that the two runqueues are in fact one and the same.

Deadlock prevention is not always possible. In particular, the ordering technique I showed cannot be used if the mutexes that need locking only become apparent one by one as the computation proceeds, such as when following a linked list or other pointer-based data structure. Thus, you need to consider coping with deadlocks, rather than only preventing them.

```
static inline
void double_rq_lock(runqueue_t *rq1, runqueue_t *rq2)
{
        if (rq1 == rq2)
                spin_lock(&rq1->lock);
        else {
                if (rq1 < rq2) {
                        spin_lock(&rq1->lock);
                        spin_lock(&rq2->lock);
                } else {
                        spin_lock(&rq2->lock);
                        spin_lock(&rq1->lock);
                }
        }
}
```

Figure 4.21   The Linux scheduler uses deadlock prevention when locking two runqueues.

4.7.3 Ex Post Facto Deadlock Detection

In order to diagnose deadlocks, you need some information about who is waiting for whom. Suppose that each mutex records not just whether it is locked or unlocked, but also which thread it is held by, if any. (This information may be useful for unrelated purposes as well, such as implementing recursive or error-checking mutexes.) Additionally, when a thread is unable to immediately acquire a mutex and is put into a waiting state, you can record which mutex it is waiting for. With this information, you can construct a *resource allocation graph*. Figure 4.22 shows an example graph for Section 4.7.1's sample deadlock between bank account transfers. Squares are threads and circles are mutexes. The arrows show which mutex each thread is waiting to acquire and which thread each mutex is currently held by. Because the graph has a cycle, it shows that the system is deadlocked.

A system can test for deadlocks periodically or when a thread has waited an unreasonably long time for a lock. In order to test for a deadlock, the system uses a standard graph algorithm to check whether the resource allocation graph contains a cycle. With the sort of mutexes described in this book, each mutex can be held by at most one thread and each thread is waiting for at most one mutex, so no vertex in the graph has an out-degree greater than 1. This allows a somewhat simpler graph search than in a fully-general directed graph.

Once a deadlock is detected, a painful action is needed in order to recover: one of the deadlocked threads must be forcibly terminated, or at least rolled back to an earlier state, so as to free up the mutexes it holds. In a general computing environment, where

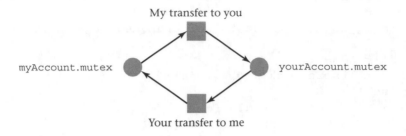

Figure 4.22 The cycle in this resource allocation graph indicates a deadlock. Each square represents a thread and each circle a mutex. An arrow from a square to a circle shows a thread waiting for a mutex, whereas an arrow from a circle to a square shows a mutex being held by a thread.

threads have no clean way to be rolled back, this is a bit akin to freeing yourself from a bear trap by cutting off your leg. For this reason, ex post facto deadlock detection is not common in general-purpose operating systems.

One environment in which ex post facto deadlock detection and recovery works cleanly is database systems, with their support for atomic transactions. I will explain atomic transactions in Chapter 5; for now, you need only understand that a transaction can cleanly be rolled back, such that all the updates it made to the database are undone. Because this infrastructure is available, database systems commonly include deadlock detection. When a deadlock is detected, one of the transactions fails and can be rolled back, undoing all its effects and releasing all its locks. This breaks the deadlock and allows the remaining transactions to complete. The rolled-back transaction can then be restarted.

Figure 4.23 shows an example scenario of deadlock detection taken from the Oracle database system. This transcript shows the time interleaving of two different sessions connected to the same database. One session is shown at the left margin, while the other session is shown indented four spaces. Command lines start with the system's prompt, SQL>, and then contain a command typed by the user. Each command line is broken on to a second line, to fit the width of this book's pages. Explanatory comments start with --. All other lines are output. In Chapter 5, I will show the recovery from this particular deadlock as part of my explanation of transactions.

4.7.4 Immediate Deadlock Detection

The two approaches to deadlocks presented thus far are aimed at the times before and after the moment when deadlock occurs. One arranges that the prerequisite circumstances leading to deadlock do not occur, while the other notices that deadlock already

```
SQL> update accounts set balance = balance - 100
                 where account_number = 1;

1 row updated.

   SQL> update accounts set balance = balance - 250
                    where account_number = 2;

   1 row updated.

SQL> update accounts set balance = balance + 100
                 where account_number = 2;
-- note no response, for now this SQL session is hanging

   SQL> update accounts set balance = balance + 250
                    where account_number = 1;
   -- this session hangs, but in the other SQL session we get
   -- the following error message:

update accounts set balance = balance + 100
             where account_number = 2
       *
ERROR at line 1:
ORA-00060: deadlock detected while waiting for resource
```

Figure 4.23   The Oracle database system detects a deadlock between two sessions connected to the same database. One session, shown at the left margin, is transferring $100 from account 1 to account 2. The other session, shown indented, is transferring $250 from account 2 to account 1. Each update statement locks the account being updated. Therefore, each session hangs when it tries locking the account that the other session has previously locked.

has occurred, so that the mess can be cleaned up. Now I will turn to a third alternative: intervening at the very moment when the system would otherwise deadlock. Because this intervention requires techniques similar to those discussed in Section 4.7.3, this technique is conventionally known as a form of deadlock detection rather than dead-lock prevention, even though from a literal perspective the deadlock is prevented from happening.

As long as no deadlock is ever allowed to occur, the resource allocation graph will remain acyclic, that is, free of cycles. Each time a thread tries to lock a mutex, the system can act as follows:

- If the mutex is unlocked, lock it and add an edge from the mutex to the thread, so as to indicate which thread now holds the lock.

Figure 4.24 In this resource graph, the solid arrows indicate that my transfer holds **myAccount.mutex**, your transfer holds **yourAccount.mutex**, and my transfer is waiting for **yourAccount.mutex**. The dashed arrow indicates a request currently being made by your transfer to lock **myAccount.mutex**. If this dashed arrow is added, a cycle is completed, indicating a deadlock. Therefore, the request will fail rather than enter a state of waiting.

- If the mutex is locked, follow the chain of edges from it until that chain dead-ends. (It must, because the graph is acyclic.) Is the end of the chain the same as the thread trying to lock the mutex?
  - If not, add an edge showing that the thread is waiting for the mutex, and put the thread into a waiting state.
  - If the end of the chain is the same thread, adding the extra edge would complete a cycle, as shown in Figure 4.24. Therefore, don't add the edge, and don't put the thread into a waiting state. Instead, return an error code from the lock request (or throw an exception), indicating that the mutex could not be locked because a deadlock would have resulted.

Notice that the graph search here is somewhat simpler than in ex post facto deadlock detection, because the graph is kept acyclic. Nonetheless, the basic idea is the same as deadlock detection, just done proactively rather than after the fact. As with any deadlock detection, some form of roll-back is needed; the application program that tried to lock the mutex must respond to the news that its request could not be granted. The application program must not simply try again to acquire the same mutex, because it will repeatedly get the same error code. Instead, the program must release the locks it currently holds and then restart from the beginning. The chance of needing to repeat this response can be reduced by sleeping briefly after releasing the locks and before restarting.

Designing an application program to correctly handle immediate deadlock detection can be challenging. The difficulty is that before the program releases its existing locks, it should restore the objects those locks were protecting to a consistent state. One case in which immediate deadlock detection can be used reasonably easily is in a program that acquires all its locks before it modifies any objects.

One example of immediate deadlock detection is in Linux and Mac OS X, for the readers/writers locks placed on files using `fcntl`. If a lock request would complete a cycle, the `fcntl` procedure returns the error code `EDEADLK`. However, this deadlock detection is not a mandatory part of the POSIX specification for `fcntl`.

4.8 The Interaction of Synchronization with Scheduling

Recall that the scheduler controls which runnable thread runs, and synchronization actions performed by the running thread control which threads are runnable. Therefore, synchronization and scheduling interact with one another. Two forms of interaction, known as priority inversion and the convoy phenomenon, are particularly interesting. Said another way, they can cause lots of grief. Each can subvert the prioritization of threads, and the convoy phenomenon can also greatly increase the context-switching rate and hence decrease system throughput.

4.8.1 Priority Inversion

When a priority-based scheduler is used, a high-priority thread should not have to wait while a low-priority thread runs. If threads of different priority levels share mutexes or other synchronization primitives, some minor violations of priority ordering are inevitable. For example, consider the following sequence of events involving two threads (high-priority and low-priority) that share a single mutex:

1. The high-priority thread goes into the waiting state, waiting for an I/O request to complete.
2. The low-priority thread runs and acquires the mutex.
3. The I/O request completes, making the high-priority thread runnable again. It pre-empts the low-priority thread and starts running.
4. The high-priority thread tries to acquire the mutex. Because the mutex is locked, the high-priority thread is forced to wait.
5. The low-priority thread resumes running.

At this point, a high-priority thread is waiting while a low-priority thread runs. However, this temporary violation of priority ordering is not a big deal, because programmers generally ensure that no thread holds a mutex for very long. As such, the low-priority thread will soon release the mutex and allow the high-priority thread to run.

However, another, more insidious problem can lead to longer-term violation of priority order (that is, *priority inversion*). Suppose there are three threads, of low, medium, and high priority. Consider this sequence of events:

1. The high- and medium-priority threads both go into the waiting state, each waiting for an I/O request to complete.

2. The low-priority thread runs and acquires the mutex.

3. The two I/O requests complete, making the high- and medium-priority threads runnable. The high-priority thread preempts the low-priority thread and starts running.

4. The high-priority thread tries to acquire the mutex. Because the mutex is locked, the high-priority thread is forced to wait.

5. At this point, the medium-priority thread has the highest priority of those that are runnable. Therefore, it runs.

In this situation, the medium-priority thread is running and indirectly keeping the high-priority thread from running. (The medium-priority thread is blocking the low-priority thread by virtue of their relative priorities. The low-priority thread is blocking the high-priority thread by holding the mutex.) The medium-priority thread could run a long time. In fact, a whole succession of medium-priority threads with overlapping lifetimes could come and go, and the high-priority thread would wait the whole time despite its higher priority. Thus, the priority inversion could continue for an arbitrarily long time.

One "solution" to the priority inversion problem is to avoid fixed-priority scheduling. Over time, a decay usage scheduler will naturally lower the priority of the medium-priority thread that is running. Eventually, it will drop below the low-priority thread, which will then run and free the mutex, allowing the high-priority thread to run. However, a succession of medium-priority threads, none of which runs for very long, could still hold up the high-priority thread arbitrarily long. Therefore, Microsoft Windows responds to priority inversion by periodically boosting the priority of waiting low-priority processes.

This first "solution" has two shortcomings. First, it may be sluggish in responding to a priority inversion. Second, fixed-priority scheduling is desirable in some applications, such as real-time systems. Therefore, a genuine solution to the priority inversion problem is needed—one that makes the problem go away, rather than just limiting the duration of its effect. The genuine solution is *priority inheritance*.

Priority inheritance is a simple idea: any thread that is waiting for a mutex temporarily "lends" its priority to the thread that holds the mutex. A thread that holds mutexes runs with the highest priority among its own priority and those priorities it has been lent by threads waiting for the mutexes. In the example with three threads, priority inheritance will allow the low-priority thread that holds the mutex to run as though it were high-priority until it unlocks the mutex. Thus, the truly high-priority thread will get to run as soon as possible, and the medium-priority thread will have to wait.

Notice that the high-priority thread has a very selfish motive for letting the low-priority thread use its priority: it wants to get the low-priority thread out of its way. The same principle can be applied with other forms of scheduling than priority scheduling. By analogy with priority inheritance, one can have *deadline inheritance* (for Earliest Deadline First scheduling) or even a lending of processor allocation shares (for proportional-share scheduling).

4.8.2 The Convoy Phenomenon

I have remarked repeatedly that well-designed programs do not normally hold any mutex for very long; thus, attempts to lock a mutex do not normally encounter contention. This is important because locking a mutex with contention is much more expensive. In particular, the big cost of a request to lock an already-locked mutex is context switching, with the attendant loss of cache performance. Unfortunately, one particularly nasty interaction between scheduling and synchronization, known as the *convoy phenomenon*, can sometimes cause a heavily used mutex to be perpetually contended, causing a large performance loss. Moreover, the convoy phenomenon can subvert scheduling policies, such as the assignment of priorities. In this subsection, I will explain the convoy phenomenon and examine some solutions.

Suppose a system has some very central data structure, protected by a mutex, which each thread operates on fairly frequently. Each time a thread operates on the structure, the thread locks the mutex before and unlocks it after. Each operation is kept as short as possible. Because they are frequent, however, the mutex spends some appreciable fraction of the time locked, perhaps 5 percent.

The scheduler may at any point preempt a thread. For example, the thread may have consumed its allocated time slice. In the example situation where the mutex is locked 5 percent of the time, it would not be very surprising if after a while, a thread were preempted while it held the mutex. When this happens, the programmer who wrote that thread loses all control over how long it holds the mutex locked. Even if the thread was going to unlock the mutex in its very next instruction, it may not get the opportunity to execute that next instruction for some time to come. If the processor is dividing its time among N runnable threads of the same priority level, the thread holding the mutex will presumably not run again for at least N times the context-switching time, even if the other threads all immediately block.

In this situation, a popular mutex is held for a long time. Meanwhile, other threads are running. Because the mutex is a popular one, the chances are good those other threads will try to acquire it. Because the mutex is locked, all the threads that try to acquire the mutex will be queued on its wait queue. This queue of threads is the *convoy*, named by analogy with the unintentional convoy of vehicles that develops behind one slow vehicle on a road with no passing lane. As you will see, this convoy spells trouble.

Eventually, the scheduler will give a new time slice to the thread that holds the mutex. Because of that thread's design, it will quickly unlock the mutex. When that happens, ownership of the mutex is passed to the first thread in the wait queue, and that thread is made runnable. The thread that unlocked the mutex continues to run, however. Because it was just recently given a new time slice, one might expect it to run a long time. However, it probably won't, because before too terribly long, it will try to reacquire the popular mutex and find it locked. ("Darn," it might say, "I shouldn't have given that mutex away to the first of the waiters. Here I am needing it again myself.") Thus, the thread takes its place at the back of the convoy, queued up for the mutex.

At this point, the new holder of the mutex gets to run, but it too gives away the mutex, and hence is unlikely to run a full time slice before it has to queue back up. This continues, with each thread in turn moving from the front of the mutex queue through a brief period of execution and back to the rear of the queue. There may be slight changes in the makeup of the convoy—a thread may stop waiting on the popular mutex, or a new thread may join—but seen in the aggregate, the convoy can persist for a very long time.

This situation causes two problems. First, the context-switching rate goes way up; instead of one context switch per time slice, there is now one context switch per attempt to acquire the popular mutex. The overhead of all those context switches will drive down the system throughput. Second, the scheduler's policy for choosing which thread to run is subverted. For example, in a priority scheduler, the priorities will not govern how the threads run. The reason for this is simple: the scheduler can choose only among the runnable threads, but with the convoy phenomenon there will be only one runnable thread; all the others will be queued up for the mutex.

When I described mutexes, I said that each mutex contains a wait queue—a list of waiting threads. I implied that this list is maintained in a first-in first-out (FIFO) basis, that is, as a true queue. If so, then the convoy threads will essentially be scheduled in a FIFO round-robin, independent of the scheduler policy (for example, priorities), because the threads are dispatched from the mutex queue rather than the scheduler's run queue.

This loss of prioritization can be avoided by handling the mutex's wait queue in priority order the same way as the run queue, rather than FIFO. When a mutex is unlocked with several threads waiting, ownership of the mutex could be passed not to the thread that waited the longest, but rather to the one with the highest priority.

Changing which one thread is moved from the mutex's waiters list to become runnable does not solve the throughput problem, however. The running thread is still going to have the experience I anthropomorphized as "Darn, I shouldn't have given that mutex away." The context-switching rate will still be one switch per lock acquisition. The convoy may reorder itself, but it will not dissipate.

Therefore, stronger medicine is needed for popular mutexes. Instead of the mutexes I showed in Figures 4.10 and 4.11 on page 87, you can use the version shown in Figure 4.25.

When a popular mutex is unlocked, *all* waiting threads are made runnable and moved from the waiters list to the runnable threads list. However, ownership of the mutex is not transferred to any of them. Instead, the mutex is left in the unlocked state, with `mutex.state` equal to 1. That way, the running thread will not have to say "Darn." It can simply relock the mutex; over the course of its time slice, it may lock and unlock the mutex repeatedly, all without context switching.

```
to lock mutex:
  repeat
    lock mutex.spinlock (in cache-conscious fashion)
    if mutex.state = 1 then
      let mutex.state = 0
      unlock mutex.spinlock
      let successful = true
    else
      add current thread to mutex.waiters
      remove current thread from runnable threads
      unlock mutex.spinlock
      yield to a runnable thread
      let successful = false
  until successful

to unlock mutex:
  lock mutex.spinlock (in cache-conscious fashion)
  let mutex.state = 1
  move all threads from mutex.waiters to runnable
  unlock mutex.spinlock
```

Figure 4.25 To protect against convoys, the unlock operation sets the mutex's state to unlocked and makes all waiting threads runnable. Each awoken thread loops back to trying to lock the mutex. This contrasts with the prior version of mutexes, in which one thread was awoken with the mutex left in its locked state.

Because the mutex is held only 5 percent of the time, the mutex will probably not be held when the thread eventually blocks for some other reason (such as a time slice expiration). At that point, the scheduler will select one of the woken threads to run. Note that this will naturally follow the normal scheduling policy, such as priority order.

The woken thread selected to run next did not have the mutex ownership directly transferred to it. Therefore, it will need to loop back to the beginning of the mutex acquisition code, as will each thread in turn when it is scheduled. However, most of the time the threads will find the mutex unlocked, so this won't be expensive. Also, because each thread will be able to run for a normal period without context-switching overhead per lock request, the convoy will dissipate.

The POSIX standard API for mutexes requires that one or the other of the two prioritization-preserving approaches be taken. At a minimum, if ownership of a mutex is directly transferred to a waiting thread, that waiting thread must be selected based on the normal scheduling policy rather than FIFO. Alternatively, a POSIX-compliant mutex implementation can simply dump all the waiting threads back into the scheduler and let it sort them out, as in Figure 4.25.

4.9 Security and Synchronization

A system can be insecure for two reasons: either because its security policies are not well designed, or because some bug in the code enforcing those policies allows the enforcement to be bypassed. For example, you saw in Chapter 3 that a denial of service attack can be mounted by setting some other user's thread to a very low priority. I remarked that as a result, operating systems only allow a thread's priority to be changed by its owner. Had this issue been overlooked, the system would be insecure due to an inadequate policy. However, the system may still be insecure if clever programmers can find a way to bypass this restriction using some low-level bug in the operating system code.

Many security-critical bugs involve synchronization, or more accurately, the lack of synchronization—the bugs are generally race conditions resulting from inadequate synchronization. Four factors make race conditions worth investigation by crackers:

- Any programmer of a complicated concurrent system is likely to introduce race bugs, because concurrency and synchronization are hard to reason about.

- Normal testing of the system is unlikely to have eliminated these bugs, because the system will still work correctly the vast majority of the time.

- Although the race might almost never occur in a normal operation, the cracker may be able to trigger the race by understanding it and carefully staging the necessary sequence of events. Even if the odds can't be improved beyond one in ten thousand (for example), the cracker can easily program a computer to loop through the attempt tens of thousands of times until the lucky timing happens.

- Races allow seemingly impossible situations, defeating the system designer's careful security reasoning.

As a hypothetical example, assume that an operating system had a feature for changing a thread's priority when given a pointer to a block of memory containing two values: an identifier for the thread to be changed and the new priority. Let's call these `request.thread` and `request.priority`. Suppose that the code looked like this:

```
if request.thread is owned by the current user then
  set request.thread's priority to request.priority
else
  return error code for invalid request
```

Can you see the race? All a cracker needs to do is start out with `request.thread` being a worthless thread he or she owns, and then modify `request.thread` to be the victim thread after the ownership check but before the priority is set. If the timing doesn't work out, no great harm is done, and the cracker can try again.

This particular example is not entirely realistic in a number of regards, but it does illustrate a particular class of races often contributing to security vulnerabilities: so-called *TOCTTOU* races, an acronym for *Time Of Check To Time Of Use*. An operating system designer would normally guard against this particular TOCTTOU bug by copying the whole request structure into protected memory before doing any checking. However, other TOCTTOU bugs arise with some regularity. Often, they are not in the operating system kernel itself, but rather in a privileged program.

For example, suppose an email delivery program is granted the privilege of writing into any file, independent of file ownership or normal protections, so that it can deliver each user's mail into that user's mail file. Before delivering mail into a mail file, it will check that the mail file is a normal file that is really in the expected location, not an indirect reference (symbolic link) to a file located elsewhere. (I will explain symbolic links in Chapter 8, when I cover file systems. The details are not important here.) That way, you cannot trick the mail delivery program into writing into some sensitive file. Or can you? Perhaps by changing from a genuine mail file to a symbolic link at just the right moment, you can exploit a TOCTTOU vulnerability. Sun Microsystems had this particular problem with their mail software in the early 1990s.

Exercises

4.1 As an example of a race condition, I showed how two threads could each dispense the last remaining ticket by each checking `seatsRemaining` before either decrements it. Show a different sequence of events for that same code, whereby starting with `seatsRemaining` being 2, two threads each dispense a ticket, but `seatsRemaining` is left as 1 rather than 0.

4.2 In the mutex-locking pseudocode of Figure 4.10 on page 87, there are two consecutive steps that remove the current thread from the runnable threads and then unlock the spinlock. Because spinlocks should be held as briefly as possible, we ought to consider whether these steps could be reversed. Explain why reversing them would be a bad idea by giving an example sequence of events where the reversed version malfunctions.

4.3 Show how to change queuing mutexes to correspond with POSIX's mutex-type `PTHREAD_MUTEX_RECURSIVE`. You may add additional components to each mutex beyond the state, waiters, and spinlock.

4.4 Explain why replacing `notifyAll` with `notify` is not safe in the `BoundedBuffer` class of Figure 4.17 on page 95. Give a concrete sequence of events under which the modified version would misbehave.

4.5 A semaphore can be used as a mutex. Does it correspond with the kind POSIX calls `PTHREAD_MUTEX_ERROR_CHECK`, `PTHREAD_MUTEX_NORMAL`, or `PTHREAD_MUTEX_RECURSIVE`? Justify your answer.

4.6 State licensing rules require a child-care center to have no more than three infants present for each adult. You could enforce this rule using a semaphore to track the remaining capacity, that is, the number of additional infants that may be accepted. Each time an infant is about to enter, a `down` operation is done first, with an `up` when the infant leaves. Each time an adult enters, you do three `up` operations, with three `down` operations before the adult may leave.

   (a) Although this system will enforce the state rules, it can create a problem when two adults try to leave. Explain what can go wrong, with a concrete scenario illustrating the problem.

   (b) The difficulty you identified in the preceding subproblem can be remedied by using a mutex as well as the semaphore. Show how.

   (c) Alternatively, you could abandon semaphores entirely and use a monitor with one or more condition variables. Show how.

4.7 I illustrated deadlock detection using a transcript taken from an Oracle database (Figure 4.23, page 107). From that transcript you can tell that the locks are at the granularity of one per row, rather than one per table.

   (a) What is the evidence for this assertion?

   (b) Suppose the locking were done per table instead. Explain why no deadlock would have ensued.

   (c) Even if locking were done per table, deadlock could still happen under other circumstances. Give an example.

4.8 Suppose you have two kinds of objects: threads and mutexes. Each locked mutex contains a reference to the thread that holds it as `mutex.owner`; if the mutex is unlocked, `mutex.owner` is `null`. Similarly, each thread that is blocked waiting for a mutex contains a reference to the mutex it is waiting for as `thread.blocker`; if the thread is not waiting for any mutex, `thread.blocker` is `null`. Suppose threads also contain a field, `thread.mark`, which is available for your use and is initialized to 0. Further, suppose you have an array of all the threads in the system as `threads[0]`, `threads[1]`, and so forth, up to `threads[threads.length-1]`. Write a pseudocode algorithm to test whether the system is deadlocked.

4.9 The main topic of this chapter (synchronization) is so closely related to the topics of Chapters 2 and 3 (threads and scheduling) that an author can hardly describe one without also describing the other two. For each of the following pairs of topics, give a brief explanation of why understanding the first topic in the pair is useful for gaining a full understanding of the second:
   (a) threads, scheduling
   (b) threads, synchronization
   (c) scheduling, synchronization
   (d) scheduling, threads
   (e) synchronization, scheduling
   (f) synchronization, threads

▤ Programming Projects

4.1 Flesh out the `TicketVendor` class from Figure 4.6 on page 83 using Figure 4.5 on page 79 for guidance. Add a simple test program that uses a `TicketVendor` from multiple threads. Temporarily remove the `synchronized` keywords and demonstrate race conditions by inserting calls to the `Thread.sleep` method at appropriate points, so that incredibly lucky timing is not necessary. You should set up one demonstration for each race previously considered: two threads selling the last seat, two threads selling seats but the count only going down by 1, and an audit midtransaction. Now reinsert the `synchronized` keyword and show that the race bugs have been resolved, even with the `sleep`s in place.

4.2 Demonstrate races and mutual exclusion as in the previous project, but using a C program with POSIX threads and mutexes. Alternatively, use some other programming language of your choice, with its support for concurrency and mutual exclusion.

4.3 Choose some simplified version of a real-world process that evolves over time, such as a bouncing ball, an investment with compound interest, or populations of predator and prey. Write a program with two threads. One thread should simulate the process you chose as time passes, possibly with some suitable scaling such as 1 second of simulator time per year of simulated time. The other thread should provide a user interface through which the user can modify the parameters of the ongoing simulation and can also pause and resume the simulation. Be sure to properly synchronize the two threads. Java would be an appropriate language for this project, but you could also use some other language with support for concurrency, synchronization, and user interfaces.

4.4 This project is identical to the previous one, except that instead of building a simulator for a real-world process, you should build a game of the kind where action continues whether or not the user makes a move.

4.5 Write a test program in Java for the **BoundedBuffer** class of Figure 4.17 on page 95.

4.6 Modify the **BoundedBuffer** class of Figure 4.17 (page 95) to call **notifyAll** only when inserting into an empty buffer or retrieving from a full buffer. Test that it still works.

4.7 Rewrite the **BoundedBuffer** class of Figure 4.17 (page 95) in C or C++ using the POSIX API. Use two condition variables, one for availability of space and one for availability of data.

4.8 Define a Java class for readers/writers locks, analogous to the **BoundedBuffer** class of Figure 4.17 (page 95). Allow additional readers to acquire a reader-held lock even if writers are waiting. As an alternative to Java, you may use another programming language with support for mutexes and condition variables.

4.9 Modify your readers/writers locks from the prior project so no additional readers may acquire a reader-held lock if writers are waiting.

4.10 Modify your readers/writers locks from either of the prior two projects to support an additional operation that a reader can use to upgrade its status to writer. (This is similar to dropping the read lock and acquiring a write lock, except that it is atomic: no other writer can sneak in and acquire the lock before the upgrading reader does.) What happens if two threads both hold the lock as readers, and each tries upgrading to become a writer? What do you think a good response would be to that situation?

4.11 Define a Java class for barriers, analogous to the **BoundedBuffer** class of Figure 4.17 (page 95). Alternatively, use another programming language, with support for mutexes and condition variables.

4.12 Define a Java class for semaphores to meet the needs of Figure 4.18 on page 100.

4.13 Rewrite the semaphore-based bounded buffer of Figure 4.18 (page 100) so that instead of using a `List`, it uses an array and a couple integer variables, just like the earlier version (Figure 4.17, page 95). Be sure to provide mutual exclusion for the portion of each method that operates on the array and the integer variables.

4.14 Translate the semaphore-based bounded buffer of Figure 4.18 (page 100) into C or C++ using the POSIX API's semaphores.

4.15 Translate the dining philosophers program of Exploration Project 4.2 into another language. For example, you could use C or C++ with POSIX threads and mutexes.

Exploration Projects

4.1 I illustrated pipes (as a form of bounded buffer) by piping the output from the `ls` command into the `tr` command. One disadvantage of this example is that there is no way to see that the two are run concurrently. For all you can tell, `ls` may be run to completion, with its output going into a temporary file, and then `tr` run afterward, with its input coming from that temporary file. Come up with an alternative demonstration of a pipeline, where it is apparent that the two commands are run concurrently because the first command does not immediately run to termination.

4.2 The Java program in Figure 4.26 simulates the dining philosophers problem, with one thread per philosopher. Each thread uses two nested `synchronized` statements to lock the two objects representing the forks to a philosopher's left and right. Each philosopher dines many times in rapid succession. In order to show whether the threads are still running, each thread prints out a message every 100000 times its philosopher dines.

(a) Try the program out. Depending on how fast your system is, you may need to change the number 100000. The program should initially print out messages, at a rate that is not overwhelmingly fast, but that keeps you aware the program is running. With any luck, after a while, the messages should stop entirely. This is your sign that the threads have deadlocked. What is your experience? Does the program deadlock on your system? Does it do so consistently if you run the program repeatedly? Document what you observed (including its variability) and the circumstances under which you observed it. If you have more than one system available that runs Java, you might want to compare them.

(b) You can guarantee the program won't deadlock by making one of the threads (such as number 0) acquire its right fork before its left fork. Explain why this

```
public class Philosopher extends Thread{

  private Object leftFork, rightFork;
  private int myNumber;

  public Philosopher(Object left, Object right, int number){
    leftFork = left;
    rightFork = right;
    myNumber = number;
  }

  public void run(){
    int timesDined = 0;
    while(true){
      synchronized(leftFork){
        synchronized(rightFork){
          timesDined++;
        }
      }
      if(timesDined % 100000 == 0)
        System.err.println("Thread " + myNumber + " is running.");
    }
  }

  public static void main(String[] args){
    final int PHILOSOPHERS = 5;
    Object[] forks = new Object[PHILOSOPHERS];
    for(int i = 0; i < PHILOSOPHERS; i++){
      forks[i] = new Object();
    }
    for(int i = 0; i < PHILOSOPHERS; i++){
      int next = (i+1) % PHILOSOPHERS;
      Philosopher p = new Philosopher(forks[i], forks[next], i);
      p.start();
    }
  }
}
```

Figure 4.26 Java program to simulate the dining philosophers.

prevents deadlock, and try it out. Does the program now continue printing messages as long as you let it run?

4.3 Search on the Internet for reported security vulnerabilities involving race conditions. How many can you find? How recent is the most recent report? Do you find any cases particularly similar to earlier ones?

Notes

The Therac-25's safety problems were summarized by Leveson and Turner [87]. Those problems went beyond the race bug at issue here, to also include sloppy software development methodology, a total reliance on software to the exclusion of hardware interlocks, and an inadequate mechanism for dealing with problem reports from the field.

When describing races, I spoke of threads' execution as being interleaved. In fact, unsynchronized programs may execute in even more bizarre ways than just interleavings. For example, one thread may see results from another thread out of order. For the Java programming language, considerable effort has gone into specifying exactly what reorderings of the threads' execution steps are legal. However, the bottom line for programmers is still that synchronization should be used to avoid races in the first place; trying to understand the race behavior is a losing battle.

Recall that my brief descriptions of the POSIX and Java APIs are no replacement for the official documentation on the web at *http://www.opengroup.org* and *http://java.sun.com*, respectively. In particular, I claimed that each Java mutex could only be associated with a single condition variable, unlike in the POSIX API. Actually, version 1.5 of the Java API gained a second form of mutexes and condition variables, contained in the `java.util.concurrent` package. These new mechanisms are not as well integrated with the Java programming language as the ones I described, but do have the feature of allowing multiple condition variables per mutex.

My spinlocks depend on an atomic exchange instruction. I mentioned that one could also use some other atomic read-and-update instruction, such as atomic increment. In fact, in 1965 Dijkstra [45] showed that mutual exclusion is also possible using only ordinary load and store instructions. However, this approach is complex and not practical; by 1972, Dijkstra [48] was calling it "only of historical interest."

Semaphores were proposed by Dijkstra in a privately circulated 1965 manuscript [46]; he formally published the work in 1968 [47]. Note, however, that Dijkstra credits Scholten with having shown the usefulness of semaphores that go beyond 0 and 1. Presumably this includes the semaphore solution to the bounded buffer problem, which Dijkstra presents.

The idea of using a consistent ordering to prevent deadlocks was published by Havender, also in 1968 [65]. Note that his title refers to "avoiding deadlock." This is potentially confusing, as today *deadlock avoidance* means something different than *deadlock prevention*. Havender describes what is today called deadlock prevention. Deadlock avoidance is a less practical approach, dating at least to Dijkstra's work in 1965 and fleshed out by Habermann in 1971 [62]. (Remarkably, Habermann's title speaks of "prevention" of deadlocks—so terminology has completely flip-flopped since the seminal papers.) I do not present deadlock avoidance in this textbook. Havender also described other approaches to preventing deadlock; ordering is simply his "Approach 1." The best of his other three approaches is "Approach 2," which calls for obtaining all necessary resources at the same time, rather than one by one. Coffman, Elphick, and Shoshani [31] published a survey of deadlock issues in 1971, which made the contemporary distinction between deadlock prevention and deadlock avoidance.

In 1971, Courtois, Heymans, and Parnas [35] described both variants of the readers/writers locks that the programming projects call for. (In one, readers take precedence over waiting writers, whereas in the other waiting writers take precedence.) They also point out that neither of these two versions prevents starvation: the only question is which class of threads can starve the other.

Resource allocation graphs were introduced by Holt in the early 1970s; the most accessible publication is number [71]. Holt also considered more sophisticated cases than I presented, such as resources for which multiple units are available, and resources that are produced and consumed rather than merely being acquired and released.

Monitors and condition variables apparently were in the air in the early 1970s. Although the clearest exposition is by Hoare in 1974 [69], similar ideas were also proposed by Brinch Hansen [23] and by Dijkstra [48], both in 1972. Brinch Hansen also designed the monitor-based programming language Concurrent Pascal, for which he later wrote a history [24].

My example of deadlock prevention in the Linux kernel was extracted from the file `kernel/sched.c` in version 2.6.0-test9.

The use of priority inheritance to limit priority inversion was explained by Sha, Rajkumar, and Lehoczky [116]. They also presented an alternative solution to the priority inversion problem, known as the priority ceiling protocol. The priority ceiling protocol sometimes forces a thread to wait before acquiring a mutex, even though the mutex is available. In return for that extra waiting, it guarantees that a high-priority thread will have to loan its priority to at most one lower-priority thread to free up a needed mutex. This allows the designer of a real-time system to calculate a tighter bound on each task's worst-case execution time. Also, the priority ceiling protocol provides a form of deadlock avoidance.

The convoy phenomenon, and its solution, were described by Blasgen et al. [21].

Dijkstra introduced the dining philosophers problem in reference [48]. He presented a more sophisticated solution that not only prevented deadlock but also ensured that each hungry philosopher got a turn to eat, without the neighboring philosophers taking multiple turns first.

The TOCTTOU race vulnerability in Sun's mail delivery software was reported in 1992 by a group known as [8lgm]. Their web site, *http://www.8lgm.org*, may or may not still be around when you read this, but you should be able to find a copy of the advisory somewhere on the web by searching for [8lgm]-Advisory-5.UNIX.mail.24-Jan-1992.

5

Atomic Transactions

5.1 Introduction

In Chapter 4, I described mutual exclusion as a mechanism for ensuring that an object undergoes a sequence of invariant-preserving transformations and hence is left in a state where the invariant holds. (Such states are called *consistent* states.) In particular, this was the idea behind monitors. Any monitor object is constructed in a consistent state. Any public operation on the monitor object will work correctly when invoked in a consistent state and will reestablish the invariant before returning. No interleaving of actions from different monitor operations is allowed, so the monitor's state advances from one consistent state to the next.

In this chapter, I will continue on the same theme of invariant-preserving state transformations. This time through, though, I will address two issues I ignored in Chapter 4:

1. Some invariants span multiple objects; rather than transforming a single object from a consistent state to another consistent state, you may need to transform a whole system of objects from one consistent state to the next. For example, suppose you use objects to form a rooted tree, with each object knowing its parent and its children, as shown in Figure 5.1. An invariant is that X has Y as a child if

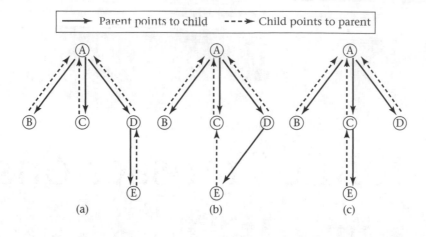

Figure 5.1 Rooted trees with pointers to children and parents: (a) example satisfying the invariant; (b) invariant violated because E's parent is now C, but E is still a child of D and not of C; (c) invariant restored because the only child pointer leading to E again agrees with E's parent pointer. The complete transformation from Part (a) to Part (c) requires modifications to nodes C, D, and E.

and only if Y has X as its parent. An operation to move a node to a new position in the tree would need to change three objects (the node, the old parent, and the new parent) in order to preserve the invariant.

2. Under exceptional circumstances an operation may *fail*, that is, be forced to give up after doing only part of its invariant-preserving transformation. For example, some necessary resource may be unavailable, the user may press a Cancel button, the input may fail a validity check, or a hardware failure may occur. Nonetheless, the system should be left in a consistent state.

An *atomic transaction* is an operation that takes a system from an observable initial state to an observable final state, without any intermediate states being observable or perturbable by other atomic transactions. If a system starts with a consistent initial state and modifies that state using only invariant-preserving atomic transactions, the state will remain consistent. Atomicity must be preserved in the face of both concurrency and failures. That is, no transaction may interact with a concurrently running transaction nor may any transaction see an intermediate state left behind by a failed transaction. The former requirement is known as *isolation*. The latter requirement lacks a generally agreed-upon name; I will call it *failure atomicity*.

Often, atomic transactions are simply called *transactions*. In fact, according to many authors, atomicity is part of the definition of a transaction. Unfortunately, there are other authors for whom transactions need not be atomic. Because of this lack of agreement on the nomenclature, I have introduced this chapter with the full phrase "atomic transactions" to make my focus clear. Henceforth, I will skip the modifier "atomic" and use only "transactions," with the understanding that they are atomic unless otherwise specified.

Many transaction systems require not only atomicity, but also *durability*. A transaction is durable if the state of a successfully completed transaction remains intact, even if the system crashes afterward and has to be rebooted. Each successful transaction ends with an explicit *commit* action, which signifies that the consistent final state has been established and should be made visible to other transactions. With durable transactions, if the system crashes after the commit action, the final transformed state will be intact after system restart. If the crash occurs before the commit action, the system will be back in the initial, unchanged state after restart.

Note that failure atomicity is slightly simpler for nondurable transactions. Atomicity across system crashes and restarts is easy to arrange: by clearing all memory on restart, you can guarantee that no partially updated state is visible after the restart—no updates at all, partial or otherwise, will remain. This clearing of memory will happen automatically if the computer's main semiconductor DRAM memory is used, because that memory is *volatile*, that is, it does not survive reboots. (Strictly speaking, volatility means the memory does not survive a loss of power; reboots with the power left on generally clear volatile memory as well, however.)

Even nondurable transactions must ensure failure atomicity for less dramatic failures in which the system is not rebooted. For example, a transaction might do some updates, then discover invalid input and respond by bailing out. To take another example, recovering from a detected deadlock might entail aborting one of the deadlocked transactions. Both situations can be handled using an explicit *abort* action, which indicates the transaction should be terminated with no visible change made to the state. Any changes already made must be concealed, by undoing them.

In 1983, Härder and Reuter coined a catchy phrase by saying that whether a system supports transactions is "the ACID test of the system's quality." The ACID acronym indicates that transactions are *atomic, consistent, isolated*, and *durable*. This acronym is quite popular, but somewhat redundant. As you have seen, a transaction system really provides only two properties: atomicity and durability. Consistency is a property of system states—a state is consistent if the invariants hold. Transactions that are written correctly (so each preserves invariants) will leave the state consistent if they execute atomically. Isolation simply is another name for atomicity in the face of concurrency: concurrent transactions must not interact.

The properties of atomicity and durability refer to transactions, independent of the objects on which the transactions operate. Returning to the earlier rooted tree example of moving a node to a new position, a transaction might modify the node, the old parent, and the new parent, all within one atomic unit. This stands in contrast to monitors, each of which controls a single object.

To obtain the requisite atomicity with monitors, the whole tree could be a single monitor object, instead of having one monitor per node. The tree monitor would have an operation to move one of its nodes. In general, this approach is difficult to reconcile with modularity. Moreover, lumping lots of data into one monitor creates a performance problem. Making the whole system (or a large chunk of it) into one monitor would prevent any concurrency. Yet it ought to be possible to concurrently move two nodes in different parts of a tree. Atomic transactions allow concurrency of this sort while still protecting the entire transformation of the system's state.

This point is worth emphasizing. Although the system's state remains consistent *as though* only one transaction were executed at a time, transactions in fact execute concurrently, for performance reasons. The transaction system is responsible for maintaining atomicity in the face of concurrency. That is, it must ensure that transactions don't interact with one another, even when running concurrently. Often the system will achieve this isolation by ensuring that no transaction reads from any data object being modified by another transaction. Enforcing this restriction entails introducing synchronization that limits, but that does not completely eliminate, the concurrency.

In Section 5.2, I will sketch several examples of the ways in which transactions are used by middleware and operating systems to support application programs. Thereafter, I present techniques used to make transactions work, divided into three sections. First, Section 5.3 explains basic techniques for ensuring the atomicity of transactions, without addressing durability. Second, Section 5.4 explains how the mechanism used to ensure failure atomicity can be extended to also support durability. Third, Section 5.5 explains a few additional mechanisms to provide increased concurrency and coordinate multiple participants cooperating on a single transaction. Finally, Section 5.6 is devoted to security issues. The chapter concludes with exercises, exploration and programming projects, and notes.

5.2 Example Applications of Transactions

The transaction concept is much more pervasive in middleware than in operating systems. Therefore, of the three examples presented in the following subsections, the first two are from middleware systems. Sections 5.2.1 and 5.2.2 explain the two most long-standing middleware applications, namely database systems and message-queuing systems. Moving into the operating systems arena, Section 5.2.3 explains the role that transactions play in journaled file systems, which are the current dominant form of file system.

5.2.1 Database Systems

The transaction concept is most strongly rooted in *database systems*; for decades, every serious database system has provided transactions as a service to application programmers. Database systems are an extremely important form of middleware, used in almost every enterprise information system. Like all middleware, database systems are built on top of operating system services, rather than raw hardware, while providing general-purpose services to application software. Some of those services are synchronization services: just as an operating system provides mutexes, a database system provides transactions.

On the other hand, transaction services are not the central, defining mission of a database system. Instead, database systems are primarily concerned with providing persistent data storage and convenient means for accessing the stored data. Nonetheless, my goal in this chapter is to show how transactions fit into relational database systems. I will cover just enough of the SQL language used by such systems to enable you to try out the example on a real system. In particular, I show the example using the Oracle database system.

Relational database systems manipulate tables of data. In Chapter 4's discussion of deadlock detection, I showed a simple example from the Oracle database system involving two accounts with account numbers 1 and 2. The scenario (as shown in Figure 4.23 on page 107) involved transferring money from each account to the other, by updating the balance of each account. Thus, that example involved a table called `accounts` with two columns, `account_number` and `balance`. That table can be created with the SQL command shown here:

```
create table accounts (
  account_number int primary key,
  balance int);
```

Similarly, you can initialize account 1 to $750 and account 2 to $2250 by using the following commands:

```
insert into accounts values (1, 750);
insert into accounts values (2, 2250);
```

At this point, you can look at the table with the `select` command:

```
select * from accounts;
```

and get the following reply:

```
ACCOUNT_NUMBER    BALANCE
--------------    ----------
             1          750
             2         2250
```

(If you are using a relational database other than Oracle, the format of the table may be slightly different. Of course, other aspects of the example may differ as well, particularly the deadlock detection response.)

At this point, to replicate the deadlock detection example from Figure 4.23, you will need to open up two different sessions connected to the database, each in its own window. In the first session, you can debit $100 from account 1, and in the second session, you can debit $250 from account 2. (See page 107 for the specific SQL commands.) Now in session one, try to credit the $100 into account 2; this is blocked, because the other session has locked account 2. Similarly, session two is blocked trying to credit its $250 into account 1, creating a deadlock, as illustrated in Figure 5.2. As you saw, Oracle detects the deadlock and chooses to cause session one's update request to fail.

Having made it through all this prerequisite setup, you are in a position to see the role that transactions play in situations such as this. Each of the two sessions is

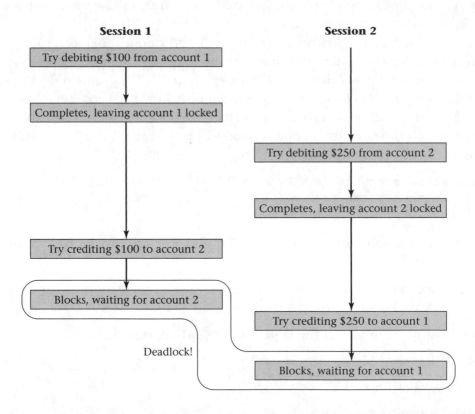

Figure 5.2 Two transfer transactions deadlock when each waits for exclusive access to the account for which the other already has obtained exclusive access. In this diagram, the vertical dimension represents the passage of time.

processing its own transaction. Recall that session one has already debited $100 from account 1 but finds itself unable to credit the $100 into account 2. The transaction cannot make forward progress, but on the other hand, you don't want it to just stop dead in its tracks either. Stopping would block the progress of session two's transaction. Session one also cannot just bail out without any cleanup: it has already debited $100 from account 1. Debiting the source account without crediting the destination account would violate atomicity and make customers angry besides.

Therefore, session one needs to abort its transaction, using the `rollback` command. Aborting will back out of the transaction's earlier debiting of $100 from account 1 and release its lock on that account. As a result, session two's attempt to credit $250 into account 1 can finally stop hanging and complete. Continuing my earlier tradition of showing session one at the left margin and session two indented four spaces, the interaction would look like:

```
SQL> rollback;

Rollback complete.

    1 row updated.
```

Of course, whoever was trying to transfer $100 from account 1 to account 2 still wants to do so. Therefore, after aborting that transaction, you should retry it:

```
SQL> update accounts set balance = balance - 100
                    where account_number = 1;
```

This command will hang, because session two's transaction now has both accounts locked. However, that transaction has nothing more it needs to do, so it can commit, allowing session one to continue with its retry:

```
    SQL> commit;

    Commit complete.

1 row updated.

SQL> update accounts set balance = balance + 100
                    where account_number = 2;

1 row updated.

SQL> commit;

Commit complete.

SQL> select * from accounts;
```

```
ACCOUNT  NUMBER      BALANCE
--------------    ----------
            1           900
            2          2100
```

Notice that at the end, the two accounts have been updated correctly. For example, account 1 does not look as though $100 was debited from it twice—the debiting done in the aborted transaction was wiped away. Figure 5.3 illustrates how the transactions recover from the deadlock.

In a large system with many accounts, there may be many concurrent transfer transactions operating on different pairs of accounts. Only rarely will a deadlock situation such as the preceding example arise. However, it is nice to know that database systems have a clean way of dealing with them. Any transaction can be aborted, due to deadlock detection or any other reason, and retried later. Moreover, concurrent transactions will never create incorrect results due to races; that was why the database system locked the accounts, causing the temporary hanging (and in one case, the deadlock) that you observed.

5.2.2 Message-Queuing Systems

Message-queuing systems form another important class of middleware, and like database systems, they support the transaction concept. Developers of large-scale enterprise information systems normally use both forms of middleware, although message-queuing systems are more avoidable than database systems. As with database systems, the primary mission of message queuing is not the support of transactions. Instead, message-queuing systems specialize in the provision of communication services. As such, I will discuss them further in Chapter 10, as part of a discussion of the broader family of middleware to which they belong: *messaging systems* or *message-oriented middleware* (*MOM*).

A straightforward application of messaging consists of a server accessed through a request queue and a response queue. As shown in Figure 5.4, the server dequeues a request message from the request queue, carries out the required processing, and enqueues a response message into the response queue. (Think about an office worker whose desk has two baskets, labeled "in" and "out," and who takes paper from one, processes it, and puts it in the other.)

These three steps (dequeue, process, enqueue) are grouped together as an atomic transaction. If any of the three steps fail, the request message is left in the input queue, ready to be retried. No request will be lost, nor will there ever be visible signs of repeated processing, such as duplicated response messages. (Of course, some causes of

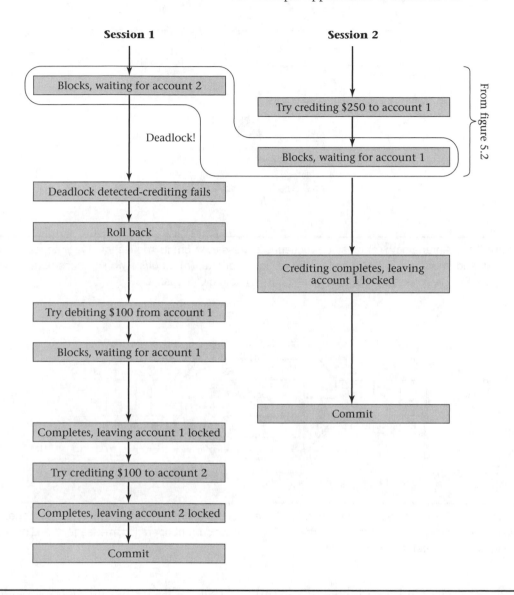

Figure 5.3 Transactions recover from their deadlock when one rolls back, releasing the lock it holds. As in the prior figure, the vertical dimension represents the passage of time.

failure will affect retries as well. For that reason, realistic systems generally keep count of retries and after a while divert the request message, for example, into a human troubleshooter's request queue.)

Message-queuing systems also provide durability, so that even if the system crashes and restarts, each request will generate exactly one response. In most systems,

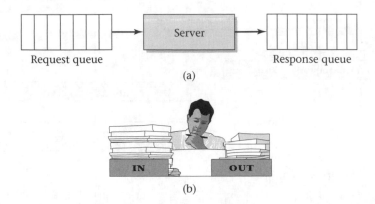

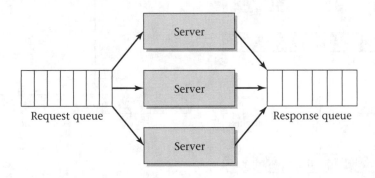

Figure 5.4 An analogy: (a) a server dequeues a message from its request queue, processes the request, and enqueues a message into the response queue; (b) an office worker takes paper from the In basket, processes the paperwork, and puts it into the Out basket.

Figure 5.5 Several message-driven servers in parallel can dequeue from a common request queue and enqueue into a common response queue. To allow concurrent operation, messages need not be provided in strict first-in, first-out order.

applications can opt out of durability in order to reduce disk traffic and thereby obtain higher performance.

To provide greater concurrency, a system may have several servers dequeuing from the same request queue, as shown in Figure 5.5. This configuration has an interesting interaction with atomicity. If the dequeue action is interpreted strictly as taking the message at the head of the queue, then you have to wait for the first transaction to commit or abort before you can know which message the second transaction should dequeue. (If the first transaction aborts, the message it tried to dequeue is still at the head of the queue and should be taken by the second transaction.) This would prevent any concurrency. Therefore, message-queuing systems generally relax queue ordering a little, allowing the second message to be dequeued even before the fate of the first message is known. In effect, the first message is provisionally removed from the queue and so is out of the way of the second message. If the transaction handling the first message aborts, the first message is returned to the head of the queue, even though the second message was already dequeued.

More advanced *workflow* systems may include several processing steps, with each processing step connected to the next by an intermediate message queue. In these systems, each processing stage is treated as a separate transaction. If the transaction commits, that stage's input is gone from its inbound queue, and its output is in the outbound queue. Seen as a whole, the workflow may not exhibit atomicity. For example, failure in a later processing stage will not roll back an earlier stage.

Consider a sale of merchandise as an example workflow, as shown in Figure 5.6. One transaction might take an incoming order, check it for validity, and generate three output messages, each into its own outbound queue: an order confirmation (back to the customer), a billing record (to the accounts receivable system), and a shipping request (to the shipping system). Another transaction, operating in the shipping

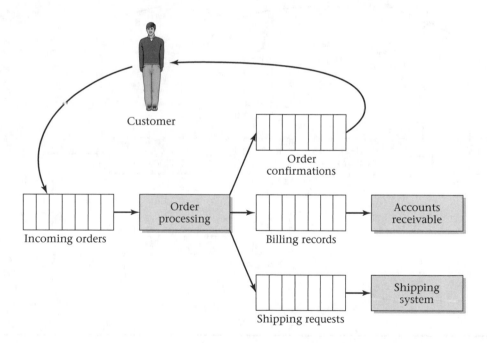

Figure 5.6 In this simplified workflow for selling merchandise, processing a single order produces three different responses. The response queues from the order-processing step are request queues for subsequent steps.

system, might dequeue the shipping request and fulfill it. If failure is detected in the shipping transaction, the system can no longer abort the overall workflow; the order confirmation and billing have already been sent. Instead, the shipping transaction has no alternative but to drive the overall workflow forward, even if in a somewhat different direction than hoped for. For example, the shipping transaction could queue messages apologizing to the customer and crediting the purchase price back to the customer's account. Figure 5.7 shows the workflow with these extra steps.

Even in a system in which one transaction may bill the customer only to have a later *compensating transaction* refund the billed amount, using atomic transactions simplifies application programming. Imagine how complex it would be to reason about a large workflow if each individual processing stage could fail midway through or could interact with other concurrently executing stages. By treating each workflow stage as an atomic transaction, a messaging system considerably reduces the application designer's cognitive burden. A diagram, such as Figure 5.7, can provide an accurate

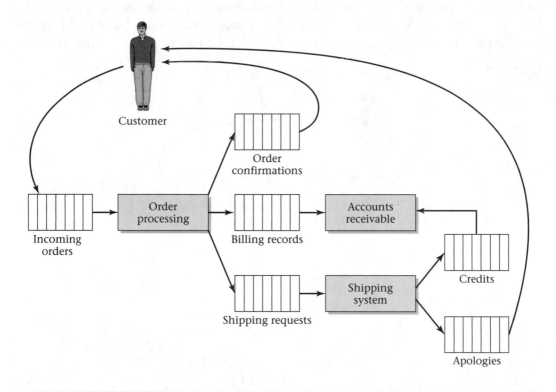

Figure 5.7 In this workflow, a failure in shipping must produce compensating responses, as it cannot abort the overall workflow. The compensating responses credit the customer's account for the previously debited amount and send an apology to the customer indicating that the previously confirmed order will not be filled after all.

abstraction of the system's observable behaviors by showing the system as processing stages linked by message queues.

Finally, consider how the sales workflow keeps track of available merchandise, customer account balances, and other information. You should be able to see that individual processing stages of a workflow will frequently have to use a database system. As such, transactions will involve both message queues and databases. Atomicity needs to cover both; if a transaction aborts, you want the database left unchanged *and* the request message left queued. In Section 5.5.2, I will explain how this comprehensive atomicity can be achieved by coordinating the systems participating in a transaction.

5.2.3 Journaled File Systems

The transaction concept has been employed in middleware both longer and more extensively than in operating systems. However, one application in operating systems has become quite important. Most contemporary operating systems provide file systems that employ atomic transactions to at least maintain the structural consistency of the file system itself, if not the consistency of the data stored in files. These file systems are known as *journaled file systems* (or *journaling file systems*) in reference to their use of an underlying mechanism known as a *journal*. I will discuss journals in Sections 5.3.2 and 5.4 under their alternative name, *logs*. Examples of journaled file systems include NTFS, used by Microsoft Windows; HFS Plus, used by Mac OS X; and ext3fs, reiserfs, JFS, and XFS, used by Linux. (The latter two originated in proprietary UNIX systems: JFS was developed by IBM for AIX, and XFS was developed by SGI for IRIX.) File systems that are not journaled need to use other techniques, which I describe in Section 8.7, to maintain the consistency of their data structures.

File systems provide a more primitive form of data storage and access than database systems. As you will see in Chapter 8, contemporary operating systems generally treat a file as an arbitrarily large, potentially extensible sequence of bytes, accessed by way of a textual name. The names are organized hierarchically into nested directories or folders. Typical operations on files include create, read, write, rename, and delete.

Underlying this simple abstraction are some largely invisible data structures, known as *metadata*, that help locate and organize the data. For example, because each file can grow in size, the file system must be free to store different parts of a file in different locations on disk. As such, the file system must store metadata for each file indicating where on disk each portion of the file is located. Moreover, the file system must store information concerning what parts of the disk are in use, so that it can allocate unused space for a file that is growing.

The existence of this metadata means that even simple file operations can involve several updates to the information stored on disk. Extending a file, for example, must update both the information about free space and the information about space allocated to that file. These structures need to be kept consistent; it would be disastrous if a portion of the disk were both used for storing a file and made available for allocation to a second file. Thus, the updates should be done as part of an atomic transaction.

Some atomic transactions may even be visible to the user. Consider the renaming of a file. A new directory entry needs to be created and an old entry removed. The user wants these two changes done atomically, without the possibility of the file having both names, or neither.

Some journaled file systems treat each operation requested by an application program as an atomic and durable transaction. On such a system, if a program asks the system to rename a file, and the rename operation returns with an indication of success, the application program can be sure that renaming has taken place. If the system crashes immediately afterward and is rebooted, the file will have its new name. Said another way, the rename operation includes commitment of the transaction. The application program can tell that the transaction committed and hence is guaranteed to be durable.

Other journaled file systems achieve higher performance by delaying transaction commit. At the time the rename operation returns, the transaction may not have committed yet. Every minute or so, the file system will commit all transactions completed during that interval. As such, when the system comes back from a crash, the file system will be in some consistent state, but maybe not a completely up-to-date one. A minute's worth of operations that appeared to complete successfully may have vanished. In exchange for this risk, the system has gained the ability to do fewer writes to disk, which improves performance. Notice that even in this version, transactions are providing some value. The state found after reboot will be the result of some sequence of operations (even if possibly a truncated sequence), rather than being a hodgepodge of partial results from incomplete and unordered operations.

Often, journaled file systems protect only metadata; the application data stored in files may be left in an inconsistent state after a crash. In particular, some writes into the files may not have taken effect, and the writes that are lost in this way are not necessarily the ones performed most recently. Even if a journaled file system does better than this, the most it will offer is a guarantee that all write operations that completed before a crash will be reflected in the state after the crash. If a program wants to do multiple writes in an atomic fashion (so that all writes take place or none do), the file system will not provide any assistance. In this regard, journaled file systems are still not as thoroughly transaction oriented as database systems are.

5.3 Mechanisms to Ensure Atomicity

Having seen how valuable atomic transactions are for middleware and operating systems, you should be ready to consider how this value is actually provided. In particular, how is the atomicity of each transaction ensured? Atomicity has two aspects: the isolation of concurrent transactions from one another and the assurance that failed transactions have no visible effect. In Section 5.3.1, you will see how isolation is formalized as serializability and how a particular locking discipline, two-phase locking, is used to ensure serializability. In Section 5.3.2, you will see how failure atomicity is assured through the use of an undo log.

5.3.1 Serializability: Two-Phase Locking

Transactions may execute concurrently with one another, so long as they don't interact in any way that makes the concurrency apparent. That is, the execution must be equivalent to a *serial* execution, in which one transaction runs at a time, committing or aborting before the next transaction starts. Any execution equivalent to a serial execution is called a *serializable* execution. In this section, I will more carefully define what it means for two executions to be equivalent and hence what it means for an execution to be serializable. In addition, I will show some simple rules for using readers/writers locks that guarantee serializability. These rules, used in many transaction systems, are known as *two-phase locking*.

Equivalence, and hence serializability, can be defined in several somewhat different ways. The definitions I give are the simplest I could find and suffice to justify two-phase locking, which is the mechanism normally used to achieve serializability in practical systems. However, you should be aware that more general definitions are needed in order to accommodate more advanced concurrency control mechanisms. The notes at the end of the chapter provide pointers to some of these more sophisticated alternatives.

Each transaction executes a sequence of actions. I will focus on those actions that read or write some stored entity (which might be a row in a database table, for example) and those actions that lock or unlock a readers/writers lock. Assume that each stored entity has its own lock associated with it. I will use the following notation:

- $r_j(x)$ means a read of entity x by transaction T_j; when I want to show the value that was read, I use $r_j(x, v)$, with v as the value.

- $w_j(x)$ means a write of entity x by transaction T_j; when I want to show the value being written, I use $w_j(x, v)$, with v as the value.

- $s_j(x)$ means an acquisition of a shared (that is, reader) lock on entity x by transaction T_j.

- $e_j(x)$ means an acquisition of an exclusive (that is, writer) lock on entity x by transaction T_j.

- $\overline{s}_j(x)$ means an unlocking of a shared lock on entity x by transaction T_j.

- $\overline{e}_j(x)$ means an unlocking of an exclusive lock on entity x by transaction T_j.

- $u_j(x)$ means an upgrade by transaction T_j of its hold on entity x's lock from shared status to exclusive status.

Each read returns the most recently written value. Later, in Section 5.5.1, I will revisit this assumption, considering the possibility that writes might store each successive value for an entity in a new location so that reads can choose among the old values.

The sequence of actions executed by a transaction is called its *history*. Because the transactions execute concurrently, if you were to write all their actions in the order they happen, the transactions' histories would be interleaved. This time-ordered interleaving of all the transactions' histories is called the system's history. All locking actions are shown at the time when the lock is granted, not at the possibly earlier time when the lock is requested. Assume that the histories include all the relevant actions. In particular, if a transaction aborts and does some extra writes at that time to undo the effect of earlier writes (as you will see in Section 5.3.2), those undo writes must be explicitly listed in the history. Note also that I am implicitly assuming the transactions have no effects other than on storage; in particular, they don't do any I/O.

Let's look at some examples. Suppose that x and y are two variables that are initially both equal to 5. Suppose that transaction T_1 adds 3 to each of the two variables, and transaction T_2 doubles each of the two variables. Each of these transactions preserves the invariant that $x = y$.

One serial history would be as follows:

$$e_1(x), r_1(x, 5), w_1(x, 8), \overline{e}_1(x), e_1(y), r_1(y, 5), w_1(y, 8), \overline{e}_1(y),$$
$$e_2(x), r_2(x, 8), w_2(x, 16), \overline{e}_2(x), e_2(y), r_2(y, 8), w_2(y, 16), \overline{e}_2(y)$$

Before you go any further, make sure you understand this notation; as directed in Exercise 5.2, write out another serial history in which transaction T_2 happens before transaction T_1. (The sequence of steps within each transaction should remain the same.)

In the serial history I showed, x and y both end up with the value 16. When you wrote out the other serial history for these two transactions, you should have obtained a different final value for these variables. Although the invariant $x = y$ again holds, the common numerical value of x and y is not 16 if transaction T_2 goes first. This makes an important point: transaction system designers do not insist on *deterministic* execution, in which the scheduling cannot affect the result. Serializability is a weaker condition.

Continuing with the scenario in which T_1 adds 3 to each variable and T_2 doubles each variable, one serializable—but not serial—history follows:

$$e_1(x), r_1(x, 5), w_1(x, 8), \bar{e}_1(x), e_2(x), r_2(x, 8), w_2(x, 16), \bar{e}_2(x),$$
$$e_1(y), r_1(y, 5), w_1(y, 8), \bar{e}_1(y), e_2(y), r_2(y, 8), w_2(y, 16), \bar{e}_2(y)$$

To convince others that this history is serializable, you could persuade them that it is equivalent to the serial history shown previously. Although transaction T_2 starts before transaction T_1 is finished, each variable still is updated the same way as in the serial history.

Because the example transactions unlock x before locking y, they can also be interleaved in a nonserializable fashion:

$$e_1(x), r_1(x, 5), w_1(x, 8), \bar{e}_1(x), e_2(x), r_2(x, 8), w_2(x, 16), \bar{e}_2(x),$$
$$e_2(y), r_2(y, 5), w_2(y, 10), \bar{e}_2(y), e_1(y), r_1(y, 10), w_1(y, 13), \bar{e}_1(y)$$

Here, the invariant $x = y$ is broken: at the end, x is equal to 16, but y is equal to 13. Thus, this history is not equivalent to either of the two serial histories.

My primary goal in this section is to show how locks can be used in a disciplined fashion that rules out nonserializable histories. (In particular, you will learn that in the previous example, x should not be unlocked until after y is locked.) First, though, I need to formalize what it means for two histories to be equivalent, so that the definition of serializability is rigorous.

I will make two assumptions about locks:

1. Each transaction correctly pairs up lock and unlock operations. That is, no transaction ever locks a lock it already holds (except upgrading from shared to exclusive status), unlocks a lock it doesn't hold, or leaves a lock locked at the end.

2. The locks function correctly. No transaction will ever be granted a lock in shared mode while it is held by another transaction in exclusive mode, and no transaction will ever be granted a lock in exclusive mode while it is held by another transaction in either mode.

Neither of these assumptions should be controversial.

Two system histories are equivalent if the first history can be turned into the second by performing a succession of equivalence-preserving swap steps. An equivalence-preserving swap reverses the order of two adjacent actions, subject to the following constraints:

- The two actions must be from different transactions. (Any transaction's actions should be kept in their given order.)

- The two actions must not be any of the following seven *conflicting* pairs:
  1. $\overline{e}_j(x), s_k(x)$
  2. $\overline{e}_j(x), e_k(x)$
  3. $\overline{s}_j(x), e_k(x)$
  4. $\overline{s}_j(x), u_k(x)$
  5. $w_j(x), r_k(x)$
  6. $r_j(x), w_k(x)$
  7. $w_j(x), w_k(x)$

Forbidding swaps of the first four pairs ensures that locks continue properly functioning: T_k may not lock x's lock until after T_j has unlocked it. The next two conflicts ensure the read actions return the correct values: swapping a read and a write would change which value the read action returns. The final conflict ensures that x is left storing the correct value.

Figure 5.8 illustrates some of the constraints on equivalence-preserving swaps. Note that in all the conflicts, the two actions operate on the same stored entity (shown as x); any two operations on different entities by different transactions can be reversed without harm. In Exercise 5.3, show that this suffices to prove that the earlier example of a serializable history is indeed equivalent to the example serial history.

Even if two actions by different transactions involve the same entity, they may be reversed without harm if they are both reads. Exercise 5.4 includes a serializable

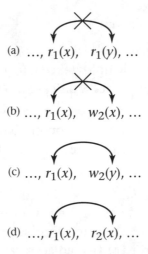

(a) ..., $r_1(x)$, $r_1(y)$, ...

(b) ..., $r_1(x)$, $w_2(x)$, ...

(c) ..., $r_1(x)$, $w_2(y)$, ...

(d) ..., $r_1(x)$, $r_2(x)$, ...

Figure 5.8   Illegal and legal swaps: (a) illegal to swap steps from one transaction; (b) illegal to swap two conflicting operations on the same entity; (c) legal to swap operations on different entities by different transactions; (d) legal to swap nonconflicting operations by different transactions.

history where reads of an entity need to be reversed in order to arrive at an equivalent serial history.

I am now ready to state the two-phase locking rules, which suffice to ensure serializability. For now, concentrate on understanding what the rules say; afterward, I will show that they suffice. A transaction obeys two-phase locking if:

- For any entity that it operates on, the transaction locks the corresponding lock exactly once, sometime before it reads or writes the entity the first time, and unlocks it exactly once, sometime after it reads or writes the entity the last time.

- For any entity the transaction writes into, either the transaction initially obtains the corresponding lock in exclusive mode, or it upgrades the lock to exclusive mode sometime before writing.

- The transaction performs all its lock and upgrade actions before performing any of its unlock actions.

Notice that the two-phase locking rules leave a modest amount of flexibility regarding the use of locks. Consider the example transactions that read and write x and then read and write y. Any of the following transaction histories for T_1 would obey two-phase locking:

- $e_1(x), r_1(x), w_1(x), e_1(y), \overline{e}_1(x), r_1(y), w_1(y), \overline{e}_1(y)$
- $e_1(x), e_1(y), r_1(x), w_1(x), r_1(y), w_1(y), \overline{e}_1(y), \overline{e}_1(x)$
- $s_1(x), r_1(x), u_1(x), w_1(x), s_1(y), r_1(y), u_1(y), w_1(y), \overline{e}_1(x), \overline{e}_1(y)$

In Exercise 5.6, you can come up with several additional two-phase possibilities for this transaction.

If the programmer who writes a transaction explicitly includes the lock and unlock actions, any of these possibilities would be valid. More commonly, however, the programmer includes only the reads and writes, without any explicit lock or unlock actions. An underlying transaction processing system automatically inserts the lock and unlock actions to make the programming simpler and less error-prone. In this case, the system is likely to use three very simple rules:

1. Immediately before any read action, acquire the corresponding lock in shared mode if the transaction doesn't already hold it.

2. Immediately before any write action, acquire the corresponding lock in exclusive mode if the transaction doesn't already hold it. (If the transaction holds the lock in shared mode, upgrade it.)

3. At the very end of the transaction, unlock all the locks the transaction has locked.

You should be able to convince yourself that these rules are a special case of two-phase locking. By holding all the locks until the end of the transaction, the system need not predict the transaction's future read or write actions.

I still need to prove that two-phase locking suffices to ensure serializability. Recall that a history is serializable if it is equivalent to a serial history. Thus, I need to show that so long as two-phase locking is followed, you can find a sequence of equivalence-preserving swaps that will transform the system history into a serial one. Please understand that this transformation of the history into a serial one is just a proof technique I am using to help understand the system, not something that actually occurs during the system's operation. Transaction systems are not in the business of forcing transactions to execute serially; concurrency is good for performance. If anything, the running transaction system is doing the reverse transformation: the programmer may have thought in terms of serial transactions, but the system's execution interleaves them. I am showing that this interleaving is equivalence-preserving by showing that you can back out of it.

To simplify the proof, I will use the following vocabulary:

- The portion of the system history starting with T_j's first action and continuing up to, but not including, T_j's first unlock action is *phase one* of T_j.

- The portion of the system history starting with T_j's first unlock action and continuing up through T_j's last action is *phase two* of T_j.

- Any action performed by T_k during T_j's phase one (with $j \neq k$) is a *phase one impurity* of T_j. Similarly, any action performed by T_k during T_j's phase two (with $j \neq k$) is a *phase two impurity* of T_j.

- If a transaction has no impurities of either kind, it is *pure*. If all transactions are pure, then the system history is serial.

My game plan for the proof is this. First, I will show how to use equivalence-preserving swaps to purify any one transaction, say, T_j. Second, I will show that if T_k is already pure, purifying T_j does not introduce any impurities into T_k. Thus, you can purify the transactions one at a time, without having to worry about wrecking the transactions purified earlier.

If T_j is impure, you can purify it by first removing any phase one impurities and then any phase two impurities. To remove the phase one impurities, you can remove the leftmost one, and then repeat with the new leftmost one, until all are gone. The leftmost phase one impurity of T_j must be preceded by an action of T_j. I will show that those two actions can be reversed by an equivalence-preserving swap. That moves the leftmost impurity further to the left. If this swapping is done repeatedly, the impurity will percolate its way further and further to the left until it passes the first operation of T_j, at which point it will cease to be an impurity of T_j. Phase two impurities can be removed similarly, starting with the rightmost one, by percolating them to the right until they pass the last operation of T_j.

I need to show that the leftmost phase one impurity of T_j can be swapped with its left-hand neighbor, and that the rightmost phase two impurity can be swapped with its right-hand neighbor. Recall that to legally swap two actions, they must be from different transactions, and they must not be one of the seven forbidden conflicting pairs. In order to be the leftmost impurity of T_j, an action must be performed by some other transaction, T_k, and have an action from T_j as its left-hand neighbor. (A similar argument applies for the rightmost impurity and its right-hand neighbor.) Thus, the actions are definitely from different transactions, and the only remaining concern is the seven conflicts.

For the leftmost phase one impurity and its left-hand neighbor, you cannot have any of these conflicts:

1. $\bar{e}_j(x), s_k(x)$
2. $\bar{e}_j(x), e_k(x)$
3. $\bar{s}_j(x), e_k(x)$
4. $\bar{s}_j(x), u_k(x)$

because transaction T_j does not do any unlock actions in phase one. (Recall the definition of phase one.) Nor can you have any of the other three conflicts:

5. $w_j(x), r_k(x)$
6. $r_j(x), w_k(x)$
7. $w_j(x), w_k(x)$

because the two-phase locking rules ensure that each read or write action is performed only with the appropriate lock held. There is no way transactions T_j and T_k can both hold the lock on x, with at least one of them being in exclusive mode. Similar arguments rule out any conflict between the rightmost phase two impurity and its right-hand neighbor; in Exercise 5.7, you can fill in the details.

You have now seen that equivalence-preserving swap steps suffice to purify T_j by percolating each of its phase one impurities out to the left and each of its phase two impurities out to the right. The goal is to serialize an arbitrary system history that complies with the two-phase locking rules. I would like to pick one of its transactions that is impure and purify it, then repeat with another and keep going until all the transactions are pure, that is, until the system history has become serial. For this plan to work, I need to be sure that purifying one transaction doesn't wreck the purity of any already pure transaction.

Purifying T_j doesn't touch any actions that don't lie between T_j's first action and its last action. Thus, the only way purifying T_j could endanger the existing purity of T_k is if T_k lies at least partly within T_j's span. However, because T_k is pure, either all of it lies within T_j's span or none of it does, so you need only consider the case that all of T_k lies within T_j's span. In fact, you should be able to convince yourself of something stronger: if any action of a pure transaction T_k lies within T_j's span, then all of T_k lies within a single one of T_j's phases (either all within phase one, or all within phase two).

If T_k's actions occupy consecutive positions within phase one, purifying T_j will percolate all of T_k's actions to the left and leave them in consecutive positions preceding the start of T_j. Similarly, if T_k is within phase two, all its actions will move to the right and wind up as a consecutive block to the right of T_j. Thus, T_k's purity is preserved.

You can conclude, then, that any system history obeying the two-phase locking rules is serializable. Recall that serializable histories are equivalent to serial histories. In a serial history composed from invariant-preserving transactions, each transaction moves the system from one consistent state to another. Thus, so long as two-phase locking is used, the system will behave as though it is moving from consistent state to consistent state. In particular, this situation can be obtained simply by locking each entity before operating on it the first time and holding all locks until the end of the transaction.

Even though serializable histories are equivalent to serial histories, they differ in one important regard. Unlike a serial history, a serializable history may include concurrency between transactions. This allows the system to achieve higher performance but entails a risk of deadlock that is not present in serial execution. If deadlock occurs, one of the deadlocked transactions needs to be aborted. This abortion is one way in which a transaction can fail. Therefore, I will next turn to the question of how atomicity is preserved in the face of transaction failures.

5.3.2 Failure Atomicity: Undo Logging

Recall that atomic transactions may temporarily put the system in an inconsistent state so long as they restore consistency before committing. For example, in the middle of a transfer from one account to another, money can temporarily "disappear" (not be in any account) so long as the money has "reappeared" in the destination account by the time the transfer is over. You have already seen one way to protect against harm from these temporary inconsistencies: by using two-phase locking, you prevent any concurrent transaction from being affected by the inconsistent state. Now you need to deal with another possible source of trouble: what if a transaction aborts after making some, but not all, of its updates to the state? How can you prevent later transactions from seeing an inconsistent state?

Transactions fail for many reasons. For example, the transfer transaction might debit money from the source account, and then before crediting it to the destination account, discover that the destination account doesn't exist. Alternatively, the system might detect a deadlock when trying to lock the destination account. Either way, the transaction is aborted after having debited the source account. To keep the transaction atomic (and thus preserve consistency), you need to undo the debit from the source account. That way, the failed transaction will have left the system's state unchanged. That is one of the two legal outcomes of an atomic transaction: all or nothing.

Without support from a transaction processing system, failure atomicity is extremely difficult to ensure. Programmers write a lot of complex and bug-prone code in attempts to provide failure atomicity on their own. To see how troublesome it can be, consider two ways to achieve failure atomicity without a transaction processing system.

One approach is to try to test for all possible causes of failure before taking any action. For example, test that the destination account exists, and can be locked, before debiting from the source account. This can lead to poor modularity. After all, the logical place to check the destination account is in association with crediting that account. In addition, the advance checking approach doesn't cope well with concurrency. What if a concurrent thread messed with the destination account after it had been checked?

Another approach is to test for each possible failure as it may occur and provide manual cleanup actions. For example, if a failure occurs while crediting the destination account, revert the money back into the source account. The problem here is that in a complicated transaction, many failure handlers are needed, as shown in Figure 5.9. The handler for the second action needs to undo the first action. The handler for the third action needs to undo actions two and one. The handler for the fourth action needs to undo actions three, two, and one. In Exercise 5.10, you can show that failure handlers must share cleanup code to prevent a quadratic increase in the amount of code for the transaction. Even if the failure handlers share cleanup code, manual cleanup actions significantly complicate the structure of the transaction.

By contrast, systems that support transactions (such as database systems) make failure atomicity completely transparent to the application programmer. If a transaction aborts, the system automatically cleans up the state so that no other transaction will observe any effects from the aborted transaction. In order to provide this service, the transaction system normally uses an *undo log*, as I will now describe.

Conceptually, each transaction has its own undo log, which records the actions needed to back out of the changes that transaction has made to the system's state. Every time the transaction writes a new value into some stored entity, it also adds an

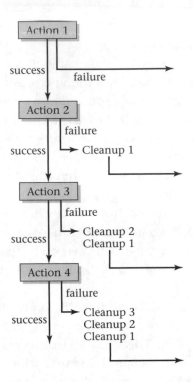

Figure 5.9 Failure atomicity can be ensured by testing for failure at each step in a process and providing appropriate failure handlers. The failure handler for each action needs to clean up all prior actions, that is, remove their effects. This approach does not scale as well as the general undo log used by transaction processing systems.

entry to the undo log, showing how the entity can be restored to its prior state. The simplest way to do this is to record the old value of the entity.

Suppose $x = 5$ and transaction T_1 asks the transaction processing system to write an 8 into x. In the prior section, you saw that behind the scenes this action might do more than just write the 8 into x: it might first acquire an exclusive lock on x. Now, you learn that the transaction processing system will do even more behind the scenes: it will also add an entry to T_1's undo log, showing that x needs to be set back to 5 to undo this step. That entry in the undo log will list x as the entity in question, and 5 as its prior value.

If a transaction aborts, the transaction processing system will read back through that transaction's undo log entries, from the most recent to the earliest, and carry out each of the reversions listed in the log. Be sure you understand why the undo log entries need to be processed in reverse chronological order. In Exercise 5.11, you can give an example where this matters.

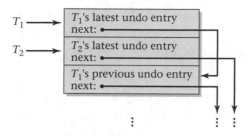

Figure 5.10   Rather than having a separate undo log for each transaction, the undo logs can be combined. In this case, the entries for any one transaction are chained together, as shown here, so that they can be efficiently processed as though in a separate log.

Notice that undoing write operations involves more writing; to undo the write of 8 into x, you write 5 back into x. This has an important consequence for two-phase locking. If a transaction writes an entity, it must hold the corresponding lock in exclusive mode until the transaction has finished aborting or committing. Shared-mode locks, for entities that the transaction only reads, can be dropped earlier, subject to the usual two-phase rules. However, the exclusive-mode locks need to be retained, because so long as the possibility of aborting exists, the possibility of more writing exists.

I mentioned that conceptually each transaction has its own undo log. Normal transaction processing systems actually store all the undo logs in one combined log, with each entry added at the end. In order to efficiently process the entries from a single transaction in reverse chronological order, each entry contains a pointer to the previous entry from the same transaction. Each transaction keeps a pointer to its latest entry, as shown in Figure 5.10. You'll see in Section 5.4 that durability requires additional logging; these extra log entries are also mixed into the same combined log with all the transactions' undo entries.

5.4 Transaction Durability: Write-Ahead Logging

Adding durability to transactions raises two new issues—one directly and one indirectly:

1. The direct issue is durability itself. When a transaction commits, all the data needs to be stored somewhere *persistent* and made available again after system restart. (Persistent storage might be battery-powered RAM or, more commonly, a disk drive.)

2. The indirect issue is that failure atomicity now needs more work. When the system is restarted, it may need to clean up after transactions that were in progress at the time the system crashed and that had already done some writing to persistent storage.

The simplest way to ensure durability itself is to store all entities in persistent storage; all writing by transactions goes directly into that persistent storage. This is not terribly efficient; consider, for example, the difference in speed between disk drives and RAM. Therefore, I will explain a more practical alternative later in this section. First, though, to have a correct (if inefficient) solution, I need to address failure atomicity.

When a transaction aborts, the undo log allows the system to roll back any writes the transaction did. If a transaction is in progress when the system crashes, the transaction should be aborted at system restart time, so that its partial updating of the system state is not visible. This abortion upon restart can be done in the usual way, by using the undo log, if four precautions are taken:

1. The undo log must be stored in persistent storage so that it will be available when the system is restarted, for use in what is called *recovery processing*.

2. Whenever a transaction writes a new value for an entity into persistent storage, it must *first* write the undo record into the persistent undo log, as shown in Figure 5.11. I previously did not emphasize the order in which these two writes occur. Now it really matters, because the system could crash between the first write and the second. Users cannot risk the possibility that the entity has been written without the undo record.

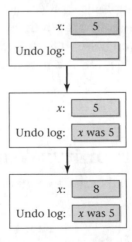

Figure 5.11   In order to allow crash recovery, the undo log entry must be made persistent before the write to the underlying object.

3. The undo operation (intended to restore an entity from its new value to its old value) must be safe to use, even if the entity already has its old value. In other words, the undo operation must be *idempotent*. Idempotency is important if the system crashes after the undo record is written, but before the entity itself is written. Recovery processing can still "undo" the write that was never done. In addition, if the system crashes again in the middle of recovery, you can start it all over again from the beginning, without harm from repeated undo processing. The form of undo record that I have shown, which records the entity's old value, naturally provides idempotency.

4. The recovery processing must have some way to figure out what transactions were in progress and hence need aborting. The usual way to do this is to keep all the undo logs in one combined log, which also includes explicit records any time a transaction commits or aborts. That way, recovery can read backward through the log, noting the completed transactions and processing the undo entries that are from other transactions.

Because persistent storage is generally slower than main memory, real transaction processing systems use a somewhat more sophisticated approach to reduce the amount of writing to persistent storage. When an entity is accessed the first time, it is copied into main memory. All reads and writes happen in main memory, for high performance. Every once in a while, the transaction system copies the latest version of the entity back into persistent storage. The system may also occasionally evict an entity from main memory, if it doesn't seem active enough to merit the space allocation. I will address this topic in Chapter 6, because it isn't particular to transactions.

Similarly, for performance reasons, log records are initially written into main memory and only later copied to persistent storage. That way, a large chunk of the log can be written to persistent storage at one time, which improves the performance of devices such as disk drives.

Incorporating these performance improvements without changing anything else would wreck atomicity and durability. When the system crashed, almost any situation would be possible. Committed transactions might have written their results only to nonpersistent memory, violating durability. Noncommitted transactions might have written some values into persistent storage, but not the corresponding undo log entries, violating atomicity. To protect against these cases, you need to put some additional machinery in place.

The simplest approach to restoring correct operation is to enforce three new rules:

1. No entity may be written back into persistent storage until the corresponding undo log entry has been written into persistent storage.

2. The commit entry in the log must be written to persistent storage before the commit operation is complete.

3. All entities must be written back into persistent storage before the commit entry is written to the log.

The first rule ensures that all undo entries needed during recovery are available at recovery time. The second rule prevents the recovery process from aborting a transaction that the user saw as committed before the crash. The third rule ensures that committed transactions are durable.

The first two rules are hard to argue with; taken together, they are called *write-ahead logging* (*WAL*). (Although these WAL rules are typical, some systems do manage to work with variants of them. The end-of-chapter notes provide pointers to the literature.) However, the third rule deserves closer scrutiny.

Durability demands that any updated value a transaction provides for an entity must be stored *somewhere* in persistent storage before that transaction can commit. However, the third rule seems to suggest a specific location: the entity must be "written back" into persistent storage, that is, stored in its usual location from which it was read. This leads to two questions: is this specific choice of location necessary, and, is it desirable?

When a transaction commits, all its updates to entities must be stored somewhere persistent. Moreover, if the updates are not stored in the entities' usual locations, they must be somewhere that the recovery process can locate. That way, if the system crashes and restarts, the recovery process can bring the entities' usual locations up to date, thereby allowing normal operation to resume. Because the recovery process does its work by reading the log, the log seems like an obvious alternative place to store committed transactions' updates.

This answers the earlier question of necessity. It is not necessary to write a transaction's updates into the main data entities' persistent storage before the transaction commits. Instead, the updates can be written to the log as *redo log* entries. As long as the redo entries are in the log before the commitment marker, and all of them are in persistent storage before the commit operation completes, the system will ensure durability. Just as an undo log entry can be as simple as a record of the data entity's old value, a redo log entry can be as simple as a copy of the new value.

I still need to address the question of desirability. Is there any advantage to writing redo log entries into persistent storage, rather than directly updating the modified entities' primary locations? To answer this, you need to understand that many systems use disk as the only persistent storage and that the slowest part of accessing a disk drive is the mechanical movements needed to reach a particular place on the disk. Therefore, writing one large block of data to a single location on disk is much faster than writing lots of smaller pieces of data at individual locations. By using redo log entries, the commit operation has to wait only for a single large write to disk: all the new portions of the log (undo, redo, and commit) can get forced out in a single disk operation. Without the redo log, the commit operation would get held up waiting for lots of individual writes.

At this point, you have seen most of the mechanisms used by real transaction processing systems, at least in simplified overview form. Perhaps the biggest performance issue I have omitted is the speed of recovery after a crash. Using the mechanisms I have described thus far, the recovery process would need to read the entire log, back to when the transaction processing system started running. This is not practical for systems that run a long time. Therefore, transaction processing systems all incorporate some mechanism that puts a limit on how much of the log needs to be processed.

These mechanisms are generally referred to as *checkpointing*, because the simplest (and historically earliest) approach is to create a *checkpoint*, that is, a point at which the main persistent storage is brought to a consistent state. No log entries prior to the checkpoint need to be retained. More sophisticated checkpointing mechanisms avoid having to bring the system into a consistent state, so that normal processing can always continue.

5.5 Additional Transaction Mechanisms

In Sections 5.3 and 5.4, you learned about the two primary mechanisms used to support transactions: two-phase locking and logging. In this section, you will extend your knowledge into two more advanced areas: how isolation can be reduced in order to increase concurrency (Section 5.5.1) and how multiple transaction participants can be coordinated using the two-phase commit protocol (Section 5.5.2).

5.5.1 Increased Transaction Concurrency: Reduced Isolation

Two-phase locking ensures serializability, but at a price in concurrency, and hence, throughput. Transactions may be forced to wait for locks. How big a problem this is depends greatly on the workload mix.

Some systems process exclusively short transactions involving only a few entities (such as the example of a transfer from one account to another). Those systems will have no problem with two-phase locking, because a transaction will lock only a small portion of the data, and never for long. Thus, there will be almost no contention.

Other systems exclusively process long-running, read-only transactions involving most of the entities in a database. For example, mining historical business data for strategically useful patterns might exhibit this behavior. Here again, two-phase locking will be no problem, because any number of read-only transactions can coexist using the shared mode of the readers/writers locks.

However, a mix of these two workloads—lots of little updates with some big analysis—could be deadly. The analysis transactions could keep much of the database locked for a long time, choking off the flow of updates. This is particularly troubling, given that the updates are likely the mission-critical part of the system. (Imagine an airline that can analyze its history thoroughly but can't book any new reservations.)

This problem is sufficiently serious that many businesses use two separate database systems. One, the operational system, handles the mission-critical short transactions, which may update the data. Periodically (such as each night), data is transferred from the operational system to a *data warehouse*. The warehouse holds historical data, generally not quite up to the present, but close enough for analysis. Analysts can run arbitrarily long read-only transactions on the warehouse. They can even directly run ad hoc queries from an interactive session, something they would never dare do on the operational system. (Imagine an analyst who types in some queries and then goes home without typing `commit`; until the interactive session exceeds a time limit and aborts, it will continue to hold locks.)

Valuable as this warehousing strategy may be, it avoids only the most obvious manifestations of a more general problem; it does not provide a complete solution. No perfect solution exists, but database systems provide one other partial solution: transaction programmers can choose to sacrifice serializability in order to attain greater concurrency.

Sacrificing serializability to increase concurrency does not mean the programmers are sacrificing correctness for performance. Serializability is a great simplification for a programmer trying to reason carefully enough about a program to ensure its correctness. However, careful reasoning is possible even for nonserializable execution, with enough additional mental labor. Because such labor is neither free nor immune from error, serializable execution ought to be the default, with other alternatives only considered where performance is demonstrably inadequate.

Recall that under two-phase locking, transactions generally hold all locks until the transaction commits or aborts. Suppose instead the transaction did this only for exclusive locks (when writing); it would acquire a shared lock before each read operation and release it immediately after the read. Many database systems (such as Microsoft SQL Server and IBM DB2) offer this as an option, called *read committed*. In fact, contrary to the SQL standard, read committed is often the default mode for transactions; programmers need to explicitly request serializability.

Even acquiring a shared lock ever so briefly has some value: it prevents reading data written by a transaction that is still in progress, because that transaction will hold the lock in exclusive mode. However, several strange phenomena are possible with this relaxed isolation, which would not be possible if serializability were enforced. The most well-known phenomenon is "nonrepeatable read." If a transaction reads an entity, and then later reads the same entity again, it may find that the value has changed. This can happen if between the two reads another transaction writes the entity and commits.

Nonrepeatable read is often spoken about as though it were the only problem arising from relaxed isolation. This is a dangerous misconception: a programmer might think that in an application that can tolerate nonrepeatable reads (for example, one that doesn't read any entity twice), serializability is superfluous. This is not true.

Consider, for example, a system with two variables, x and y. Transaction T_1 reads x's value and writes it into y. Transaction T_2 does the reverse: it copies y into x. Someone doing both of these transactions would expect x and y to be equal afterward—either of the transactions would suffice to achieve that. Yet with short read locks, doing the two transactions concurrently could result in swapping x and y's old values, as shown in Figure 5.12, rather than making the two equal. In Exercise 5.12, you can come up with a system history exhibiting this phenomenon.

Other database systems, such as Oracle and PostgreSQL, take a more radical approach to relaxed isolation, known as *multiversion concurrency control (MVCC)*. Each write action stores the new value for an entity in a different location than the old value. Thus, a read action need not read the most recent version: it can read an older version. In particular, a transaction can read all entities (other than those it has written itself) from the version that was most recently committed when the transaction started. Any writes done since then by other transactions—whether committed or otherwise—are completely ignored. No read locks are needed at all. This is known as *snapshot isolation*. When a transaction using snapshot isolation obtains a write lock and the entity

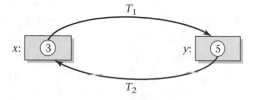

Figure 5.12 If transactions release each read lock as soon as they are done reading the corresponding object, the execution may not be serializable. For example, two transactions could swap x and y's values, as shown here.

being written was modified by some other transaction that committed since the writing transaction started, the write request is aborted with an error condition. The writing transaction must roll back and restart.

It should be clear that snapshot isolation provides repeatable reads. Therefore, some people, forgetting that nonrepeatable reads are only one symptom of relaxed isolation, think that snapshot isolation suffices for serializability. Regrettably, both Oracle and PostgreSQL foster this belief by calling their snapshot isolation mode "serializable." Neither offers true serializability, even as an option. For example, on either of these systems, one transaction could copy x to y while another was copying y to x, even at the highest isolation level.

5.5.2 Coordinated Transaction Participants: Two-Phase Commit

A transaction processing system can be built using the mechanisms I have described thus far: two-phase locking and a write-ahead log containing undo and redo entries. However, you need one more mechanism if you want to be able to coordinate multiple subsystems working together on shared transactions. That mechanism is the *two-phase commit* protocol, which I describe in this section. (Two-phase commit and two-phase locking are unrelated, other than that each happens to contain two phases.)

As an example of coordination, a system might include both a message-queuing system and a relational database. Each uses the mechanisms I have previously described in order to provide atomic and durable transactions. However, you would like to be able to have a single transaction that first dequeues a request message from one queue, then does some database operations, and finally writes a response message into another queue. All of this should be atomic and durable, as a unit. For example, if something goes wrong during database processing, the rollback not only should undo any database changes, but also should restore the request message to its queue.

Transaction processing systems generally include a module specializing in this coordination, known as a *transaction manager*, as well as the various *resource managers*, such as message-queuing and database systems. The managers communicate with one another using the two-phase commit protocol in order to ensure that all participants agree whether a transaction has aborted or committed. In particular, if the transaction commits, it must be durable in each resource manager.

Gray pointed out that the essence of two-phase commit is the same as a wedding ceremony. First, the officiating party asks all the participants whether they really want to go ahead with the commitment. After each of them says "I do," the officiating party announces that the commitment has taken place.

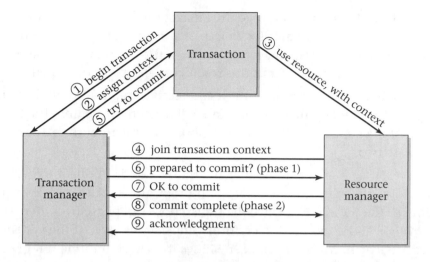

Figure 5.13 The two-phase commit protocol coordinates transaction participants, as shown here and enumerated in the accompanying text. This diagram shows only the case in which all resource managers indicate that it is OK to commit, and so the transaction is committed.

In somewhat greater detail, the steps in the two-phase commitment protocol are as follows, and as shown in Figure 5.13, for the case of a successful commitment:

1. When a new transaction begins, it registers with the transaction manager.

2. In return, the transaction manager assigns an identifying *transaction context*.

3. Whenever the transaction uses the services of a resource manager, it presents its transaction context. (If the resource manager subcontracts to another resource manger, it passes the transaction context along.)

4. When a resource manager sees a new transaction context for the first time, it registers with the transaction manager as being involved in that transaction. This is known as joining the transaction.

5. When the transaction wishes to commit, it contacts the transaction manager.

6. The transaction manager knows all the involved resource managers because of their earlier join messages. The transaction manager starts phase one by asking each of those resource managers whether it is prepared to commit.

7. When a resource manager is asked to prepare to commit, it checks whether it has any reason not to. (For example, a database system might check whether any consistency constraints were violated.) If the resource manager detects a problem, it replies to the transaction manager that the transaction should be aborted. If there

is no problem, the resource manager first makes sure the transaction's updates are all stored in persistent storage (for example, in redo log records). Then, once this is complete, the resource manager indicates to the transaction manager that the transaction can commit, so far as this resource manager is concerned.

8. The transaction manager waits until it has received replies from all the resource managers. If the replies indicate unanimous agreement to commit, the transaction manager logs a commitment record and notifies all the resource managers, which starts phase two.

9. When a resource manager hears that the transaction is in phase two of commitment, it logs its own commit record and drops any exclusive locks it has been holding for the transaction. Once the transaction is in phase two, there is no possibility it will abort and need to perform undo actions. Even if the system crashes and restarts, the transaction manager will see its own commitment log record and go forward with phase two.

   Each resource manager then sends an acknowledgment to the transaction manager, indicating completion of the phase two activity. When all of these acknowledgments are received, the transaction manager logs completion of the commit. That way, after a crash and restart, it will know not to bother redoing phase two.

On the other hand, if in phase one the transaction manager hears a request to abort from any resource manager or is forced to recover after a crash and finds no commitment record, then it notifies the resource managers to roll back the transaction, using their undo logs.

5.6 Security and Transactions

Transaction processing systems are often used for an enterprise's mission-critical operations. As such, a great deal of thought has gone into security issues in transaction processing systems. However, many of the issues that arise in these systems are not actually particular to the transaction mechanism, per se. Here I will focus on security implications that stem from using atomic transactions.

One security consequence of atomic transactions is salutary. A system constructed out of atomic transactions is much easier to reason about than a more general system would be. You saw in Chapter 4 that crackers can exploit race conditions, which would otherwise almost never happen, in order to subvert a system's security design. A similar trick can be played by forcing a non-atomic operation to fail after doing only some of its actions. By using atomic transactions, the system's designer excludes both of these entire categories of vulnerabilities.

Furthermore, security is enhanced by using a general-purpose transaction processing infrastructure, rather than trying to achieve atomicity through ad hoc means. Nothing is more prone to security vulnerabilities than complex code that is rarely used. You saw that achieving failure atomicity without a general mechanism, such as the undo log, often involves considerable complex, nonmodular code. (For example, see Exploration Project 5.7, which has you examine some Linux kernel source code.) And yet, this messy, bug-prone code is never tested under normal circumstances, because it comes into play only in the case of a failure. As such, bugs in it could go undetected for years, until some cracker goes looking for them.

By contrast, a general-purpose infrastructure (such as is included in a reputable database system) has presumably been well tested, for two reasons. First, its correct operation is a central concern for its authors, rather than peripheral. Second, the exact same infrastructure comes into play in all situations; for example, undo logs are processed in deadlock recovery, user-initiated aborts, and other failure situations. As such, testing the mechanism in one common situation provides some assurance of correct operation in other, less common situations.

You have seen that one security guideline regarding transactions is simple: they should be used. Are there other, less simple and less positive interactions between transactions and security? Unfortunately, yes. Transactions are a very powerful abstraction mechanism; that is, they hide a great deal of complexity behind a simple interface. An application programmer can think in terms of the simple interface and totally ignore the complex underpinnings—except when those complex underpinnings have security implications. That is the great danger of any abstraction mechanism, transactions included: it can blind you to what is really going on. Thus, another security guideline is to go beyond the abstract view of transactions and consider the underlying mechanisms discussed in this chapter.

One instance in which you need to think about transactions' underpinnings occurs when you are reasoning about your system's vulnerability to denial of service attacks. Transaction processing systems do a great deal of locking behind the scenes. Generally, they provide not only deadlock detection, but also timeouts on locks. However, this doesn't mean that a subverted transaction couldn't bring other transactions to their knees. Do you really want to wait the full timeout period for each lock acquisition?

Worse, the usual way of handling locking problems is to roll back the involved transactions and then restart them. If the problems are caused by fluky coincidences, they will almost surely not recur on the second try. However, if your system is being manipulated by a cracker, might you be put in the position of repeatedly rolling back and retrying the same transactions? If so, you not only are making no headway, but also are consuming great quantities of resources, such as processing time and log space. After how many retries should you give up?

Even aside from locking and retries, you need to understand your transactions' consumption of log space and other resources to be able to reason about denial of service attacks. Could an attacker trick you into filling up your log space on disk?

Another pitfall would be to lose track of exactly what degree of isolation your transactions enjoy relative to other concurrent computations. For example, suppose you have a transaction that temporarily stores some confidential information into a widely readable data entity, but then deletes the information before committing. (Alternatively, the transaction may store the information and then abort upon discovering the information is confidential.) Does this suffice to protect the information from disclosure? Maybe, maybe not. If your transaction is running in serializable isolation (that is, with full two-phase locking), *and so are all the concurrent computations*, then the information is protected. However, if you allow an adversary to run transactions that don't acquire locks (for example, SQL's "read uncommitted" isolation level), then you have not protected the confidential information, no matter how serializable your own transaction is and how careful it is to clean up all the data before committing.

Similarly, suppose your transactions rely on keeping the database consistent (maintaining invariant properties) in order to operate correctly. Specifically, if the database becomes inconsistent, your transactions can be tricked into violating security policy. Are you safe if all the transactions have been declared to use the "serializable" isolation level, and adversaries are prevented from introducing additional transactions? Not necessarily. As I mentioned earlier, if you are using the Oracle or PostgreSQL database system, the "serializable" isolation level doesn't actually provide serializability; it provides only snapshot isolation. If you don't understand that, and exactly what snapshot isolation entails, you have no way to reason about the kind of situations into which a cracker could manipulate your transactions. Perhaps the cracker could arrange for your transactions to run in a nonserializable fashion that leaves the database inconsistent in a way that creates a security vulnerability.

Most transaction processing systems are closed environments, where crackers cannot easily introduce extra transactions or even analyze the existing transactions. This makes them somewhat resistant to attack. Perhaps as a result, the risks mentioned here have generally remained theoretical to date. No known exploits take advantage of programmers' confusion between snapshot isolation and true serializability, for example. Nonetheless, it is important to remember that abstraction can be dangerous. Unless you understand what your system is really doing, you will not understand its vulnerabilities.

One final pitfall for unwary programmers, with possible security implications, is that a transaction manager can provide atomicity only for those actions under its control. For example, throughout this chapter, I have assumed that transactions don't do any I/O. Mature, full-featured transaction processing systems also allow controlled

I/O from transactions. Until a transaction commits, all its output is kept impounded. Only upon commit is the output actually produced. (Some systems go so far as to use special I/O hardware that can be tested after a crash to see whether the output was produced yet.) In contrast to these full-featured systems, many programmers build web-accessible applications (in particular) with only a transactional database as support. In these systems, as in this textbook, I/O is not automatically included in the transactional protection. The application programmer needs to take responsibility for not printing a valuable ticket and then allowing the purchase to be aborted, for example.

Exercises

5.1 In the example of deadlock detection and recovery in a database, each of the two transactions tried to update two account balances, then commit. Suppose you add another step to the beginning of each transaction: immediately before the first update, display the full table, using **select**. Other than displaying the table, will this have any impact on how the scenario plays out? Explain what will happen if the transactions are executed in a system that is enforcing serializability using two-phase locking. (Note that this cannot be tested using Oracle, because it uses MVCC, rather than two-phase locking.)

5.2 I introduced serial histories with an example where transaction T_1 added 3 to x and y and then transaction T_2 doubled x and y. Write out the other serial history, in which T_2 comes first. Leave the sequence of steps within each transaction the same as in the text, but change the values appropriately.

5.3 Prove that the example serializable history is equivalent to the example serial history by showing the result of each equivalence-preserving swap step along the way from the serializable history to the serial history.

5.4 For each of the following histories, if the history is serializable, give an equivalent serial history. Rather than listing all the steps in the serial history, you can just list the transaction numbers (1 and 2; or 1, 2, and 3) in the appropriate order. If the history is not serializable, say so.

(a) $s_1(x), r_1(x), \overline{s}_1(x), e_1(z), w_1(z), \overline{e}_1(z), s_2(y), r_2(y), \overline{s}_2(y),$
$e_2(x), w_2(x), \overline{e}_2(x), s_1(v), r_1(v), \overline{s}_1(v), e_1(y), w_1(y), e_1(y)$

(b) $s_1(v), s_2(v), r_1(v), s_2(x), r_2(x), e_2(z), w_2(z), \overline{e}_2(z), \overline{s}_2(x),$
$s_1(z), e_1(x), r_1(z), w_1(x), r_2(v), e_2(y), w_2(y), \overline{e}_1(x), \overline{s}_1(z),$
$\overline{s}_1(v), \overline{s}_2(v), \overline{e}_2(y)$

(c) $s_1(x), s_1(y), s_2(x), s_2(z), s_3(y), s_3(z), r_1(x), r_2(x), r_2(z), r_3(z),$
$r_3(y), r_1(y), \overline{s}_1(x), \overline{s}_1(y), \overline{s}_2(x), \overline{s}_2(z), \overline{s}_3(y), \overline{s}_3(z)$

(d) $c_1(x), w_1(x), \overline{e}_1(x), e_2(x), w_2(x), \overline{e}_2(x), e_2(z), w_2(z), \overline{e}_2(z),$
$e_3(z), w_3(z), \overline{e}_3(z), e_3(y), w_3(y), \overline{e}_3(y), e_1(y), w_1(y), \overline{e}_1(y)$

(e) $e_1(x), r_1(x), s_2(y), r_2(y), \overline{s}_2(y), w_1(x), e_1(y), w_1(y), \overline{e}_1(y), \overline{e}_1(x),$
$s_3(x), e_3(y), r_3(x), w_3(y), \overline{e}_3(y), \overline{s}_3(x)$

5.5 Of the serializable histories in Exercise 5.4, which ones obey the two-phase locking rules?

5.6 As an example of two-phase locking, page 141 showed three different two-phase histories for transaction T_1, which reads and writes x and then reads and writes y. Come up with at least five more histories for this transaction that also obey the two-phase locking rules.

5.7 Explain why the rightmost phase two impurity of T_j cannot conflict with its right-hand neighbor.

5.8 Explain why a pure transaction, T_k, with any of its actions occurring as an impurity within the span of T_j must lie entirely within T_j's phase one or entirely within T_j's phase two.

5.9 Some particular collections of transactions may not need two-phase locking to ensure serializability. However, this is generally a fragile situation, which can be disturbed by the addition of another transaction—even one obeying two-phase locking.

(a) Give two transaction histories, neither of which obeys the two-phase locking rules, but which nonetheless always produce a serializable system history, no matter how they are interleaved.

(b) Come up with a third transaction history, this one obeying two-phase locking, such that when interleaved with the first two, a nonserializable system history can result.

5.10 I mentioned that providing failure atomicity without an undo log results in complex code. For example, putting an explicit succession of cleanup actions into each action's failure handling code can result in a quadratic increase in code size. Flesh out the details of this argument by proving that if Figure 5.9 on page 146 were extended to include n actions, it would contain $\Theta(n^2)$ cleanup steps.

5.11 Give an example of a transaction where it matters that undo log entries are processed in reverse chronological order.

5.12 Suppose you use relaxed-isolation locking rules, where shared locks are held only for the duration of the read action and then are released immediately afterward. (Exclusive locks are still held until the end of the transaction.) Give a system history of two transactions, each complying with these locking rules, in which one copies x's value to y and the other copies y's value to x. Starting with $x = 3$ and $y = 5$, you should wind up with $x = 5$ and $y = 3$.

5.13 Redo Exercise 5.1, but instead of two-phase locking, assume that the isolation level known as "read committed" is used and is implemented with short read locks. Then do the exercise a third time, assuming snapshot isolation. Only the latter can be tested using Oracle. (Oracle's read committed level doesn't use short read locks.) To test snapshot isolation using Oracle, start each transaction with the following command:

```
set transaction isolation level serializable;
```

5.14 Suppose that when a stored value is increased by 1, an undo record is written that does not include the old value. Instead, the undo record indicates that to undo the operation, the value should be decreased by 1. Is this idempotent? What problems might arise for crash recovery?

▨ Programming Project

5.1 Build a simple, inefficient Java class to support transactions that are atomic (under both concurrency and failure) but not durable, and without deadlock detection. The class should provide some state on which the transactions can operate; for example, it might encapsulate an array of integers, with **put** and **get** operations that the transactions can use to modify and access slots within the array. The transactions need to limit themselves to this state, accessed through these operations, in order to receive the guarantee of atomic execution.

You can use Java's **Thread**s as the transactions; your class can find out which one is currently running using **Thread.currentThread()**. Your class should take care of automatically acquiring and releasing readers/writers locks (from Programming Project 4.10), in accordance with two-phase locking. You will need to keep track (perhaps in a **Map**) of the locks each transaction holds. You will also need to keep an undo log for each transaction.

One design option would be to provide three methods used to signal the start of a transaction and its termination by commitment or abortion. Another, more object-oriented, option would be to encapsulate each transaction using an interface analogous to **Runnable** in the Java API, with a **run** method that carries out the whole transaction. If that method returns, the transaction commits; on the other hand, if the method throws an exception, the transaction aborts.

As a client application for your class, you could write a program that has multiple threads transferring money between bank accounts. The encapsulated array of integers could be used to store account balances, with the array indexes serving as account numbers.

Exploration Projects

5.1 Work through the examples in Chapter 25 ("Transactions") of the *J2EE 1.4 Tutorial*.

5.2 On a Linux system that uses an ext3 file system, for which you have permission to change mount options, experiment with the performance impact of journaling options. In particular, test a write-intensive workload after mounting the file system with each of the options `journal=data`, `journal=ordered`, and `journal=writeback`. These control how much protection is provided for file data (as opposed to metadata). With the first, all file operations are atomic and durable. With the second, a crash may occasionally leave data updated without the corresponding metadata update. With the third, it is even possible for metadata to be updated but still be pointing at old data. Write a report carefully explaining what you did and in which hardware and software system context you did it, so that someone else could replicate your results.

5.3 Carry out the scenario from Exercise 5.12 using a relational database system. You should use two interactive sessions, in each of which you have given the command `set transaction isolation level read committed`. Be sure to end your commands in each session with `commit` before you inspect the outcome.

5.4 Carry out the same scenario as in the previous project using Oracle or PostgreSQL, with the `transaction isolation level` set to `serializable`.

5.5 Try the same scenario as in the previous project, using Microsoft SQL Server or IBM DB2, with the `transaction isolation level` set to `serializable`. You should find that x and y are not swapped. What happens instead? Does this depend on how you interleave the commands in the two sessions?

5.6 Come up with a plausible scenario where using snapshot isolation rather than serializability results in a security vulnerability. You needn't show detailed SQL code, just an English description of what the data would be and what the transactions would do with it. (Some more formality might be helpful, of course.) Explain what an adversary would need to do in order to exploit the vulnerability.

5.7 The quadratic growth in code size in Exercise 5.10 stems from the assumption that each action's failure handler has its own disjoint cleanup code. This results in lots of repetitions of the same cleanup actions. One way to keep explicit per-action cleanup code (rather than a general undo log) and yet avoid quadratic growth is to share the common cleanup code, so that each cleanup action appears only once. Failures later in the transaction just execute more of that shared cleanup code than failures earlier in the transaction do. An example of this pattern can be found in the procedure `copy_process` in the Linux kernel source file `kernel/fork.c`. Skim this code (you don't need to understand most of it) and write a description of what programming language mechanism it uses to execute the appropriate amount of cleanup code, based on how late the failure occurs. Can you think of an alternative programming language mechanism that could serve the same purpose? (This exercise was written when the kernel was at version 2.6.0-test11; however, the relevant aspects of this procedure seem to be stable across quite a few versions.)

Notes

My treatment of transactions barely scratches the surface. If you are interested in transactions, you should read at least one book devoted entirely to the topic. The best to start with is probably by Bernstein and Newcomer [19]. After that, you can get a more detailed treatment of the underlying principles from Weikum and Vossen [134] or of the practical details (with lots of code) from Gray and Reuter [60].

The earliest electronic transaction processing systems are poorly documented in the open literature; apparently companies regarded techniques for achieving atomicity and durability as proprietary. (Gray has suggested the developers merely prioritized code over papers.) Only in the mid to late 1970s did techniques such as I explain begin showing up in publications; references [50, 107, 85, 59] still make good reading today. A longer, less polished work by Gray [56] was quite influential; today, it is primarily of interest to historians, as much of the same material appears in more polished form in his book with Reuter [60].

Härder and Reuter [63] introduced the acronym ACID. In the terminology I presented, isolation is subsumed under atomicity. You should be aware that some other authors instead treat atomicity as meaning only atomicity in the face of failures. Lampson and Sturgis [85] use *unitary* to mean atomic with respect to failures; however, this term does not seem to have caught on.

The specific software versions used for the examples were Oracle Database 9i, PostgreSQL 7.4, and J2EE 1.4. Documentation is available from *http://otn.oracle.com*, *http://www.postgresql.org*, and *http://java.sun.com*, respectively.

I showed how workflow systems can be configured with message queues connecting the processing stages. A popular alternative is to connect each processing stage with a centralized process manager, which coordinates the workflow. For example, upon receiving a message from order processing, the manager would send messages out to accounts receivable, shipping, and the customer. The process manager allows centralized monitoring and control. Process managers are sold as part of Enterprise Application Integration (EAI) products such as TIBCO's BusinessWorks.

I mentioned that my definitions of history, equivalence, and serializability were chosen for simplicity and would not accommodate more sophisticated concurrency control methods. If you wish to pursue this, the previously cited book by Weikum and Vossen [134] provides a good foundation. Classic works on the topic include those by Bernstein and Goodman [17, 18] and by Stearns and Rosenkrantz [121]. Several works I will cite with regard to relaxed isolation are also relevant here.

Two-phase locking seems to have first been published by Eswaran et al. [50]. That same 1976 paper also brought to the fore a difficult aspect of serializability in relational databases, which I have glossed over. Normally, locking is done at the granularity of individual rows in database tables. Suppose a transaction is operating on all accounts with zero balances. On the surface, you might think it locks just those rows of the accounts table. However, what if a concurrent transaction is doing a withdrawal that brings another account's balance down to zero? Or inserting a new account with zero balance? This introduces the problem known as *phantoms*; a transaction's assumptions can be invalidated not only by changes to the rows the transaction has read, but also by the addition of new rows. Eswaran et al.'s proposed solution, *predicate locks*, was impractical if taken too literally but provided the foundation for more practical techniques.

In describing durability and failure atomicity in the face of system crashes, I differentiated volatile storage from persistent storage. Real systems need to consider these issues in even greater detail. For example, a system failure while overwriting a block on disk may result in the disk having neither the old nor the new version available. This necessitates precautions, such as writing two copies of critical blocks. A good starting point for this topic would be the works cited at the beginning of these notes.

Key papers on snapshot isolation and other relaxations of isolation include those by Berenson et al. [15]; by Kempster, Stirling, and Thanisch [78]; and by Adya, Liskov, and O'Neil [1]. Historically, the original treatment of relaxed isolation was by Gray et al. [58].

I attributed the wedding analogy for two-phase commit to Gray. He seems to have first introduced it in a conference paper [57] and then reused it in his book with Reuter [60].

6

Virtual Memory

6.1 Introduction

In Chapters 4 and 5, you have seen that synchronization (including transactions) can control the interactions between concurrent threads. For example, synchronization can ensure that only one thread at a time updates the memory locations holding a shared data structure. Now you will learn about another form of control, which can provide each thread with its own private storage, rather than regulating the threads' access to shared storage.

In this chapter, I will present a mechanism, *virtual memory*, that can be used to provide threads with private storage, thereby controlling their interaction. However, virtual memory turns out to be a very general-purpose abstraction, useful for many goals other than just giving threads some privacy. Therefore, after using this introductory section to present the basic concept of virtual memory, I will devote Section 6.2 to surveying the applications of virtual memory. Only afterward will I turn to the details of mechanisms and policies; you'll find the related discussions in Sections 6.3 and 6.4. The chapter concludes with the standard features: security issues in Section 6.5, then exercises, programming and exploration projects, and notes.

The essence of virtual memory is to decouple the addresses that running programs use to identify objects from the addresses that the memory uses to identify storage

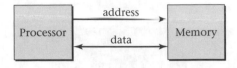

Figure 6.1   In a system without virtual memory, the processor sends addresses directly to the memory.

locations. The former are known as *virtual addresses* and the latter as *physical addresses*. As background for understanding this distinction, consider first a highly simplified diagram of a computer system, without virtual memory, as shown in Figure 6.1. In this system, the processor sends an address to the memory whenever it wants to store a value into memory or load a value from memory. The data being loaded or stored is also transferred in the appropriate direction. Each load operation retrieves the most recent value stored with the specified address. Even though the processor and memory are using a common set of addresses to communicate, the role played by addresses is somewhat different from the perspective of the processor than from the perspective of the memory, as I will now explain.

From the perspective of the processor (and the program the processor is executing), addresses are a way of differentiating stored objects from one another. If the processor stores more than one value, and then wishes to retrieve one of those values, it needs to specify which one should be retrieved. Hence, it uses addresses essentially as names. Just as an executive might tell a clerk to "file this under 'widget suppliers' " and then later ask the clerk to "get me that document we filed under 'widget suppliers'," the processor tells the memory to store a value with a particular address and then later loads from that address. Addresses used by executing programs to refer to objects are known as *virtual addresses*.

Of course, virtual addresses are not arbitrary names; each virtual address is a number. The processor may make use of this to give a group of related objects related names, so that it can easily compute the name of any object in the group. The simplest example of this kind of grouping of related objects is an array. All the array elements are stored at consecutive virtual addresses. That allows the virtual address of any individual element to be computed from the base virtual address of the array and the element's position within the array.

From the memory's perspective, addresses are not identifying names for objects, but rather are spatial locations of storage cells. The memory uses addresses to determine which cells to steer the data into or out of. Addresses used by the memory to specify storage locations are known as *physical addresses*. Figure 6.2 shows the processor's and memory's views of addresses in a system like that shown in Figure 6.1, where

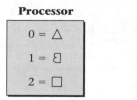

Figure 6.2 In a system without virtual memory, virtual addresses (the processor's names for objects) equal physical addresses (the memory's storage locations).

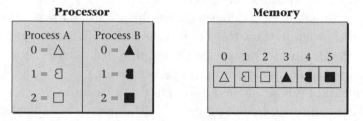

Figure 6.3 When two processes each use the same virtual addresses as names for their own objects, the virtual addresses cannot equal the physical addresses, because each process's objects need to be stored separately.

the physical addresses come directly from the virtual addresses, and so are numerically equal.

The difference between the processor's and memory's perspectives becomes apparent when you consider that the processor may be dividing its time between multiple computational processes. Sometimes the processes will each need a private object, yet the natural name to use will be the same in more than one process. Figure 6.3 shows how this necessitates using different addresses in the processor and the memory. That is, virtual addresses can no longer be equal to physical addresses. To make this work, general-purpose computers are structured as shown in Figure 6.4. Program execution within the processor works entirely in terms of virtual addresses. However, when a load or store operation is executed, the processor sends the virtual address to an intermediary, the *memory management unit* (*MMU*). The MMU translates the virtual address into a corresponding physical address, which it sends to the memory.

In Figure 6.3, each process uses the virtual address 0 as a name for its own triangle. This is a simplified model of how more complicated objects are referenced by real processes. Consider next a more realistic example of why each process might use the same virtual addresses for its own objects. Suppose several copies of the same spreadsheet

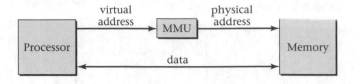

Figure 6.4 The memory management unit (MMU) translates the processor's virtual addresses into the memory's physical addresses.

program are running. Each copy will naturally want to refer to "the spreadsheet," but it should be a different spreadsheet object in each process. Even if each process uses a numerical name (that is, a virtual address), it would be natural for all running instances of the spreadsheet program to use the same address; after all, they are running the same code. Yet from the memory's perspective, the different processes' objects need to be stored separately—hence, at different physical addresses.

The same need for private names arises, if not quite so strongly, even if the concurrent processes are running different programs. Although in principle each application program could use different names (that is, virtual addresses) from all other programs, this requires a rather unwieldy amount of coordination.

Even for shared objects, addresses as names behave somewhat differently from addresses as locations. Suppose two processes are communicating via a shared bounded buffer; one is the producer, while the other is the consumer. From the perspective of one process, the buffer is the "output channel," whereas for the other process, it is the "input channel." Each process may have its own name for the object; yet, the memory still needs to store the object in one location. This holds true as well if the names used by the processes are numerical virtual addresses.

Thus, once again, virtual addresses and physical addresses should not be forced to be equal; it should be possible for two processes to use the same virtual address to refer to different physical addresses or to use different virtual addresses to refer to the same physical address.

You have seen that the MMU maps virtual addresses to physical addresses. However, I have not yet discussed the nature of this mapping. So far as anything up to this point goes, the mapping could be as simple as computing each physical address as twice the virtual address. However, that would not yield the very general mechanism known as virtual memory. Instead, virtual memory must have the following additional properties:

- The function that maps virtual addresses to physical addresses is represented by a table, rather than by a computational rule (such as doubling). That way, the mapping can be much more general.

- However, to keep its size manageable, the table does not independently list a physical address for each virtual address. Instead, the virtual addresses are grouped together into blocks known as *pages*, and the table shows for each page of virtual addresses the corresponding *page frame* of physical addresses. I'll explain this in greater detail in Section 6.3. In that same section, I also briefly consider an alternative, *segmentation.*

- The contents of the table are controlled by the operating system. This includes both incremental adjustments to the table (for purposes you will see in Section 6.2) and wholesale changes of the table when switching between threads. The latter allows each thread to have its own private virtual address space, in which case, the threads belong to different processes, as explained in Section 6.2.1.

- The table need not contain a physical address translation for every page of virtual addresses; in effect, some entries can be left blank. These undefined virtual addresses are illegal for the processor to use. If the processor generates an illegal address, the MMU interrupts the processor, transferring control to the operating system. This interrupt is known as a *page fault.* This mechanism serves not only to limit the usable addresses but also to allow address translations to be inserted into the table only when needed. By creating address translations in this demand-driven fashion, many applications of virtual memory arrange to move data only when necessary, thereby improving performance.

- As a refinement of the notion of illegal addresses, some entries in the table may be marked as legal for use, but only in specific ways. Most commonly, it may be legal to read from some particular page of virtual addresses but not to write into that page. The main purpose this serves is to allow trouble-free sharing of memory between processes.

In summary, then, virtual memory consists of an operating system–defined table of mappings from virtual addresses to physical addresses (at the granularity of pages), with the opportunity for intervention by the operating system on accesses that the table shows to be illegal. You should be able to see that this is a very flexible mechanism. The operating system can switch between multiple views of the physical memory. Parts of physical memory may be completely invisible in some views, because no virtual addresses map to those physical addresses. Other parts may be visible in more than one view, but appearing at different virtual addresses. Moreover, the mappings between virtual and physical addresses need not be established in advance. By marking pages as illegal to access, and then making them available when an interrupt indicates that they are first accessed, the operating system can provide mappings on a demand-driven basis. In Section 6.2, you will see several uses to which this general mechanism can be put.

6.2 Uses for Virtual Memory

This section contains a catalog of uses for virtual memory, one per subsection. The applications of virtual memory enumerated are all in everyday use in most general-purpose operating systems. A comprehensive list would be much longer and would include some applications that have thus far been limited to research systems or other esoteric settings.

6.2.1 Private Storage

The introductory section of this chapter has already explained that each computation running on a computer may want to have its own private storage, independent of the other computations that happen to be running on the same computer. This goal of private storage can be further elaborated into two subgoals:

- Each computation should be able to use whatever virtual addresses it finds most convenient for its objects, without needing to avoid using the same address as some other computation.

- Each computation's objects should be protected from accidental (or malicious) access by other computations.

Both subgoals—independent allocation and protection—can be achieved by giving the computations their own virtual memory mappings. This forms the core of the process concept.

A *process* is a group of one or more threads with an associated protection context. I will introduce processes more fully in Chapter 7. In particular, you will learn that the phrase "protection context" is intentionally broad, including such protection features as file access permissions, which you will study in Chapters 7 and 8. For now, I will focus on one particularly important part of a process's context: the mapping of virtual addresses to physical addresses. In other words, for the purposes of this chapter, a process is a group of threads that share a virtual address space.

As I will describe in Chapter 7, the computer hardware and operating system software collaborate to achieve protection by preventing any software outside the operating system from updating the MMU's address mapping. Thus, each process is restricted to accessing only those physical memory locations that the operating system has allocated as page frames for that process's pages. Assuming that the operating system allocates different processes disjoint portions of physical memory, the processes will have no ability to interfere with one another. The physical memory for the processes need only be disjoint at each moment in time; the processes can take turns using the same physical memory.

This protection model, in which processes are given separate virtual address spaces, is the mainstream approach today; for the purposes of the present chapter, I will take it for granted. In Chapter 7, I will also explore alternatives that allow all processes to share a single address space and yet remain protected from one another.

6.2.2 Controlled Sharing

Although the norm is for processes to use disjoint storage, sometimes the operating system will map a limited portion of memory into more than one process's address space. This limited sharing may be a way for the processes to communicate, or it may simply be a way to reduce memory consumption and the time needed to initialize memory. Regardless of the motivation, the shared physical memory can occupy a different range of virtual addresses in each process. (If this flexibility is exercised, the shared memory should not be used to store pointer-based structures, such as linked lists, because pointers are represented as virtual addresses.)

The simplest example of memory-conserving sharing occurs when multiple processes are running the same program. Normally, each process divides its virtual address space into two regions:

- A read-only region holds the machine language instructions of the program, as well as any read-only data the program contains, such as the character strings printed for error messages. This region is conventionally called the *text* of the program.

- A read/write region holds the rest of the process's data. (Many systems actually use two read/write regions, one for the stack and one for other data.)

All processes running the same program can share the same text. The operating system maps the text into each process's virtual memory address space, with the protection bits in the MMU set to enforce read-only access. That way, the shared text does not accidentally become a communication channel.

Modern programs make use of large libraries of supporting code. For example, there is a great deal of code related to graphical user interfaces that can be shared among quite different programs, such as a web browser and a spreadsheet. Therefore, operating systems allow processes to share these libraries with read-only protection, just as for main programs. Microsoft refers to shared libraries as *dynamic-link libraries (DLLs)*.

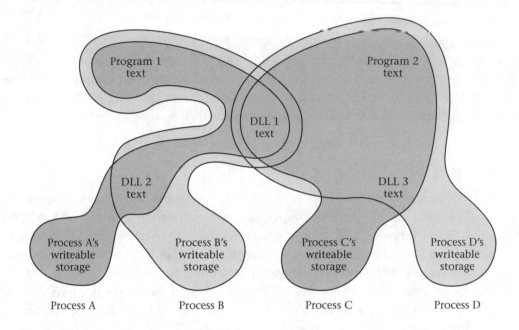

Figure 6.5 The address space of a process includes the text of the program the process is running, the text of any DLLs used by that program, and a writable storage area for data. Because processes A and B are both running program 1, which uses DLLs 1 and 2, their address spaces share these components. Processes C and D are running program 2, which uses DLLs 1 and 3. Because both programs use DLL 1, all four processes share it.

Figure 6.5 illustrates how processes can share in read-only form both program text and the text of DLLs. In this figure, processes A and B are running program 1, which uses DLLs 1 and 2. Processes C and D are running program 2, which uses DLLs 1 and 3. Each process is shown as encompassing the appropriate program text, DLLs, and writable data area. In other words, each process encompasses those areas mapped into its virtual address space.

From the operating system's perspective, the simplest way to support interprocess communication is to map some physical memory into two processes' virtual address spaces with full read/write permissions. Then the processes can communicate freely; each writes into the shared memory and reads what the other one writes. Figure 6.6 illustrates this sharing of a writable area of memory for communication.

Simple as this may be for the operating system, it is anything but simple for the application programmers. They need to include mutexes, readers-writers locks, or some similar synchronization structure in the shared memory, and they need to take scrupulous care to use those locks. Otherwise, the communicating processes will exhibit races, which are difficult to debug.

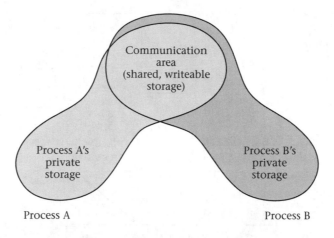

Figure 6.6 Two processes can communicate by sharing a writable storage area.

Therefore, some operating systems (such as Mac OS X) use virtual memory to support a more structured form of communication, known as *message passing*, in which one process writes a message into a block of memory and then asks the operating system to send the message to the other process. The receiving process seems to get a copy of the sent message. For small messages, the operating system may literally copy the message from one process's memory to the other's. For efficiency, though, large messages are not actually copied. Instead, the operating system updates the receiver's virtual memory map to point to the same physical memory as the sender's message; thus, sender and receiver both have access to the message, without it being copied. To maintain the ease of debugging that comes from message passing, the operating system marks the page as read-only for both the sender and the receiver. Thus, they cannot engage in any nasty races. Because the sender composes the message before invoking the operating system, the read-only protection is not yet in place during message composition and so does not stand in the way.

As a final refinement to message passing by read-only sharing, systems such as Mac OS X offer *copy on write* (*COW*). If either process tries to write into the shared page, the MMU will use an interrupt to transfer control to the operating system. The operating system can then make a copy of the page, so that the sender and receiver now have their own individual copies, which can be writable. The operating system resumes the process that was trying to write, allowing it to now succeed. This provides the complete illusion that the page was copied at the time the message was sent, as shown in Figure 6.7. The advantage is that if the processes do not write into most message pages, most of the copying is avoided.

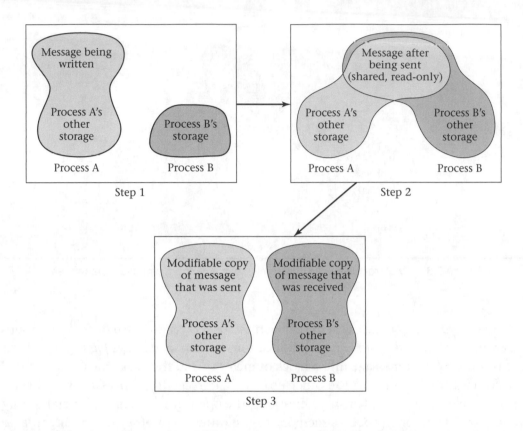

Figure 6.7 To use copy on write (COW) message passing, process A writes a message into part of its private memory (Step 1) and then asks the operating system to map the memory containing the message into process B's address space as well (Step 2). Neither process has permission to write into the shared area. If either violates this restriction, the operating system copies the affected page, gives each process write permission for its own copy, and allows the write operation to proceed (Step 3). The net effect is the same as if the message were copied when it was sent, but the copying is avoided if neither process writes into the shared area.

6.2.3 Flexible Memory Allocation

The operating system needs to divide the computer's memory among the various processes, as well as retain some for its own use. At first glance, this memory allocation problem doesn't seem too difficult. If one process needs 8 megabytes (MB) and another needs 10, the operating system could allocate the first 8 MB of the memory (with the lowest physical addresses) to the first process and the next 10 MB to the second. However, this kind of contiguous allocation runs into two difficulties.

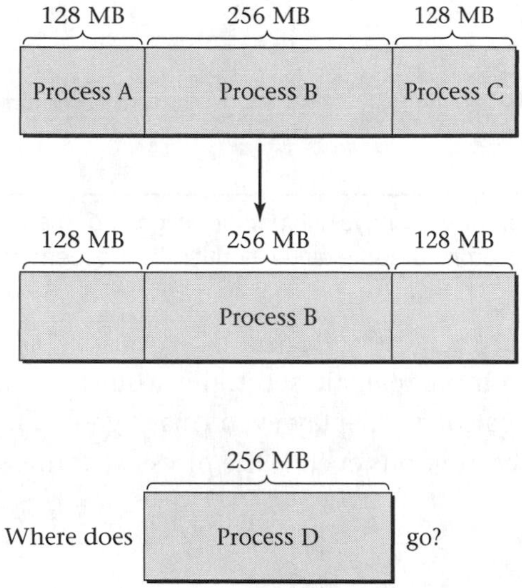

Figure 6.8 Contiguous allocation leads to external fragmentation. In this example, there is no contiguous 256-MB space available for process D, even though the termination of processes A and C has freed up a total of 256 MB.

The first problem with contiguous allocation is that the amount of memory that each process requires may grow and shrink as the program runs. If the first process is immediately followed in memory by the second process, what happens if the first process needs more space?

The second problem with contiguous allocation is that processes exit, and new processes (with different sizes) are started. Suppose you have 512 MB of memory available and three processes running, of sizes 128 MB, 256 MB, and 128 MB. Now suppose the first and third processes terminate, freeing up their 128-MB chunks of memory. Suppose a 256-MB process now starts running. There is enough memory available, but not all in one contiguous chunk, as illustrated in Figure 6.8. This situation is known as *external fragmentation*. I will discuss external fragmentation more carefully in Chapter 8, because contiguous allocation is important for disk space. (I will also define the contrasting term, internal fragmentation, in that same chapter.)

Because all modern general-purpose systems have virtual memory, these contiguous allocation difficulties are a non-issue for main memory. The operating system can allocate any available physical page frames to a process, independent of where they are located in memory. For example, the conundrum of Figure 6.8 could be solved as

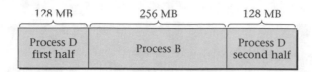

Figure 6.9 With virtual memory, the physical memory allocated to a process need not be contiguous, so process D can be accommodated even without sufficient memory in any one place.

shown in Figure 6.9. In a more realistic setting, it would be surprising for the pattern of physical memory allocation to display even this degree of contiguity. However, the virtual addresses can be contiguous even if the physical addresses are scattered all over the memory.

6.2.4 Sparse Address Spaces

Just as virtual memory provides the operating system with flexibility in allocating physical memory space, it provides each application program (or process) with flexibility in allocating virtual address space. A process can use whatever addresses make sense for its data structures, even if there are large gaps between them. This provides flexibility for the compiler and runtime environment, which assign addresses to the data structures.

Suppose, for example, that a process has three data structures (S1, S2, and S3) that it needs to store. Each needs to be allocated in a contiguous range of addresses, and each needs to be able to grow at its upper end. The picture might look like this, with addresses in megabytes:

S1	free	S2	free	S3	free

```
0      2              6     8            12    14                18
```

In this example, only one third of the 18-MB address range is actually occupied. If you wanted to allow each structure to grow more, you would have to position them further apart and wind up with an even lower percentage of occupancy. Many real processes span an address range of several gigabytes without using anywhere near that much storage. (Typically, this is done to allow one region to grow up from the bottom of the address space and another to grow down from the top.)

In order to allow processes to use this kind of *sparse address space* without wastefully occupying a corresponding amount of physical memory, the operating system simply doesn't provide physical address mappings for virtual addresses in the gaps.

6.2.5 Persistence

Any general-purpose operating system must provide some way for users to retain important data even if the system is shut down and restarted. Most commonly, the data is kept in files, although other kinds of persistent objects can be used. The persistent objects are normally stored on disk. For example, as I write this book, I am storing it in files on disk. That way, I don't have to retype the whole book every time the computer is rebooted. I will consider persistence in more detail in Chapter 8; for now, the only question is how it relates to virtual memory.

When a process needs to access a file (or other persistent object), it can ask the operating system to map the file into its address space. The operating system doesn't actually have to read the whole file into memory. Instead, it can do the reading on a demand-driven basis. Whenever the process accesses a particular page of the file for the first time, the MMU signals a page fault. The operating system can respond by reading that page of the file into memory, updating the mapping information, and resuming the process. (For efficiency reasons, the operating system might choose to fetch additional pages at the same time, on the assumption they are likely to be needed soon. I discuss this possibility in Section 6.4.1.)

If the process writes into any page that is part of a mapped file, the operating system must remember to write the page back to disk, in order to achieve persistence. For efficiency, the operating system should not write back pages that have not been modified since they were last written back or since they were read in. This implies the operating system needs to know which pages have been modified and hence are not up to date on disk. (These are called *dirty* pages.)

One way to keep track of dirty pages, using only techniques I have already discussed, is by initially marking all pages read-only. That way, the MMU will generate an interrupt on the first attempt to write into a clean page. The operating system can then make the page writable, add it to a list of dirty pages, and allow the operation to continue. When the operating system makes the page clean again, by writing it to disk, it can again mark the page read-only.

Because keeping track of dirty pages is such a common requirement and would be rather inefficient using the approach just described, MMUs generally provide a more direct approach. In this approach, the MMU keeps a *dirty bit* for each page. Any write into the page causes the hardware to set the dirty bit without needing operating system intervention. The operating system can later read the dirty bits and reset them. (The Intel Itanium architecture contains a compromise: the operating system sets the dirty bits, but with some hardware support. This provides the flexibility of the software approach without incurring so large a performance cost.)

6.2.6 Demand-Driven Program Loading

One particularly important case in which a file gets mapped into memory is when running a program. Each executable program is ordinarily stored as a file on disk. Conceptually, running a program consists of reading the program into memory from disk and then jumping to the first instruction.

However, many programs are huge and contain parts that may not always be used. For example, error handling routines will get used only if the corresponding errors occur. In addition, programs often support more features and optional modes than any one user will ever need. Thus, reading in the whole program is quite inefficient.

Even in the rare case that the whole program gets used, an interactive user might prefer several short pauses for disk access to one long one. In particular, reading in the whole program initially means that the program will be slow to start, which is frustrating. By reading in the program incrementally, the operating system can start it quickly at the expense of brief pauses during operation. If each of those pauses is only a few tens of milliseconds in duration and occurs at the time of a user interaction, each will be below the threshold of human perception.

In summary, operating system designers have two reasons to use virtual memory techniques to read in each program on a demand-driven basis: in order to avoid reading unused portions and in order to quickly start the program's execution. As with more general persistent storage, each page fault causes the operating system to read in more of the program.

One result of demand-driven program loading is that application programmers can make their programs start up more quickly by grouping all the necessary code together on a few pages. Of course, laying out the program text is really not a job for the human application programmer, but for the compiler and linker. Nonetheless, the programmer may be able to provide some guidance to these tools.

6.2.7 Efficient Zero Filling

For security reasons, as well as for ease of debugging, the operating system should never let a process read from any memory location that contains a value left behind by some other process that previously used the memory. Thus, any memory not occupied by a persistent object should be cleared out by the operating system before a new process accesses it.

Even this seemingly mundane job—filling a region of memory with zeros—benefits from virtual memory. The operating system can fill an arbitrarily large amount of virtual address space with zeros using only a single zeroed-out page frame of physical memory. All it needs to do is map all the virtual pages to the same physical page frame and mark them as read-only.

In itself, this technique of sharing a page frame of zeros doesn't address the situation where a process writes into one of its zeroed pages. However, that situation can be handled using a variant of the COW technique mentioned in Section 6.2.2. When the MMU interrupts the processor due to a write into the read-only page of zeros, the operating system can update the mapping for that one page to refer to a separate read/write page frame of zeros and then resume the process.

If it followed the COW principle literally, the operating system would copy the read-only page frame of zeros to produce the separate, writable page frame of zeros. However, the operating system can run faster by directly writing zeros into the new page frame without needing to copy them out of the read-only page frame. In fact, there is no need to do the zero filling only on demand. Instead, the operating system can keep some spare page frames of zeros around, replenishing the stock during idle time. That way, when a page fault occurs from writing into a read-only page of zeros, the operating system can simply adjust the address map to refer to one of the spare prezeroed page frames and then make it writable.

When the operating system proactively fills spare page frames with zeros during idle time, it should bypass the processor's normal cache memory and write directly into main memory. Otherwise, zero filling can seriously hurt performance by displacing valuable data from the cache.

6.2.8 Substituting Disk Storage for RAM

In explaining the application of virtual memory to persistence, I showed that the operating system can read accessed pages into memory from disk and can write dirty pages back out to disk. The reason for doing so is that disk storage has different properties from main semiconductor memory (RAM). In the case of persistence, the relevant difference is that disk storage is nonvolatile; that is, it retains its contents without power. However, disk differs from RAM in other regards as well. In particular, it is a couple orders of magnitude cheaper per gigabyte. This motivates another use of virtual memory, where the goal is to simulate having lots of RAM using less-expensive disk space. Of course, disk is also five orders of magnitude slower than RAM, so this approach is not without its pitfalls.

Many processes have long periods when they are not actively running. For example, on a desktop system, a user may have several applications in different windows—a word processor, a web browser, a mail reader, a spreadsheet—but focus attention on only one of them for minutes or hours at a time, leaving the others idle. Similarly, within a process, there may be parts that remain inactive. A spreadsheet user might look at the online help once, and then not again during several days of spreadsheet use.

This phenomenon of inactivity provides an opportunity to capitalize on inexpensive disk storage while still retaining most of the performance of fast semiconductor memory. The computer system needs to have enough RAM to hold the *working set*—the active portions of all active processes. Otherwise, the performance will be intolerably slow, because of disk accesses made on a routine basis. However, the computer need not have enough RAM for the entire storage needs of all the processes: the inactive portions can be shuffled off to disk, to be paged back in when and if they again become active. This will incur some delays for disk access when the mix of activity changes, such as when a user sets the word processor aside and uses a spreadsheet for the first time in days. However, once the new working set of active pages is back in RAM, the computer will again be as responsive as ever.

Much of the history of virtual memory focuses on this one application, dating back to the invention of virtual memory in the early 1960s. (At that time, the two memories were magnetic cores and magnetic drum, rather than semiconductor RAM and magnetic disk.) Even though this kind of paging to disk has become only one of many roles played by virtual memory, I will still pay it considerable attention. In particular, some of the most interesting policy questions arise only for this application of virtual memory. When the operating system needs to free up space in overcrowded RAM, it needs to guess which pages are unlikely to be accessed soon. I will come back to this topic (so-called replacement policies) after first considering other questions of mechanism and policy that apply across the full spectrum of virtual memory applications.

6.3 Mechanisms for Virtual Memory

Address mapping needs to be flexible, yet efficient. As I mentioned in Section 6.1, this means that the mapping function is stored in an explicit table, but at the granularity of pages rather than individual bytes or words. Most systems today use fixed-size pages, perhaps with a few exceptions for the operating system itself or hardware access, though research suggests that more general mixing of page sizes can be beneficial.

Typical page sizes have grown over the decades, for reasons you can explore in Exercises 6.3 and 6.4; today, the most common is 4 kilobytes (KB). Each page of virtual memory and each page frame of physical memory is this size, and each starts at an

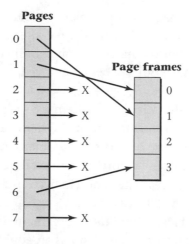

Figure 6.10 In this example mapping of eight pages to four page frames, page 0 has been allocated page frame 1, page 1 has been allocated page frame 0, and page 6 has been allocated page frame 3. The Xs indicate that no page frame is assigned to hold pages 2–5 or page 7. Page frame 2 is unused.

address that is a multiple of the page size. For example, with 4-KB pages, the first page (or page frame) has address 0, the next has address 4096, then 8192, and so forth.

Each page of virtual memory address space maps to an underlying page frame of physical memory or to none. For example, Figure 6.10 shows one possible mapping, on a system with unrealistically few pages and page frames. The numbers next to the boxes are page numbers and page frame numbers. The starting addresses are these numbers multiplied by the page size. At the top of this figure, you can see that page 0 is stored in page frame 1. If the page size is 4 KB, this means that virtual address 0 translates to physical address 4096, virtual address 100 translates to physical address 4196, and so forth. The virtual address of the last 4-byte word in page 0, 4092, translates to the physical address of the last word in page frame 1, 8188. Up until this point, all physical addresses were found by adding 4096 to the virtual address. However, the very next virtual address, 4096, translates to physical address 0, because it starts a new page, which is mapped differently. Note also that page frame 2 is currently not holding any page, and that pages 2–5 and page 7 have no translation available. In Exercise 6.5, you can gain experience working with this translation of virtual addresses into physical addresses by translating the addresses for page 6.

Of course, a realistic computer system will have many more page frames of physical memory and pages of virtual address space. Often there are tens or hundreds of thousands of page frames and at least hundreds of thousands of pages. As a result, operating system designers need to think carefully about the data structure used to store the table that maps virtual page numbers to physical page frame numbers. Sections 6.3.2 through 6.3.4 will be devoted to presenting three alternative structures that are in current use for page tables: linear, multilevel, and hashed. (Other alternatives that have fallen out of favor, or have not yet been deployed, are briefly mentioned in the end-of-chapter notes.)

Whatever data structure the operating system uses for its page table, it will need to communicate the mapping information to the hardware's MMU, which actually performs the mapping. The nature of this software/hardware interface constrains the page table design and also provides important context for comparing the performance of alternative page table structures. Therefore, in Section 6.3.1, I will explain the two forms the software/hardware interface can take.

Finally, Section 6.3.5 provides a brief look at segmentation, which was historically important both as an alternative to paging and as an adjunct to it.

6.3.1 Software/Hardware Interface

You have seen that the operating system stores some form of page table data structure in memory, showing which physical memory page frame (if any) holds each virtual memory page. Although I will present several possible page table structures shortly, the most important design issue applies equally to all of them: the page table should almost never be used.

Performance considerations explain why such an important data structure should be nearly useless (in the literal sense). Every single memory access performed by the processor generates a virtual address that needs translation to a physical address. Naively, this would mean that every single memory access from the processor requires a lookup operation in the page table. Performing that lookup operation would require at least one more memory access, even if the page table were represented very efficiently. Thus, the number of memory accesses would at least double: for each real access, there would be one page table access. Because memory performance is often the bottleneck in modern computer systems, this means that virtual memory might well make programs run half as fast—unless the page table lookup can be mostly avoided. Luckily, it can.

The virtual addresses accessed by realistic software are not random; instead, they exhibit both *temporal locality* and *spatial locality*. That is, addresses that are accessed once are likely to be accessed again before long, and nearby addresses are also likely to be accessed soon. Because a nearby address is likely to be on the same page, both kinds of locality wind up creating temporal locality when considered at the level of whole pages. If a page is accessed, chances are good that the same page will be accessed again soon, whether for the same address or another.

The MMU takes advantage of this locality by keeping a quickly accessible copy of a modest number of recently used virtual-to-physical translations. That is, it stores a limited number of pairs, each with one page number and the corresponding page frame number. This collection of pairs is called the *translation lookaside buffer* (*TLB*). Most memory accesses will refer to page numbers present in the TLB, and so the MMU will be able to produce the corresponding page frame number without needing to access the page table. This happy circumstance is known as a *TLB hit*; the less fortunate case, where the TLB does not contain the needed translation, is a *TLB miss*.

The TLB is one of the most performance-critical components of a modern microprocessor. In order for the system to have a fast clock cycle time and perform well on small benchmarks, the TLB must be very quickly accessible. In order for the system's performance not to fall off sharply on larger workloads, the TLB must be reasonably large (perhaps hundreds of entries), so that it can still prevent most page table accesses. Unfortunately, these two goals are in conflict with one another: chip designers know how to make lookup tables large or fast, but not both. Coping as well as possible with this dilemma requires cooperation from the designers of hardware, operating system, and application software:

- The hardware designers ameliorate the problem by including *two* TLBs, one for instruction fetches and one for data loads and stores. That way, these two categories of memory access don't need to compete for the same TLB.

- The hardware designers may further ameliorate the problem by including a hierarchy of TLBs, analogous to the cache hierarchy. A small, fast level-one (L1) TLB makes most accesses fast, while a larger, slower level-two (L2) TLB ensures that the page table won't need to be accessed every time the L1 TLB misses. As an example, the AMD Opteron microprocessor contains 40-entry L1 instruction and data TLBs, and it also contains 512-entry L2 instruction and data TLBs.

- The hardware designers also give the operating system designers some tools for reducing the demand for TLB entries. For example, if different TLB entries can provide mappings for pages of varying sizes, the operating system will be able to map large, contiguously allocated structures with fewer TLB entries, while still retaining flexible allocation for the rest of virtual memory.

- The operating system designers need to use tools such as variable page size to reduce TLB entry consumption. At a minimum, even if all application processes use small pages (4 KB), the operating system itself can use larger pages. Similarly, a video frame buffer of many consecutive megabytes needn't be carved up into 4-KB chunks. As a secondary benefit, using larger pages can reduce the size of page tables.

- More fundamentally, all operating system design decisions need to be made with an eye to how they will affect TLB pressure, because this is such a critical performance factor. One obvious example is the normal page size. Another, less obvious, example is the size of the scheduler's time slices: switching processes frequently will increase TLB pressure and thereby hurt performance, even if the TLB doesn't need to be flushed at every process switch. (I will take up that latter issue shortly.)

- The application programmers also have a role to play. Programs that exhibit strong locality of reference will perform much better, not only because of the cache hierarchy, but also because of the TLB. The performance drop-off when your program exceeds the TLB's capacity is generally quite precipitous. Some data structures are inherently more TLB-friendly than others. For example, a large, sparsely occupied table may perform much worse than a smaller, more densely occupied table. In this regard, theoretical analyses of algorithms may be misleading, if they assume all memory operations take a constant amount of time.

At this point, you have seen that each computer system uses two different representations of virtual memory mappings: a page table and a TLB. The page table is a comprehensive but slow representation, whereas the TLB is a selective but fast representation. You still need to learn how entries from the page table get loaded into the TLB. This leads to the topic of the software/hardware interface.

In general, the MMU loads page table entries into the TLB on a demand-driven basis. That is, when a memory access results in a TLB miss, the MMU loads the relevant translation into the TLB from the page table, so that future accesses to the same page can be TLB hits. The key difference between computer architectures is whether the MMU does this TLB loading autonomously, or whether it does it with lots of help from operating system software running on the processor.

In many architectures, the MMU contains hardware, known as a *page table walker*, that can do the page table lookup operation without software intervention. In this case, the operating system must maintain the page table in a fixed format that the hardware understands. For example, on an IA-32 processor (such as the Pentium 4), the operating system has no other realistic option than to use a multilevel page table, because the hardware page table walker expects this format. The software/hardware interface consists largely of a single register that contains the starting address of the page table. The operating system just loads this register and lets the hardware deal with loading individual TLB entries. Of course, there are some additional complications. For example, if the operating system stores updated mapping information into the page table, it needs to flush obsolete entries from the TLB.

In other processors, the hardware has no specialized access to the page table. When the TLB misses, the hardware transfers control to the operating system using an interrupt. The operating system software looks up the missing address translation in the page table, loads the translation into the TLB using a special instruction, and resumes normal execution. Because the operating system does the page table lookup, it can use whatever data structure its designer wishes. The lookup operation is done not with a special hardware walker, but with normal instructions to load from memory. Thus, the omission of a page table walker renders the processor more flexible, as well as simpler. However, TLB misses become more expensive, as they entail a context switch to the operating system with attendant loss of cache locality. The MIPS processor, used in the Sony PlayStation 2, is an example of a processor that handles TLB misses in software.

Architectures also differ in how they handle process switches. Recall that each process may have its own private virtual memory address space. When the operating system switches from one process to another, the translation of virtual addresses to physical addresses needs to change as well. In some architectures, this necessitates flushing all entries from the TLB. (There may be an exception for global entries that are not flushed, because they are shared by all processes.) Other architectures tag the TLB entries with a process identifying number, known as an *address space identifier* (*ASID*). A special register keeps track of the current process's ASID. For the operating system to switch processes, it simply stores a new ASID into this one register; the TLB need not be flushed. The TLB will hit only if the ASID and page number both match, effectively ignoring entries belonging to other processes.

For those architectures with hardware page table walkers, each process switch may also require changing the register pointing to the page table. Typically, linear page tables and multilevel page tables are per process. If an operating system uses a hashed page table, on the other hand, it may share one table among all processes, using ASID tags just like in the TLB.

Having seen how the MMU holds page translations in its TLB, and how those TLB entries are loaded from a page table either by a hardware walker or operating system software, it is time now to turn to the structure of page tables themselves.

6.3.2 Linear Page Tables

Linear page tables are conceptually the simplest form of page table, though as you will see, they turn out to be not quite so simple in practice as they are in concept. A linear page table is an array with one entry per page in the virtual address space. The first entry in the table describes page 0, the next describes page 1, and so forth. To find the information about page n, one uses the same approach as for any array access: multiply n by the size of a page table entry and add that to the base address of the page table.

Recall that each page either has a corresponding page frame or has none. Therefore, each page table entry contains, at a minimum, a *valid bit* and a page frame number. If the valid bit is 0, the page has no corresponding frame, and the page frame number is

Valid	Page Frame
1	1
1	0
0	X
0	X
0	X
0	X
1	3
0	X

Figure 6.11   In a linear page table, the information about page *n* is stored at position number *n*, counting from 0. In this example, the first row, position 0, shows that page 0 is stored in page frame 1. The second-to-last row, position 6, shows that page 6 is stored in page frame 3. The rows with valid bit 0 indicate that no page frame holds the corresponding pages, numbers 2–5 and 7. In these page table entries, the page frame number is irrelevant and can be any number; an X is shown to indicate this.

unused. If the valid bit is 1, the page is mapped to the specified page frame. Real page tables often contain other bits indicating permissions (for example, whether writing is allowed), dirtiness, and so forth.

Figure 6.10 on page 181 showed an example virtual memory configuration in which page 0 was held in page frame 1, page 1 in page frame 0, and page 6 in page frame 3. Figure 6.11 shows how this information would be expressed in a linear page table. Notice that the page numbers are not stored in the linear page table; they are implicit in the position of the entries. The first entry is implicitly for page 0, the next for page 1, and so forth, on down to page 7. If each page table entry is stored in 4 bytes, this tiny page table would occupy 32 consecutive bytes of memory. The information that page 3 has no valid mapping would be found 12 bytes after the base address of the table.

The fundamental problem with linear page tables is that real ones are much larger than this example. For a 32-bit address space with 4-KB pages, there are 2^{20} pages, because 12 of the 32 bits are used to specify a location within a page of 4 KB or 2^{12} bytes. Thus, if you again assume 4 bytes per page table entry, you now have a 4-MB page table. Storing one of those per process could use up an undesirably large fraction of a computer's memory. (My computer is currently running 70 processes, for a hypothetical total of 280 MB of page tables, which would be 36 percent of my total RAM.) Worse yet, modern processors are moving to 64-bit address spaces. Even if you assume larger pages, it is hard to see how a linear page table spanning a 64-bit address space could be stored. In Exercise 6.8, you can calculate just how huge such a page table would be.

This problem of large page tables is not insurmountable. Linear page tables have been used by 32-bit systems (for example, the VAX architecture, which was once quite commercially important), and even 64-bit linear page tables have been designed— Intel supports them as one option for its current Itanium architecture. Because storing such a huge page table is inconceivable, the secret is to find a way to avoid storing most of the table.

Recall that virtual memory address spaces are generally quite sparse: only a small fraction of the possible page numbers actually have translations to page frames. (This is particularly true on 64-bit systems; the address space is billions of times larger than for 32-bit systems, whereas the number of pages actually used may be quite comparable.) This provides the key to not storing the whole linear page table: you need only store the parts that actually contain valid entries.

On the surface, this suggestion seems to create as big a problem as it solves. Yes, you might now have enough memory to store the valid entries, but how would you ever find the entry for a particular page number? Recall that the whole point of a linear page table is to directly find the entry for page n at the address that is n entries from the beginning of the table. If you leave out the invalid entries, will this work any more? Not if you squish the addresses of the remaining valid entries together. So, you had better not do that.

You need to avoid wasting memory on invalid entries, and yet still be able to use a simple array-indexing address calculation to find the valid entries. In other words, the valid entries need to stay at the same addresses, whether there are invalid entries before them or not. Said a third way, although you want to be thrifty with storage of the page table, you cannot be thrifty with addresses. This combination is just barely possible, because storage and addressing need not be the same.

Divorcing the storage of the page table from the allocation of addresses for its entries requires three insights:

- The pattern of address space usage, although sparse, is not completely random. Often, software will use quite a few pages in a row, leave a large gap, and then use many more consecutive pages. This clumping of valid and invalid pages means that you can decide which portions of the linear page table are worth storing at a relatively coarse granularity and not at the granularity of individual page table entries. You can store those chunks of the page table that contain any valid entries, even if there are also a few invalid entries mixed in, and not store those chunks that contain entirely invalid entries.

- In fact, you can choose your chunks of page table to be the same size as the pages themselves. For example, in a system with 4-KB pages and 4-byte page table entries, each chunk of page table would contain 1024 page table entries. Many of these chunks won't actually need storage, because there are frequently 1024 unused pages in a row. Therefore, you can view the page table as a bunch of consecutive pages, some of which need storing and some of which don't.

- Now for the trick: use virtual memory to store the page table. That way, you decouple the addresses of page table entries from where they are stored—if anywhere. The virtual addresses of the page table entries will form a nice orderly array, with the entry for page n being n entries from the beginning. The physical addresses are another story. Recall that the page table is divided into page-sized chunks, not all of which you want to store. For those you want to store, you allocate page frames, wherever in memory is convenient. For those you don't want to store, you don't allocate page frames at all.

If this use of virtual memory to store the virtual memory's page table seems dizzying, it should. Suppose you start with a virtual address that has been generated by a running application program. You need to translate it into a physical address. To do so, you want to look up the virtual page number in the page table. You multiply the application-generated virtual page number by the page table entry size, add the base address, and get another virtual address: the virtual address of the page table entry. So, now what? You have to translate the page table entry's virtual address to a physical address. If you were to do this the same way, you would seem to be headed down the path to infinite recursion. Systems that use linear page tables must have a way out of this recursion. In Figure 6.12, the box labeled "?" must not be another copy of the whole diagram. That is where the simple concept becomes a not-so-simple reality.

Most solutions to the recursion problem take the form of using two different representations to store the virtual-to-physical mapping information. One (the linear page table) is used for application-generated virtual addresses. The other is used for the translation of page table entries' virtual addresses. For example, a multilevel page table can be used to provide the mapping information for the pages holding the main linear page table; I will describe multilevel page tables in Section 6.3.3.

This may leave you wondering what the point of the linear page table is. If another representation is going to be needed anyway, why not use it directly as the main page table, for mapping all pages, rather than only indirectly, for mapping the page table's pages? To answer this, you need to recall that the MMU has a TLB in which it keeps track of recently used virtual-to-physical translations; repeated access to the same

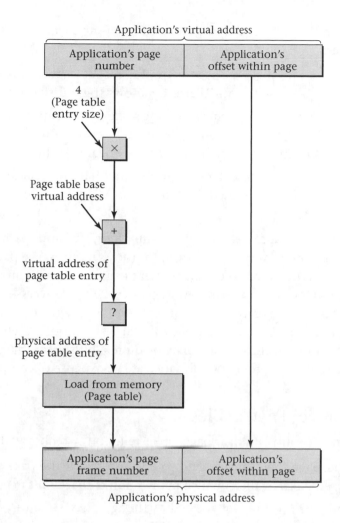

Figure 6.12 This diagram shows how a virtual address, generated by an application process, is translated into a physical address using a linear page table. At one point in the translation procedure, indicated by a "?" in this diagram, the virtual address of the page table entry needs to be translated into a physical address. This must be done using a method that is different from the one used for the application's virtual address, in order to avoid an infinite recursion. To see this, imagine inserting another copy of the whole diagram in place of the "?" box. A second "?" would result, which would require further substitution, and so forth to infinity.

virtual page number doesn't require access to the page table. Only when a new page number is accessed is the page table (of whatever kind) accessed. This is true not only when translating the application's virtual address, but also when translating the virtual address of a page table entry.

Depending on the virtual address generated by the application software, there are three possibilities:

1. For an address within the same page as another recent access, no page table lookup is needed at all, because the MMU already knows the translation.

2. For an address on a new page, but within the same chunk of pages as some previous access, only a linear page table lookup is needed, because the MMU already knows the translation for the appropriate page of the linear page table.

3. For an address on a new page, far from others that have been accessed, both kinds of page table lookup are needed, because the MMU has no relevant translations cached in its TLB.

Because virtual memory accesses generally exhibit temporal and spatial locality, most accesses fall into the first category. However, for those accesses, the page table organization is irrelevant. Therefore, to compare linear page tables with alternative organizations, you should focus on the remaining accesses. Of those accesses, spatial locality will make most fall into the second category rather than the third. Thus, even if there is a multilevel page table behind the scenes, it will be used only rarely. This is important, because the multilevel page table may be quite a bit slower than the linear one. Using the combination improves performance at the expense of complexity.

6.3.3 Multilevel Page Tables

Recall that the practicality of linear page tables relies on two observations:

• Because valid page table entries tend to be clustered, if the page table is divided into page-sized chunks, there will be many chunks that don't need storage.

• The remaining chunks can be located as though they were in one big array by using virtual memory address translation to access the page table itself.

These two observations are quite different from one another. The first is an empirical fact about most present-day software. The second is a design decision. You could accept the first observation while still making a different choice for how the stored chunks are located. This is exactly what happens with *multilevel page tables* (also known as *hierarchical page tables* or *forward-mapped page tables*). They too divide the page table into page-sized chunks, in the hopes that most chunks won't need storage. However, they locate the stored chunks without recursive use of virtual memory by using a tree data structure, rather than a single array.

For simplicity, start by considering the two-level case. This suffices for 32-bit architectures and is actually used in the extremely popular IA-32 architecture, the architecture of Intel's Pentium and AMD's Athlon family microprocessors. The IA-32

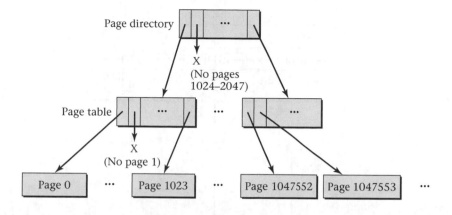

Figure 6.13   The IA-32 two-level page table has a page directory that can point to 1024 chunks of the page table, each of which can point to 1024 page frames. The leftmost pointer leading from the leftmost chunk of the page table points to the page frame holding page 0. Each entry can also be marked invalid, indicated by an X in this diagram. For example, the second entry in the first chunk of the page table is invalid, showing that no page frame holds page 1. The same principle applies at the page directory level; in this example, no page frames hold pages 1024–2047, so the second page directory entry is marked invalid.

architecture uses 4-KB pages and has page table entries that occupy 4 bytes. Thus, 1024 page-table entries fit within one page-sized chunk of the page table. As such, a single chunk can span 4 MB of virtual address space. Given that the architecture uses 32-bit virtual addresses, the full virtual address space is 4 gigabytes (GB) (that is, 2^{32} bytes); it can be spanned by 1024 chunks of the page table. All you need to do is locate the storage of each of those 1024 chunks or, in some cases, determine that the chunk didn't merit storage. You can do that using a second-level structure, much like each of the chunks of the page table. It, too, is 4 KB in size and contains 1024 entries, each of which is 4 bytes. However, these entries in the second-level *page directory* point to the 1024 first-level chunks of the page table, rather than to individual page frames. See Figure 6.13 for an illustration of the IA-32 page table's two-level hierarchy, with branching factor 1024 at each level. In this example, page 1 is invalid, as are pages 1024–2047. You can explore this example further in Exercise 6.9 and can consider a modified version of this page table format in Exercise 6.10.

The operating system on an IA-32 machine stores the physical base address of the page directory in a special register, where the hardware's page table walker can find it. Suppose that at some later point, the processor generates a 32-bit virtual address and presents it to the MMU for translation. Figure 6.14 shows the core of the translation

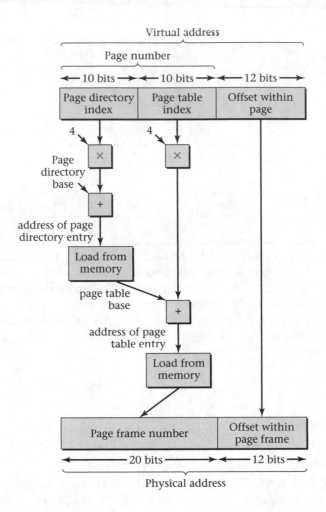

Figure 6.14 This diagram shows only the core of IA-32 paged address mapping, omitting the TLB and validity checks. The virtual address is divided into a 20-bit page number and 12-bit offset within the page; the latter 12 bits are left unchanged by the translation process. The page number is subdivided into a 10-bit page directory index and a 10-bit page table index. Each index is multiplied by 4, the number of bytes in each entry, and then added to the base physical address of the corresponding data structure, producing a physical memory address from which the entry is loaded. The base address of the page directory comes from a register, whereas the base address of the page table comes from the page directory entry.

process, omitting the TLB and the validity checks. In more detail, the MMU follows the following translation process:

1. Initially divide the 32-bit virtual address into its left-hand 20 bits (the page number) and right-hand 12 bits (the offset within the page).

2. Look up the 20-bit page number in the TLB. If a TLB hit occurs, concatenate the resulting page frame number with the 12-bit offset to form the physical address. The process is over.

3. On the other hand, if a TLB miss occurred, subdivide the 20-bit page number into its left-hand 10 bits (the page directory index) and its right-hand 10 bits (the page table index).

4. Load the page directory entry from memory; its address is four times the page directory index plus the page directory base address, which is taken from the special register.

5. Check the page directory entry's valid bit. If it is 0, then there is no page frame holding the page in question—or any of its 1023 neighbors, for that matter. Interrupt the processor with a page fault.

6. Conversely, if the valid bit is 1, the page directory entry also contains a physical base address for a chunk of page table.

7. Load the page table entry from memory; its address is four times the page table index plus the page table base address, which comes from the previous step.

8. Check the page table entry's valid bit. If it is 0, then there is no page frame holding the page in question. Interrupt the processor with a page fault.

9. On the other hand, if the valid bit is 1, the page table entry also contains the physical page frame number. Load the TLB and complete the memory access.

This description, although somewhat simplified, shows the key feature of the IA-32 design: it has a compact page directory, with each entry covering a span of 4 MB. For the 4-MB regions that are entirely invalid, nothing further is stored. For the regions containing valid pages, the page directory entry points to another compact structure containing the individual page table entries.

The actual IA-32 design derives some additional advantages from having the page directory entries with their 4-MB spans:

- Each page directory entry can optionally point directly to a single large 4-MB page frame, rather than pointing to a chunk of page table entries leading indirectly to 4-KB page frames, as I described. This option is controlled by a page-size bit in the page directory entry. By using this feature, the operating system can more efficiently provide the mapping information for large, contiguously allocated structures.

- Each page directory entry contains permission bits, just like the page table entries do. Using this feature, the operating system can mark an entire 4-MB region of virtual address space as being read-only more quickly, because it doesn't need to set the read-only bits for each 4-KB page in the region. The translation process outlined earlier is extended to check the permission bits at each level and signal a page fault interrupt if there is a permission violation at either level.

The same principle used for two-level page tables can be expanded to any greater number of levels. If you have taken a course on data structures, you may have seen this structure called a *trie* (or perhaps a *digital tree* or *radix tree*). The virtual page number is divided into groups of consecutive bits. Each group of bits forms an index for use at one level of the tree, starting with the leftmost group at the top level. The indexing at each level allows the chunk at the next level down to be located.

For example, the AMD64 architecture (used in the Opteron and Athlon 64 processors and later imitated by Intel under the name IA-32e) employs four-level page tables of this kind. Although the AMD64 is nominally a 64-bit architecture, the virtual addresses are actually limited to only 48 bits in the current version of the architecture. Because the basic page size is still 4 KB, the rightmost 12 bits are still the offset within a page. Thus, 36 bits remain for the virtual page number. Each page table entry (or similar entry at the higher levels) is increased in size to 8 bytes, because the physical addresses are larger than in IA-32. Thus, a 4-KB chunk of page table can reference only 512 pages spanning 2 MB. Similarly, the branching factor at each higher level of the tree is 512. Because 9 bits are needed to select from 512 entries, it follows that the 36-bit virtual page number is divided into four groups of 9 bits each, one for each level of the tree.

Achieving adequate performance with a four-level page table is challenging. The AMD designers will find this challenge intensified if they extend their architecture to full 64-bit virtual addresses, which would require two more levels be added to the page table. Other designers of 64-bit processors have made different choices: Intel's Itanium uses either linear page tables or hashed page tables, and the PowerPC uses hashed page tables.

6.3.4 Hashed Page Tables

You have seen that linear page tables and multilevel page tables have a strong family resemblance. Both designs rely on the assumption that valid and invalid pages occur in large clumps. As a result, each allows you to finesse the dilemma of wanting to store page table entries for successive pages consecutively in memory, yet not wanting to waste storage on invalid entries. You store page table entries consecutively within each chunk of the table and omit storage for entire chunks of the table.

Suppose you take a radical approach and reject the starting assumption. You will still assume that the address space is sparsely occupied; that is, many page table entries are invalid and should not be stored. (After all, no one buys 2^{64} bytes of RAM for their 64-bit processor.) However, you will no longer make any assumption about clustering of the valid and invalid pages—they might be scattered randomly throughout the whole address space. This allows greater flexibility for the designers of runtime environments. As a consequence, you will have to store individual valid page table entries, independent of their neighbors.

Storing only individual valid page table entries without storing any of the invalid entries takes away the primary tool used by the previous approaches for locating entries. You can no longer find page n's entry by indexing n elements into an array—not even within each chunk of the address space. Therefore, you need to use an entirely different approach to locating page table entries. You can store them in a hash table, known as a *hashed page table*.

A hashed page table is an array of *hash buckets*, each of which is a fixed-sized structure that can hold some small number of page table entries. (In the Itanium architecture, each bucket holds one entry, whereas in the PowerPC, each bucket holds eight entries.) Unlike the linear page table, this array of buckets does not have a private location for each virtual page number; as such, it can be much smaller, particularly on 64-bit architectures.

Because of this reduced array size, the page number cannot be directly used as an index into the array. Instead, the page number is first fed through a many-to-one function, the *hash function*. That is, each page gets assigned a specific hash bucket by the hash function, but many different pages get assigned the same bucket. The simplest plausible hash function would be to take the page number modulo the number of buckets in the array. For example, if there are 1000000 hash buckets, then the page table entries for pages 0, 1000000, 2000000, and so forth would all be assigned to bucket 0, while pages 1, 1000001, 2000001, and so forth would all be assigned to bucket 1.

The performance of the table relies on the assumption that only a few of the pages assigned to a bucket will be valid and hence have page table entries stored. That is, the assumption is that only rarely will multiple valid entries be assigned to the same bucket, a situation known as a *hash collision*. To keep collisions rare, the page table size needs to scale with the number of valid page table entries. Luckily, systems with lots of valid page table entries normally have lots of physical memory and therefore have room for a bigger page table.

Even if collisions are rare, there must be some mechanism for handling them. One immediate consequence is that each page table entry will now need to include

Valid	Page	Page Frame
1	0	1
1	1	0
1	6	3
0	X	X

Figure 6.15 Each entry in a hashed page table is in a location determined by feeding the page number through a hash function. In this example, the hash function consists of taking the page number modulo the number of entries in the table, 4. Consider the entry recording that page 6 is held by page frame 3. This entry is in position 2 within the table (counting from 0) because the remainder when 6 is divided by 4 is 2.

an indication of which virtual page number it describes. In the linear and multilevel page tables, the page number was implicit in the location of the page table entry. Now, any one of many different page table entries could be assigned to the same location, so each entry needs to include an identifying tag, much like in the TLB.

For an unrealistically small example of using a hashed page table, we can return to Figure 6.10 on page 181. Suppose you have a hashed page table with four buckets, each capable of holding one entry. Each of the four entries will contain both a virtual page number and a corresponding physical page number. If the hash function consists of taking the page number modulo 4, the table would contain approximately the information shown in Figure 6.15.

The possibility of collisions has another consequence, beyond necessitating page number tags. Even if collisions occur, each valid page table entry needs to be stored somewhere. Because the colliding entries cannot be stored in the same location, some alternative location needs to be available. One possibility is to have alternative locations within each hash bucket; this is why the PowerPC has room for eight page table entries in each bucket. Provided no collision involves more than this number of entries, they can all be stored in the same bucket. The PowerPC searches all entries in the bucket, looking for one with a matching tag.

If a collision involving more than eight entries occurs on a PowerPC, or any collision at all occurs on an Itanium processor, the collision cannot be resolved within the hash bucket. To handle such collisions, the operating system can allocate some extra memory and chain it onto the bucket in a linked list. This will be an expensive but rare occurrence. As a result, hardware page table walkers do not normally handle this case. If the walker does not find a matching tag within the bucket, it uses an interrupt to transfer control to the operating system, which is in charge of searching through the linked list.

You have now seen two reasons why the page table entries in hashed page tables need to be larger than those in linear or multilevel page tables. The hashed page table entries need to contain virtual page number tags, and each bucket needs a pointer to an overflow chain. As a result of these two factors and the addition of some extra features, the Itanium architecture uses 32-byte entries for hashed page tables versus 8-byte entries for linear page tables.

Incidentally, the fact that the Itanium architecture supports two different page table formats suggests just how hard it is to select one. Research continues into the relative merits of the different formats under varying system workloads. As a result of this research, future systems may use other page table formats beyond those described here, though they are likely to be variants on one of these themes. Architectures such as MIPS that have no hardware page table walker are excellent vehicles for such research, because they allow the operating system to use any page table format whatsoever.

Some operating systems treat a hashed page table as a *software TLB*, a table similar to the hardware's TLB in that it holds only selected page table entries. In this case, no provision needs to be made for overfull hash buckets; the entries that don't fit can simply be omitted. A slower multilevel page table provides a comprehensive fallback for misses in the software TLB. This alternative is particularly attractive when porting an operating system (such as Linux) that was originally developed on a machine with multilevel page tables.

6.3.5 Segmentation

Thus far, I have acted as though virtual memory were synonymous with paging. Today, that is true. However, when virtual memory was first developed in the 1960s, there were two competing approaches: paging and *segmentation*. Some systems (notably Multics) also included a hybrid of the two. Thus, seen historically, segmentation was both a competitor and a collaborator of paging. Today, segmentation remains only in vestigial form. The IA-32 architecture still contains full support for segmentation, but no common operating system uses it, and the successor architectures (Itanium and AMD64) have dropped it. As such, this subsection can be omitted with no great loss.

Recall that the basic premise of virtual memory is that a process uses addresses as names for objects, whereas memory uses addresses as routing information for storage locations. The defining property of segmentation is that the processor's virtual addresses name objects using two granularities: each virtual address names both an aggregate object, such as a table or file, and a particular location within that object, such as a table entry or a byte within a file. This is somewhat analogous to my name, "Max Hailperin," which identifies both the family to which I belong (Hailperin), and the particular person within that family (Max).

The aggregate objects, such as tables or files, that have names akin to family names are called *segments*. Each process refers to its segments by segment number. Each virtual address is divided into two parts: some number of bits are a segment number, and the remaining bits are a location within that segment.

On the surface, segmented virtual addresses may not seem very different from paged ones. After all, you saw that paged virtual addresses are also divided into two parts: a page number and an offset within that page. For example, a 32-bit address might be divided into a 20-bit page number and a 12-bit offset within the page. The key difference is that pages are purely an implementation detail; they do not correspond to logical objects such as files, stacks, or tables.

Because segments correspond to logical objects, they cannot have a fixed size, such as 4 KB. Each segment will have its own natural size. For example, each file a process accesses might be mapped into the virtual address space as its own segment. If so, the segment sizes will need to match the file sizes, which could be quite arbitrary.

A system employing pure segmentation maps each segment into a contiguous range of physical memory. Instead of a page table, the system uses a segment table, which specifies for each segment number the starting physical address, the size, and the permissions.

Unlike paging, pure segmentation does not provide for flexible allocation of physical memory; external fragmentation may occur, where it is hard to find enough contiguous free memory to accommodate a segment. In addition, pure segmentation does not provide good support for moving inactive information to disk, because only an entire segment can be transferred to or from disk.

Because of these and similar problems, segmentation can be combined with paging. Each process uses two-part addresses containing segment numbers and offsets. The MMU translates each of these addresses in two stages using both a segment table and a page table. The end result is an offset within a physical memory page frame. Thus, each segment may occupy any available page frames, even if they are not contiguous, and individual pages of the segment may be moved to disk.

Systems have combined segmentation with paging in two slightly different ways, one exemplified by the IA-32 architecture and the other by the Multics system. The key difference is whether all the segments share a single page table, as in the IA-32, or are given individual page tables, as in Multics.

Figure 6.16 shows how segmentation and paging are used together in the IA-32 architecture's MMU. When the IA-32 MMU translates a virtual address, it starts by

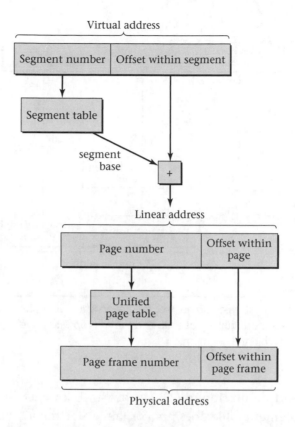

Figuro 6.16 The IA-32 architecture combines segmentation and paging using a single page table for all the segments. The segment table is used to translate the segment number into a base address, to which the offset within the segment is added, yielding a linear address. The linear address is then translated to a physical address using the unified page table, as shown in greater detail in Figure 6.14.

looking up the segment number in a segment table, yielding a starting address for the segment, a length, and permissions, just like in systems that use pure segmentation. Assuming the permissions are OK and the offset is legal with regard to the length, the MMU adds the segment's starting address to the offset. However, rather than treating the sum as a physical address, the MMU treats it as a paged virtual address, of the sort I have described in previous subsections. In IA-32 terminology, this address is known as a *linear address*. The MMU looks up the linear address in a single page table, shared by all the segments, in order to locate the appropriate page frame.

Figure 6.17 shows an alternative method of combining segmentation and paging, which was used in the Multics system. The Multics approach also starts by looking up the segment number in a segment table, which again provides information on the

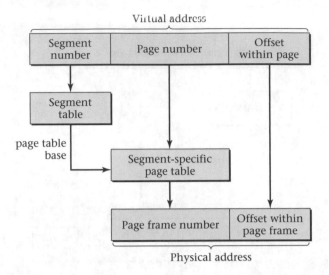

Figure 6.17   The Multics system combines segmentation and paging using a separate page table for each segment. The segment table is used to find the appropriate page table, which is then used to translate the address within the segment.

segment's length and permissions to allow the MMU to check the access for legality. However, this segment table does not contain a starting address for the segment; instead, it contains a pointer to the segment's private page table. The MMU uses this segment-specific page table to translate the offset within the segment, using techniques of the sort you saw in previous subsections. The end result is again an offset within a page frame.

Which approach is simpler for the operating system to manage? On the surface, the IA-32 approach looks simpler, because it uses only a single page table instead of one per segment. However, it has a significant disadvantage relative to the Multics approach. Remember that both approaches allow space in physical memory to be flexibly allocated in individual, non-contiguous page frames. However, the IA-32 approach forces each segment to be allocated a single contiguous region of address space at the level of linear addresses. Thus, the IA-32 approach forces the operating system to deal with the complexities of contiguous allocation, with its potential for external fragmentation.

Unlike pure segmentation, which is undeniably inferior to paging, the combination of segmentation and paging seems attractive, as it combines segmentation's meaningful units for protection and sharing with paging's smaller units for space allocation and data transfer. However, many of the same protection and sharing features can be simulated using paging alone. Probably as a result of this, many hardware designers decided the cost of segmentation, in both money and performance, was not worth the gain. Therefore, they provided support only for paging. This created a disincentive for the use of segmentation in operating systems; all popular operating systems (such as UNIX, Microsoft Windows, and Linux) are designed to be portable across multiple hardware architectures, some of which don't support segmentation. As a result, none of these operating systems makes any use of segmentation, even on systems where it is supported. This completes a cycle of disincentives; designers of modern architectures have no reason to support segmentation, because modern operating systems do not use it.

Although modern architectures no longer support segmentation, they do have one feature that is reminiscent of the combination of segmentation and paging. Recall that TLBs and hashed page tables use ASIDs to tag page translations so that translations from different processes can coexist. I said that a special register holds the ASID of the current process. In actuality, many modern architectures allow each process to use several different ASIDs; the top few bits of each virtual address select one of a group of ASID registers. Thus, address translation occurs in two steps. First, the top bits of the address are translated to an ASID; then the ASID and the remaining bits are translated into a page frame and offset. If the operating system sets up several processes to use the same ASID for a shared library, they will wind up sharing not only the page frames, but also the page table and TLB entries. This is akin to processes sharing a segment. However, unlike segmentation, it is invisible at the application level. Also, the number of segments (ASIDs) per process may be quite limited; eight on the Itanium and 16 on the 32-bit version of PowerPC.

6.4 Policies for Virtual Memory

Thus far, I have defined virtual memory, explained its usefulness, and shown some of the mechanisms typically used to map pages to page frames. Mechanisms alone, however, are not enough. The operating system also needs a set of policies describing how the mechanisms are used. Those policies provide answers for the following questions:

- At what point is a page assigned a page frame? Not until the page is first accessed, or at some earlier point? This decision is particularly performance critical if the page needs to be fetched from disk at the time it is assigned a page frame. For this reason, the policy that controls the timing of page frame assignment is normally called the *fetch policy*.

- Which page frame is assigned to each page? I have said that each page may be assigned any available frame, but some assignments may result in improved performance of the processor's cache memory. The policy that selects a page frame for a page is known as the *placement policy*.

- If the operating system needs to move some inactive page to disk in order to free up a page frame, which page does it choose? This is known as the the *replacement policy*, because the page being moved to disk will presumably be replaced by a new page—that being the motivation for freeing a page frame.

All of these policies affect system performance in ways that are quite workload dependent. For example, a replacement policy that performs well for one workload might perform terribly on another; for instance, it might consistently choose to evict a page that is accessed again a moment later. As such, these policies need to be chosen and refined through extensive experimentation with many real workloads. In the following subsections, I will focus on a few sample policies that are reasonably simple and have performed adequately in practice.

6.4.1 Fetch Policy

The operating system has wide latitude regarding when each page is assigned a page frame. At one extreme, as soon as the operating system knows about a page's existence, it could assign a page frame. For example, when a process first starts running, the operating system could immediately assign page frames for all the pages holding the program and its statically allocated data. Similarly, when a process asks the operating system to map a file into the virtual memory address space, the operating system could assign page frames for the entire file. At the other extreme, the operating system could wait for a page fault caused by an access to a page before assigning that page a page frame. In between these extremes lies a range of realistic fetch policies that try to stay just a little ahead of the process's needs.

Creating all page mappings right away would conflict with many of the original goals for virtual memory, such as fast start up of programs that contain large but rarely used portions. Therefore, one extreme policy can be discarded. The other, however, is a reasonable choice under some circumstances. A system is said to use *demand paging* if it creates the mapping for each page in response to a page fault when accessing that page. Conversely, it uses *prepaging* if it attempts to anticipate future page use.

Demand paging has the advantage that it will never waste time creating a page mapping that goes unused; it has the disadvantage that it incurs the full cost of a page fault for each page. On balance, demand paging is particularly appropriate under the following circumstances:

- If the process exhibits limited spatial locality, the operating system is unlikely to be able to predict what pages are going to be used soon. This makes paging in advance of demand less likely to pay off.

- If the cost of a page fault is particularly low, even moderately accurate predictions of future page uses may not pay off, because so little is gained each time a correct prediction allows a page fault to be avoided.

The Linux operating system uses demand paging in exactly the circumstances suggested by this analysis. The fetch policy makes a distinction between zero-filled pages and those that are read from a file, because the page fault costs are so different. Linux uses demand paging for zero-filled pages because of their comparatively low cost. In contrast, Linux ordinarily uses a variant of prepaging (which I explain in the remainder of this subsection) for files mapped into virtual memory. This makes sense because reading from disk is slow. However, if the application programmer notifies the operating system that a particular memory-mapped file is going to be accessed in a "random" fashion, then Linux uses demand paging for that file's pages. The programmer can provide this information using the `madvise` procedure.

The most common form of prepaging is *clustered paging*, in which each page fault causes a cluster of neighboring pages to be fetched, including the one incurring the fault. Clustered paging is also called *read around*, because pages around the faulting page are read. (By contrast, *read ahead* reads the faulting page and later pages, but no earlier ones.)

The details of clustered paging vary between operating systems. Linux reads a cluster of sixteen pages aligned to start with a multiple of 16. For example, a page fault on any of the first sixteen pages of a file will cause those sixteen pages to be read. Thus, the extra fifteen pages can be all before the faulting page, all after it, or any mix. Microsoft Windows uses a smaller cluster size, which depends in part on the kind of page incurring the fault: instructions or data. Because instruction accesses generally exhibit more spatial locality than data accesses, Windows uses a larger cluster size for instruction pages than for data pages.

Linux's read around is actually a slight variant on the prepaging theme. When a page fault occurs, the fault handler fetches a whole cluster of pages into RAM but only updates the faulting page table entry. The other pages are in RAM but not mapped into any virtual address space; this status is known as the *page cache*. Subsequent page faults can quickly find pages in the page cache. Thus, read around doesn't decrease the total number of page faults, but converts many from *major page faults* (reading disk) to *minor page faults* (simply updating the page table).

Because reading from disk takes about 10 milliseconds and because reading sixteen pages takes only slightly longer than reading one, the success rate of prepaging doesn't need to be especially high for it to pay off. For example, if the additional time needed to read and otherwise process each prepaged page is half a millisecond, then reading a cluster of sixteen pages, rather than a single page, adds 7.5 milliseconds. This would be more than repaid if even a single one of the fifteen additional pages gets used, because the prepaging would avoid a 10-millisecond disk access time.

6.4.2 Placement Policy

Just as the operating system needs to determine when to make a page resident (on demand or in advance), it needs to decide where the page should reside by selecting one of the unused page frames. This choice influences the physical memory addresses that will be referenced and can thereby influence the miss rate of the cache memory hardware.

Although cache performance is the main issue in desktop systems, there are at least two other reasons why the placement policy may matter. In large-scale multiprocessor systems, main memory is distributed among the processing nodes. As such, any given processor will have some page frames it can more rapidly access. Microsoft Windows Server 2003 takes this effect into account when allocating page frames. Another issue, likely to become more important in the future, is the potential for energy savings if all accesses can be confined to only a portion of memory, allowing the rest to be put into standby mode.

To explain why the placement policy influences cache miss rate, I need to review cache memory organization. An idealized cache would hold the *n* most recently accessed blocks of memory, where *n* is the cache's size. However, this would require each cache access to examine all *n* blocks, looking to see if any of them contains the location being accessed. This approach, known as *full associativity*, is not feasible for realistically large caches. Therefore, real caches restrict any given memory location to only a small set of positions within the cache; that way, only those positions need to be searched. This sort of cache is known as *set-associative*. For example, a two-way set-associative cache has two alternative locations where any given memory block can be stored.

Consider what would happen if a process repeatedly accesses three blocks of memory that have the misfortune of all competing for the same set of a two-way set-associative cache. Even though the cache may be large—capable of holding far more than the three blocks that are in active use—the miss rate will be very high. The standard description for this situation is to say the cache is suffering from *conflict misses* rather than *capacity misses*. Because each miss necessitates an access to the slower main memory, the high rate of conflict misses will significantly reduce performance.

The lower the cache's associativity, the more likely conflict misses are to be a problem. Thus, careful page placement was more important in the days when caches were external to the main microprocessor chips, as external caches are often of low associativity. Improved semiconductor technology has now allowed large caches to be integrated into microprocessors, making higher associativity economical and rendering placement policy less important.

Suppose, though, that an operating system does wish to allocate page frames to reduce cache conflicts. How would it know which pages are important to keep from conflicting? One common approach is to assume that pages that would not conflict without virtual memory address translation should not conflict even with address translation; this is known as *page coloring*. Another common approach is to assume that pages that are mapped into page frames soon after one another are likely to also be accessed in temporal proximity; therefore, they should be given nonconflicting frames. This is known as *bin hopping*.

The main argument in favor of page coloring is that it leaves intact any careful allocation done at the level of virtual addresses. Some compiler authors and application programmers are aware of the importance of avoiding cache conflicts, particularly in high-performance scientific applications, such as weather forecasting. For example, the compiler or programmer may pad each row of an array with a little wasted space so that iterating down a column of the array won't repeatedly access the same set of the cache. This kind of cache-conscious data allocation will be preserved by page coloring.

The main argument in favor of bin hopping is that experimental evidence suggest it performs better than page coloring does, absent cache-conscious data allocation. This may be because page coloring is less flexible than bin hopping, providing only a way of deciding on the most preferred locations in the cache for any given page, as opposed to ranking all possible locations from most preferred to least.

6.4.3 Replacement Policy

Conceptually, a replacement policy chooses a page to evict every time a page is fetched with all page frames in use. However, operating systems typically try to do some eviction in advance of actual demand, keeping an inventory of free page frames. When the inventory drops below a *low-water mark*, the replacement policy starts freeing up page frames, continuing until the inventory surpasses a *high-water mark*. Freeing page frames in advance of demand has three advantages:

- Last-minute freeing in response to a page fault will further delay the process that incurred the page fault. In contrast, the operating system may schedule proactive work to maintain an inventory of free pages when the hardware is otherwise idle, improving response time and throughput.

- Evicting dirty pages requires writing them out to disk first. If the operating system does this proactively, it may be able to write back several pages in a single disk operation, making more efficient use of the disk hardware.

- In the time between being freed and being reused, a page frame can retain a copy of the page it most recently held. This allows the operating system to inexpensively recover from poor replacement decisions by retrieving the page with only a minor page fault instead of a major one. That is, the page can be retrieved by mapping it back in without reading it from disk. You will see that this is particularly important if the MMU does not inform the replacement policy which pages have been recently referenced.

In a real operating system, a page frame may go through several temporary states between when it is chosen for replacement and when it is reused. For example, Microsoft Windows may move a replaced page frame through the following four inventories of page frames, as illustrated in Figure 6.18:

- When the replacement policy first chooses a dirty page frame, the operating system moves the frame from a process's page table to the *modified page list*. The modified page list retains information on the previous page mapping so that a minor page fault can retrieve the page. (Microsoft calls this a *soft page fault*.)

- If a page frame remains in the modified page list long enough, a system thread known as the *modified page writer* will write the contents out to disk and move the frame to the *standby page list*. A page frame can also move directly from a process's page table to the standby page list if the replacement policy chooses to evict a clean page. The standby page list again retains the previous mapping information so that a soft page fault can inexpensively recover a prematurely evicted page.

- If a page frame remains on standby for long enough without being faulted back into use, the operating system moves it to the *free page list*. This list provides page frames for the system's *zero page thread* to proactively fill with zeros, so that zero-filled pages will be available to quickly respond to page faults, as discussed earlier. The operating system also prefers to use a page frame from the free list when reading a page in from disk.

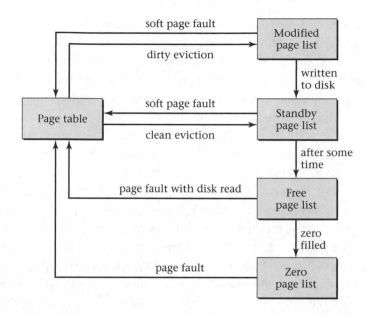

Figure 6.18 Each page frame in Microsoft Windows that is not referenced from a page table is included in one of the four page lists. Page frames circulate as shown here. For example, the system can use a soft page fault to recover a page frame from the modified or standby page list, if the page contained in that page frame proves to still be needed after having been evicted by the replacement policy.

- Once the zero page thread has filled a free page frame with zeros, it moves the page frame to the *zero page list*, where it will remain until mapped back into a process's page table in response to a page fault.

Using a mechanism such as this example from Windows, an operating system keeps an inventory of page frames and thus need not evict a page every time it fetches a page. In order to keep the size of this inventory relatively stable over the long term, the operating system balances the rate of page replacements with the rate of page fetches. It can do this in either of two different ways, which lead to the two major categories of replacement policies, *local replacement* and *global replacement*.

Local replacement keeps the rate of page evictions and page fetches balanced individually for each process. If a process incurs many page faults, it will have to relinquish many of its own page frames, rather than pushing other process's pages out of their frames. The replacement policy chooses which page frames to free only from those held by a particular process. A separate allocation policy decide how many page frames each process is allowed.

Global replacement keeps the rate of page evictions and page fetches balanced only on a system-wide basis. If a process incurs many page faults, other process's pages may be evicted from their frames. The replacement policy chooses which page frames to free from all the page frames, regardless which processes they are used by. No separate page frame allocation policy is needed, because the replacement policy and fetch policy will naturally wind up reallocating page frames between processes.

Of the operating systems popular today, Microsoft Windows uses local replacement, whereas all the members of the UNIX family, including Linux and Mac OS X, use global replacement. Microsoft's choice of a local replacement policy for Windows was part of a broader pattern of following the lead of Digital Equipment Corporation's VMS operating system, which has since become HP's OpenVMS. The key reason why VMS's designers chose local replacement was to prevent poor locality of reference in one process from greatly hurting the performance of other processes. Arguably, this performance isolation is less relevant for a typical Windows desktop or server workload than for VMS's multi-user real-time and timesharing workloads. Global replacement is simpler, and it more flexibly adapts to processes whose memory needs are not known in advance. For these reasons, it tends to be more efficient.

Both local and global replacement policies may be confronted with a situation where the total size of the processes' working sets exceeds the number of page frames available. In the case of local replacement, this manifests itself when the allocation policy cannot allocate a reasonable number of page frames to each process. In the case of global replacement, an excessive demand for memory is manifested as *thrashing*, that is, by the system spending essentially all its time in paging and process switching, producing extremely low throughput.

The traditional solution to excess memory demand is *swapping*. The operating system picks some processes to evict entirely from memory, writing all their data to disk. Moreover, it removes those processes' threads from the scheduler's set of runnable threads, so that they will not compete for memory space. After running the remaining processes for a while, the operating system swaps some of them out and some of the earlier victims back in. Swapping adds to system complexity and makes scheduling much choppier; therefore, some global replacement systems such as Linux omit it and rely on users to steer clear of thrashing. Local replacement systems such as Microsoft Windows, on the other hand, have little choice but to include swapping. For simplicity, I will not discuss swapping further in this text. You should know what it is, however, and should also understand that some people incorrectly call paging swapping; for example, you may hear of Linux swapping, when it really is paging. That is, Linux is moving individual pages of a process's address space to disk and back, rather than moving the entire address space.

Having seen some of the broader context into which replacement policies fit, it is time to consider some specific policies. I will start with one that is unrealistic but which provides a standard against which other, more realistic policies can be measured. If the operating system knew in advance the full sequence of virtual memory accesses, it could select for replacement the page that has its next use furthest in the future. This turns out to be more than just intuitively appealing: one can mathematically prove that it optimizes the number of demand fetches. Therefore, this replacement policy is known as *optimal replacement (OPT)*.

Real operating systems don't know future page accesses in advance. However, they may have some data that allows the probability of different page accesses to be estimated. Thus, a replacement policy could choose to evict the page estimated to have the longest time until it is next used. As one special case of this, consider a program that distributes its memory accesses across the pages randomly but with unequal probabilities, so that some pages are more frequently accessed than others. Suppose that these probabilities shift only slowly. In that case, pages which have been accessed frequently in the recent past are likely to be accessed again soon, and conversely, those that have not been accessed in a long while are unlikely to be accessed soon. As such, it makes sense to replace the page that has gone the longest without being accessed. This replacement policy is known as *Least Recently Used (LRU)*.

LRU replacement is more realistic than OPT, because it uses only information about the past, rather than about the future. However, even LRU is not entirely realistic, because it requires keeping a list of page frames in order by most recent access time and updating that list on every memory access. Therefore, LRU is used much as OPT is, as a standard against which to compare other policies. However, LRU is not a gold standard in the same way that OPT is; while OPT is optimal among all policies, LRU may not even be optimal among policies relying only on past activity. Real processes do not access pages randomly with slowly shifting probability distributions. For example, a process might repeatedly loop through a set of pages, in which case LRU will perform terribly, replacing the page that will be reused soonest. Nonetheless, LRU tends to perform reasonably well in many realistic settings; therefore, many other replacement policies try to approximate it. While they may not replace the least recently used page, they will at least replace a page that hasn't been used very recently.

Before considering realistic policies that approximate LRU, I should introduce one other extremely simple policy, which can serve as a foundation for an LRU-approximating policy, though it isn't one itself. The simple policy is known as *first in, first out replacement (FIFO)*. The name tells the whole story: the operating system chooses for replacement whichever page frame has been holding its current page the longest. Note the difference between FIFO and LRU; FIFO chooses the page that was

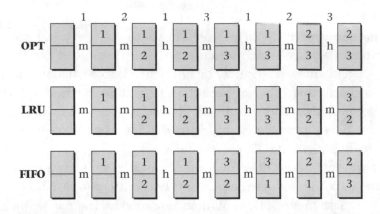

Figure 6.19 In this comparison of the OPT, LRU, and FIFO replacement policies, each pair of boxes represents the two page frames available on an unrealistically small system. The numbers within the boxes indicate which page is stored in each page frame. The numbers across the top are the reference sequence, and the letters h and m indicate hits and misses. In this example, LRU performs better than FIFO, in that it has one more hit. OPT performs even better, with three hits.

fetched the longest ago, even if it continues to be in frequent use, whereas LRU chooses the page that has gone the longest without access. Figure 6.19 shows an example where LRU outperforms FIFO and is itself outperformed by OPT. This performance ordering is not universal; in Exercises 6.11 and 6.12, you can show that FIFO sometimes outperforms LRU and that OPT does not always perform strictly better than the others.

FIFO is not a very smart policy; in fact, early simulations showed that it performs comparably to random replacement. Beyond this mediocre performance, one sign that FIFO isn't very smart is that it suffers from *Belady's anomaly:* increasing the number of page frames available may increase the number of page faults, rather than decreasing it as one would expect. In Exercise 6.13, you can generate an example of this counterintuitive performance phenomenon.

Both OPT and LRU are immune from Belady's anomaly, as are all other member of the class of *stack algorithms*. A stack algorithm is a replacement policy with the property that if you run the same sequence of page references on two systems using that replacement policy, one with n page frames and the other with $n + 1$, then at each point in the reference sequence the n pages that occupy page frames on the first system will also be resident in page frames on the second system. For example, with the LRU policy, the n most recently accessed pages will be resident in one system, and the $n + 1$ most recently accessed pages will be resident in the other. Clearly the $n + 1$ most recently accessed pages include the *n* most recently accessed pages. In Exercise 6.14, you can come up with a similar justification for my claim that OPT is a stack algorithm.

Recall that at the beginning of this subsection, I indicated that page frames chosen for replacement are not immediately reused, but rather enter an inventory of free page frames. The operating system can recover a page from this inventory without reading from disk, if the page is accessed again before the containing page frame is reused. This refinement turns out to dramatically improve the performance of FIFO. If FIFO evicts a page that is frequently used, chances are good that it will be faulted back in before the page frame is reused. At that point, the operating system will put it at the end of the FIFO list, so it will not be replaced again for a while. Essentially, the FIFO policy places pages on probation, but those that are accessed while on probation aren't actually replaced. Thus, the pages that wind up actually replaced are those that were not accessed recently, approximating LRU. This approximation to LRU, based on FIFO, is known as *Segmented FIFO (SFIFO)*.

To enable smarter replacement policies, some MMUs provide a *reference bit* in each page table entry. Every time the MMU translates an address, it sets the corresponding page's reference bit to 1. (If the address translation is for a write to memory, the MMU also sets the dirty bit that I mentioned earlier.) The replacement policy can inspect the reference bits and set them back to 0. In this way, the replacement policy obtains information on which pages were recently used. Reference bits are not easy to implement efficiently, especially in multiprocessor systems; thus, some systems omit them. However, when they exist, they allow the operating system to find whether a page is in use more cheaply than by putting it on probation and seeing whether it gets faulted back in.

One replacement policy that uses reference bits to approximate LRU is *clock replacement*. In clock replacement, the operating system considers the page frames cyclically, like the hand of a clock cycling among the numbered positions. When the replacement policy's clock hand is pointing at a particular page, the operating system inspects that page's reference bit. If the bit is 0, the page has not been referenced recently and so is chosen for replacement. If the bit is 1, the operating system resets it to 0 and moves the pointer on to the next candidate. That way, the page has a chance to prove its utility, by having its reference bit set back to 1 before the pointer comes back around. As a refinement, the operating system can also take the dirty bit into account, as follows:

- reference = 1: set reference to 0 and move on to the next candidate
- reference = 0 and dirty = 0: choose this page for replacement
- reference = 0 and dirty = 1: start writing the page out to disk and move on to the next candidate; when the writing is complete, set dirty to 0

Replacement policies such as FIFO and clock replacement can be used locally to select replacement candidates from within a process, as well as globally. For example, some versions of Microsoft Windows use clock replacement as the local replacement policy on systems where reference bits are available, and FIFO otherwise.

6.5 Security and Virtual Memory

Virtual memory plays a central role in security because it provides the mechanism for equipping each process with its own protected memory. Because this is the topic of Chapter 7, I will not discuss it further here. I will also defer most other security issues to that chapter, because they have close relationships with the process concept and with protection. However, there is one classic virtual memory security issue that I can best discuss here, which is particularly relevant to application programmers.

Recall that the most traditional use of virtual memory is to simulate having lots of RAM by moving inactive pages to disk. This can create a security problem if a program processes confidential data that should not be permanently stored. For high-security applications, you may not want to rely on the operating system to guard the data that is on disk. Instead, you may want to ensure the sensitive information is never written to disk. That way, even if an adversary later obtains physical possession of the disk drive and can directly read all its contents, the sensitive information will not be available.

Many cryptographic systems are designed around this threat model, in which disks are presumed to be subject to theft. As a familiar example, most systems do not store login passwords on disk. Instead, they store the results of feeding the passwords through a one-way function. That suffices for checking entered passwords without making the passwords themselves vulnerable to exposure. Programs such as the login program and the password-changing program store the password only temporarily in main memory.

Application programmers may think their programs keep sensitive data only temporarily in volatile main memory and never store it out to disk. The programmers may even take care to overwrite the memory afterward with something safe, such as zeros. Even so, a lasting record of the confidential data may be on the disk if the virtual memory system wrote out the page in question during the vulnerable period. Because the virtual memory is intentionally operating invisibly behind the scenes, the application programmers will never know.

To protect your programs against this vulnerability, you need to forbid the operating system from writing a sensitive region of memory out to disk. In effect, you want to create an exception to the normal replacement policy, in which certain pages are never chosen for replacement. The POSIX standard API contains two procedures you can use for this purpose, `mlock` and `mlockall`. Unfortunately, overuse of these procedures could tie up all the physical memory, so only privileged processes are allowed to use them. Of course, some programs handling sensitive information, such as the login program, need to run with special privileges anyway for other reasons.

Exercises

6.1 In Section 6.1, I introduced an analogy with an executive and a file clerk. Extend this analogy to a clerk serving multiple executives. Give a plausible scenario where the clerk might need to understand that two executives are referring to two different documents, even though they are using the same name for the documents. Give another plausible scenario where two executives would use different names to refer to the same document. Explain how the clerk would cope with these scenarios. What is the connection to virtual memory?

6.2 The file containing an executable program generally contains not only the read-only text of the program, but also the initial contents for some writable data structures. Explain how and why COW could be used for this writable region.

6.3 I mentioned that typical page sizes have grown over the decades. Brainstorm considerations that would make smaller pages better than larger pages and other considerations that would make larger pages better than smaller. Now think about what has changed over the decades. Can you identify any argument favoring small pages that has weakened over time? Can you identify any argument favoring large pages that has strengthened over time? Presumably, these factors account for the historical trend in page sizes. On the other hand, you may also be able to identify one or more factors that would have suggested the reverse trend; if so, they were presumably outweighed.

6.4 The previous exercise concerns factors influencing the historical trend in page sizes. On the other hand, there are also real-world influences causing page sizes to remain unchanged for many years. Can you think of what some of these influences might be?

6.5 Assume a page size of 4 KB and the page mapping shown in Figure 6.10 on page 181. What are the virtual addresses of the first and last 4-byte words in page 6? What physical addresses do these translate into?

6.6 Suppose the rightmost k bits within an address are used to represent an offset within a page, with the remaining bits used for the page number. Consider the location at offset j within page n. Give a mathematical formula for the address of this location.

6.7 Suppose the rightmost k bits within a virtual or physical address are used to represent an offset within a page or page frame, with the remaining bits used for the page number or page frame number. Suppose that for all integers n, page number n is mapped by the page table into page frame number $f(n)$. Give a mathematical formula for the physical address that corresponds with virtual address v.

6.8 Suppose an architecture uses 64-bit virtual addresses and 1-MB pages. Suppose that a linear page table is stored in full for each process, containing a page table entry for every page number. Suppose that the size of each page table entry is only 4 bytes. How large would each page table be?

6.9 At the lower right of Figure 6.13 on page 191 are page numbers 1047552 and 1047553. Explain how these page numbers were calculated.

6.10 My discussion of IA-32 multilevel page tables is based on the original version of the architecture, which limited physical addresses to 32 bits. Newer IA-32 processors offer an optional *Physical Address Extension* (*PAE*) mode in order to address up to sixteen times as much RAM. One consequence of this is that page table entries (and page directory entries) are increased to 8 bytes instead of 4. Each page and chunk of page table is still 4 KB.
   (a) How many entries can each chunk of page table or page directory now hold?
   (b) How big a virtual address range does each chunk of page table now span? (A page directory entry can also directly point to a large page frame this size, just as without PAE it can directly point to a 4-MB page frame.)
   (c) How big a virtual address range can each page directory now span?
   (d) Because each page directory can no longer span the full 4-GB virtual address range, PAE requires adding a third level to the top of the tree. The newly added root node doesn't have as large a branching factor as you calculated in part (a) for the preexisting two levels. How many page directories does the root point to?
   (e) Draw a diagram analogous to Figure 6.13 on page 191 for PAE mode.

6.11 Figure 6.19 on page 210 shows a small example where LRU has a lower miss rate than FIFO replacement. Develop an example of similar size in which FIFO has a lower miss rate than LRU.

6.12 In Figure 6.19 on page 210, both LRU and FIFO replacement have higher miss rates than OPT. Develop an example of similar size in which at least one of LRU and FIFO has as low a miss rate as OPT does.

6.13 Show a small example of Belady's anomaly. That is, give a small integer, n, and a short sequence of page number references such that when the FIFO replacement policy is given n initially empty page frames, fewer misses result from the reference sequence than when $n + 1$ initially empty page frames are used.

6.14 Justify my claim that OPT is a stack algorithm. You may assume that ties are broken by replacing the lowest numbered page of those involved in the tie.

6.15 When conducting measurement studies, it is always good to conduct multiple trials of any experiment, rather than reporting data only from a single run. In the particular case of a study of how much paging is caused by a particular activity, why is it important to reboot between each experimental run and the next?

▣ Programming Projects

6.1 Write a program that loops many times, each time using an inner loop to access every 4096th element of a large array of bytes. Time how long your program takes per array access. Do this with varying array sizes. Are there any array sizes when the average time suddenly changes? Write a report in which you explain what you did, and the hardware and software system context in which you did it, carefully enough that someone could replicate your results.

6.2 On a system (such as Linux or most versions of UNIX, including Mac OS X) that supports the `mmap` and `madvise` (or `posix_madvise`) system calls, read the online manual pages for them and write four simple C test programs that map a large file into virtual memory. Two programs should use `madvise` to indicate random access; one of them should then genuinely access the file randomly, whereas the other should access all of it sequentially. The other two programs should use `madvise` to indicate sequential access; again, one should behave sequentially and one randomly. Time the programs, rebooting the computer before each run. Write a report in which you explain what you did, and the hardware and software system context in which you did it, carefully enough that someone could replicate your results. Your report should draw some conclusions from your experiments: does the correct use of `madvise` seem important to the performance of your test system?

◯ Exploration Projects

6.1 On a Linux system, you can find the files mapped into a process's address space by typing a command of the following form:

```
cat /proc/n/maps
```

where n is the process's ID number. Read the documentation for `proc` in Section 5 of the online manual in order to understand the output format. Then look through the various processes' maps to see if you can find a case where the same file is mapped into two processes' address spaces, but at different virtual addresses. (On most Linux systems with a variety of networking software and so forth, such cases will exist.)

6.2 On a Linux or UNIX system, including Mac OS X, you can find information about processes by using the **ps** command. To include all processes, you need to provide the option letters **ax**. If you give the letter **l** as an option, you will receive additional columns of information about each process, including **SIZE** or **VSZ** (the virtual memory size) and **RSS** (the resident set size, in physical memory). Use the **ps axl** command and note the sizes. Presumably, the virtual size is always bigger than the resident set size. If you calculate a ratio of the two sizes for each process, what range do the ratios span? What is the median ratio?

6.3 If you compile and run the C program in Figure 6.20 on a Linux or UNIX system (including Mac OS X), it will run the **ps l** command as in the preceding project, and in the output you will be able to see its own virtual memory and resident set sizes. The program contains a large zero-filled array, **large_array**, most of which goes unused. How do the virtual and resident set sizes of this process compare? If you change the size of **large_array** and recompile and run, which size changes? What does the unit of measure seem to be?

6.4 Use the same command as in Exploration Project 6.1 to determine how sparse some processes' address spaces are. What fraction of the range from lowest mapped address to highest mapped address belongs to any mapping? How many contiguous address ranges are occupied and how many unoccupied holes are there? Are the holes large enough that a linear or multilevel page table could plausibly take advantage of them?

```c
#include <stdlib.h>

int large_array[10000000];

int main(int argc, char *argv[]){
  system("ps l"); /* note: letter l */
  return large_array[0];
}
```

Figure 6.20 This C program, **own-size.c**, shows its own size, including the size of a large array of zeros, by running the **ps** command.

6.5 In Section 6.2.8, I estimated the relative price per gigabyte and speed of disk versus RAM. Look up some prices and specifications on the web and make your own estimates of these ratios. Explain the assumptions you make and data you use.

6.6 As explained in the text, Linux normally uses a form of clustered paging, also known as read around. Using the `madvise` procedure, you can override this normal behavior for a particular region of virtual memory, marking it as randomly accessed (which turns off all prepaging) or sequentially accessed (which switches to a variant form of prepaging). Instead of experimenting with these modes selectively, as in Programming Project 6.2, you can experiment with changing all virtual memory to use one of them, provided you have a system on which you can build and install Linux kernels. Near the top of the kernel source file `include/linux/mm.h`, you will find the definitions of `VM_NormalReadHint(v)`, `VM_SequentialReadHint(v)`, and `VM_RandomReadHint(v)`. Change these definitions so that one of them is defined as `1` and the other two are defined as `0`. Now all virtual memory areas will be treated in accordance with the mode you defined as `1`, independent of any uses of `madvise`. Build the kernel with your change and conduct an experiment in which you compare the performance of some programs running under your variant kernel with their performance running under a normal kernel. (You may want to build more than one variant kernel in order to try out more than one of the modes.) Write a report clearly presenting your results and carefully explaining what you did, and in which hardware and software system context you did it, so that someone else could replicate your results. (This project was written when the kernel was at version 2.6.11; however, the relevant aspects of the source code seem to be stable across quite a few versions.)

6.7 In the end-of-chapter notes, I trace paging back to seminal articles published in the early 1960s by the designers of the Atlas computer, and I also report that this computer was the first to use a small fast memory and a large slow memory to simulate a large fast memory. However, in those same notes, I also cite a recent article by Jessen, which brought to light an unpublished doctoral dissertation by Güntsch from 1956. This dissertation proposed a similar approach to simulating a large fast memory. Read these articles and write a comparison of Güntsch's work with that of the Atlas team. Beyond the dates, the most obvious difference is that one was an unpublished proposal for an unbuilt machine and had no apparent influence, whereas the other resulted in both an actual machine and publications that were frequently referenced by later writers. However, you should go beyond these surface issues and compare the substance of the two proposals. Which is more like today's virtual memory?

Notes

I introduced the virtual memory concept by stressing the distinction between addresses as names for information and as locations of storage. Fotheringham made this point in one of the earliest papers on virtual memory, concerning the pioneering Atlas computer [53]. Dennis made the same point at greater length a few years later [43]. These two papers from the 1960s were seminal with regard to paging and segmentation, respectively. At the end of that decade, Denning wrote an influential survey of the whole virtual memory field, including both paging and segmentation [42].

Many of the uses I list for virtual memory can be traced back to the earliest papers. Most famously, the simulation of a large fast memory by a small fast memory and a large slow external storage device was first used in the Atlas computer [53, 80]. (See also Exploration Project 6.7 with regard to a related mechanism proposed even earlier by Güntsch, which Jessen has recently described [76].) In this context, Denning developed the working set concept [41]. One virtual memory application of more modern vintage is message passing with COW; for a recent example, see Mac OS X [6].

While discussing applications of virtual memory, I touched on a couple of implementation issues. The compromise approach to dirty bits (and reference bits) employed in Itanium can be found in reference [75]. A readable example of the performance impact of cache bypassing when prezeroing pages can be found in a paper on Linux for the PowerPC [49].

In introducing the representations of address mappings, I mentioned that mixing page sizes can be beneficial. One important body of research on this topic is Talluri's dissertation [127].

Specific information on each of the example systems I mentioned is available: VAX/VMS [88], Itanium [75], AMD64 (including IA-32 compatibility) [3], Multics [14, 38], and Microsoft Windows [109].

Hashed page tables are part of an interesting historical design progression, starting with the Atlas and continuing on past hashed page tables to clustered page tables, which have yet to be deployed commercially. The Atlas [53, 80] used a fully associative *inverted page table*. That is, it had an array with one storage location per page frame; element n contained the page number resident in page frame n. To locate a given page number (for address translation), special hardware checked all the entries in the inverted page table in parallel. This hardware does not scale up to large numbers of page frames. Therefore, the IBM System/38 replaced the parallel search with a hash table, while still retaining the inverted page table itself [72]. Each entry in the hash table pointed to an entry in the inverted page table. HP originally adopted this same approach for their Precision Architecture, but then recognized that the hash table and the inverted page table could be merged together, forming today's hashed page table, as described by Huck and Hays [74]. (Huck and Hays also introduced the notion of software TLB.)

Recall that linear and multilevel page tables store page table entries consecutively for a chunk of sequential page numbers (for example, 1024 pages). These chunks may contain some unused entries, wasting space. Hashed page tables, on the other hand, store each page table entry individually, so that no space is wasted on unused entries. However, each entry needs to be significantly larger. The optimal balance point for space might be somewhere between the two extremes. Also, if page table references exhibit spatial locality, keeping at least a small cluster of consecutive pages' entries adjacent could speed access. Based on these observations, Talluri, Hill, and Khalidi [126] proposed *clustered page tables*, a variant of hashed page tables where each entry in the hash table contains page table entries for several consecutive pages.

Kessler and Hill [79] evaluated page coloring and bin hopping, as well as other approaches to cache-conscious page placement.

Belady [11] published an early comparison of replacement policies, including FIFO, LRU, and a more complex version of OPT he called MIN. In a separate publication [12], he and coworkers showed that FIFO was subject to the anomaly which has come to bear his name; see also reference [100]. Mattson et al. [92] refined OPT to its modern form, proved its optimality, introduced the concept of stack algorithms, and proved they were immune from Belady's anomaly. Aho, Denning, and Ullman [2] analyzed optimality under probabilistic models; in particular, they showed that LRU approximates optimal replacement given slowly varying reference probabilities. Turner and Levy [130] showed how Segmented FIFO page replacement can approximate LRU. Their work was in the context of VMS's local replacement. A similar replacement policy, again using cheap reclamation of recently freed pages as a substitute for reference bits, but this time global and patterned on clock replacement, was used by Babaoglu and Joy [8] shortly thereafter.

7

Processes and Protection

7.1 Introduction

At this point, having seen both the threads that perform computations and the virtual memory spaces in which those computations take place, you are finally prepared to synthesize the notion of *process*. Processes play a central role in the view of an operating system as experienced by most system administrators, application programmers, and other moderately sophisticated computer users. In particular, the technical concept of process comes the closest to the informal idea of a running program.

The concept of process is not entirely standardized across different operating systems. Not only do some systems use a different word (such as "task"), but also the details of the definition vary. Nonetheless, most mainstream systems are based on definitions that include the following:

One or more threads Because a process embodies a running program, often the process will be closely associated with a single thread. However, some programs are designed to divide work among multiple threads, even if the program is run only once. (For example, a web browser might use one thread to download a web page while another thread continues to respond to the user interface.)

Virtual memory accessible to those threads The word "accessible" implies that some sort of protection scheme ensures that the threads within a process access only the memory for which that process has legitimate access rights. As you will see, the mainstream protection approach is for each process to have its own virtual memory address space, shared by the threads within that process. However, I will also present an alternative, in which all processes share a single address space, but with varying access rights to individual objects within that address space. In any case, the access rights are assigned to the process, not to the individual threads.

Other access rights A process may also hold the rights to resources other than memory. For example, it may have the right to update a particular file on disk or to service requests arriving over a particular network communication channel. I will address these issues in Chapters 8 and 9. For now, I will sketch two general approaches by which a process can hold access rights. Either the process can hold a specific *capability*, such as the capability to write a particular file, or it can hold a general *credential*, such as the identification of the user for whom the process is running. In the latter case, the credential indirectly implies access rights, by way of a separate mechanism, such as *access control lists*.

Resource allocation context Limited resources (such as space in memory or on disk) are generally associated with a process for two reasons. First, the process's termination may serve to implicitly release some of the resources it is holding, so that they may be reallocated. Operating systems generally handle memory in this way. Second, the process may be associated with a limited resource quota or with a billing account for resource consumption charges. For simplicity, I will not comment on these issues any further.

Miscellaneous context Operating systems often associate other aspects of a running program's state with the process. For example, systems such as Linux and UNIX (conforming to the POSIX standard) keep track of each process's current working directory. That is, when any thread in the process accesses a file by name without explicitly indicating the directory containing the file, the operating system looks for the file starting from the process's current working directory. For historical reasons, the operating system tracks a single current working directory per process, rather than one per thread. Yet this state might have been better associated with the individual threads, as it is hard to see why a change-directory operation in one thread should upset file operations underway in another concurrently running thread. Because there is no big master narrative to these items of miscellaneous context, I won't consider them further in this chapter.

From this list, you can see that many of the key aspects of processes concern protection, and these are the aspects on which I will focus. Before diving into a consideration of various approaches to protection, however, I will devote Section 7.2 to the basics of how the POSIX process management API can be used, such as how a thread running in one process creates another process and how a process exits. This section should serve to make the use of processes more concrete. Studying this API will also allow you to understand how the shell (command interpreter) executes user commands.

After studying the basics of POSIX process management, you will spend the remaining sections of the chapter learning various aspects of protection. Keep in mind that protection is a large and diverse area; although I will introduce several different protection mechanisms in this chapter, I will leave many topics for later chapters. I postpone some protection questions specific to file systems to Chapter 8. Also, protection is intimately related to security, which I cover in Chapter 11. In particular, my emphasis here will be on basic mechanisms. I will defer to Chapter 11 all questions of how those mechanisms are deployed to enforce chosen security policies.

I will divide this current chapter's treatment of protection among three sections. Section 7.3 addresses the fundamental question of limiting each process's access to memory. After showing how processors provide two distinct execution modes to serve as the foundation for any protection system, I will present two approaches to memory protection: one with a separate address space for each process, and one with a single address space. Moving beyond memory protection, Section 7.4 first presents the fundamentals of access rights, then examines the two approaches I mentioned for representing access rights: capabilities and the combination of credentials with access control lists. The assumption throughout these two sections is that protection operates at the granularity of processes. Section 7.5 examines two alternatives, of finer and coarser granularity. The finer-grained protection approach protects parts of processes from each other. The coarser-grained approach, on the other hand, protects entire simulated machines from one another, with each simulated machine running its own operating system.

In Section 7.6, the chapter concludes with an examination of some of the security issues most directly raised by material in the earlier sections.

7.2 POSIX Process Management API

All operating systems provide mechanisms for creating new processes, terminating existing processes, and performing related actions. The details vary from system to system. To provide a concrete example, I will present relevant features of the POSIX API, which is used by Linux and UNIX, including by Mac OS X.

In the POSIX approach, each process is identified by a *process ID number*, which is a positive integer. Each process (with one exception) comes into existence through the *forking* of a *parent process*. The exception is the first process created when the operating system starts running. A process forks off a new process whenever one of the threads running in the parent process calls the **fork** procedure. In the parent process, the call to **fork** returns the process ID number of the new child process. (If an error occurs, the procedure instead returns a negative number.) The process ID number may be important to the parent later, if it wants to exert some control over the child or find out when the child terminates.

Meanwhile, the child process can start running. The child process is in many regards a copy of the parent process. For protection purposes, it has the same credentials as the parent and the same capabilities for such purposes as access to files that have been opened for reading or writing. In addition, the child contains a copy of the parent's address space. That is, it has available to it all the same executable program code as the parent, and all of the same variables, which initially have the same values as in the parent. However, because the address space is copied instead of shared, the variables will start having different values in the two processes as soon as either performs any instructions that store into memory. (Special facilities do exist for sharing some memory; I am speaking here of the normal case.) Of course, the operating system doesn't need to actually copy each page of the address space. It can use copy on write (COW) to avoid (or at least postpone) most of the copying.

Because the child process is nearly identical to the parent, it starts off by performing the same action as the parent; the **fork** procedure returns to whatever code called it. However, application programmers generally don't want the child to continue executing all the same steps as the parent; there wouldn't be much point in having two processes if they behaved identically. Therefore, the **fork** procedure gives the child process an indication that it is the child so that it can behave differently. Namely, **fork** returns a value of 0 in the child. This contrasts with the return value in the parent process, which is the child's process ID number, as mentioned earlier.

The normal programming pattern is for any **fork** operation to be immediately followed by an **if** statement that checks the return value from **fork**. That way, the same program code can wind up following two different courses of action, one in the parent and one in the child, and can also handle the possibility of failure, which is signaled by a negative return value. The C++ program in Figure 7.1 shows an example of this; the parent and child processes are similar (both loop five times, printing five messages at one-second intervals), but they are different enough to print different messages, as shown in the sample output in Figure 7.2. Keep in mind that this output is only one possibility; not only can the ID number be different, but the interleaving of output from the parent and child can also vary from run to run. This example program also illustrates that the processes each get their own copy of the **loopCount** variable. Both start with the initial value, 5, which was established before the fork. However, when each process decrements the counter, only its own copy is affected. In Programming Projects 7.1 and 7.2, you can write variants of this program.

```cpp
#include <unistd.h>
#include <stdio.h>
#include <iostream>
using namespace std;

int main(){
  int loopCount = 5; // each process will get its own loopCount
  cout << "I am still only one process." << endl;
  pid_t returnedValue = fork();
  if(returnedValue < 0){
    // still only one process
    perror("error forking"); // report the error
    return -1;
  } else if (returnedValue == 0){
    // this must be the child process
    while(loopCount > 0){
      cout << "I am the child process." << endl;
      loopCount--; // decrement child's counter only
      sleep(1); // wait a second before repeating
    }
  } else {
    // this must be the parent process
    while(loopCount > 0){
      cout << "I am the parent process; my child's ID is "
           << returnedValue << "." << endl;
      loopCount--; // decrement parent's counter only
      sleep(1);
    }
  }
  return 0;
}
```

Figure 7.1 This C++ program, `forker.cpp`, demonstrates process creation using `fork`. The program prints eleven lines of output, including five each from the parent and child process after the call to `fork`.

In early versions of UNIX, only one thread ever ran in each process. As such, programs that involved concurrency needed to create multiple processes using `fork`. In situations such as that, it would be normal to see a program like the one in Figure 7.1, which includes the full code for both parent and child. Today, however, concurrency within a program is normally done using a multi-threaded process. This leaves only the other big use of `fork`: creating a child process to run an entirely different program. In this case, the child code in the forking program is only long enough to load in the

```
I am still only one process.
I am the child process.
I am the parent process; my child's ID is 23307.
I am the parent process; my child's ID is 23307.
I am the child process.
I am the parent process; my child's ID is 23307.
I am the child process.
I am the parent process; my child's ID is 23307.
I am the child process.
I am the parent process; my child's ID is 23307.
I am the child process.
```

Figure 7.2   This sample output from the `forker` program of Figure 7.1 shows just one possible sequence of events.

new program and start it running. This happens, for example, every time you type a program's name at a shell prompt; the shell forks off a child process in which it runs the program. Although the program execution is distinct from the process forking, the two are used in combination. Therefore, I will turn next to how a thread running in a process can load a new program and start that program running.

The POSIX standard includes six different procedures, any one of which can be used to load in a new program and start it running. The six are all variants on a theme; because they have names starting with **exec**, they are commonly called the *exec family*. Each member of the exec family must be given enough information to find the new program stored in a file and to provide the program with any arguments and environment variables it needs. The family members differ in exactly how the calling program provides this information. Because the family members are so closely related, most systems define only the **execve** procedure in the kernel of the operating system itself; the others are library procedures written in terms of **execve**.

Because **execl** is one of the simpler members of the family, I will use it for an example. The program in Figure 7.3 prints out a line identifying itself, including its own process ID number, which it gets using the **getpid** procedure. Then it uses **execl** to run a program, named **ps**, which prints out information about running processes. After the call to **execl** comes a line that prints out an error message, saying that the execution failed. You may find it surprising that the error message seems to be issued unconditionally, without an **if** statement testing whether an error in fact occurred. The reason for this surprising situation is that members of the exec family return only if an error occurs; if all is well, the new program has started running, replacing the old program within the process, and so there is no possibility of returning in the old program.

```
#include <unistd.h>
#include <stdio.h>
#include <iostream>
using namespace std;

int main(){
  cout << "This is the process with ID " << getpid()
       << ", before the exec." << endl;
  execl("/bin/ps", "ps", "axl", NULL);
  perror("error execing ps");
  return -1;
}
```

Figure 7.3 This C++ program, `execer.cpp`, illustrates how the procedure `execl` (a member of the exec family) can be used to change which program the current process is running. The same process ID that this program reports as its own is later shown by the `ps` program as being its own, because the same process starts running the `ps` program. Note also the unconditional error message after the call to `execl`; only if `execl` fails does the calling program continue to run.

Looking in more detail at the example program's use of `execl`, you can see that it takes several arguments that are strings, followed by the special **NULL** pointer. The reason for the **NULL** is to mark the end of the list of strings; although this example had three strings, other uses of `execl` might have fewer or more. The first string specifies which file contains the program to run; here it is `/bin/ps`, that is, the `ps` program in the `/bin` directory, which generally contains fundamental programs. The remaining strings are the so-called "command-line arguments," which are made available to the program to control its behavior. Of these, the first is conventionally a repeat of the command's name; here, that is `ps`. The remaining argument, `axl`, contains both the letters `ax` indicating that all processes should be listed and the letter `1` indicating that more complete information should be listed for each process. As you can see from the sample output in Figure 7.4, the exact same process ID that is mentioned in the initial message shows up again as the ID of the process running the `ps axl` command. The process ID remains the same because `execl` has changed what program the process is running without changing the process itself.

One inconvenience about `execl` is that to use it, you need to know the directory in which the program file is located. For example, the previous program will not work if `ps` happens to be installed somewhere other than `/bin` on your system. To avoid this problem, you can use `execlp`. You can give this variant a filename that does not include a directory, and it will search through a list of directories looking for the file, just like the shell does when you type in a command. This can be illustrated with an example program that combines `fork` with `execlp`, as shown in Figure 7.5.

```
This is the process with ID 3849, before the exec.
  UID    PID   ...   COMMAND
.
.
.
   0   3849   ...   ps axl
.
.
.
```

Figure 7.4   This sample output from the **execer** program in Figure 7.3 was made narrower and shorter by omitting many of the columns of output produced by the **ps axl** command as well as many of its lines of output. The remaining output suffices to show that the process had process ID (**PID**) 3849 before it executed **ps axl**, and that the same process became the process running the **ps axl** command.

```
#include <unistd.h>
#include <stdio.h>

int main(){
  pid_t returnedValue = fork();
  if(returnedValue < 0){
    perror("error forking");
    return -1;
  } else if (returnedValue == 0){
    execlp("xclock", "xclock", NULL);
    perror("error execing xclock");
    return -1;
  } else {
    return 0;
  }
}
```

Figure 7.5   This C program, **launcher.c**, runs **xclock** without waiting for it. The program does so by forking off a child process and executing **xclock** in that child process. The result is that **xclock** continues to run in its own window while the parent process exits, allowing the shell from which this program was run to prompt for another command.

This example program assumes you are running the X Window System, as on most Linux or UNIX systems. It runs **xclock**, a program that displays a clock in a separate window. If you run this program from a shell, you will see the clock window appear, and your shell will prompt you for the next command to execute while the clock keeps running. This is different than what happens if you type **xclock** directly to the shell. In that case, the shell waits for the `xclock` program to exit before prompting for another command. Instead, the example program is more similar to typing `xclock &` to the shell. The `&` character tells the shell not to wait for the program to exit; the program is said to run "in the background." The way the shell does this is exactly the same as the sample program: it forks off a child process, executes the program in the child process, and allows the parent process to go on its way. In the shell, the parent loops back around to prompt for another command.

When the shell is not given the `&` character, it still forks off a child process and runs the requested command in the child process, but now the parent does not continue to execute concurrently. Instead, the parent waits for the child process to terminate before the parent continues. The same pattern of fork, execute, and wait would apply in any case where the forking of a child process is not to enable concurrency, but rather to provide a separate process context in which to run another program.

In order to wait for a child process, the parent process can invoke the `waitpid` procedure. This procedure takes three arguments; the first is the process ID of the child for which the parent should wait, and the other two can be zero if all you want the parent to do is to wait for termination. As an example of a process that waits for each of its child processes, Figure 7.6 shows a very stripped-down shell. This shell can be used to run the user's choice of commands, such as `date`, `ls`, and `ps`, as illustrated in Figure 7.7. A real shell would allow command line arguments, offer background execution as an option, and provide many other features. Nonetheless, you now understand the basics of how a shell runs programs. In Programming Projects 7.3 and 7.4, you can add some of the missing features.

The exec family of procedures interacts in an interesting fashion with protection mechanisms. When a process executes a program file, there is ordinarily almost no impact on the process's protection context. Any capabilities (for reading and writing files, for example) remain intact, and the process continues to operate with the same user identification credentials. This means that when you run a program, generally it is acting on your behalf, with the access rights that correspond to your user identification. However, there is one important exception. A program file can have a special *set user ID* (*setuid*) bit set on it, in which case, a process that executes the program acquires the credential of the file's owner.

Because a setuid program can check which user ran it, and can check all sorts of other data (the time of day, for example), the setuid mechanism provides an extremely general mechanism for granting access rights. You can grant any subset of your rights to any other users you choose, under any conditions that you can program, by writing a setuid program that tests for the conditions and then performs the controlled access. As a mundane example, you can create a game program that has the ability to write into a file of high scores, no matter who is running it, even though other users

```cpp
#include <unistd.h>
#include <stdio.h>
#include <sys/wait.h>
#include <string>
#include <iostream>
using namespace std;

int main(){
  while(1){ // loop until return
    cout << "Command (one word only)> " << flush;
    string command;
    cin >> command;
    if(command == "exit"){
      return 0;
    } else {
      pid_t returnedValue = fork();
      if(returnedValue < 0){
        perror("error forking");
        return -1;
      } else if (returnedValue == 0){
        execlp(command.c_str(), command.c_str(), NULL);
        perror(command.c_str());
        return -1;
      } else {
        if(waitpid(returnedValue, 0, 0) < 0){
          perror("error waiting for child");
          return -1;
        }
      }
    }
  }
}
```

Figure 7.6 This C++ program, `microshell.cpp`, is a stripped-down shell that waits for each child process.

are forbidden from directly writing into the file. A similar program you have likely encountered is the one you use to change your password. That program can update a password database that you do not have permission to directly modify. As I will discuss in Section 7.6, the setuid mechanism's flexibility makes it useful for enforcing security policies; however, I will also point out in Section 7.6 that the same mechanism is the source of many security pitfalls. (Even ordinary program execution, with credentials left unchanged, can be a security problem, as I will discuss.)

```
Command (one word only)> date
Thu Feb 12 09:33:26 CST 2004
Command (one word only)> ls
microshell  microshell.cpp  microshell.cpp~
Command (one word only)> ps
  PID TTY          TIME CMD
23498 pts/2     00:00:00 bash
24848 pts/2     00:00:00 microshell
24851 pts/2     00:00:00 ps
Command (one word only)> exit
```

Figure 7.7 This sample interaction shows the `date`, `ls`, and `ps` commands being run within the `microshell` from Figure 7.6.

At this point, you have seen many of the key elements of the process life cycle. Perhaps the most important omission is that I haven't shown how processes can terminate, other than by returning from the main procedure. A process can terminate itself by using the `exit` procedure (in Java, `System.exit`), or it can terminate another process using the `kill` procedure (see the documentation for details). Rather than exploring process programming further here, I will move on to the mechanisms that operating systems use to protect the memory occupied by processes. If you want to pursue application programming further, the notes section at the end of the chapter suggests additional reading.

7.3 Protecting Memory

Memory protection is the most fundamental barrier between processes, as well as between each process and the operating system. If a process could freely write into the operating system's data structures, the operating system would be unable to enforce any other kind of protection. Moreover, if processes could freely write into each other's memory, a process without ability to write a file (for example) could manipulate another into doing so for it. Thus, to understand any other kind of protection, you need to first understand how memory is protected.

Section 7.3.1 explains the foundation of this protection, which is the processor's ability to switch between a restricted and an unrestricted mode of operation. Sections 7.3.2 and 7.3.3 explain how memory protection can be built on that foundation in either of two ways: by giving each process its own virtual memory address space or by giving the processes differing access rights within a single address space.

7.3.1 The Foundation of Protection: Two Processor Modes

Whether the operating system gives each process its own address space, or instead gives each process its own access rights to portions of a shared address space, the operating system needs to be privileged relative to the processes. That is, the operating system must be able to carry out actions, such as changing address spaces or access rights, that the processes themselves cannot perform. Otherwise, the processes wouldn't be truly contained; they could get access to each other's memory the same way the operating system does.

For this reason, every modern processor can run in two different modes, one for the operating system and one for the application processes. The names of these modes vary from system to system. The more privileged mode is sometimes called *kernel mode*, *system mode*, or *supervisor mode*. Of these, *kernel mode* seems to be in most common use, so I will use it. The less privileged mode is often called *user mode*.

When the processor is in kernel mode, it can execute any instructions it encounters, including ones to change memory accessibility, ones to directly interact with I/O devices, and ones to switch to user mode and jump to an instruction address that is accessible in user mode. This last kind of instruction is used when the operating system is ready to give a user process some time to run.

When the processor is in user mode, it will execute normal instructions, such as add, load, or store. However, any attempt to perform hardware-level I/O or change memory accessibility interrupts the process's execution and jumps to a handler in the operating system, an occurrence known as a *trap*. The same sort of transfer to the operating system occurs for a page fault or any interrupt, such as a timer going off or an I/O device requesting attention. Additionally, the process may directly execute an instruction to call an operating system procedure, which is known as a *system call*. For example, the process could use system calls to ask the operating system to perform the `fork` and `execve` operations that I described in Section 7.2. System calls can also request I/O, because the process doesn't have unmediated access to the I/O devices. Any transfer to an operating system routine changes the operating mode and jumps to the starting address of the routine. Only designated entry points may be jumped to in this way; the process can't just jump into the middle of the operating system at an arbitrary address.

The operating system needs to have access to its own portion of memory, as well as the memory used by processes. The processes, however, must not have access to the operating system's private memory. Thus, switching operating modes must also entail a change in memory protection. How this is done varies between architectures.

Some architectures require the operating system to use one address space for its own access, as well as one for each process. For example, if a special register points at the base of the page table, this register may need to be changed every time the operating mode changes. The page table for the operating system can provide access to pages that are unavailable to any of the processes.

Many other architectures allow each page table entry to contain two different protection settings, one for each operating mode. For example, a page can be marked as readable, writable, and executable when in kernel mode, but totally inaccessible when in user mode. In this case, the page table need not be changed when switching operating modes. If the kernel uses the same page table as the user-mode process, then the range of addresses occupied by the kernel will be off limits to the process. The IA-32 architecture fits this pattern. For example, the Linux operating system on the IA-32 allows each user-mode process to access up to 3 GB of its 4-GB address space, while reserving 1 GB for access by the kernel only.

In this latter sort of architecture, the address space doesn't change when switching from a user process to a simple operating system routine and back to the same user process. However, the operating system may still need to switch address spaces before returning to user mode if its scheduler decides the time has come to run a thread belonging to a different user-mode process. Whether this change of address spaces is necessary depends on the overall system design: one address space per process or a single shared address space. Sections 7.3.2 and 7.3.3 address these alternatives.

Having described the distinction between kernel mode and user mode, I am also now in a position to explain the three ways in which threads can be implemented using those modes. Figure 7.8 shows the three options in schematic form; I explain them in the following paragraphs.

As described in Chapters 2 and 6, operating system kernels use threads for their own internal purposes, such as zeroing out unused page frames or flushing dirty pages

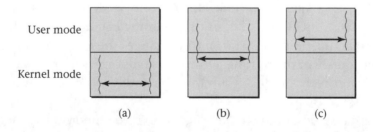

Figure 7.8 Three relationships are possible between threads, the scheduling and dispatching code that switches threads, and the operating modes: (a) the threads can be part of the kernel, along with the kernel's scheduler and dispatcher; (b) the threads can run mostly in user mode, but be scheduled and dispatched in the kernel; (c) the threads can run in user mode along with a user-level scheduler and dispatcher.

out to disk. In these circumstances, the threads may execute entirely within kernel mode; they are called *kernel threads*. As shown in Figure 7.8(a), the processor can run a first kernel thread, the kernel's scheduling and thread dispatching code, and then a second kernel thread, all without leaving kernel mode.

An operating system kernel's scheduler may also choose to run a thread that is part of a user-mode process. As shown in Figure 7.8(b), switching between user threads requires two mode switches, even if the threads are in the same process. First, a switch from user mode to kernel mode is needed when moving from one user thread to the scheduler. Second, a switch from kernel mode back to user mode is needed when the kernel dispatches the next user thread. Nomenclature for these kernel-supported user threads is not standardized; the most common term seems to be *native threads*, or simply *threads* when the context is clear.

To avoid mode-switching costs when switching threads within a process, some middleware systems provide scheduling and dispatching mechanisms analogous to the kernel's but residing within the user-level code, that is, the code running in user mode. As shown in Figure 7.8(c), this allows the outgoing thread, the scheduler, and the incoming thread to all execute in user mode with no mode switch—provided the two threads are in the same process. These threads are commonly called *user-level threads*, but I prefer Microsoft's name, *fibers*. This name makes clear that I am not talking about Figure 7.8(b)'s threads, which also contain user-level code. Moreover, the name provides a nice metaphor, suggesting that multiple fibers exist within one native, kernel-supported thread. As shown in Figure 7.9, the kernel's scheduler divides the processor between threads, but within each thread, there can also be a user-level scheduler switching between fibers.

Although you needed to understand the two processor modes in order to appreciate the preceding three kinds of threads, you should keep in mind that I introduced

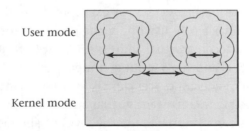

Figure 7.9 Multiple user-level threads can be enclosed in each kernel-supported native thread. The kernel's scheduler switches between the enclosing native threads. Within each of them, user-level dispatching also occurs. This creates what Microsoft calls fibers within the threads.

you to the processor modes for a different reason. Namely, the processor modes provide the foundation for the protection of processes. For example, the processor modes allow each process to be confined within its own address space in a multiple address space system.

7.3.2 The Mainstream: Multiple Address Space Systems

Most operating systems (including Linux, Microsoft Windows, and Mac OS X) provide memory protection by giving each process its own virtual memory address space. Unless the application programmer makes special arrangements, these address spaces are completely disjoint. However, the programmer can explicitly ask the operating system to map the same file, or the same block of shared memory space, into several processes' address spaces.

The multiple address space design is particularly appropriate on architectures with comparatively narrow addresses. For example, a 32-bit address can reference only a 4-GB address space. If a 32-bit system is going to run several processes, each of which has a couple gigabytes of data to access, the only way to obtain enough space is by using multiple address spaces. This motivation for multiple address spaces goes away (for present practical purposes) on 64-bit systems.

Regardless of address size, the multiple address space design confers other advantages, which I mentioned in Section 6.1, where I provided a rationale for virtual memory. Each process can allocate virtual addresses independently from the others. This means that a compiler can build addresses into a program, even though several concurrent processes may be running the same program; each will be able to use the predetermined addresses for its own copy of data. Moreover, procedures to dynamically allocate memory (for example, when creating objects) can work independently in the different processes. Even shared memory can independently appear at the most convenient virtual address for each process. For example, several processes running the same program can all consistently use one virtual address for their input channels, and all consistently use a second virtual address for their output channels, even if one process's output channel is another's input channel.

However, independent address spaces can also confer disadvantages. I briefly mentioned one in Section 6.2.2: inconsistent virtual addresses for shared memory means pointer-based structures can't be shared. At the level of abstraction provided by programming languages, objects are linked together by pointers (as in C++) or references (as in Java). At the lower level of abstraction executed by the computer, these language constructs generally are represented by virtual addresses; one object contains the virtual address of another. With separate address spaces, virtual addresses are meaningful only within one process. Thus, while a shared memory region can contain a simple data structure, such as a contiguous array of characters, it cannot contain anything complex enough to need pointers, such as a linked list or tree. Strictly speaking, pointers can be used as long as they are represented other than as virtual addresses (which most compilers won't do) or the processes take care to map the shared memory into the same locations (which is difficult to square with their independent allocation of other memory). Pointer-based data structures that span multiple shared-memory regions are even more problematic.

You can see one important variant of the pointer problem if you recognize that memory holds code as well as data. Instructions sometimes include virtual addresses: either the virtual address of another instruction to jump to or the virtual address of a data location to load or store. The virtual addresses included within instructions suffer the same fate as pointers: either they need to be kept local to one process or the processes need to coordinate their assignments of virtual addresses. However, if the processes need to coordinate address allocation, you have already traded away one of the advantages of separate address spaces.

Another disadvantage to separate address spaces is that addresses cannot be used as the ultimate system-wide name for objects. For example, suppose two processes are communicating, and one of them wants to suggest to the other that it map some new object into its address space. The sending process can't specify the object in question by address (even though it may have an address for the object), because the receiving process doesn't yet have an address for the object. Instead, the communication needs to be in terms of some other, address-neutral nomenclature, such as filenames. Similarly, virtual addresses can't play any role in persistent storage of objects, because their validity is confined to a single executing process.

None of these disadvantages has been sufficiently severe as to displace multiple address space systems from the mainstream. However, the disadvantages have been sufficient to cause system designers to explore the alternative, which is for all processes to share a single address space. Single address space systems have even been commercially deployed—in one case with considerable success. Therefore, I will move next to a consideration of such systems.

7.3.3 An Alternative: Single Address Space Systems

There is no need to consider in detail the advantages and disadvantages of a single address space; they are the exact opposite of those for multiple address spaces. Processes can share and store addresses freely but need to coordinate on their allocation. Instead of rehearsing the case for and against a single address space system, I will consider how one could still protect memory with such a system.

Beyond questions of security, memory protection is critical because programs contain bugs. Debugging is challenging enough even if the result of a bug in one process always manifests itself as a symptom in that same process. However, without memory protection, a bug in one process can cause a symptom in another process, because the bug can take the form of writing into memory being used by the other process. This situation, in which a process's data seems to spontaneously change as a result of a bug in an unrelated process, is a debugging nightmare. Thus, even in a single address space system, processes must have varying access rights to memory. The goal in moving to a single address space is simply to decouple the question of accessibility from that of addressability. The latter concerns whether a memory location can be named, whereas the former concerns whether the location can be read and written.

In a multiple address space system, the processes are protected from one another through addressability; each process will typically have no ability to name the memory locations being used by the others. Even when two address spaces share a particular region of memory, the accessibility of that region is seldom modulated independently for the individual processes. For example, it would be rare for a shared-memory region to be marked read-only for one process but not another. By contrast, the processes in a single address space system are not separated at all by addressability; they can all name any memory location. Instead, the processes differ with regard to the memory regions they have permission to read and write.

Intel's Itanium architecture contains a representative mechanism for supporting protection in a shared address space. Each page table entry (in a hashed page table) contains a protection key, which is a number. The idea is that all pages that are to be protected in the same way have the same key. In particular, if a data structure spans several pages, all the pages would have the same key. Giving a process the right to read pages with that key would give that process the right to read the whole structure. A collection of at least sixteen special registers holds protection keys possessed by the currently executing process. Every memory access is checked: does the process have a key that matches the accessed page? If not, the hardware traps to an operating system handler, much like for a page fault.

Processes may need access to more independently protected memory regions than the number of protection key registers. Therefore, the operating system will normally use those registers as only a cache of recently accessed structures' keys, much like a TLB. When a protection key miss fault occurs, the operating system will not immediately assume the access was illegal. Instead, it will first search a comprehensive list of the process's keys. If the missing key is found there, the operating system will load it into one of the key registers and resume execution. Only if the process truly doesn't have the key does the operating system cope with the illegal access, such as by terminating the process.

Each protection key register contains not only a key number, but also a set of access control bits for read, write, and execute permissions. Recall that each page table entry also has access control bits. A process can access a page only if it has the appropriate permission in its key register and the page table entry also allows the access. Thus, the page table entry can specify the maximum access for any process, whereas the protection key registers can provide modulated access for individual processes. For example, a process may only be able to read a group of pages that some other process can write.

Although single address space systems remain outside the mainstream, at least one has proved to be commercially viable. In the 1970s, IBM chose the single address space design for an innovative product line, the System/38, aimed at small businesses. In 1988, they issued a revised version of the same basic design, the AS/400, and in 2000 they renamed the AS/400 the iSeries. Whatever it may be called, the design has proved successful; as of June 2005, IBM reports that more than 400,000 iSeries servers are installed worldwide.

7.4 Representing Access Rights

In Sections 7.4.2 and 7.4.3, I will present the two principle approaches to representing access rights. First, though, I will use Section 7.4.1 to clarify the vocabulary used for discussing protection systems.

7.4.1 Fundamentals of Access Rights

A protection system controls access to *objects* by *subjects*. An object is whatever kind of entity needs protection: a region of memory, a file, a service that translates names to addresses, or anything else. A subject is the active entity attempting to make use of an object; I will generally assume that it is a process, because each thread within the process has the same access rights. Each kind of object has its own repertory of *operations* that a subject can perform on it, if the protection system permits: for example, a memory region may have read and write operations, whereas a naming service may have lookup, insert, and modify operations. Each subject is also an object, because operations can be performed on subjects, such as the operation of terminating a process.

Although protection mechanisms normally operate in terms of access rights given to subjects (that is, processes within the computer), those access rights ultimately should reflect the external authority of human users. To capture this notion, I will say that each subject is acting on behalf of a *principal*. For most purposes, you can equate the word "principal" with "user."

I use the technical word "principal" because occasionally the principal will be an organization rather than an individual, and because a server process may treat client processes as principals, for its purposes, even though the client processes are really only intermediaries, themselves operated by users. The distinguishing feature of a principal is that its rights are completely a question of policy, not of technical mechanism. If organizational policy directs a web server to grant some rights to particular client web browsers (such as those at on-campus addresses), then it is treating those browsers as principals. If, on the other hand, the organizational policy directs the web server to attempt to identify the human sitting at the web browser and grant access rights on that basis, then the human is the principal and the web browser is just an intermediary subject.

As my example of a web server indicates, a subject may operate on behalf of one principal at one time and a different principal at a different time. One common, but unsatisfactory, design is for the operating system's protection mechanism to give the subject the union of all the access rights it needs for all the principals. The subject then has the responsibility to enforce more specific protections. A better design would be for the operating system's protection mechanism to allow the server to switch from one set of access rights to another. In this case, the subject is said to move from one *protection domain* to another; a protection domain is simply the set of access rights possessed by a subject.

Some subjects may also need to switch domains in order to obtain extra access rights that would not normally be available to the principal. I have already mentioned one form this can take. In systems such as Linux and UNIX, when a process executes a program that has the setuid bit set, the process switches protection domains by taking on the identity of the program file's owner, with all the corresponding access rights.

At any one time, you can look at one subject (call it S) and one object (call it O) and say that S is allowed to perform some particular set of operations on O. To generalize this to the whole system, one can picture the instantaneous state of a protection system as an *access matrix*, with one row for each subject and one column for each object. The entry in row S and column O of the matrix is the set of operations that S can perform on O, as shown in Figure 7.10. Any attempt by a subject to perform an operation can be checked for legality by reference to the matrix.

The access matrix in most systems is very dynamic; it gains and loses columns and rows, and the operations listed in individual cells of the matrix change over time. For example, forking off a new process would add a row and a column to the matrix, because the new process is both a subject and an object. If the process executes a setuid program, many of the entries in that process's row of the matrix would change, because the new user identity conveys different access rights to many objects.

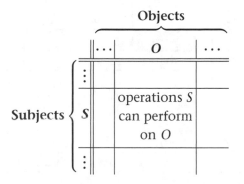

Figure 7.10 An access matrix has one row for each subject, one column for each object, and entries showing which operations each subject can perform on each object.

	F	P_1	P_2	⋯
P_1	change accessibility		transfer rights	
P_2	change accessibility			
⋮				

Figure 7.11 An access matrix can contain rights that control changes to the matrix itself. In this example, the processes P_1 and P_2 have the right to change the accessibility of file F, that is, to change entries in F's column of the access matrix. Process P_1 also has the right to transfer rights to process P_2, that is, to copy any access right from the P_1 row of the matrix to the corresponding entry in the P_2 row. Notice that the representation of the right to transfer rights relies upon that fact that each subject is also an object.

Some changes to the access matrix also reflect explicit protection operations, such as making a formerly private file readable by everyone or passing an access right held by one process to another process. These protection operations can themselves be regulated by access rights listed in the access matrix, as illustrated in Figure 7.11. Changing a file's accessibility would be an operation on that file, contained in some entries within that file's column of the matrix. Normally, this operation would not appear in every entry of the column, because only some processes should be able to change the file's accessibility. If only processes P_1 and P_2 have the right to change file F's accessibility, then the corresponding change-accessibility access right would show up in the matrix in two spots, exactly where rows P_1 and P_2 intersect with column F. Similarly, if process P_1 can pass an access right along to process P_2, there might be an entry in row P_1 and column P_2 conferring that transfer-rights permission. (Recall that subjects, such as P_2, are also objects, and hence have columns as well as rows.)

(a)

	F_1	F_2	JDoe	P_1	...
JDoe	read	write			
P_1	read	write			
⋮					

(b)

	F_1	F_2	JDoe	P_1	...
JDoe	read	write			
P_1			use the rights of		
⋮					

Figure 7.12   If access rights are initially granted to a principal, such as *JDoe*, then there are two options for how those rights can be conveyed to a process, such as P_1, operating on behalf of that principal. In option (a), when the process P_1 is created, all of *JDoe*'s rights are copied to P_1's row of the matrix; in this example, the rights are to read file F_1 and write file F_2. In option (b), P_1 is given just a special right to indirectly use the rights of *JDoe*.

In order to fit common protection mechanisms into the access matrix model, some slight contortions are necessary. For example, many mechanisms include access rights granted to principals (users), independent of whether they are running any computations at the time. Thus, it becomes necessary to add the principals themselves as subjects, in addition to their processes. Access rights can then go in both the row for the principal and the rows (if any) for the processes running on behalf of the principal. When a principal starts running a new process, the protection system can initialize the newly added row with rights taken from the principal's row. Alternatively, the process can just have rights to a special operation on the principal object, allowing it to indirectly use the principal's rights. Figure 7.12 illustrates both alternatives.

The access matrix model is very general: protections are established by sets of operations contained in an access matrix, which include operations to change the matrix itself. This generality suggests that one could construct an elegant mathematical theory of protection systems, which would work independently from the specifics of concrete systems. Unfortunately, the model's generality itself limits the results such a mathematical theory can provide. Harrison, Ruzzo, and Ullman showed that under very basic assumptions, the general access matrix model can simulate a Turing machine, with the matrix playing the role of the Turing machine's tape. Fundamental questions, such as whether a particular access right leaks out, turn out to be equivalent to the halting problem and, as such, are undecidable. Even restricting the problems enough to render them decidable may not make them practically solvable; for example, some fall into the class of PSPACE-complete problems. As explained in the end-of-chapter notes, this classification from computational complexity theory contains only very hard problems for which efficient solution algorithms are unlikely to exist. Thus, concrete protection systems need to be analyzed individually, rather than by reference to general results about the access matrix model.

Access matrices can represent very different security policies, depending on their contents. If you focus on the operations that allow modification of the matrix, you can distinguish two broad categories of policies: *Discretionary Access Control* (*DAC*) and *Mandatory Access Control* (*MAC*).

Most mainstream systems (such as Linux, Microsoft Windows, and Mac OS X) are usually configured to use DAC, so you are probably familiar with that class of policies, even if you are not familiar with the name. In a DAC system, each object is considered to be owned by a principal; when one of your processes creates an object (such as a file), you become its owner. The owner has broad rights to control the object's accessibility. As the owner of a file, you can choose whether to let other users read or write the file. In some DAC systems, you can go even further than giving away arbitrary access rights to your files; you can give away transferable rights, allowing other users to further propagate access to your files.

By contrast, an object's creator in a MAC system does not obtain control over access rights to the object. Instead, the access rights are determined by an explicit security policy and can be changed only within the parameters of that policy, often only by a designated security officer, rather than by an ordinary user. For example, consider a MAC system that enforces the military policy with regard to classified documents. If you are using such a system and have created a classified document, the fact that you are the creator does not give you any special control. You cannot choose to give access to users who are not cleared for the document's classification level. The only way the document can be made readable to those users is by declassifying it, an operation that only security officers can perform.

I will postpone further comparison between DAC and MAC systems until Section 7.6. Even there, I will include only the basics, leaving more detailed treatment for Chapter 11. For now, I will explain the two techniques that are used to keep track of access rights, independent of what sort of policy those rights are enforcing. The first technique is the use of capabilities, which I explain in Section 7.4.2. The second technique is the use of access control lists and credentials, which I explain in Section 7.4.3.

7.4.2 Capabilities

A *capability* is an indirect reference to an object, much like a pointer. The key distinction is that a capability includes not only the information needed to locate the object, but also a set of access rights. For example, two processes could possess capabilities for the same file, but one of them might have a read-only capability to the file, whereas the other might have a capability that permitted both reading and writing. A process that possesses capabilities has a tangible representation of entries from its row of the access matrix.

Nomenclature, as always, is not standardized. Although the word "capability" dates back to the mid-1960s and is popular in the academic literature, other names are used by today's mainstream operating systems. Microsoft Windows refers to capabilities as *handles*, and POSIX systems such as Linux and UNIX refer to them as *descriptors*. Continuing with the example of files, a Windows process could have a file handle that permitted reading only, and a Linux process could have a file descriptor that permitted reading only. (As you will see shortly, the handles and descriptors are actually even more indirect than capabilities; however, for everyday purposes, programmers can and do think about them in the same way as capabilities.)

To further confuse matters, the designers of Linux and UNIX systems have recently started using the word "capability" in a somewhat different sense. A capability in this new sense of the word confers rights, but does not refer to a specific object. For example, a process might hold a capability that allows it to access any file, or one that allows it to kill any process. To distinguish the two senses, these new object-independent capabilities are sometimes called "POSIX capabilities," even though the draft standard that would have made them part of POSIX was in fact abandoned. I will not use the word "capability" in this sense.

A process can store its capabilities in either of two ways, depending on the design of the operating system. Most systems give each process a special storage area just for capabilities, independent of the normal virtual memory address space of the process. Microsoft Windows and the POSIX systems take this approach. The alternative approach, taken by the iSeries, is for a process's capabilities to be stored in normal memory, just like any other data.

A separate storage area for capabilities is called a *C-list*, which is short for capability list. You will also frequently see C-lists called by system-specific names, such as *handle tables* in Microsoft Windows and *descriptor tables* in POSIX systems. Systems with C-lists provide special system calls to put entries into the C-list or otherwise operate on it, because normal load and store operations are not applicable. Entries in the C-list are referred to by their integer positions within the list. For example, an operation to read from a file takes an integer argument, which must be the position within the C-list of a file capability that includes the read permission. An operation to open a file for reading adds an entry to the C-list and returns the integer index of that entry.

It is these integer indices into the C-list that serve as handles in Microsoft Windows or as descriptors in POSIX. The integers can be stored anywhere in the process's memory; however, they do not have any significance outside the process, and so cannot be used for interprocess communication or for persistent storage. In order to pass a capability from one process to another, you need to use a special system call. The sending process specifies the capability to send by its integer index, and the receiving process is notified of its newly acquired capability as an integer index. However, the receiving process will in general be given a different integer than the sending process sent, because the two processes each have their own C-lists. In POSIX systems, descriptors are sent using `sendmsg` and received using `recvmsg`.

The capability model is incomplete as an explanation of POSIX file descriptors. As I will explain in Chapter 8, to fully understand file descriptors, you need to consider not only their capability-like properties, but also how the operating system keeps track of other information associated with each open file, especially the current position within the file for reading or writing. For the present chapter, however, I prefer to continue with the topic of capabilities, explaining another option for how they can be stored.

Instead of segregating the capabilities into a C-list for each process and forcing each process to use positions within its C-list as surrogates for the capabilities, an operating system can give the processes direct possession of the capabilities. In particular, IBM chose this approach for the System/38 and carried it forward into the AS/400 and iSeries. I call these nonsegregated capabilities *addressable capabilities*, because they are stored within the address space.

Capabilities that are addressable values are considerably more flexible than the C-list variety. By storing addressable capabilities within objects, software can use them to link several independently protected objects together into a larger structure, just as pointers would be used to make a more traditional structure of linked objects. This flexibility is particularly valuable in the iSeries, because (as I mentioned in Section 7.3.3) it is a single address space system.

The major difficulty with addressable capabilities is how to prevent an application program from forging them. (Recall that in the C-list approach, the operating system stores capabilities in memory inaccessible to the process, so forgery is a nonissue.) Normally, the capabilities should come from trusted system calls. However, if the capabilities are stored in ordinary memory locations, what is to stop a program from writing the appropriate set of bits to look like a capability and then using that forged capability to perform a protected operation?

Three basic approaches exist to prevent capability forgery. The approach used by the iSeries relies on special hardware features. Each memory word is supplemented by a tag bit indicating whether the word contains part of a capability. All normal instructions set the bit to 0, whereas capability operations set it to 1. Only words with their tag bits set to 1 can be used as a capability.

An alternative approach uses cryptographic techniques to achieve a high probability that forgeries will be detected, without needing special hardware. If each capability is represented by a large string of essentially random bits, and the operating system can check whether a given string of bits is valid, the only way to forge a capability would be by an incredibly lucky guess.

The third approach to preventing capability forgery forces all user programs to be processed by a trusted translator that enforces a strong type system. The type system prevents capability forgery the same way as any other type error. Interestingly, the iSeries does put all user programs through a trusted translator; apparently its type system is simply too weak to function without special tagging hardware. You will see an example of a stronger type system providing protection in Section 7.5.1, where I discuss the use of the Java Virtual Machine to provide protection at a finer granularity than operating system processes.

With the iSeries's combination of a single address space and addressable capabilities, determining the set of all capabilities available to a given process is not an easy job. They are not all in one place, unlike with a C-list. Nor can one just scan the process's address space looking for capabilities, because the process does not have an individual address space. Instead, it has access to those portions of the shared address space that are reachable through its capabilities. That is, each capability the process has available leads to an object, which can in turn contain more capabilities, leading to more objects. Some capabilities might lead back to already discovered objects. Thus, to find all the capabilities would require a general directed graph traversal algorithm, similar to what is needed for a garbage collector.

Regardless of how easy- or hard-to-find a process's capabilities are, one can recognize this set of capabilities as being the link to the abstract model of protection systems, which is the access matrix. Each process's set of capabilities corresponds with one row of the access matrix, because it records one subject's rights to objects. For a hypothetical system that provided protection purely through capabilities, the correspondence between access matrix rows and capability sets would be exact. The correspondence is less direct in real systems, which blend capability-based protection with access control lists, a topic I consider in Section 7.4.3. Because of this hybridization of protection representations, a process's set of capabilities holds only a portion of the contents of an access matrix row.

In all common operating systems, capabilities can be selectively granted but not selectively revoked. As an example of the selective granting of capabilities, an operating system will not allow just any process to open up a file of private information and obtain the corresponding capability. (You will see in Section 7.4.3 how the system achieves this.) However, once a process has the capability—whether by successfully opening the file or by being passed the capability by another, more privi-leged, process—it can continue to operate on the file. The file's owner cannot revoke the capability, short of destroying the file itself. (In POSIX systems, the owner can't even destroy the open file, but just its contents and any names it has.)

Several systems (such as Multics and various research systems) have supported selective revocation, in which some capabilities to an object can be revoked, while others remain valid. One approach is to keep track of the location of all copies of a capability; they can be invalidated by overwriting them. Another approach is to check whether a capability is still valid each time it is used to request an operation. For example, if capabilities are large random strings of bits, each object can contain a list of the valid capabilities.

Irrevocable capabilities are difficult to reconcile with system security. For this rea-son, the architects of the AS/400 made a change (relative to the original design taken from System/38) and eliminated all use of capabilities except within the operating system itself.

The POSIX systems take a more pragmatic approach to the problem of irrevocable capabilities. These systems use capabilities only for short-term storage of access rights while a process is running. As such, any excess access rights caused by the irrevocable capabilities will go away when the system is rebooted, in the worst case. Long-term storage of access rights is provided by access control lists, which are the next topic of this chapter.

7.4.3 Access Control Lists and Credentials

As you have seen, a capability list collects together the access rights held by a process. This row-wise slice of the access matrix is natural when considering the instantaneous rights of a process as it executes. However, it is much less natural when setting down (or auditing) longer-term policy regarding access rights. For those purposes, most systems use a mechanism based on user credentials and access control lists.

An *access control list* (*ACL*) is essentially a column-wise slice of the access matrix, listing for one object what subjects may access the object, and in what manner. Rather than listing the subjects at the fine granularity of individual processes, an ACL specifies rights for users (that is, principals) or for named groups of users.

I can show you an example of an ACL on a Microsoft Windows system by pulling up the Properties dialog box for a folder and selecting the Security tab on that dialog box. The visual form of the dialog boxes is dependent on the particular version of Windows, but the principles apply to all modern versions. As shown in Figure 7.13, the folder named "max" has an ACL with three entries: two for groups of users

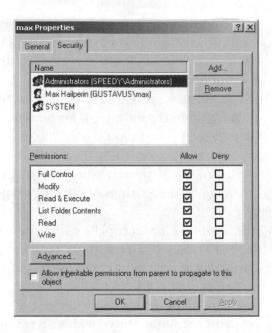

Figure 7.13 This is the initial dialog box summarizing a Microsoft Windows ACL, found in the Security tab of a Properties dialog box.

(Administrators and SYSTEM) and one for an individual user (myself). In the bottom part of the dialog box, you can see that any process running with a credential from the Administrators group is allowed Full Control over this folder. The permissions (such as Full Control) listed here are actually abbreviations for sets of permissions; to see the individual permissions, one needs to click the Advanced button (which gives the dialog box in Figure 7.14) and then the View/Edit button, producing the result shown in Figure 7.15. As you can see, Full Control actually is a set of thirteen different permissions. Some of these permissions (those with slashes in their names) have different interpretations when applied to folders than when applied to files.

One subtlety in Figures 7.13 and 7.15 concerns the presence of the Deny column of check boxes; this column is to the right of the Allow column. You might suspect that this is redundant, with the Deny box checked whenever the Allow box is unchecked. Although that is a reasonable suspicion, it is wrong. You can see in Figure 7.16 that the Users group has been neither allowed nor denied the ability to create files in the Program Files folder. To understand ACLs, you need to understand the difference between denying a permission and not allowing it.

As you have seen, an ACL entry can allow a permission, deny it, or neither. (Although the graphical user interface looks as though an entry could both allow and

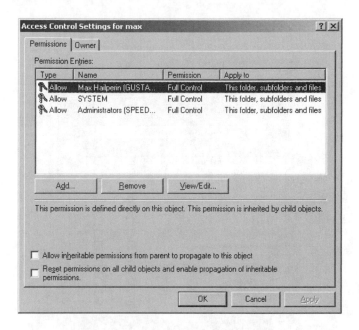

Figure 7.14   Clicking the Advanced button on the dialog box shown in Figure 7.13 produces this dialog box, which in turn gives you the opportunity to click the View/Edit button to obtain the detailed view shown in Figure 7.15.

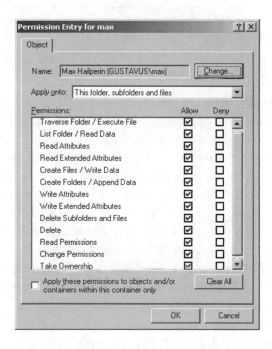

Figure 7.15   This detailed view of a Microsoft Windows ACL entry allows you to see that Full Control really is a summary name for thirteen different permissions.

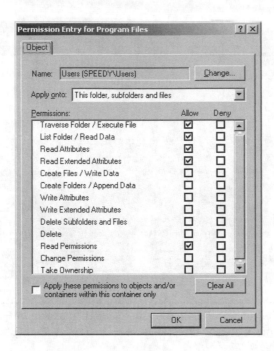

Figure 7.16 In the Microsoft Windows ACL entry shown in this detailed view, some permissions are neither allowed nor denied. In this circumstance, other ACL entries are allowed to control access.

deny the same permission, in fact this is not possible. Checking one box unchecks the other.) Keep in mind that your rights as a user derive both from ACL entries specifically for your user identity and from other ACL entries for groups to which you belong. In combining together these various ACL entries, having three options makes sense for the same reason as in parliamentary procedure one can vote yes, no, or abstain. An ACL entry that abstains (neither allows nor denies a permission) is permitting the other ACL entries to decide the question. In Figure 7.16, simply being a member of the Users group is not determinative one way or the other with regard to creating files. A member of the Users group *may* be able to create files in this folder, depending on what the other ACL entries say and depending on what other groups the user belongs to. This is the meaning of having neither the Allow box nor the Deny box checked. If all applicable ACL entries abstain, then access is denied.

What if one ACL entry that applies to a user specifies that a permission should be allowed, while another ACL entry that also applies to the same user specifies that the permission should be denied? In this case, a key difference arises between ACLs

	Allow	Deny	Neither
Allow	Allow	Deny	Allow
Deny	Deny	Deny	Deny
Neither	Allow	Deny	Neither

Figure 7.17 This table shows the rule for combining two Microsoft Windows ACL entries. The same rule is used repeatedly to combine any number of ACL entries. However, if the final result of combining all applicable entries is Neither, it is treated as Deny. (As the text explains, a different rule is used at a lower level. This figure explains the usual interface.)

and parliamentary procedure: the majority of the non-abstaining votes does not win with ACLs. Instead, a single vote to deny access will overrule any number of votes to allow access, much like the veto power possessed by permanent members of the United Nations Security Council. This allows an ACL to include exceptions; for example, all members of some group can be given access (without listing them individually), except one specific user who is denied access. Figure 7.17 summarizes the rule for combining ACL entries.

Within the Windows kernel, ACL entries are actually combined according to a different rule. If one ACL entry that applies to a user specifies that a permission should be allowed, while another ACL entry that also applies to the same user specifies that the permission should be denied, the kernel obeys whichever ACL entry is listed first. However, the API procedures that are generally used to maintain ACLs take care that all Deny entries precede any Allow entries. This effectively results in the rule shown in Figure 7.17, that a Deny entry always overrides an Allow entry. In particular, the graphical user interface shown in the preceding figures makes use of the API that gives precedence to Deny entries. In Exercise 7.8, you can analyze the relative merits of the two rules for combining ACL entries.

Although details vary from operating system to operating system, the Microsoft Windows version of ACLs is typical of all systems with full-fledged ACLs, dating back at least to Multics in the 1960s. Rather than looking at any other examples with full ACLs, I will consider a popular alternative, which is to use a highly restricted form of ACL. In particular, I will explain the file permissions portion of the POSIX specification, implemented by Linux, Mac OS X, and other versions of UNIX. (Some POSIX systems also offer the option of full ACLs; I will focus here on the traditional, required permission system.)

In common with Microsoft Windows, POSIX has a concept of user groups. Each file is owned by a particular user (usually its creator) and also has an owning group.

The ACL for any file always has exactly three entries:

- One entry specifies the permissions for the user who owns the file.
- The second entry specifies the permissions for all users who are members of the owning group, except for the owning user.
- The third entry specifies the permissions for all other users, who are neither the owner nor members of the owning group.

Note that unlike Windows, where several ACL entries may contribute to a single user's permissions, only one of these three will apply to any user. Thus, each permission can be treated in a binary fashion (granted or not granted), without need for the three-way distinction of allow/deny/neither. (Because of the way the three ACL entries are defined, you can perform odd stunts like giving everyone but yourself permission to access one of your files.)

Each of the three entries in a POSIX ACL can specify only three permissions: read, write, and "execute," which as you'll see can also mean "traverse directory." These three permissions are abbreviated by the single letters **r**, **w**, and **x**. A file has a total of nine permission bits: **r**, **w**, and **x** for the owner; **r**, **w**, and **x** for the rest of the owning group; and **r**, **w**, and **x** for everyone else. You can see these nine bits in the output from the **ls** directory listing program, when given the **-l** option (the letter **l** indicates you want a long-format listing, with lots of information). For example, in listing my home directory, I see a line that starts with

```
drwxr-x---      4 max        mc27fac
```

followed by the size, date, time, and name of the directory entry. The letter **d** at the beginning indicates that this is an entry for a subdirectory. The next nine characters are the permissions; I have full **rwx** permission, the other members of group **mc27fac** have only **r** and **x** (but not **w**), and other users have no permissions at all.

For an ordinary file, the **rwx** permissions are relatively self-explanatory. However, many people are confused as to what they mean for directories. For a directory:

- The **r** permission allows its possessor to find out what names are listed in the directory. This permission is neither necessary nor sufficient to get access to one of those named files. With only the **r** permission on one of your directories, another user would just be able to observe your taste in filenames.
- The **w** permission allows its possessor to create, delete, or rename files in the directory. Note, in particular, that a user who doesn't have permission to write into one of your files may still have permission to delete the file and create a new one with the same name.

- The **x** permission allows its possessor to use a filename in the directory as part of getting access to a file, subject to that file's own permissions. The **x** permission allows a user to *traverse* a directory, that is, to look up a given name in the directory and determine what it is a name for. Even without the **r** permission, a user can access one of the files in the directory if the user already knows (or can guess) its name, has the appropriate permission to the file itself, and has the **x** permission.

As a simple rule, you should always use the **r** and **x** permissions together on directories, unless you really know what you are doing. Giving **x** permission without **r** can be very frustrating, because it will break many modern programs with graphical user interfaces. These interfaces present users with a list of files to pick from, rather than making the user type the filename in. The only value of **x** without **r** is for security, but a security design that relies on other users not knowing your obscure choices of filenames is probably not very wise. On the other hand, **x** without **r** is at least more useful than **r** without **x**. You would need to think quite creatively to find value in letting people see your filenames but not make any use of them. (In Exercise 7.10, you have the opportunity to be that creative.) For most normal purposes, directory permissions should be **rwx** (for yourself, and sometimes for a group you really trust a lot), **r-x** (for others you want to use the directory), or **---** (for others you want to keep out).

As described in the preceding bulleted list, having **w** permission on a directory is quite powerful, in that it allows you to delete and replace an existing file within that directory, even if you couldn't overwrite the file. However, this power can be kept in check. Each directory has a bit, alongside the nine **rwx** permission bits constituting the ACL, which can be used to limit the power of the **w** permission. If this so-called *sticky bit* is set, then a file may be deleted from the directory only by the owner of the file, the owner of the directory, or the system administrator. The same limitation applies to renaming files.

Access control lists, of either the full variety or the simplified owner-group-other kind, are generally used in conjunction with capabilities. When a POSIX process wants to read or write a file, for example, it starts by using the **open** procedure to translate the filename into a file descriptor, which refers to a capability.

The **open** procedure takes as arguments both the filename (a string) and an integer encoding a set of flags. That set of flags contains information as to whether the process intends to read the file, write the file, or both. For example, **open("alpha/beta", O_RDONLY)** would attempt to obtain a read-only capability for the file named **beta** in the directory named **alpha** in the current directory.

The **open** procedure uses the process's user and group credentials to check whether the process has the necessary permissions: **x** permission on the current directory and the subdirectory named **alpha**, and **r** permission on the file named **beta** within **alpha**. If the process has executed a setuid program, these permission checks are done using the effective user ID, adopted from the program's ownership information. Similarly, the permission checks take the effective group ID from the program's owning group if an analogous *set group ID* (*setgid*) feature is used. Assuming the permissions are granted, the **open** procedure creates a read-only capability for the file and returns an integer file descriptor providing access to that capability. From this point on, the ACLs cease to be relevant. The **x** bit could be removed from **alpha** or the **r** bit from **beta**, and the open file descriptor would continue to function. That is, an open file descriptor is an irrevocable capability, as described in Section 7.4.2.

7.5 Alternative Granularities of Protection

Sections 7.3 and 7.4 showed how an operating system can protect processes from unwanted interaction with one another. Section 7.5.1 considers the possibility of providing analogous control over interaction even for objects within a single process, and Section 7.5.2 considers protecting entire operating system environments from one another, within a single computer.

7.5.1 Protection Within a Process

When I described what a process is, I indicated that it is the unit of granularity for protection provided by the operating system. That is, operating systems protect processes from each other, but generally do not protect components within a process from each other. This does not mean that protection within a process isn't important or can't be achieved. Instead, such protection is normally a job for middleware, rather than for the operating system.

Consider, for example, the Java objects that are used in application servers. Because a large number of objects collaborate within web-based applications, you wouldn't want to pay the overhead cost of an operating system process per object. Instead, application servers allow numerous objects to exist within a single operating system process. On the other hand, an application server may contain objects assembled together from many different sources. If they were not protected from one another, you would have the same sort of debugging and security nightmares that you would have if processes were unprotected.

In order to protect objects from one another, even if they coexist within a single process, the process runs the *Java Virtual Machine* (*JVM*), which provides protection and other basic support for Java objects. Thus, the JVM provides a good example of how middleware can provide protection for components within a process.

To protect Java objects from one another, the JVM makes sure that the Java code it is executing obeys certain restrictions. A typical restriction is that no method may ever read from an uninitialized local variable, that is, one into which it has not previously written. This prevents the method from picking up some value left in memory by a previously executed method, which might have been in an object from a different source.

In principle, the JVM could enforce its restrictions by carefully monitoring each step of the Java program as it is executing. For example, the JVM could maintain a set of initialized local variables as the program runs. Any assignment to a local variable would add it to the set. Any use of a local variable would be preceded by a check whether the variable is in the set.

The problem with this approach is that it would make all Java code run like molasses in winter. Each instruction in the program would be preceded by hundreds of other instructions checking whether various restrictions were satisfied. As such, the program would be running hundreds of times more slowly.

Therefore, real JVMs take a smarter approach. As each class is loaded, a JVM component called the *verifier* mathematically proves that everywhere along all paths through the code, no uninitialized variable is ever read. The verifier also checks other restrictions similarly. Having proved that all paths are safe (in the checked senses), the JVM can then run the code full speed ahead.

The verifier cannot check potential paths through the code one by one, because there may be a great number of paths, or even infinitely many. (Consider, for example, a method with a `while` loop in the middle. There is one path from the beginning of the method to the end that goes around the loop zero times, one that goes around the loop one time, and so forth.) Therefore, the verifier constructs its safety proofs using the same sort of dataflow analysis that compilers have traditionally used for optimization. This analysis involves finding the greatest fixed-point solution of a system of simultaneous equations. An important general theorem regarding dataflow analysis shows that the greatest fixed-point solution gives a set of security guarantees that can be counted on to hold at a point, independent of which path is taken to that point. Therefore, the verifier can check all paths for safety at once. In Exercise 7.13, you will prove this theorem.

7.5.2 Protection of Entire Simulated Machines

You have seen that the JVM allows you to zoom in and create a whole collection of protected domains within a single operating system process. Similarly, you can zoom out and treat a whole operating system, complete with all its processes, as just one protected domain among many within a larger *Virtual Machine Monitor* (*VMM*). A VMM uses the computer it runs on to simulate the execution of several similar computers, each of which can then run its own operating system with its own processes.

Two commercially significant VMMs are VMware's ESX Server and IBM's z/VM. ESX Server uses IA-32 hardware to simulate multiple IA-32 servers; for example, a single four-way multiprocessor server might simulate six uniprocessor servers, each with its own operating system, such as Microsoft Windows or Linux. The six simulated processors take turns executing on the four real processors, under control of the VMM. Similarly, z/VM uses IBM's mainframe zSeries to simulate multiple zSeries machines, each of which could be running one of IBM's legacy mainframe operating systems or could be running Linux.

To see how a VMM can be used, you can look at the example in Figure 7.18. Each box indicates a hardware or software component. At the bottom is the Xeon hardware, a member of the Pentium family, which supplies the IA-32 interface upward to the next layer. That next layer is a VMM (specifically the ESX Server), which simulates three virtual machines, each also providing the IA-32 interface. The leftmost virtual machine is running Linux 2.6, the middle one is running Windows 2003, and the rightmost one is running an older version of Linux, 2.4. The presence of Microsoft Windows and Linux on the same hardware may have come about through server consolidation; perhaps two different groups within the enterprise had settled on different software environments but now are being hosted on common hardware to reduce total cost of ownership. The two versions of Linux may reflect a similar story, or may be a case where a new version is being tested while an older version continues to be in production use. In the particular case shown in the figure, the Linux 2.6 virtual

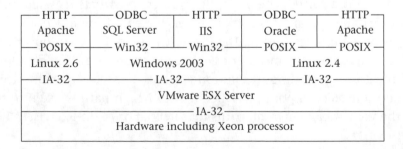

Figure 7.18 This example shows a VMM, the VMware ESX Server, supporting multiple operating systems. The label within each box identifies a component, whereas the label on each horizontal dividing line identifies an interface. Unlike the operating systems, the VMM provides upward the same IA-32 interface that it relies upon from below.

machine is running a single process (the Apache web server), whereas the other two virtual machines are running two processes apiece (in each case, a database server and a web server).

Notice that processes can benefit from two levels of protection, one provided by the operating system and another by the VMM. For example, Windows 2003 is responsible for isolating the SQL Server process from the IIS process. If someone finds a way to subvert Windows's protection mechanism, this isolation may fail. However, the processes running on the other two virtual machines will remain isolated, so long as the ESX Server software continues to do its job. Consider another explanation for why two versions of Linux are running on the same machine: one group, with a lot at stake, might choose to run the latest version with all available security patches, while another group, with less at stake, might choose to stick with an older, less secure version so as to avoid the disruption of an upgrade. The high-stakes group need not fear consequences from an attacker breaking into the low-stakes group's system any more than if the two were on different hardware machines. The VMM provides that assurance.

The operation of a VMM is similar to that of an operating system. Like an operating system, it uses scheduling to divide processing time and uses page mapping to divide memory. The key difference is that it doesn't support any higher-level APIs, such as the file operations found in POSIX or Win32. Instead, the VMM supports an interface similar to a real machine's, complete with I/O devices.

Because the virtual machines use the same instruction set architecture as the real hardware, the VMM does not need to simulate their execution on an instruction-by-instruction basis. Most instructions can be directly executed by the real hardware. The only issue is with privileged instructions, of the kind used by operating systems for such tasks as managing I/O hardware or changing page tables.

Recall that processors generally have two operating modes, a kernel mode in which all instructions are legal, and a user mode, in which dangerous instructions trap to an operating system handler. I need to explain how these two modes can be used to support three levels of execution: the VMM, the operating system, and the application processes.

The VMM runs in kernel mode. When the underlying processor executes instructions from one of the virtual machines, on the other hand, it does so in user mode. That way, the VMM is in complete control and can protect the virtual machines from one another. However, the virtual machines still need to support a simulated kernel mode so that they can run operating systems. Therefore, the VMM keeps track of each virtual machine's simulated mode, that is, whether the virtual machine is in simulated kernel mode or simulated user mode.

If a virtual machine executes a privileged instruction (for example, to manage I/O hardware), a trap to the VMM occurs, as shown in Figure 7.19. The VMM then

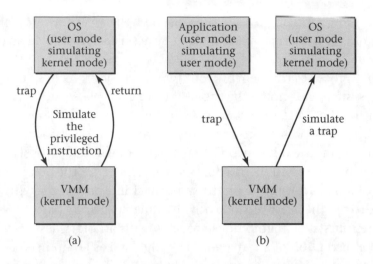

Figure 7.19 When an attempt is made to execute a privileged instruction within a virtual machine, a trap to the VMM occurs, whether the virtual machine is executing operating system code or application code, because the hardware is in user mode in either case. However, the VMM knows whether the virtual machine is in simulated kernel mode or simulated user mode and responds accordingly. In (a), the virtual machine is in simulated kernel mode, so the VMM simulates the privileged instruction and then returns from the trap. In (b), the virtual machine is in simulated user mode, so the VMM simulates the trap that would have occurred on a real machine: it switches to simulated kernel mode and jumps to the operating system trap handler within the virtual machine.

checks whether the virtual machine was in simulated kernel mode. If so, the privileged instruction was attempted by the virtual machine's operating system, and the VMM carries out the intent of the instruction, for example, by doing the requested I/O. If, on the other hand, the virtual machine was in simulated user mode, then the VMM simulates a trap within the virtual machine by switching it to simulated kernel mode and jumping to the trap handler within the virtual machine's operating system. In Exercise 7.14, you can consider how the trap handler within the virtual machine's operating system can later return control to the application program.

One particularly interesting design question is how virtual memory is handled. The operating system running within a virtual machine sets up a page table mapping virtual page numbers into what it thinks of as physical page frame numbers. However, the VMM does another level of mapping, translating the virtual machine's "physical" page frames into the truly physical page frames of the hardware. That way, the VMM can allocate the hardware's memory among the virtual machines and can do tricks like using copy on write (COW) to transparently share memory across the virtual machines.

In order to efficiently support this double translation of addresses, the VMM computes the functional composition of the two address translations and provides that composition to the hardware's MMU. That is, if the virtual machine's simulated page table would map A into B, and the VMM wants to map B into C, then the VMM puts a translation directly from A to C into the real page table used by the hardware MMU.

7.6 Security and Protection

Protection plays an essential role in security. If I were to take the title of this section literally, it could be a very long section. Instead, I will simply highlight a few key security issues directly raised by the material in this chapter.

Perhaps the most important take-home message is that although protection is essential to security, it is not the same as security. The two are easily confused. For example, security includes maintaining confidentiality, and protection includes the use of access control lists to limit read access permissions. Surely these are the same, right? Wrong. If the data in question is on a disk drive that is in an unlocked room, then all the access control lists in the world won't keep it confidential. An adversary simply needs to steal the drive and read it on his own machine, which is programmed to ignore ACLs. In Chapter 11, I will address some of the broader security picture.

Many nasty security pitfalls arise from the distinction between a principal and a subject, or in simplified terms, between a user and a process. A process that is operating with the credentials of a user may carry out actions that the user would not approve of. One way this could happen is if the user authentication system is weak enough for someone else to log in as you. I will not consider that topic further here, instead concentrating on the problems that remain even if the system knows which human is behind each keyboard.

In discussing POSIX processes, I mentioned that user credentials are retained when a process forks and also when it executes a program. Thus, any program you run will be acting with your credentials. (The same is true in other systems, such as Microsoft Windows.) This immediately raises the possibility of a *Trojan horse*, a program that has some apparent benign purpose but that also has a hidden nefarious intent. Suppose someone gives you a program and tells you it shows a really funny animation of Bart Simpson impersonating Bill Gates. You run it, enjoy the animation, and chuckle merrily. Unfortunately, you aren't the only one laughing; so is the programmer who knows what else the program does other than showing the animation. Remember: whatever the program does, "you" are doing, because the process is acting with your user credentials. If you have the ability to send all your private data over the network (which you probably do), then so does the Trojan horse.

One variant of the general Trojan horse theme is the *email worm*. Suppose you receive an email with an attached program. When you run the program, it can do anything it wants with your credentials. Suppose what it does is send new email to everyone in your address book, with the same attachment. (After all, the protection system thinks you have every right to read your address book and to send email with your return address.) In this way, the same malicious program can be spread to many computers all over the world. Of course, the worm can perform other actions as well.

Suppose you never knowingly run gift programs. Does that make you safe from Trojan horses? Not necessarily. Recall my discussion of **execlp**. I mentioned that it looks through a sequence of directories until it finds the program file, just as the shell does. This search means that even when you type in as simple a command as **ps** (to list your processes), you don't necessarily know what program is being run; it might not be **/bin/ps**, if some other program named **ps** is in one of the other directories that comes before **/bin** in the search path. In particular, it was once common for UNIX users to have search paths that started with the current directory (named **.**), before any system-wide directories. That has ceased to be popular, because it is an open invitation to Trojan horses planted by adversaries who don't have write access to any of the system-wide directories. Even putting the current directory last in the search path (as many users still do) is not completely safe; a clever adversary could plant a Trojan horse named with a common misspelling or with a program name that is installed on some systems, but not the one under attack. The only really safe alternative is to leave the current directory out of your search path. When you want to run a program in your current directory, you will need to specify an explicit pathname. For example, to run the **microshell** program from Figure 7.6, you might compile it in your current directory and then run **./microshell**.

An attacker who wants to plant a Trojan horse for you to run may not even need to take advantage of search paths, if one of the programs you run has file access permissions set so that other people can overwrite the file with a modified version. Similarly, if the directory containing the program is writable, the program can be deleted and replaced. Setting programs (or the containing directories) to be writable seems like such an obvious invitation for Trojan horses that you might find it difficult to imagine such situations arise. Yet I have repeatedly encountered installer programs for commercial application software that set the installed programs or directories to be writable by all users of the system. In the face of such installers, a system administrator needs to be vigilant and manually change the permissions.

The Trojan horse problem is far more dangerous in a system with Discretionary Access Control (DAC) than one with Mandatory Access Control (MAC), because there is far more that "you" (actually, the Trojan horse) can do in a DAC system. For example, in a MAC system that enforces military classification levels, no Trojan horse can possibly read from a top secret file and then write a copy into an unclassified file; the operating system forbids any process from reading and writing in this way. Notice that using MAC rather than DAC is only partially intended to guard against computer users making unwise decisions. Far more, MAC is guarding against the organization needing to trust all programs' authors. (Trust in the people running the programs can come from nontechnical sources, like keeping an eye out for employees who seem to have too much money. For external program authors, this would be more difficult.)

Another security pitfall comes from the ability of a setuid program to propagate its owner's credentials. Suppose that an adversary briefly has the ability to act with your credentials, using some means other than setuid. (This could be through a Trojan horse, but alternatively the adversary might simply use your keyboard while you are getting coffee.) You cannot assume that the adversary's ability to do damage is over when the initial access method is removed (when you return from getting coffee). A smart adversary will use the brief access to create a setuid shell, owned by you and executable by the adversary. Then, at any convenient later time, the adversary can run any programs whatsoever with your credentials. A real-world analogy would be if leaving your door unlocked made it easy for a burglar to retrofit a secret entrance into your house.

System administrators fight back against unwanted setuid programs with measures such as turning the setuid feature off for file systems that normal users can write into, as well as regularly scanning the file systems looking for setuid files. These measures are valuable but are treating a symptom of a bigger problem. The setuid mechanism, in its elegant generality, is a fundamental mismatch for most organizational security policies. In most organizations, authorization can flow only from the top down; low-level employees are not empowered to pass their authority on to someone else.

Setuid programs raise an additional set of issues, which are in a sense the opposite of the Trojan horse problem. Security problems arise whenever the person providing authority is different from the person deciding how that authority will be used. A Trojan horse tricks the user running the program into providing credentials for actions specified by the program's author. Conversely, a setuid program provides the author's credentials, but might unintentionally allow the user running it to control what actions it carries out. Either way, there is a mismatch between the source of authority and the source of control.

Programming oversights explain most cases where a setuid program cedes control to the user running it. For example, suppose the designer of a setuid program wants it to print out a file and wants the user running the program to specify the name of the printer (but not of the file). The program might execute a shell command like `lpr -Pprintername` *filename*, where the *printername* comes from the user's input and the *filename* is controlled by the setuid program itself. This seemingly innocent command could be compromised in several ways, such as the following:

- If the adversary can control the directory search path, the `lpr` command might be executing a program of the adversary's choice, rather than the normal printing command.

- If the adversary can input a printer name that contains a space, the print command might gain an extra argument, which would be taken as another filename to print, this one specified by the adversary.

- If the adversary can input a printer name that contains a semicolon, the print command might turn into two separate commands, one to run `lpr` and one to run some totally different program of the adversary's choice.

UNIX system programmers have developed a whole body of lore on how to write setuid (or setgid) programs without falling into traps such as the preceding example. Some of this lore addresses particular pitfalls, such as interpolating arbitrary user input into shell commands. However, there are also some more fundamental steps you can take to reduce the risk of a program being exploited. Keep in mind that risk is a function both of the chance of exploitation and of the damage that can be done:

- You can reduce the opportunity for exploitation by making each setuid (or setgid) program as small and simple as possible and by making it executable by as few users as possible.

- You can reduce the damage an exploitation could do by having each setuid (or setgid) program owned by a special user (or group) that exists just for that one purpose and that has only the relevant permissions. The program should not be owned by a normal user or group that has many other unrelated permissions. (The worst choice is if the setuid program is owned by the special system administration account, `root`, which has permission to do absolutely anything.)

On the positive side, setuid programs can be very valuable in enforcing security policies that go beyond what basic owner-group-other permissions (or even full ACLs) can represent. For example, suppose you want to allow a group of employees to write into a file, but only with the following limitations:

- These employees may only add entries to the end of the file, not modify existing entries.

- Each entry must include a time stamp and the name of the employee making the addition.

- These employees may make additions only during normal business hours, when they are subject to physical observation, so as to provide greater protection against impersonation.

A sophisticated protection system might have special accommodation for some of these needs; for example, you saw that Microsoft Windows has separate permissions for "append data" versus "write data." However, it is unlikely that any system would directly support the whole package of application-specific policies. Instead, you could funnel this group's access through a setuid program that enforces the policies. Database programmers commonly use a similar technique: rather than granting users permission to directly access a table, they grant the users permission to run a stored procedure or to access a specialized view of the table.

Because I showed Microsoft Windows's ACLs through the graphical user interface, I have a good opportunity to point out the importance of user interface design to security. A protection system does not enhance security by virtue of being *able* to correctly enforce a security policy; instead, it enhances security only if it *is actually used* to correctly enforce the policy. In general, the more sophisticated a mechanism, the lower the chance that users will actually figure out how to use it correctly. If they make mistakes that result in overly restrictive protections, someone will notice and complain. If they make mistakes that result in insufficiently restrictive permissions, no one is likely to complain. Thus, the user interface design must help the user manage complexity and reduce the chance of errors. Microsoft has done this in several ways, such as providing a simplified interface to common groupings of permissions, with the individual underlying permissions visible only on request. Also, the uniform rule that deny permissions take precedence over allow permissions is less likely to result in accidental underprotection than the lower-level rule of processing the allow and deny permissions in a user-specified order.

My description of the meaning of **rwx** permission bits on directories ignored an important issue. When I discuss file naming in Chapter 8, you will see that a single file can have multiple filenames, listed in multiple directories. Thus, saying that the **x** permission bit on a directory controls access to files in that directory is an oversimplification. This directory permission controls whether names in that directory can be used to access files—but the same files may in any case be accessible through other names in other directories. Unless you know that a file only has one name, the only sure-fire way to restrict its access is with its own permission bits, not with an ancestor directory's **x** bit.

In discussing Virtual Machine Monitors, I remarked that a VMM can keep processes running in separate virtual machines isolated from one another, even in the face of a security breach in one or both virtual machines' operating systems. This sounds on the surface like an example of *defense in depth*, the general security principle of providing multiple independent safeguards, so that even if one is breached, the others prevent a system security failure. However, this view is not entirely correct, because a VMM has complete power over the virtual machines; if the VMM's security is breached, the security of the operating systems becomes irrelevant. Therefore, isolating two processes with a VMM and operating systems will not necessarily result in better protection than an operating system alone, because an attacker need only subvert the VMM. Of course, it may be that the VMM is more secure than the operating system, because it is much simpler. However, the enhanced security, if there is any, comes from substitution of a better protection mechanism, rather than from the cumulative contribution of an additional protection mechanism.

Exercises

7.1 Consider how `fork` is typically used today. On a uniprocessor system, would it make more sense to schedule the child process to run immediately after a fork or continue to run the parent process? Explain why. Be sure to take COW into account.

7.2 I described access matrices as containing access permissions for individual processes, rather than only for users. Give an example of how a POSIX process could have access permissions different from those of any user.

7.3 What is the difference between a DAC system and a MAC system? Give an example of a circumstance under which you would prefer a DAC system, and explain why. Give an example of a circumstance under which you would prefer a MAC system, and explain why.

7.4 Explain the relationship between access matrices, C-lists, and ACLs.

7.5 Explain the relationship between handles, C-lists (or handle tables), and capabilities in a system like Microsoft Windows.

7.6 Compare C-list capabilities with addressable capabilities. Which is more powerful for the application programmer? Which is simpler for the operating system designer? Justify your answers.

7.7 Suppose the processes on a computer occupy a total of 8 GB of virtual memory, half of which is occupied by addressable capabilities. Suppose that each capability is represented by a random string of 256 bits, subject to the constraint that no two of the capabilities are equal. What is the probability that a randomly generated string of 256 bits would equal one of the capabilities?

7.8 On a Microsoft Windows system, suppose there are two user groups, `big` and `small`, with the property that all users who belong to `small` also belong to `big`.

Suppose, further, that user **jdoe** belongs to **small** (and hence to **big**). You are not to know what other users belong to the groups.

(a) Explain how a file's ACL could be set to allow read access only to users who are members of **big** but not of **small**.

(b) Explain why the file's ACL cannot be modified using the ordinary user interface to additionally allow **jdoe** read access, without changing any other user's access rights.

(c) Explain how the alternative rule used within the Windows kernel for combining allow and deny permissions would make the goal stated in the previous part possible.

(d) Make an argument why this alternative is superior to the one used in the Microsoft Windows interface.

(e) Make an argument why the permission combining rule from the Microsoft Windows interface is superior to the alternative from the kernel.

(f) Which argument do you find more persuasive? Why?

7.9 For combining permissions from multiple applicable ACL entries, it is desirable to use a combining operation that is associative and commutative.

(a) Show that the combining operation specified by the table in Figure 7.17 on page 249 is associative and commutative.

(b) Show that if the operation is changed so that Neither combined with Neither yields Deny, the operation is no longer associative.

7.10 Think creatively and come up with a scenario where it would be valuable for the owner of a POSIX directory to grant someone **r** permission to that directory but not **x** permission.

7.11 On a POSIX system, a file and a directory are both owned by user 37 and group 53, and both have permissions **rw-r-x--x**; that is, **rw-** for the owner, **r-x** for the group, and **--x** for others. The members of group 53 are users 37, 42, and 71.

(a) Which user(s) may read the file?

(b) Which user(s) may write the file?

(c) Which user(s) may execute the file?

(d) When the file is executed by user 85, what are the two possibilities for the effective user ID?

(e) What determines which of these two possible user IDs is used?

(f) Which of the following are true?

    i. User 37 may list the contents of the directory.

    ii. User 37 may use the directory in a pathname to access files under it, subject to those files' permissions.

    iii. User 42 may list the contents of the directory.

    iv. User 42 may use the directory in a pathname to access files under it, subject to those files' permissions.

    v. User 85 may list the contents of the directory.

    vi. User 85 may use the directory in a pathname to access files under it, subject to those files' permissions.

7.12 What is the function of the sticky bit on a directory in a POSIX system?

7.13 In this exercise, you will prove a theorem relied upon by the JVM verifier. Let S be a set of security properties, and let (V,E) be a directed graph with vertices V and edges $E \subseteq V \times V$. (The graph represents a program; the vertices are points in the program and the edges are possible control flows.) Let v_0 be a distinguished element of V, the start vertex. If the edge (u,v) is in E, one says u is a predecessor of v; the set $Pred(v)$ consists of all predecessors of v. For each edge $(u,v) \in E$, let f_{uv} be a monotone function from 2^S to 2^S. That is, f_{uv} is a function such that if $A \subseteq B \subseteq S$, then $f_{uv}(A) \subseteq f_{uv}(B) \subseteq S$. If $v_0 v_1 \cdots v_n$ is a (possibly cyclic) path in the digraph from the start vertex v_0 to v_n, then define the security properties that hold after the path to be $H(v_0 v_1 \cdots v_n) = f_{v_{n-1} v_n}(f_{v_{n-2} v_{n-1}}(\cdots f_{v_0 v_1}(\emptyset) \cdots))$. Define the security properties that are guaranteed at vertex v to be $G(v)$, where G is some function that satisfies the following equations:

$$G(v_0) = \emptyset$$
$$G(v) = \bigcap_{p \in Pred(v)} f_{pv}(G(p)), \ v \neq v_0.$$

Use induction on the length of the path $v_0 v_1 \cdots v_{n-1} v_n$, $n \geq 0$, to prove that $G(v_n) \subseteq H(v_0 v_1 \cdots v_{n-1} v_n)$, that is, after any path leading to v_n, all the security properties guaranteed at v_n hold.

7.14 Part (b) of Figure 7.19 on page 256 shows how a hardware-level trap to the VMM is used to simulate a trap to the operating system running within a virtual machine. The accompanying text also describes this situation. When the trap handler in the operating system finishes and executes a return-from-trap instruction, how is control transferred back to the application program? What mode changes, both real and simulated, occur?

▣ Programming Projects

7.1 Write and test a variant of the **forker** program from Figure 7.1 on page 224, in which as much code as possible is shared between the parent and child processes.

7.2 Write a variant of the **forker** program from Figure 7.1 on page 224, in which the parent and child processes are more dissimilar from one another than in the given program.

7.3 Learn enough C++, if you don't already know it, to be able to read in a line of text and break it into whitespace-separated words. Then modify the microshell of Figure 7.6 on page 229 to accept multi-word commands and use **execvp** to pass the words as command line arguments.

7.4 Modify your microshell from the previous project so that if the last word in a command is **&**, that word is not passed as a command line argument. Instead, your program should skip the **waitpid**.

7.5 From the behavior of the **forker** program in Figure 7.1 on page 224, you can tell that each parent and child process gets its own copy of the **loopCount** variable. Are the two copies at equal virtual addresses or different virtual addresses? Testing this might help you determine whether you are using a single address space system or a multiple address space system. Modify the program so that each process prints out **&loopCount**, the address of **loopCount**. What can you conclude from the results you observe?

Exploration Projects

7.1 Figure 7.20 contains a simple C program that loops three times, each time calling the **fork** system call. Afterward it **sleep**s for 30 seconds. Compile and run this program, and while it is in its 30-second sleep, use the **ps** command in a second terminal window to get a listing of processes. How many processes are shown running the program? Explain by drawing a "family tree" of the processes, with one box for each process and a line connecting each (except the first one) to its parent.

```
#include <unistd.h>

int main(int argc, char **argv){
  int i;
  for(i = 0; i < 3; i++){   /* loops 3 times */
    fork();                 /* each time calling fork */
  }
  sleep(30);                /* then sleeps 30 seconds */
}
```

Figure 7.20 This C program, **multiforker.c**, loops three times and each time forks. At the end, it sleeps 30 seconds so that you have time to run the **ps** command and see how many copies of the process are running.

7.2 On a Linux or UNIX system, read the documentation for the `find` command. Use it to search for setuid or setgid programs. In as many cases as possible, determine why the program needs to be setuid or setgid. In each case, try to determine whether the file is owned by a special-purpose user or group that owns only the file and a few related ones.

7.3 Browse the web for cases where buggy setuid programs have constituted security vulnerabilities. Write up a summary of the cases you find; look in particular for recurrent themes.

7.4 Occasionally an adversary will gain control of an FTP or web server from which widely used software is distributed. Explain why this is a particular source of concern, in terms of one of the security issues discussed in this chapter. Read CERT Advisory CA-2002-28 (which you can find on the web) for an example. What countermeasures are suggested in that advisory? How does each of them help mitigate this sort of problem?

7.5 On a Linux or UNIX system, use the same `find` program as in Exploration Project 7.2 to search for files that are executable by someone and writable by all users, as well as to identify directories that are writable by all users. Do you find any opportunities for the installation of Trojan horses?

7.6 Suppose you carefully check the source code of all programs you run, and you make sure to run only versions that you have compiled yourself from the source code you check. Are you then safe against Trojan horses? Think this through for yourself, and then read Thompson's Turing Award lecture, cited in the notes at the end of this chapter. Write a brief summary explaining how Thompson has influenced your thinking on this topic or why he hasn't.

Notes

The idea that a process is a group of threads sharing a protection context dates back at least to a seminal 1966 paper by Dennis and Van Horn [44]. The terminology has shifted over the decades, however. They (and other early authors) used the word "process" for what today is called a thread and "computation" for what today is called a process.

You can supplement my brief introduction to the POSIX API for process management in two ways. One is by reading the official documentation; the POSIX standard is on the web at *http://www.opengroup.org*, and the documentation for specific implementations (such as Linux) is also easily available. The other approach, which is likely to be more useful at first, would be to read a book on the topic. Two good choices are those by Stevens and Rago [123] and by Robbins and Robbins [105].

Multics was a very influential multiple address space system. Although processes could share individual memory segments (named with filenames in a directory tree), each process used its own segment numbers for addressing, rather than the shared segment names. Segments were protected using a combination of ACLs and capabilities. See, for example, Daley and Dennis's article [38] and the later retrospective by Saltzer [110].

Another interesting feature of the Multics system, which made its way into the IA-32 architecture, was the use of intermediate processor protection modes between the kernel and user modes I describe. The availability of multiple protection modes joins segmentation as an underutilized feature of the IA-32 architecture.

The case for single address space systems has been made by Chase et al. [26]. The Itanium mechanism is described in Intel's documentation [75]. A good source of information on the AS/400 is Soltis's book [119]. Other relevant sources are papers on the System/38 [20, 118, 73].

Harrison, Ruzzo, and Ullman [64] use the access matrix model to show that theoretical results independent of specific protection systems are pessimistic. As mentioned in the text, they showed some important problems to be undecidable and others to be PSPACE-complete. A decision problem is PSPACE-complete if it satisfies two criteria. First, the problem must be in PSPACE, which means it is solvable using a polynomially-bounded amount of memory and unlimited time. Second, the problem must have the property that if a polynomial-time algorithm exists to solve it, then such an algorithm also exists for every other problem in PSPACE. Because of this definition, either all problems in PSPACE have polynomial-time solutions, or no PSPACE-complete problem has a polynomial-time solution. The general consensus is that the latter is the more plausible possibility.

Capabilities were introduced by Dennis and Van Horn [44] in the limited context of C-lists, where they remain in today's mainstream systems. The greater power of addressable capabilities was explored by Fabry [51] and Linden [89]. Variants of these ideas were incorporated into various research systems, of which Hydra [137, 32] and CAP [96] are well known. The most direct influence of the ideas, however, seems to be on the design of IBM's commercial System/38 and AS/400 systems, for which citations were given previously.

The JVM verifier is specified by Lindholm and Yellin [90]. The VMware ESX Server VMM is described in an article by Waldspurger [131], which does a wonderful job of showing how operating system concepts are applied to a practical design problem.

A good overview of current directions in VMM technology appeared in May of 2005 as a special issue of *Computer* magazine [52].

I said that z/VM is a VMM that simulates zSeries machines. Strictly speaking, the VMM is just one component of z/VM, the one called CP, which is short for

Control Program. Also, the simulated architecture is technically called z/Architecture, the zSeries consists of particular hardware implementations of that architecture, analogous to the Pentium family being implementations of IA-32.

IBM's z/VM has evolved from its roots in the 1960s. In particular, the early version of CP-67 described by Meyer and Seawright [95] made use of paging for its own operation but did not allow paging within the virtual machines. Two years later, Parmelee et al. [99] describe a version of CP-67 that did provide paging within the virtual machines. The evolution of CP-67 into VM/370 is described by Seawright and MacKinnon [114] and by Creasy [36]. VM/370 itself evolved into today's z/VM, by way of VM/XA and VM/ESA.

One of the most devious forms of Trojan horse was explained by Thompson in the lecture he gave upon receiving the Turing Award [129].

CHAPTER

8

Files and Other Persistent Storage

8.1 Introduction

In this chapter, you will study two different kinds of service, each of which can be provided by either an operating system or middleware, and each of which can take several different forms. *Persistence* services provide for the retention of data for periods of time that are long enough to include system crashes, power failures, and similar disruptions. *Access* services provide application programs the means to operate on objects that are identified by name or by other attributes, such as a portion of the contents. In principle, these two kinds of service are independent of one another: persistent objects can be identified by numeric address rather than by name, and naming can be applied to non-persistent objects. However, persistence and access services are often provided in concert, as with named files stored on disk. Therefore, I am addressing both in a single chapter.

Any kind of object that stores data can be persistent, whether the object is as simple as a sequence of bytes or as complex as an application-specific object, such as the representation of a retirement portfolio in a benefits management system. In contemporary mainstream systems, the three most common forms of persistent storage are as follows:

- A *file*, which is an array of bytes that can be modified in length, as well as read and written at any numerically specified position. (Historically, the word has had other meanings, but this definition has become dominant.) File storage is normally provided by operating systems and will serve as my primary example in this chapter.

- A *table*, which in a relational database system is a multiset of *rows* (also known as *tuples* or *records*). Each row provides an appropriately typed value for each of the table's *columns*. For example, a table of chapters might have a title column, which holds character strings, and a number column, which holds integers. Then an individual row within that table might contain the title `"Files and Other Persistent Storage"` and the number `8`. Database storage is normally provided by middleware, rather than by an operating system.

- A *persistent object*, which is an application-specific object of the sort associated with object-oriented programming languages. For example, Java objects can be made persistent. Persistent objects are normally supported by middleware using one of the previous two types of persistent storage. Unfortunately, there are many competing approaches to supporting persistent objects; even the Java API does not yet have a single standardized approach. Therefore, I will not discuss persistent objects any further.

Access services can also take a variety of forms, from a single directory of unique names to the sort of sophisticated full-text search familiar from the web. I will concentrate on two access options that are popular in operating systems and middleware:

- Hierarchical *directories* map names into objects, each of which can be a subdirectory, thereby forming a tree of directories (or nested file folders). In some variants, objects can be accessible through multiple names, either directly (multiple names refer to one object) or indirectly (one name refers to another name, which refers to an object). Operating systems generally use hierarchical directories to provide access to files.

- *Indexes* provide access to those objects that contain specified data. For example, an index on a table of orders could be used to find those rows that describe orders placed by a particular customer. Relational database middleware commonly uses indexes to provide access to rows. Files can also be indexed for fast searching.

The design of persistent storage mechanisms is influenced not only by the service being provided, but also by the underlying hardware technology. For many years the dominant technology has been moving-head magnetic disk drives; most experts expect this dominance to continue for years to come. Therefore, Section 8.2 summarizes the key performance characteristics of disk drives; this summary serves as background for the design decisions explained in the remainder of the chapter.

Then, in Section 8.3, I will present an external view of a persistence service, looking at the file operations made available by POSIX operating systems. This material is of practical value (you are more likely to use a file system than to design one) and serves to motivate the examination of file system design in subsequent sections. Only once you understand what requirements a persistence service needs to meet will it make sense to consider the internal mechanisms it uses to do so.

Moving into the underlying mechanisms for persistence, Sections 8.4 and 8.5 examine the techniques used to allocate disk space and the metadata used to package the allocated space into usable objects. For simplicity, these two sections make reference only to file systems. However, the techniques used to provide space for a database table are fundamentally no different than for a file.

Next, I turn in Section 8.6 to the primary mechanisms for locating data: directories and indexes. Initially, I explain how these mechanisms are used in the traditional context of file directories and database indexes, and I point out that they are variations on the common theme of providing access through search keys. I then give a brief example of how these mechanisms can be merged to provide index-based file access. Before leaving the high-level view of access services, I explain one topic of particular interest to system administrators and application programmers: the ways in which multiple names can refer to the same file. Moving into the internals, I then present the data structures commonly used to store the directories or indexes for efficient access.

Persistent storage needs to retain its integrity in the face of system crashes. For example, no disk space should ever be both assigned to a file and marked as free for other use, even if the system crashed just as the space was being allocated. Similar properties are needed for directories and indexes; if a crash occurs while a file is being renamed, the file should have either its old name or its new name, but not both or neither. Because Chapter 5 covered the use of logs to provide durable atomic transactions, you have already seen the primary mechanism used to ensure integrity in contemporary persistent storage systems. Nonetheless, I devote Section 8.7 to the topic of metadata integrity so that I can sketch the alternative approaches to this problem.

Many operating systems allow file systems of varying designs to be mixed together. A Linux system might use one disk partition to store a Linux-specific file system, while another partition holds a file system designed for Microsoft Windows or Mac OS X. This mixing of file systems provides a valuable case study of *polymorphism*, that is, the use of multiple implementations for a common interface. I devote Section 8.8 to this topic.

Finally, I give some attention to security issues in Section 8.9 before closing with the usual selection of exercises, projects, and bibliographic notes.

8.2 Disk Storage Technology

A disk drive stores fixed-sized blocks of data known as *sectors*; a typical sector size is 512 bytes. The interface between a contemporary disk drive and a computer is conceptually quite simple, essentially just a large array of sectors. Just like in any array, the sectors are consecutively numbered, from 0 up to a maximum that depends on the capacity of the drive. The computer can ask the disk controller to perform two basic operations:

- The computer can request that the controller *write* data from a specified physical address in the main memory (RAM) to a specified sector number on the disk. For reasons you will see in the remainder of this section, the write request can also specify a number of consecutive sectors to be transferred.

- The computer can request that the controller *read* data from a specified sector number to a specified physical address in the main memory. Again, the read request can specify that multiple consecutive sectors be transferred.

This view of the disk drive as one large array of sectors suffices for writing correct software, but not for writing software that performs well. Because some disk accesses involve far more mechanical movement than others, the access time can vary substantially. In particular, contemporary disk drives can sustain data transfer rates measured in tens of megabytes per second if accessed optimally, but only tens of kilobytes per second if accessed randomly. To understand what the software needs to do to avoid this performance penalty of three orders of magnitude, it helps to look inside the black box at the internal structure of a disk drive, as in Figure 8.1.

A disk drive contains a stack of platters mounted on a common spindle and spinning at a fixed rotational speed, such as 10,000 revolutions per minute. Data is recorded onto the surface of the platters and read back off using heads, one recording and playback head per surface. The heads are supported by an arm that can pivot so as to position the heads nearer or further from the central spindle; Figure 8.1 shows the relationship between the platters, the spindle, and the head arm. If the arm is left in a fixed position, the rotation of the disks causes a circular region of each disk surface to pass under the corresponding head. This circular region of a single disk surface is known as a *track*; each track is divided into hundreds of sectors. The collection of tracks, one per disk surface, accessible at a particular position of the head arm is called a *cylinder*.

Only one head can be active at any time. Depending on which head is active and the position of the head arm, a single track's worth of sectors can be read or written. In order to access more data than can fit in a single track, there are two options. A *head switch* changes the active head and thereby provides access to another track in the

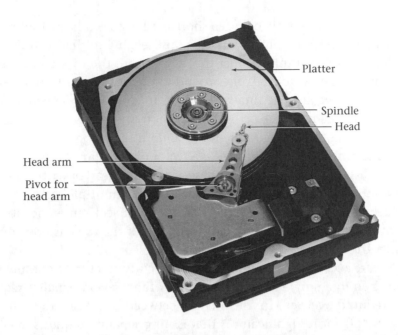

Platter

Spindle

Head

Head arm

Pivot for
head arm

Figure 8.1 In this photo of an opened disk drive, a stack of four platters is visible at the top, with a head arm extending into the platter area. The part you can see is the topmost layer of the head arm, holding the head for the top surface of the top platter. Similar layers are stacked below it; for example, the next layer down has heads for the bottom of the top platter and the top of the second platter. Photo copyright by and reprinted by courtesy of Seagate Technology LLC.

same cylinder. A *seek* moves the arm to a position closer or further from the spindle in order to provide access to another cylinder. As it happens, the head switch time on a modern drive is quite similar to the time needed to seek to an adjacent cylinder—a fraction of a millisecond—so the distinction is not important; henceforth, I'll talk only about seeking.

The seek time is larger for tracks that are further apart, but not proportionately so, for some of the same reasons as the duration of an automobile trip is not proportional to its distance. Just as an automobile needs to accelerate at the beginning of a trip, decelerate at the end of the trip, and then painstakingly pull into a parking spot, so too a disk arm needs to accelerate, decelerate, and home in on the exact position of the destination track. The net result of this is that seeking to a track tens of thousands of cylinders away may take 5 milliseconds, only ten times as long as seeking to an adjoining track. Seeking to an adjoining track already takes long enough that tens of kilobytes of data could have been transferred were the drive not busy seeking.

Even the ten-fold speed ratio between short and long seeks is misleading, however, because accessing a sector involves more than just seeking to that sector's track. Once the appropriate track is spinning under the active head, the disk controller needs to wait for the appropriate sector to come around to the head's position, a delay known as *rotational latency*. Because the time a disk takes to complete one revolution is comparable to the time taken to seek across tens of thousands of cylinders, the rotational latency can bring the total access time for a random sector on an adjoining track to within a small factor of the access time for a sector on a distant track.

Once an access is underway, additional sectors can be read or written at high speed as they pass under the head assembly. Even a request for multiple sectors that happens to cross a track boundary will pay only the penalty of seek time and not the larger penalty of rotational latency, because the first sector of the track is positioned so that it passes under the head just after the seek completes.

If the software accesses a large number of consecutive sectors, there are two advantages for doing so in a single large request rather than several smaller requests. One advantage is reduced overhead in the interface between computer and disk. The other difference, which is more significant, is that issuing separate requests may cost additional disk revolutions, particularly for writes; missing the timing for a sector means waiting a full revolution for it to come around again. (Reads are less of a problem because disk drives contain on-board RAM, known as *cache buffers*, to hold data that has passed under the active head, so that it can be accessed without waiting for it to come around again. Disks can use the cache buffers for writes as well, but only if the software is designed to tolerate some loss of recently written data upon system crash.)

Thus, the secrets to attaining a disk drive's full potential are locality, locality, and locality:

- Accessing a sector with a similar identifying number to the most recently accessed one will generally be faster than accessing a sector with a greatly different number.

- Accessing consecutive sectors will generally be faster than accessing sectors that have even small differences in their sector numbers.

- Accessing consecutive sectors in one large request will be faster than accessing them in several smaller requests.

You should keep these performance issues related to locality in mind when considering topics such as how disk space is allocated.

There is one other performance issue, less directly related to locality, which I will only briefly mention here. (Seeing how it influences software design would be interesting, but beyond the level of this book.) The software should not wait for the disk drive to complete each request before issuing the next request, which may be from a different thread. Disk drives are capable of queuing up multiple requests and then handling them in whichever order best utilizes the mechanical components. For example, if several accesses to the same track are queued, the disk drive can perform them in the order the sectors happen to pass under the head.

Throughout this chapter, I will focus on systems that employ a single disk drive, for the sake of simplicity. Using multiple drives to divide or replicate data raises interesting trade-offs of reliability and performance; the notes section at the end of the chapter suggests some readings if you want to explore this area.

8.3 POSIX File API

All UNIX-like systems (including Linux and Mac OS X) support a rather complicated set of procedures for operating on files, which has evolved over the decades, eventually becoming part of the POSIX standard. For most everyday purposes, programmers can and should ignore this API, instead using one of the cleaner, higher-level APIs built on top of it, such as those included in the Java and C++ standards. Nonetheless, I will introduce the POSIX API here, because in many important systems, it forms the interface between the operating system kernel and software running in user-level application processes, even if the latter is encapsulated in libraries.

8.3.1 File Descriptors

Files are referred to in two different ways: by character-string *pathnames* (such as `microshell.c` or `/etc/passwd`) and by integer *file descriptors* (such as 0, 1, or 17). A pathname is a name of a file, optionally including a sequence of directories used to reach it. A file descriptor, on the other hand, provides no information about the file's name or location; it is just a featureless integer.

Many operations require file descriptors; in particular, to read data from a file or write data into a file requires a file descriptor. If a process happens to have inherited a file descriptor when it was forked from its parent (or happens to have received the file descriptor in a message from another process), then it can read or write the file without ever knowing a name for it. Otherwise, the process can use the **open** procedure to obtain a file descriptor for a named file. When the process is done with the file descriptor, it can **close** it. (When a process terminates, the operating system automatically closes any remaining open file descriptors.)

File descriptors can refer not only to open files, but also to other sources and destinations for input and output, such as the keyboard and the display screen. Some procedures will work only for regular files, whereas others work equally well for hardware devices, network communication ports, and so forth. I will flag some places these distinctions matter; however, my primary focus will be on regular files, stored on disk.

By convention, all processes inherit at least three file descriptors from their parent. These file descriptors, known as the *standard input*, *standard output*, and *standard error output*, are numbered 0, 1, and 2, respectively. Rather than remembering the numbers, you should use the symbolic names defined in `unistd.h`, namely, `STDIN_FILENO`, `STDOUT_FILENO`, and `STDERR_FILENO`.

When you run a program from a shell and don't make special arrangements, standard input generally is your keyboard, while the standard output and error output are both directed to the shell's window on your display screen. You can redirect the standard input or output to a file by using the shell's `<` and `>` notations. For example, the shell command

```
ps l >my-processes
```

runs the `ps` program with the `l` option to generate a list of processes, as you saw in Chapter 7. However, rather than displaying the list on your screen, this command puts the list into a file called `my-processes`. The `ps` program doesn't need to know anything about this change; it writes its output to the standard output in either case. Only the shell needs to do something different, namely, closing the preexisting standard output and opening the file in its place before executing the `ps` program. If the `ps` program has any error messages to report, it outputs them to the standard error output, which remains connected to your display screen. That way, the error messages aren't hidden in the `my-processes` file.

Figure 8.2 contains a program illustrating how the shell would operate in the preceding example, with a child process closing its inherited standard output and then opening `my-processes` before executing `ps`. The most complicated procedure call is the one to `open`. The first argument is the name of the file to open. Because this character string does not contain any slash characters (`/`), the file is found in the process's current directory. (Every process has a current *working directory*, which can be changed using the `chdir` procedure.) If the name contained one or more slashes, such as `alpha/beta/gamma` or `/etc/passwd`, then the operating system would traverse one or more directories to find the file to open. In particular, `alpha/beta/gamma` would start with the current directory, look for the subdirectory `alpha`, look in `alpha` for `beta`, and finally look in `beta` for the file `gamma`. Because `/etc/passwd` starts with a slash, the search for this file would begin by looking in the root directory for `etc` and then in that directory for `passwd`. In Section 8.6, I will discuss file naming further, including related aspects of the POSIX API, such as how a file can be given an additional name or have a name removed.

The second argument to `open` specifies the particular way in which the file should be opened. Here, the `O_WRONLY` indicates the file should be opened for writing only (as opposed to `O_RDONLY` or `O_RDWR`), the `O_CREAT` indicates that the file should be

```cpp
#include <unistd.h>
#include <stdio.h>
#include <iostream>
#include <fcntl.h>
#include <sys/wait.h>
#include <sys/stat.h>
using namespace std;

int main(){
  pid_t returnedValue = fork();
  if(returnedValue < 0){
    perror("error forking");
    return -1;
  } else if (returnedValue == 0){
    if(close(STDOUT_FILENO) < 0){
      perror("error closing standard output");
      return -1;
    }
    // When there is no error, open returns the smallest file
    // descriptor not already in use by this process, so having
    // closed STDOUT_FILENO, the open should reuse that number.
    if(open("my-processes", O_WRONLY | O_CREAT | O_TRUNC,
            S_IRUSR | S_IWUSR) < 0){
      perror("error opening my-processes");
      return -1;
    }
    execlp("ps", "ps", "l", NULL);  // ps with option letter l
    perror("error executing ps");
    return -1;
  } else {
    if(waitpid(returnedValue, 0, 0) < 0){
      perror("error waiting for child");
      return -1;
    }
    cout << "Note the parent still has the old standard output."
        << endl;
  }
}
```

Figure 8.2 This C++ program, `file-processes.cpp`, illustrates how the shell runs the command `ps l >my-processes`. After forking, the child process closes the inherited standard output and in its place opens `my-processes` before executing `ps`.

created if it doesn't already exist (rather than signaling an error), and the O_TRUNC indicates that the file should be truncated to zero length before writing; that is, all the old data (if any) should be thrown out. Because the O_CREAT option is specified, the third argument to open is needed; it specifies the access permissions that should be given to the file, if it is created. In this case, the access permissions are read and write for the owning user only, that is, rw-------.

Even setting aside open and close, not all operations on files involve reading or writing the contents of the file. Some operate on the *metadata attributes*—attributes describing a file—such as the access permissions, time of last modification, or owner. A variety of procedures, such as chmod, utime, and chown, allow these attributes to be set; I won't detail them. I will, however, illustrate one procedure that allows the attributes of a file to be retrieved. The C++ program in Figure 8.3 uses the fstat procedure to retrieve information about its standard input. It then reports just a few

```cpp
#include <unistd.h>
#include <time.h>
#include <sys/stat.h>
#include <stdio.h>
#include <iostream>
using namespace std;

int main(){
  struct stat info;
  if(fstat(STDIN_FILENO, &info) < 0){
    perror("Error getting info about standard input");
    return -1;
  }
  cout << "Standard input is owned by user number "
       << info.st_uid << endl;
  cout << "and was last modified " << ctime(&info.st_mtime);
  if(S_ISREG(info.st_mode)){
    cout << "It is a " << info.st_size << "-byte file." << endl;
  } else {
    cout << "It is not a regular file." << endl;
  }
  return 0;
}
```

Figure 8.3 This C++ program, fstater.cpp, describes its standard input, using information retrieved using fstat. That information includes the owner, last modification time, and whether the standard input is from a regular file. In the latter case, the size of the file is also available.

of the attributes from the larger package of information. After printing the owner and modification time stamp, the program checks whether the standard input is from a regular file, as it would be if the shell were told to redirect standard input, using `<`. Only in this case does the program print out the file's size, because the concept of size doesn't make any sense for the stream of input coming from the keyboard, for example. If this program is compiled in a file called **fstater**, then the shell command

```
./fstater </etc/passwd
```

would give you information about the **/etc/passwd** file, which you could verify using the command **ls -ln /etc/passwd**.

Moving on to actually reading or writing the contents of a file, the low-level POSIX API provides three different choices. A file (or a portion thereof) can be mapped into the process's address space using the **mmap** procedure, allowing normal memory loads and stores to do the reading and writing. Alternatively, the file can be left outside the address space, and individual portions explicitly read or written using procedures that copy from the file into memory or from memory into the file. One version of these procedures (**pread** and **pwrite**) needs to be told what position within the file to read or write, whereas the other version (**read** and **write**) operates sequentially, with each operation implicitly using the portion of the file immediately after the preceding operation. I'll discuss all three possibilities at least briefly, because each has its virtues. Because **mmap** is the simplest procedure, I will start with it.

8.3.2 Mapping Files into Virtual Memory

The use of **mmap** is illustrated by the C++ program in Figures 8.4 and 8.5, which copies the contents of one file to another. The program expects to be given the names of the input and output files as **argv[1]** and **argv[2]**, respectively. It uses the **open** procedure to translate these into integer file descriptors, **fd_in** and **fd_out**. By using **fstat** (as in Figure 8.3), it finds the size of the input file. This size (**info.st_size**) plays three roles. One is that the program makes the output file the same size, using **ftruncate**. (Despite its name, **ftruncate** does not necessarily make a file shorter; it sets the file's size, whether by truncating it or by padding it out with zero bytes.) Another use of the input file's size is for the two calls to **mmap**, which map the input and output files into virtual memory, with read-only and write-only protections, respectively. The returned values, **addr_in** and **addr_out**, are the virtual addresses at which the two files start in the process's address space. The third use of the input file size is to tell the library procedure **memcpy** how many bytes to copy from **addr_in** to **addr_out**. The **memcpy** procedure is a loop that executes load and store instructions to copy from one place in virtual memory to another. (This loop could be written explicitly in C++, but would

```
#include <unistd.h>
#include <fcntl.h>
#include <sys/stat.h>
#include <sys/mman.h>
#include <stdio.h>
#include <string.h>
#include <iostream>
using namespace std;

int main(int argc, char *argv[]){
  if(argc != 3){
    cerr << "Usage: " << argv[0] << " infile outfile" << endl;
    return -1;
  }
  int fd_in = open(argv[1], O_RDONLY);
  if(fd_in < 0){
    perror(argv[1]);
    return -1;
  }
  struct stat info;
  if(fstat(fd_in, &info) < 0){
    perror("Error stating input file");
    return -1;
  }
  void *addr_in =
    mmap(0, info.st_size, PROT_READ, MAP_SHARED, fd_in, 0);
  if(addr_in == MAP_FAILED){
    perror("Error mapping input file");
    return -1;
  }
```

Figure 8.4 This is the first portion of `cpmm.cpp`, a C++ program using virtual memory mapping to copy a file. The program is continued in the next figure.

be less clear and likely less efficient as well, because the library routine is very carefully tuned for speed.)

Of course, I haven't explained all the arguments to `mmap`, or many other details. My intent here is not to provide comprehensive documentation for these API procedures, nor to provide a complete tutorial. Instead, the example should suffice to give you some feel for file I/O using `mmap`; files are opened, then mapped into the virtual address space, and then accessed as any other memory would be, for example, using `memcpy`.

The underlying idea behind virtual memory-based file access (using `mmap`) is that files are arrays of bytes, just like regions of virtual address space; thus, file access can be

```
  int fd_out =
    open(argv[2], O_RDWR | O_CREAT | O_TRUNC, S_IRUSR | S_IWUSR);
  if(fd_out < 0){
    perror(argv[2]);
    return -1;
  }
  if(ftruncate(fd_out, info.st_size) < 0){
    perror("Error setting output file size");
    return -1;
  }
  void *addr_out =
    mmap(0, info.st_size, PROT_WRITE, MAP_SHARED, fd_out, 0);
  if(addr_out == MAP_FAILED){
    perror("Error mapping output file");
    return -1;
  }
  memcpy(addr_out, addr_in, info.st_size);
  return 0;
}
```

Figure 8.5   This is the second portion of **cpmm.cpp**, a C++ program using virtual memory mapping to copy a file. The program is continued from the previous figure.

treated as virtual memory access. The next style of file I/O to consider accepts half of this argument (that files are arrays of bytes) but rejects the other half (that they should therefore be treated the same as memory). In Section 8.3.4, you will see a third style of I/O, which largely rejects even the first premise.

8.3.3 Reading and Writing Files at Specified Positions

Although convenient, accessing files as virtual memory is not without disadvantages. In particular, writing files using **mmap** raises two problems:

- The process has no easy way to control the time at which its updates are made persistent. Specifically, there is no simple way for the process to ensure that a data structure is written to disk only after it is in a consistent state, rather than in the middle of a series of related updates.

- A process can write a file only if it has read permission as well as write permission, because all page faults implicitly read from the file, even if the page faults occur in the course of writing data into the file's portion of virtual memory.

For these and other reasons, some programmers prefer to leave files separate from the virtual memory address space and use procedures in the POSIX API that explicitly copy data from a file into memory or from memory into a file. The `pread` and `pwrite` procedures take as arguments a file descriptor, a virtual address in memory, a number of bytes to copy, and a position within the file. Each procedure copies bytes starting from the specified position in the file and the specified address in memory—`pread` from the file to the memory and `pwrite` from the memory to the file. These procedures are somewhat tricky to use correctly, because they may copy fewer bytes than requested, and because they may signal error conditions that go away upon retrying the operation. Therefore, they always need to be put in carefully designed loops. For this reason, I will not devote space to an example here.

8.3.4 Sequential Reading and Writing

Both `mmap` and the `pread`/`pwrite` pair rely on the ability to access arbitrary positions within a file; that is, they treat the file as an array of bytes. As such, neither interface will work for other sources of input and destinations for output, such as keyboards and network connections. Instead, one needs to use a sequential style of I/O, where each read or write operation takes place not at a specified position, but wherever the last one left off.

Sequential I/O is also quite convenient for many purposes, even when used with files. For example, suppose you give the following command in a shell:

```
(ls; ps) > information
```

This opens the file named `information` for writing as the standard output and then runs two programs in succession: `ls` to list the files in the current directory and `ps` to list processes. The net result is that `information` contains both listings, one after the other. The `ps` command does not need to take any special steps to direct its output to the position in the file immediately after where `ls` stopped. Instead, by using the sequential I/O features of the POSIX API, each of the two processes naturally winds up writing each byte of output to the position after the previously written byte, whether that previous byte was written by the same process or not.

A process can perform sequential I/O using the `read` and `write` procedures, which are identical to `pread` and `pwrite`, except that they do not take an argument specifying the position within the file. Instead, each implicitly is directed to read or write at the current *file offset* and to update that file offset. The file offset is a position for reading and writing that is maintained by the operating system.

For special files such as keyboard input, sequential input is intrinsic, without needing an explicit file offset. For regular files stored on disk, however, the file offset is a numeric position within the file (of the same kind `pread` and `pwrite` take as arguments) that the operating system keeps track of behind the scenes. Whenever a file is opened, the operating system creates an *open file description*, a capability-like structure that includes the file offset, normally initialized to 0. Any file descriptors descended from that same call to `open` share the same open file description. For example, in the previous example of `ls` and `ps` writing to the `information` file, each of the two processes has its own file descriptor, but they are referring to the same open file description, and hence share the same file offset. If a process independently calls `open` on the same file, however, it will get a separate file offset.

A process implicitly increases the file offset whenever it does a `read` or `write` of more than zero bytes. It can also explicitly change the file offset using the `lseek` procedure. The `lseek` procedure can set the file offset anywhere within the file (for a regular disk file). As such, a process can use the combination of `lseek` and `read` or `write` to simulate `pread` or `pwrite`. However, this simulation is prone to races if multiple threads or processes share the same open file description, unless they use some synchronization mechanism, such as a mutex.

Normally `lseek` is used only infrequently, with sequential access predominating. For example, a process may read a whole file sequentially, using `read`, and then use `lseek` to set it back to the beginning to read a second time. The conceptual model is based on a tape drive, where ordinary reads and writes progress sequentially through the tape, but rewinding or skipping forward is also possible.

The `read` and `write` procedures share the same difficulty as `pread` and `pwrite`: the necessity of looping until all bytes have been transferred. It is much easier to use the I/O facilities defined in the standard libraries for higher level programming languages, such as Java or C++. Behind the scenes, these libraries are using `read` and `write` and doing the looping (and other details) for you.

8.4 Disk Space Allocation

A file system is analogous to a virtual memory system, in that each uses a level of indirection to map objects into storage locations. In virtual memory, the mapping is from virtual addresses within address spaces to physical addresses within memory. In a file system, the mapping is from positions within files to locations on disk. For efficiency, the mapping is done at a coarse granularity, several kilobytes at a time. In virtual memory, each page is mapped into a page frame; in a file system, each block of a file is mapped into a disk block. (You will see that blocks are typically several kilobytes in size, spanning multiple sectors.)

When discussing virtual memory, I remarked that the operating system was free to assign any unused page frame of physical memory to hold each page of virtual memory. However, although any allocation policy would be correct, some might cause cache memory to perform better.

Persistent storage faces a similar allocation problem, but the performance issues are considerably more pronounced. A file system has the freedom to store data in any otherwise unused disk block. The choices it makes determine how accesses to files translate into accesses to disk. You have already seen that the pattern of disk access can make a huge performance difference (three orders of magnitude). Thus, I will examine allocation policies here more closely than I examined placement policies in Chapter 6.

Before I get into allocation policies themselves and their embodiment in allocation mechanisms, I will look at the key objectives for allocation: minimizing wasted space and time. As you will see in Sections 8.4.1 and 8.4.2, these goals can be expressed as minimizing fragmentation and maximizing locality.

8.4.1 Fragmentation

The word *fragmentation* is used in two different senses. First, consider the definition I will *not* be using. For some authors, fragmentation refers to the degree to which a file is stored in multiple noncontiguous regions of the disk. A file that is stored in a single contiguous sequence of disk blocks (called an *extent*) is not fragmented at all, by this definition. A file stored in two separate extents would be slightly fragmented. If the file's blocks are individually scattered across the disk, then the file is maximally fragmented, by this definition. A *defragmentation* program moves files' blocks around on disk so as to leave each file in a single extent. To allow future allocations to be non-fragmented, the defragmentation program also arranges the files so that the free space on the disk is clustered together.

The contiguity and sequentiality issues mentioned in the preceding paragraph are important for speed of access; I will discuss them in Section 8.4.2 under the broader heading of locality. However, I will not refer to them as fragmentation, because I will use another definition that is well established in the operating systems field. By this alternative definition, fragmentation concerns space efficiency. A highly fragmented disk is one in which a large proportion of the storage capacity is unavailable for allocation to files. I will explain in the remainder of this subsection the phenomena that cause space to be unusable.

One source of waste is that space is allocated only in integer multiples of some file system block size. For example, a file system might allocate space only in units of 4 KB. A file that is too big to fit in a single 4-KB unit will be allocated 8 KB of space—even if it is only a single byte larger than 4 KB. The unused space in the last file block is called *internal fragmentation*. The amount of internal fragmentation depends not only on the desired file sizes, but also on the file system block size. As an analogy, consider parallel parking in an area where individual parking spaces are marked with painted lines, and where drivers actually respect those lines. The amount of wasted space depends on the cars being parked, but it also depends on how far apart the lines are painted. Larger parking spaces will generally result in more wasted space.

The file system block size is always some multiple of the underlying disk drive's sector size; no file system ever subdivides the space within a single disk sector. Generally, the file system blocks span several consecutive disk sectors; for example, eight disk sectors of 512 bytes each might be grouped into each 4-KB file system block. Larger file system blocks cause more internal fragmentation, but are advantageous from other perspectives. In particular, you will see that a larger block size tends to reduce external fragmentation. Additionally, a larger block size implies that there are fewer blocks to keep track of, which reduces bookkeeping overhead.

Once a space allocation request has been rounded up to the next multiple of the block size, the operating system must locate the appropriate number of unused blocks. In order to read or write the file as quickly as possible, the blocks should be in a single consecutive extent. For the moment, I will consider this to be an absolute requirement. Later, I will consider relaxing it.

Continuing with my earlier example, suppose you need space for a file that is just one byte larger than 4 KB and hence has been rounded up to two 4-KB blocks. The new requirement of contiguity means that you are looking for somewhere on the disk where two consecutive 4-KB blocks are free. Perhaps you are out of luck. Maybe the disk is only half full, but the half that is full consists of every even-numbered file system block with all the odd-numbered ones available for use. This situation, where there is lots of space available but not enough grouped together in any one place, is *external fragmentation*. So long as you insist on contiguous allocation, external fragmentation is another cause of wasted space: blocks that are free for use, but are too scattered to be usable.

On the surface, it appears that external fragmentation would result only from very strange circumstances. My example, in which every second file system block is occupied, would certainly fit that description. To start with, it implies that you allocated lots of small files and now suddenly want to allocate a larger file. Second, it implies that you either were really dumb in choosing where those small files went (skipping every other block), or had phenomenally bad luck in the user's choice of which files to delete.

However, external fragmentation can occur from much more plausible circumstances. In particular, you can wind up with only small gaps of space available even if all the allocations have been for much larger amounts of space and even if the previous allocations were done without leaving silly gaps for no reason.

For a small scenario that illustrates the phenomenon, consider a disk that has room for only 14 file system blocks. Suppose you start by allocating three four-block files. At this point, the space allocation might look as follows:

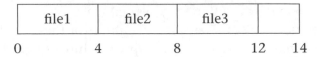

Suppose file2 is now deleted, resulting in a four-block gap, with another two blocks free at the end of the disk:

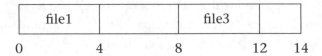

If, at this point, a three-block file (file4) is created, it can go into the four-block gap, leaving one block unused:

Now there are three unused blocks, but there is no way to satisfy another three-block allocation request, because the three unused blocks are broken up, with one block between files 4 and 3, and two more blocks at the end of the disk.

Notice that you wound up with a one-block gap not because a one-block file was created and later deleted (or because of stupid allocation), but because a four-block file was replaced by a three-block file. The resulting gap is the difference in the file sizes. This means that even if a disk is used exclusively for storing large files, it may still wind up with small gaps, which cannot hold any large files. This is the fundamental problem of external fragmentation.

Returning to the parallel parking analogy, consider an area where no parking spaces are marked on the pavement, leaving drivers to allocate their own spaces. Even if they are courteous enough not to leave any pointless gaps, small gaps will arise as cars of varying sizes come and go. A large car may vacate a space, which is then taken by a smaller car. The result is a gap equal to the difference in car sizes, too small for even the smallest cars to use. If this situation happens repeatedly at different spots along a block, there may be enough total wasted space to accommodate a car, but not all in one place.

Earlier, I mentioned that increasing the file system block size, which increases internal fragmentation, decreases external fragmentation. The reason for this is that with a larger block size, there is less variability in the amount of space being allocated. Files that might have different sizes when rounded up to the next kilobyte (say, 14 KB and 15 KB) may have the same size when rounded to the next multiple of 4 KB (in this case, 16 KB and 16 KB). Reduced variability reduces external fragmentation; in the extreme case, no external fragmentation at all occurs if the files are all allocated the same amount of space.

Suppose you relax the requirement that a file be allocated a single extent of the disk. Using file metadata, it is possible to store different blocks of the file in different locations, much as a virtual memory address space can be scattered throughout physical memory. Does this mean that external fragmentation is a nonissue? No, because for performance reasons, you will still want to allocate the file contiguously as much as possible. Therefore, external fragmentation will simply change from being a space-efficiency issue (free space that cannot be used) to a time-efficiency issue (free space that cannot be used without file access becoming slower). This gets us into the next topic, locality.

8.4.2 Locality

Recall that disks provide their fastest performance when asked to access a large number of consecutive sectors in a single request at a location nearby to the previous access request. Most file system designers have interpreted these conditions for fast access as implying the following locality guidelines for space allocation:

1. The space allocated for each file should be broken into as few extents as possible.

2. If a file needs to be allocated more than one extent, each extent should be nearby to the previous one.

3. Files that are commonly used in close succession (or concurrently) should be placed near one another.

The connection between fast access and these three guidelines is based on an implicit assumption that the computer system's workload largely consists of accessing one file at a time and reading or writing each file in its entirety, from beginning to end. In many cases, this is a reasonable approximation to the truth, and so the preceding locality guidelines do result in good performance. However, it is important to remember that the guidelines incorporate an assumption about the workload as well as the disk performance characteristics. For some workloads, a different allocation strategy may be appropriate.

As an example of a different allocation strategy that might make sense, Rosenblum and Ousterhout suggested that blocks should be allocated space on disk in the order they are written, without regard to what files they belong to or what positions they occupy within those files. By issuing a large number of consecutive writes to the disk in a single operation, this allows top performance for writing. Even if the application software is concurrently writing to multiple files, and doing so at random positions within those files, the write operations issued to disk will be optimal, unlike with the more conventional file layout. Of course, read accesses will be efficient only if they are performed in the same order as the writes were. Fortunately, some workloads do perform reads in the same order as writes, and some other workloads do not need efficient read access. In particular, the efficiency of read access is not critical in a workload that reads most disk blocks either never or repeatedly. Those blocks that are never read are not a problem, and those that are read repeatedly need only suffer the cost of disk access time once and can thereafter be kept in RAM.

Returning to the more mainstream strategy listed at the beginning of this subsection, the primary open question is how to identify files that are likely to be accessed contemporaneously, so as to place them nearby to one another on disk. One approach, used in UNIX file systems, is to assume that files are commonly accessed in conjunction with their parent directory or with other (sibling) files in the same directory. Another approach is to not base the file placement on assumptions, but rather on observed behavior. (One assumption remains: that future behavior will be like past behavior.) For example, Microsoft introduced a feature into Windows with the XP version, in which the system observes the order of file accesses at system boot time and also at application startup time, and then reorganizes the disk space allocation based on those observed access orders. Mac OS X does something similar as of version 10.3: it measures which files are heavily used and groups them together.

8.4.3 Allocation Policies and Mechanisms

Having seen the considerations influencing disk space allocation (fragmentation and locality), you are now in a better position to appreciate the specific allocation mechanism used by any particular file system and the policy choices embodied in that mechanism. The full range of alternatives found in different file systems is too broad to consider in any detail here, but I will sketch some representative options.

Each file system has some way of keeping track of which disk blocks are in use and which are free to be allocated. The most common representation for this information is a *bitmap*, that is, an array of bits, one per disk block, with bit i indicating whether block i is in use. With a bitmap, it is easy to look for space in one particular region of the disk, but slow to search an entire large disk for a desired size extent of free space.

Many UNIX and Linux file systems use a slight variant on the bitmap approach. Linux's ext3fs file system can serve as an example. The overall disk space is divided into modest-sized chunks known as *block groups*. On a system with 4-KB disk blocks, a block group might encompass 128 MB. Each block group has its own bitmap, indicating which blocks within that group are free. (In Exercise 8.8, you can show that in the example given, each block group's bitmap fits within a single block.) Summary information for the file system as a whole indicates how much free space each block group has, but not the specific location of the free space within the block groups. Thus, allocation can be done in two steps: first find a suitable block group using the summary information, and then find a suitable collection of blocks within the block group, using its bitmap.

I remarked earlier that UNIX and Linux file systems generally try to allocate each file near its parent directory. In particular, regular files are placed in the same block group as the parent directory, provided that there is any space in that group. If this rule were also followed for subdirectories, the result would be an attempt to cram the entire file system into one block group. Therefore, these file systems use an alternative rule to choose a block group for a subdirectory.

When creating a subdirectory, early versions of ext3fs and similar file systems selected a block group containing a lot of free space. This spread the directories, with their corresponding files, relatively evenly through the whole disk. Because each new directory went into a block group with lots of free space, there was a good chance that the files contained in that directory would fit in the same block group with it. However, traversing a directory tree could take a long time with these allocation policies, because each directory might be nowhere near its parent directory.

Therefore, more recent versions of ext3fs and similar file systems have used a different allocation policy for directories, developed by Orlov. A subdirectory is allocated in the parent directory's block group, provided that it doesn't get too crowded. Failing that, the allocation policy looks through the subsequent block groups for one that isn't too crowded. This preserves locality across entire directory trees without stuffing any block group so full of directories that the corresponding files won't fit. The result can be significant performance improvements for workloads that traverse directory trees.

Once a file system decides to locate a file within a particular block group, it still needs to allocate one or more extents of disk blocks to hold the file's data. (Hopefully those extents will all lie within the chosen block group, although there needs to be a way for large files to escape from the confines of a single block group.)

The biggest challenge in allocating extents is knowing how big an extent to allocate. Some older file systems required application programmers to specify each file's size at the time the file was created, so that the system could allocate an extent of corresponding size. However, modern systems don't work this way; instead, each file grows automatically to accommodate the data written into it.

To meet this challenge, modern operating systems use a technique known as *delayed allocation*. As background, you need to understand that operating systems do not normally write data to disk the moment an application program issues a write request. Instead, the data is stored in RAM and written back to disk later. This delay in writing yields two options for when the disk space is allocated: when the data goes into RAM or later when it gets written to disk.

Without delayed allocation, the operating system needs to choose a disk block to hold the data at the time it goes into RAM. The system tags the data in RAM with the disk block in which that data belongs. Later, the system writes the data out to the specified location on disk. This approach is simple, but requires the operating system to allocate space for the first block of data as soon as it is generated, before there is any clue how many more blocks will follow.

Delayed allocation puts off the choice of disk block until the time of actually writing to disk; the data stored in RAM is tagged only with the file it should be written to and the position within that file. Now the operating system does not need to guess how much data a program is going to write at the time when it generates the first block. Instead, it can wait and see how much data gets written and allocate an extent that size.

Once the operating system knows the desired extent size, it needs to search the data structure that records the available space. Bitmaps (whether in individual block groups or otherwise) are not the only option for tracking free space. The XFS file system, which was particularly designed for large file systems, takes an alternative approach. It uses balanced search trees, known as B-trees, to track the free extents of disk space. One B-tree stores the free extents indexed by their location while another indexes them by their size. That way, XFS can quickly locate free space near a specified location on disk or can quickly locate a desired amount of space. Technically, the trees used by XFS are a slight variant of B-trees, known as B^+-trees. I'll describe this data structure in Section 8.5.1.

With free extents indexed by size in a B^+-tree, the XFS allocator can naturally use a *best-fit* policy, where it finds the smallest free extent bigger than the desired size. (If the fit is not exact, the extra space can be broken off and left as a smaller free extent.) With a bitmap, on the other hand, the most natural allocation policy is *first-fit*, the policy of finding the first free extent that is large enough. Each policy has its merits; you can compare them in Exercise 8.9.

8.5 Metadata

You have seen that a file system is analogous to a virtual memory system. Each has an allocation policy to select concrete storage locations for each chunk of data. Continuing the analogy, I will now explain the *metadata* that serves as the analog of page tables. Recall that in a system with separate address spaces, each process has its own page table, storing the information regarding which page frame holds that process's page 0, page 1, and so forth. Similarly, each file has its own metadata storing the information regarding which disk block holds that file's block 0, block 1, and so forth. You will see that, as with page tables, there are several choices for the data structure holding this mapping information. I discuss these alternative structures in Section 8.5.1.

Metadata is data about data. Information regarding where on disk the data is stored is one very important kind of metadata. However, I will also more briefly enumerate other kinds. First, in Section 8.5.2, I will revisit access control, a topic I considered from another perspective in Chapter 7. In Section 8.5.2, the question is not how access control information is enforced during access attempts, but how it is stored in the file system. Second, I will look in Section 8.5.3 at the other more minor, miscellaneous kinds of metadata (beyond data location and access control), such as access dates and times.

Some authors include file names as a kind of metadata. This makes sense in those file systems where each file has exactly one name. However, most modern file systems do not fit this description; a file might have no names, or might have multiple names. Thus, you are better off thinking of a name not as a property of a file, but as a route that can lead to a file. Similarly, in other persistence services, data may be accessed through multiple routes, such as database indexes. Therefore, I will not include naming in this section on metadata, instead including it in Section 8.6 on directories and indexing.

8.5.1 Data Location Metadata

The simplest representation for data location metadata would be an array of disk block numbers, with element i of the array specifying which disk block holds block i of the file. This would be analogous to a linear page table. Traditional UNIX file systems (including Linux's ext2fs and ext3fs) use this approach for small files. Each file's array of disk block numbers is stored in the file's metadata structure known as its *inode* (short for *index node*). For larger files, these file systems keep the inodes compact by using indirect blocks, roughly analogous to multilevel page tables. I discuss the traditional form of inodes and indirect blocks next. Thereafter, I discuss two alternatives used in some more modern file systems: extent maps, which avoid storing information about individual blocks, and B-trees, which provide efficient access to large extent maps.

Inodes and Indirect Blocks

When UNIX was first developed in the early 1970s, one of its many innovative features was the file system design, a design that has served as the model for commonly used UNIX and Linux file systems to the present day, including Linux's ext3fs. The data-location metadata in these systems is stored in a data structure that can better be called expedient than elegant. However, the structure is efficient for small files, allows files to grow large, and can be manipulated by simple code.

Each file is represented by a compact chunk of data called an inode. The inode contains the file's metadata if the file is small or an initial portion of the metadata if the file is large. By allowing large files to have more metadata elsewhere (in indirect blocks), the inodes are kept to a small fixed size. Each file system contains an array of inodes, stored in disk blocks set aside for the purpose, with multiple inodes per block. Each inode is identified by its position in the array. These inode numbers (or *inumbers*) are the fundamental identifiers of the files in a file system; essentially, the files are identified as file 0, file 1, and so forth, which indicate the files with inodes in position 0, 1, and so forth. Later, in Section 8.6, you'll see how file names are mapped into inode numbers.

Each inode provides the metadata for one file. The metadata includes the disk block numbers holding that file's data, as well as the access permissions and other metadata. These categories of metadata are shown in Figure 8.6. In this simplified diagram, the inode directly contains the mapping information specifying which disk block contains each block of the file, much like a linear page table. Recall, however, that inodes are a small, fixed size, whereas files can grow to be many blocks long. To resolve this conflict, each inode directly contains the mapping information only for the first dozen or so blocks. (The exact number varies between file systems, but is consistent within any one file system.) Thus, a more realistic inode picture is as shown in Figure 8.7.

Before I go into detail on how further disk blocks are indirectly accessed, I should emphasize one aspect of the inode design. The low-numbered blocks of a file are mapped in the exact same way (directly in the inode) regardless of whether they are the only blocks in a small file or the first blocks of a large file. This means that large files have a peculiar asymmetry, with some blocks more efficiently accessible than others.

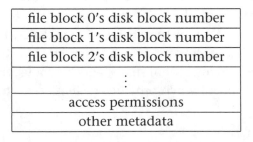

Figure 8.6 This initial approximation of an inode shows the principle categories of metadata. However, this diagram is unrealistic in that the list of disk block numbers seems to be unlimited, whereas actual inodes have only a limited amount of space.

file block 0's disk block number
⋮
file block 11's disk block number
indirect access to file block 12 through the end of the file
access permissions
other metadata

Figure 8.7 In this limited-size inode, blocks from number 12 to the end of the file are indirectly referenced.

Inode

file block 0's disk block number
⋮
file block 11's disk block number
indirect block's block number
access permissions
other metadata

Indirect block

file block 12's disk block number
⋮
file block 1035's disk block number

Figure 8.8 If an inode were used with a single indirect block, the block numbers would be stored as shown here. Note that the indirect block is actually considerably larger than the inode, contrary to its appearance in the figure.

The advantage is that when a file grows and transitions from being a small file to being a large one, the early blocks' mapping information remains unchanged.

Because most files are small, the inodes are kept small, a fraction of a block in size. (If inodes were full blocks, the overhead for single-block files would be 100 percent.) For those files large enough to overflow an inode, however, one can be less stingy in allocating space for metadata. Therefore, if the system needs more metadata space, it doesn't allocate a second inode; it allocates a whole additional disk block, an *indirect block*. This provides room for many more block numbers, as shown in Figure 8.8. The exact number of additional block numbers depends on how big blocks and block numbers are. With 4-KB blocks and 4-byte block numbers, an indirect block could hold 1 K block numbers (that is, 1024 block numbers), as shown in the figure. This kind of indirect block is more specifically called a *single indirect block*, because it adds only a single layer of indirection: the inode points to it, and it points to the data blocks.

In this example with 4-KB blocks, the single indirect block allows you to accommodate files slightly more than 4 MB in size. To handle yet-larger files, you can use

Inode

file block 0's disk block number
⋮
file block 11's disk block number
single indirect block's number
double indirect block's number
access permissions
other metadata

Single indirect block

file block 12's disk block number
⋮
file block 1035's disk block number

Double indirect block

indirect block 1's block number
⋮
indirect block 1024's block number

Indirect block 1

file block 1036's disk block number
⋮
file block 2059's disk block number

Indirect blocks 2–1024: similar to indirect block 1

Figure 8.9 If an inode were used with single and double indirect blocks, the block numbers would be stored as shown here.

a multilevel tree scheme, analogous to multilevel page tables. The inode can contain a block number for a double indirect block, which contains block numbers for many more single indirect blocks, each of which contains many data block numbers. Figure 8.9 shows this enhancement to the inode design, which retains the dozen direct blocks and the original single indirect block, while adding a double indirect block.

Because the double indirect block points at many indirect blocks, each of which points at many data blocks, files can now grow quite large. (In Exercise 8.10, you can figure out just how large.) However, many UNIX file systems go one step further by allowing the inode to point to a triple indirect block as well, as shown in Figure 8.10. Comparing this with multilevel page tables is illuminating; the very unbalanced tree used here allows a small, shallow tree to grow into a large, deeper tree in a straightforward way. Later you'll see that B-trees grow somewhat less straightforwardly, but without becoming so imbalanced.

Having presented this method of mapping file blocks into disk blocks, I will shortly turn to an alternative that avoids storing information on a per-block basis. First, however, it is worth drawing one more analogy with page tables. Just as a page table need not provide a page frame number for every page (if some pages are not in memory), an inode or indirect block need not provide a disk block number for every block of the

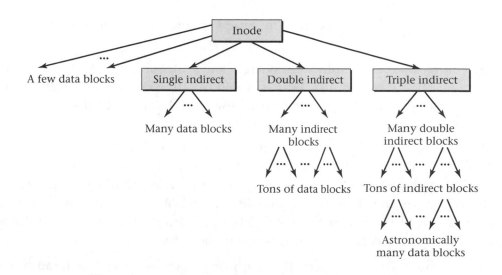

Figure 8.10 The full structure of a file starts with an inode and continues through a tree of single, double, and triple indirect blocks, eventually reaching each of the data blocks.

file. Some entries can be left blank, typically by using some reserved value that cannot be mistaken for a legal disk block number. This is valuable for *sparse files*, also known as files with *holes*. A sparse file has one or more large portions containing nothing but zeros, usually because those portions have never been written. By not allocating disk blocks for the all-zero file blocks, the file system can avoid wasting space and time.

Extent Maps

You have seen that traditional inodes and indirect blocks are based around the notion of a *block map*, that is, an array specifying a disk block number for each file block. A block map is completely general, in that each file block can be mapped to any disk block. File block n can be mapped somewhere totally different on disk from file block $n - 1$. Recall, however, that file system designers prefer not to make use of this full generality. For performance reasons, consecutive file blocks will normally be allocated consecutive disk blocks, forming long extents. This provides the key to a more efficient data structure for storing the mapping information.

Suppose you have a file that is 70 blocks long and that occupies disk blocks 1000–1039 and 1200–1229. A block map would contain each one of those 70 disk block numbers. An *extent map*, on the other hand, would contain only two entries, one for each of the file's extents, just as the opening sentence of this paragraph contains two ranges of block numbers. Each entry in the extent map needs to contain enough information to describe one extent. There are two alternatives for how this can be done:

- Each entry can contain the extent's length and starting disk block number. In the example, the two extent map entries would be (40, 1000) and (30, 1200). These say the file contains 40 blocks starting at disk block 1000 and 30 blocks starting at disk block 1200.

- Each entry can contain the extent's length, starting file block number, and starting disk block number. In the example, the two extent map entries would be (40, 0, 1000) and (30, 40, 1200). The first entry describes an extent of 40 blocks, starting at position 0 in the file and occupying disk blocks starting with number 1000. The second entry describes an extent of 30 blocks, starting at position 40 in the file and occupying disk blocks starting with number 1200.

The first approach is more compact. The second approach, however, has the advantage that each extent map entry can be understood in isolation, without needing to read the preceding extent map entries. This is particularly useful if the extent map is stored in a B-tree, as I will discuss subsequently. For simplicity, I will assume the second approach in the remainder of my discussion, though there are systems that use each.

At first, it may not be obvious why extent maps are a big improvement. A typical block map system might use a 4-byte block number to refer to each 4-KB block. This is less than one-tenth of one percent space overhead, surely affordable with today's cheap disk storage. What reason do file system designers have to try to further reduce such an already small overhead? (I will ignore the possibility that the extent map takes more space than the block map, which would happen only if the file is scattered into lots of tiny extents.)

The key fact is that disk space efficiency turns into time efficiency, which is a much more precious commodity. Indirect blocks result in extra disk I/O operations. Consider, for example, reading a file that is stored in a single 20-block extent. With the block map approach, the file system would need to do at least two disk read operations: one to read the single indirect block and one to read the data blocks. This assumes the inode is already cached in memory, having been read in along with other inodes in its disk block, and that the file system is smart enough to read all 20 data blocks in a single operation. With an extent map, the entire mapping information would fit in the inode; if you again assume the inode is cached, a single read operation suffices. Thus, the system can read files like this twice as fast. Admittedly, this is a somewhat artificial best-case example. However, even with realistic workloads, a significant speedup is possible.

Several modern file systems use extent maps, including Microsoft Windows' NTFS, Mac OS X's HFS Plus, and XFS, which was ported into Linux from SGI's IRIX version of UNIX. For files that have only a handful of extents (by far the most common case), all three store the sequence of extent map entries in the inode or (in Windows and Mac OS X) in the corresponding inode-like structure. The analogs of inodes in NTFS are large enough (1 KB) that they can directly store entire extent maps for most files, even those with more than a few extents. The other two file systems use smaller inodes (or inode-like structures) and so provide an interesting comparison of techniques for handling the situation where extra space is needed for a large extent map.

HFS Plus takes an approach quite reminiscent of traditional UNIX inodes: the first eight extent map entries are stored directly in the inode-like structure, whether they are the only ones or just the first few of a larger number. Any additional entries are stored elsewhere, in a single B-tree that serves for all the files, as I will describe subsequently. XFS, on the other hand, stores all the extent map entries for a file in a file-specific B-tree; the space in the inode is the root node of that tree. When the tree contains only a few extents, the tree is small enough that the root of the tree is also a leaf, and so the extents are directly in the inode, just as with HFS Plus. When the extent map grows larger, however, all the entries move down into descendant nodes in the tree, and none are left in the inode, unlike HFS Plus's special treatment of the first eight.

B-Trees

The *B-tree* data structure is a balanced search tree structure generally configured with large, high-degree nodes forming shallow, bushy trees. This property makes it well suited to disk storage, where transferring a large block of data at once is efficient (hence, large nodes), but performing a succession of operations is slow (hence, a shallow tree). You may have encountered B-trees before, in which case my summary will be a review, with the exception of my description of specific applications for which this structure is used.

Any B-tree associates search keys with corresponding values, much like a dictionary associates words with their definitions or a phone book associates names with phone numbers. The keys can be textual strings organized in alphabetic order (as in these examples) or numbers organized by increasing value; all that is required is that there is some way to determine the relative order of two keys.

The B-tree allows entries to be efficiently located by key, as well as inserted and deleted. Thus far, the same could be said for a hash table structure, such as is used for hashed page tables. Where B-trees (and other balanced search trees) distinguish themselves is that they also provide efficient operations based on the ordering of keys, rather than just equality of keys. For example, if someone asks you to look up "Smit" in a phone book, you could reply, "There is no Smit; the entries skip right from Smirnoff to Smith." You could do the same with a B-tree, but not with a hash table.

This ability to search for neighbors of a key, which need not itself be present in the tree, is crucial when B-trees are used for extent maps. Someone may want information about the extent containing file block 17. There may be no extent map entry explicitly mentioning 17; instead, there is an entry specifying a 10-block extent starting with file block 12. This entry can be found as the one with the largest key that is less than or equal to 17.

B-trees can play several different roles in persistence systems. In Section 8.6, you'll see their use for directories of file names and for indexes of database contents; both are user-visible data access services. In the current section, B-trees play a more behind-the-scenes role, mapping positions within a file to locations on disk. Earlier, in Section 8.4.3, you saw another related use, the management of free space for allocation. The data structure fundamentals are the same in all cases; I choose to introduce them here, because extent maps seem like the simplest application. Free space mapping is complicated by the dual indexing (by size and location), and directories are complicated by the use of textual strings as keys.

You are probably already familiar with binary search trees, in which each tree node contains a root key and two pointers to subtrees, one with keys smaller than the root key, and one with keys larger than the root key. (Some convention is adopted for which subtree contains keys equal to the root key.) B-tree nodes are similar, but rather than using a single root key to make a two-way distinction, they use N root keys to make an $N + 1$ way distinction. That is, the root node contains N keys (in ascending order) and $N + 1$ pointers to subtrees, as shown in Figure 8.11. The first subtree contains keys smaller than the first root key, the next subtree contains keys between the first and second root keys, and so forth. The last subtree contains keys larger than the last root key.

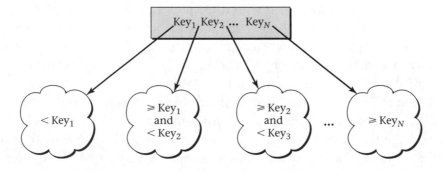

Figure 8.11 A B-tree node contains N keys and $N + 1$ pointers to the subtrees under it. Each subtree contains keys in a particular range.

If a multi-kilobyte disk block is used to hold a B-tree node, the value of N can be quite large, resulting in a broad, shallow tree. In fact, even if a disk block were only half full with root keys and subtree pointers, it would still provide a substantial branching factor. This observation provides the inspiration for the mechanism used to maintain B-trees as entries are inserted.

Each node is allowed to be anywhere between half full and totally full. This flexibility means one can easily insert into a node, so long as it is less than full. The hard case can be handled by splitting nodes. As a special exception, the root node is not required to be even half full. This exception allows you to build a tree with any number of nodes, and it adds at most one level to the height of the tree.

Consider, for example, inserting one more entry into an already full node. After insertion, you have $N + 1$ keys but only room for N. The node can be replaced with two nodes, one containing the $N/2$ smallest keys and the other the $N/2$ largest keys. Thus, you now have two half-full nodes. However, you have only accounted for N of the $N + 1$ keys; the median key is still left over. You can insert this median key into the parent node, where it will serve as the divider between the two half-full nodes, as shown in Figure 8.12.

When you insert the median key into the parent node, what if the parent node is also full? You split the parent as well. The splitting process can continue up the tree, but because the tree is shallow, this won't take very long. If the node being split has no parent, because it is the root of the tree, it gains a new parent holding just the median key. In this way the tree grows in height by one level.

In Bayer and McCreight's 1972 paper introducing B-trees, they suggested that each node contain key/value pairs, along with pointers to subtrees. Practical applications today instead use a variant, sometimes called B^+-*trees*. In a B^+-tree, the nonleaf nodes contain just keys and pointers to subtrees, without the keys having any associated values. The keys in these nodes are used solely for navigation to a subtree. The leaves

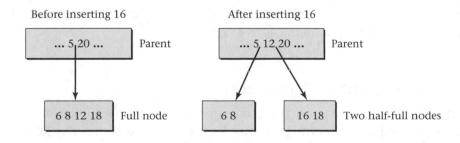

Figure 8.12 Inserting 16 into the illustrated B-tree, which has node-capacity 4, causes a node to split, with the median key moving into the parent.

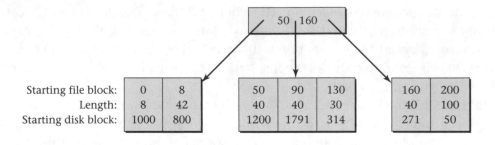

Figure 8.13 This small B^+-tree extent map contains information that can be used to find each extent's range of file block numbers and range of disk block numbers. Because the tree is a B^+-tree rather than a B-tree, all the extents are described in the leaves, with the nonleaf node containing just navigational information.

contain the key/value pairs that are the actual contents of the data structure. For example, a small B^+-tree of extent map entries might be organized as shown in Figure 8.13. As an additional refinement, each leaf node usually contains pointers to the neighboring leaf nodes to its left and right. This speeds operations such as traversing the extents in order.

This sort of B^+-tree can store the extent map for a single file, as is done in XFS. For Mac OS X's HFS Plus, a slightly different approach is needed, because all files' extent maps are combined into a single B^+-tree. (Recall, though, that the first eight extents of each file are not included in this tree.)

Each entry in this file system's B^+-tree describes an extent map entry for some position within some file. That is, the entry contains a file number (analogous to an inode number), a starting block number within the file, a length in blocks, and a starting disk block number. The concatenation of file number and starting file block number serves as the key. That way, all the entries for a particular file appear consecutively in the tree, in order by their position within the file.

The insertion algorithm for B^+-trees is a slight variant of the one for pure B-trees; you can work through the differences in Exercise 8.13.

8.5.2 Access Control Metadata

The complexity of the data structures storing access control information is directly related to the sophistication of the protection system. Recall that the POSIX specification, followed by UNIX and Linux, provides for only fixed-length access control lists (ACLs), with permissions for a file's owner, owning group, and others. This information can be stored compactly in the file's inode. Microsoft Windows, on the other hand, allows much more general ACLs. Thus, the designers of NTFS have faced a more interesting challenge and, in fact, have revisited their design decision, as you will see.

For POSIX-compliant access control, an inode can contain three numbers: one identifying the file's owning user, one identifying the file's owning group, and one containing nine bits, representing the `rwx` permissions for the owning user, the owning group, and other users. This third number, containing the nine permission bits, is called the file's *mode*. Rather than waste all but nine bits in the mode, the others are used to encode additional information, such as whether the file is a regular file, a directory, an I/O device, and so forth. Figure 8.14 shows how the permissions can be determined by extracting an inode's mode using the `stat` system call. (This system call differs only slightly from `fstat`, which you saw earlier. The file is specified by name, rather than by a numerical file descriptor.) If you compile this C++ program and call the resulting executable `stater`, then a command like `./stater somefile` should produce information you could also get with `ls -l somefile`.

Early versions of NTFS stored the full ACL for each file independently. If the ACL was small enough to fit in the inode-like structure, it was stored there. Otherwise, it was stored in one or more extents of disk blocks, just like the file's data, and the inode-like structure contained an extent map for the ACL.

As of Windows 2000, Microsoft redesigned NTFS to take advantage of the fact that many files have identical ACLs. The contents of the ACLs are now stored in a centralized database. If two files have identical ACLs, they can share the same underlying representation of that ACL.

8.5.3 Other Metadata

Because files can be of any length, not just a multiple of the block size, each inode (or equivalent) contains the file's size in bytes. (The program in Figure 8.3 on page 278 showed how you can retrieve this information.) Other metadata is much more system-specific. For example, POSIX specifies that each file has three time stamps, recording when the file was last accessed, last written, and last modified in any way. Modification includes not only writing the data, but also making changes in permissions and other metadata attributes. NTFS records whether the file should be hidden in ordinary directory listings. HFS Plus has many metadata attributes supporting the graphical user interface; for example, each file records its icon's position.

One metadata attribute on POSIX systems connects with file linking, that is, the use of multiple names for one file, which is the topic of Section 8.6.3. Each file's inode contains a count of how many names refer to the file. When that count reaches zero and the file is not in use by any process, the operating system deletes the file. The

```cpp
#include <unistd.h>
#include <time.h>
#include <sys/stat.h>
#include <stdio.h>
#include <iostream>
using namespace std;

static void print_bit(int test, char toPrint){
  if(test)
    cout << toPrint;
  else
    cout << '-';
}

int main(int argc, char *argv[]){
  if(argc != 2){
    cerr << "Usage: " << argv[0] << " filename" << endl;
    return -1;
  }
  struct stat info;
  if(stat(argv[1], &info) < 0){
    perror(argv[1]);
    return -1;
  }
  print_bit(info.st_mode & S_IRUSR, 'r');
  print_bit(info.st_mode & S_IWUSR, 'w');
  print_bit(info.st_mode & S_IXUSR, 'x');
  print_bit(info.st_mode & S_IRGRP, 'r');
  print_bit(info.st_mode & S_IWGRP, 'w');
  print_bit(info.st_mode & S_IXGRP, 'x');
  print_bit(info.st_mode & S_IROTH, 'r');
  print_bit(info.st_mode & S_IWOTH, 'w');
  print_bit(info.st_mode & S_IXOTH, 'x');
  cout << endl;
  return 0;
}
```

Figure 8.14 This C++ program, `stater.cpp`, uses `stat` to retrieve access control metadata for whichever file is specified by the command-line argument `argv[1]`.

operation users normally think of as deleting a file actually just removes a name; the underlying file may or may not be deleted as a consequence.

8.6 Directories and Indexing

Having seen how file systems provide the storage for files, you are now ready to consider how those systems allow files to be located by name. As a similar question regarding database systems, you can consider how those systems provide indexed lookup. In Section 8.6.1, I set the stage for this discussion by presenting a common framework for file directories and database indexes, showing the ways in which they differ. In Section 8.6.2, I show how the separation between file directories and database indexes is currently weakening with the introduction of indexing mechanisms for locating files. Having shown the basic principles of both directories and indexes, I use Section 8.6.3 to dig into one particular aspect of file directories in more detail: the ways in which multiple names can refer to a single file. Finally, in Section 8.6.4, I take you behind the scenes to look at typical data structures used for directories and indexes.

8.6.1 File Directories Versus Database Indexes

Traditionally, file systems include *directories*, which provide access to files by name. Databases, on the other hand, include *indexes*, which provide access to entries in the database based on a portion of the contents. This clean distinction between file systems and databases is currently blurring, as alternative file-access techniques based on indexes become available. In particular, Apple introduced such a feature in Mac OS X version 10.4 under the name Spotlight. I describe Spotlight in Section 8.6.2. Microsoft has announced that Windows Vista will contain a similar feature and that a more ambitious integration of database and file system technology, known as WinFS, will follow in a subsequent update to Windows. This trend makes it even more important to see what directories and indexes have in common and what distinguishes them.

Both directories and indexes provide a mapping from keys to objects. The keys in a directory are names, which are external to the object being named. You can change the contents of a file without changing its name or change the name without changing the contents. In contrast, the keys in an index are attributes of the indexed objects, and so are intrinsic to those objects. For example, an index on a database table of chapters might allow direct access to the row with the title `"Files and Other Persistent Storage"` or with the number `8`. If the row were updated to show a change in this chapter's title or number, the index would need to be updated accordingly. Similarly, any update to the index must be in the context of a corresponding change to the indexed row; it makes no sense to say that you want to look up the row under chapter number **1**, but there find that the real chapter number is still **8**.

Each name in a directory identifies a unique file. Two files may have the same name in different directories, but not in the same directory. Database indexes, on the other hand, can be either for a unique attribute or a non-unique one. For example, it may be useful to index a table of user accounts by both the unique login name and the non-unique last name. The unique index can be used to find the single record of information about the user who logs in as **"jdoe"**, whereas the non-unique index can be used to find all the records of information about users with last name **"Doe"**. An index can also use a combination of multiple attributes as its key. For example, a university course catalog could have a unique index keyed on the combination of department and course number.

The final distinction between file directories and database indexes is the least fundamental; it is the kind of object to which they provide access. Traditionally, directories provide access to entire files, which would be the analog of tables in a relational database. Indexes, on the other hand, provide access not to entire tables, but rather to individual rows within those tables. However, this distinction is misleading for two reasons:

- Database systems typically have a meta-table that serves as a catalog of all the tables. Each row in this meta-table describes one table. Therefore, an index on this meta-table's rows is really an index of the tables. Access to its rows is used to provide access to the database's tables.

- As I mentioned earlier, operating system developers are incorporating indexes in order to provide content-based access to files. This is the topic of Section 8.6.2.

8.6.2 Using Indexes to Locate Files

As I have described, files are traditionally accessed by name, using directories. However, there has been considerable interest recently in using indexes to help users locate files by content or other attributes. Suppose that I could not remember the name of the file containing this book. That would not be a disaster, even leaving aside the possibility that the world might be better off without the book. I could search for the file in numerous ways; for example, it is one of the few files on my computer that has hundreds of pages. Because the Mac OS X system that I am using indexes files by page count (as well as by many other attributes), I can simply ask for all files with greater than 400 pages. Once I am shown the five files meeting this restriction, it is easy to recognize the one I am seeking.

The index-based search feature in Mac OS X, which is called Spotlight, is not an integral component of the file system in the way directories and filenames are. Instead, the indexing and search are provided by processes external to the operating system, which can be considered a form of middleware.

The file system supports the indexing through a generic ability to notify processes of events such as the creation or deletion of a file, or a change in a file's contents. These events can be sent to any process that subscribes to them and are used for other purposes as well, such as keeping the display of file icons up to date. The Spotlight feature uses it to determine when files need reindexing. When I save out a new version of my book, the file system notifies Spotlight that the file changed, allowing Spotlight to update indexes such as the one based on page count. Unlike file directories, which are stored in a special data structure internal to the file system, the indexes for access based on contents or attributes like page counts are stored in normal files in the `/.Spotlight-V100` directory.

Apple refers to the indexed attributes (other than the actual file contents) as metadata. In my book example, the number of pages in a document would be one piece of metadata. This usage of the word "metadata" is rather different from its more traditional use in file systems. Every file has a fixed collection of file system metadata attributes, such as owner, permissions, and time of last modification. By contrast, the Spotlight metadata attributes are far more numerous, and the list of attributes is open-ended and specific to individual types of files. For example, while the file containing my book has an attribute specifying the page count, the file containing one of my vacation photos has an attribute specifying the exposure time in seconds. Each attribute makes sense for the corresponding file, but would not make sense for the other one.

As you have seen, the metadata attributes that need indexing are specific to individual types of files. Moreover, even common attributes may need to be determined in different ways for different types of files. For example, reading a PDF file to determine its number of pages is quite different from reading a Microsoft Word file to determine its number of pages—the files are stored in totally different formats. Therefore, when the indexing portion of Spotlight receives notification from the file system indicating that a file has changed, and hence should be indexed, it delegates the actual indexing work to a specialist indexing program that depends on the type of file. When you install a new application program on your system, the installation package can include a matching indexing program. That way you will always be able to search for files on your system using relevant attributes, but without Apple having had to foresee all the different file types.

8.6.3 File Linking

Indexed attributes, such as page counts, are generally not unique. My system may well have several five-page documents. By contrast, you have already seen that each name within a directory names a unique file. Just because each pathname specifies a single file does not mean the converse is true, however. In this subsection, I will explain two different ways in which a file can be reachable through multiple names.

The most straightforward way in which multiple names can reach a single file is if the directory entry for each of the names specifies the same file. Figure 8.15 shows a directory with two names, both referring to the same file. In interpreting this figure, you should understand that the box labeled as the file does not denote just the data contained in the file, but also all of the file's metadata, such as its permissions. In the POSIX API, this situation could have arisen in at least two different ways:

- The file was created with the name `alpha`, and then the procedure call `link("alpha", "beta")` added the name `beta`.

- The file was created with the name `beta`, and then the procedure call `link("beta", "alpha")` added the name `alpha`.

No matter which name is the original and which is added, the two play identical roles afterward, as shown in Figure 8.15. Neither can be distinguished as the "real" name. Often people talk of the added name as a *link* to the file. However, you need to understand that *all* file names are links to files. There is nothing to distinguish one added with the `link` procedure.

POSIX allows a file to have names in multiple directories. In the previous illustration (Figure 8.15), `alpha` and `beta` in the current directory named one file. Instead, I could have had directory entries in multiple directories all pointing at the same file. For example, in Figure 8.16, I show a situation where `/alpha/beta` is a name for the same file as `/gamma/delta`.

To keep the directory structure from getting too tangled, POSIX systems ordinarily do not allow a directory to have more than one name. One exception is that each directory contains two special entries: one called `.` that is an extra link to that directory itself and one called `..` that is an extra link to its parent directory.

Just as `link` adds a name for a file, `unlink` removes a name. For example, `unlink("/alpha/beta")` would eliminate one of the two routes to the file in Figure 8.16 by removing the `beta` entry from the directory `alpha`. As mentioned earlier, removing a name only implicitly has anything to do with removing a file. The

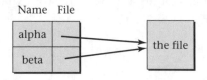

Figure 8.15 A directory can contain two names for one file.

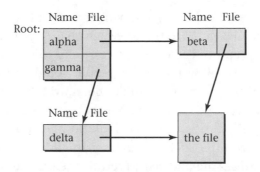

Figure 8.16 A file can have two different names, each in its own directory. In this example, the two pathnames **/alpha/beta** and **/gamma/delta** both lead to the same file.

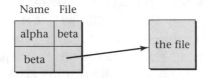

Figure 8.17 A symbolic link allows a file name to refer to a file indirectly, by way of another file name.

operating system removes the file when it no longer has any names and is no longer in use by any process. (An open file can continue to exist without any names, as you can demonstrate in Exploration Project 8.10.)

POSIX also supports another alternative for how multiple names can lead to one file. One name can refer to another name and thereby indirectly refer to the same file as the second name. In this situation, the first name is called a *symbolic link*. Figure 8.17 shows an example, where **alpha** is specified as a symbolic link to **beta**, and thereby refers to whatever file **beta** does. (Symbolic links are also sometimes called *soft links*. Ordinary links are called *hard links* when it is important to emphasize the difference.) In this figure, I show that a directory can map each name to one of two options: either a pointer to a file (which could be represented as an Inode number) or another name. The code that looks up filenames, in procedures such as **open**, treats these two options differently. When it looks up **alpha** and finds **beta**, it recursively looks up **beta**, so as to find the actual file. The symbolic link shown in Figure 8.17 could be created by executing **symlink("beta", "alpha")**.

Symbolic links are somewhat tricky, because they can form long chains, dangling references, or loops. In the preceding example, you could form a longer chain by adding **gamma** as a symbolic link to **alpha**, which is already a symbolic link to **beta**. The code for looking up files needs to traverse such chains to their end. However, there may not be a file at the end of the chain. If you were to execute **unlink("beta")**, then you would have a dangling reference: **gamma** would still be a symbolic link to **alpha**, which would still be a symbolic link to **beta**, which wouldn't exist any more. Worse, having deleted **beta**, you could reuse that name as a symbolic link to **alpha**, creating a loop. All POSIX procedures that look up files must return a special error code, **ELOOP**, if they encounter such a situation. In addition to returning **ELOOP** for true loops, these procedures are allowed to return the same error code for any chain of symbolic links longer than some implementation-defined maximum.

You can create either a symbolic link or an ordinary hard link from within a shell by using the **ln** command. This command runs a program that will invoke either the **link** procedure or the **symlink** procedure. You can explore this command and the results it produces in Exploration Projects 8.9 and 8.11.

Some file systems outside the UNIX tradition store the metadata for a file directly in that file's directory entry, rather than in a separate structure such as an inode. This tightly binds the name used to reach the file together with the identity of the file itself. In effect, the name becomes an attribute of the file, rather than just a means of accessing the file. In systems of this kind, symbolic links can still be used, but there is no easy analog for hard links. This leads to an interesting situation when one of these systems needs to be retrofitted for POSIX compliance.

For example, Apple's HFS Plus was developed before Mac OS became based on UNIX, which happened in Mac OS X. The underlying design assumes that each file has exactly one name and fuses together the directory and metadata structures. Yet Mac OS X is a UNIX system and so needs to support files with multiple names (created with **link**) or no names (if still in use when unlinked). To accommodate this, Apple puts any file that is in either of these situations into a special invisible directory with a random number as its name. Any other names for the file are provided by a special kind of symbolic link, which is made completely invisible to the POSIX API, even to those procedures that normally inspect symbolic links rather than simply following them to their targets.

8.6.4 Directory and Index Data Structures

The simplest data structure for a directory or index is an unordered linear list of key/value pairs. Whereas this is never used for a database index, it is the most traditional approach for directories in UNIX-family file systems and remains in use in many systems to this day. With this structure, the only way to find a directory entry is through linear search. (For a database, unordered linear search is available without any index at all by searching the underlying rows of the database table.)

For small directories, a linear search can perform quite reasonably. Therefore, system administrators often design directory trees so that each directory remains small. For example, my home directory is not `/home/max`, but rather `/home/m/a/max`, where the `m` and `a` come from the first two letters of my username. That way, the `/home` directory has only 26 entries, each of which in turn has 26 entries, each of which has only one small fraction of the thousands of users' home directories. As you will see shortly, this kind of directory tree is no longer necessary with a modern file system. On a modern system, my files could be in `/home/max`, and similarly for the thousands of other users, without a major slowdown—unless, of course, someone listed the contents of `/home`.

A second alternative structure is a *hash table*. A hash table is a numerically indexed array of key/value pairs where software can directly access entry number i without looking at the preceding entries. The trick is to know (most of the time) which entry would contain a particular key; this knowledge comes from using a hash function of the key as the entry number. So long as no two keys collide and are assigned the same location, looking up a particular entry (such as the one for `max` inside the `/home` directory) is a constant-time operation, independent of the table size. All that is necessary is to hash the key into a numerical hash code and use that code to directly access the appropriate entry. If it contains the desired key (`max`), the lookup is complete. If it contains no key at all, the lookup is also complete and can report failure. If, due to a collision, the entry contains some other key than the one being looked for, the system must start searching through alternative locations. That searching, however, can be kept very rare, by ensuring that the table is never very full.

Hash tables are occasionally used for database indexes; in particular, they are an option in PostgreSQL. However, as I mentioned in Section 8.5.1, they have the disadvantage relative to B-trees of not supporting order-based accesses. For example, there is no way to use a hash table index to find all rows in an accounting table for payments made within a particular range of dates. Hash indexes may also not perform as well as B-tree indexes; the PostgreSQL documentation cites this as a reason to discourage their use.

Hash tables are also occasionally used for indexing file system directories. In particular, the FFS file system used in BSD versions of UNIX supports a directory hashing extension. This feature builds a hash table in memory for large directories at the time they are accessed. However, the on-disk data structure remains an unsorted linear list.

B-trees are the dominant structure for both database indexes and contemporary file systems' directories. I already discussed the structure of B-trees in Section 8.5.1 and showed how they provide highly efficient access. As examples, B-trees are used for directories in Microsoft's NTFS, in SGI's XFS, and (in a different form) in Apple's HFS Plus.

In most systems, each index or directory is represented by its own B-tree. HFS Plus instead puts all the directories' entries together in one big B-tree. The keys in this tree are formed by concatenating together the identifying number of the parent directory with the name of the particular child file (or subdirectory). Thus, all the entries within a single directory appear consecutively within the tree.

8.7 Metadata Integrity

When a system crashes, any data held in the volatile main memory (RAM) is lost. In particular, any data that the file system was intending to write to disk, but was temporarily buffering in RAM for performance reasons, is lost. This has rather different implications depending on whether the lost data is part of what a user was writing into a file or is part of the file system's metadata:

- Some user data is noncritical, or can be recognized by a human as damaged and therefore restored from a backup source. Other user data is critical and can be explicitly flushed out to disk under control of the application program. For example, when a relational database system is committing a transaction and needs to ensure that all the log entries are on disk, it can use the POSIX API's `fsync` procedure to force the operating system to write the log file to disk.

- If the last few metadata operations before a crash are cleanly lost in their entirety, this can often be tolerated. However, users cannot tolerate a situation where a crash in the middle of metadata updates results in damage to the integrity of the metadata structures themselves. Without those structures to organize the disk blocks into meaningful files, the disk's contents are just one big pile of bits. There wouldn't even be any individual files to check for damage.

Therefore, all file systems contain some mechanism to protect the integrity of metadata structures in the face of sudden, unplanned shutdowns. (More extreme hardware failures are another question. If your machine room burns down, you better have an off-site backup.)

Metadata integrity is threatened whenever a single logical transformation of the metadata from one state to another is implemented by writing several individual blocks to disk. For example, extending a file by one data block may require two metadata blocks be written to disk: one containing the inode (or indirect block) pointing at the new data block and another containing the bitmap of free blocks, showing that the allocated block is no longer free. If the system crashes when only one of these two updates has happened, the metadata will be inconsistent. Depending on which update was written to disk, you will either have a lost block (no longer free, but not part of the file either) or, more dangerously, a block that is in use, but also still "free" for another file to claim.

Although having a block "free" while also in use is dangerous, it is not irreparable. If a file system somehow got into this state, a consistency repair program could fix the free block bitmap by marking the block as not free. By contrast, if the situation were to progress further, to the point of the "free" block being allocated to a second file, there would be no clean repair. Both files would appear to have equal rights to the block.

Based on the preceding example, I can distinguish three kinds of metadata integrity violation: irreparable corruption, noncritical reparable corruption, and critical reparable corruption. Irreparable corruption, such as two files using the same block, must be avoided at all costs. Noncritical reparable corruption, such as a lost block, can be repaired whenever convenient. Critical reparable corruption, such as a block that is both in use and "free," must be repaired before the system returns to normal operation.

Each file system designer chooses a strategy for maintaining metadata integrity. There are two basic strategies in use, each with two main variants:

- Each logical change to the metadata state can be accomplished by writing a single block to disk.
  - The single block can be the commit record in a write-ahead log, as I discussed in Section 5.4. Other metadata blocks may be written as well, but they will be rolled back upon reboot if the commit record is not written. Thus, only the writing of the commit block creates a real state change. This approach is known as *journaling*.
  - Alternatively, if the system always creates new metadata structures rather than modifying existing ones, the single block to write for a state change is the one pointing to the current metadata structure. This approach is known as *shadow paging*.
- Each logical change to the metadata state can be accomplished by writing multiple blocks to disk. However, the order of the updates is carefully controlled so that after a crash, any inconsistencies in the metadata will always be of the reparable kind. A consistency repair program is run after each crash to restore the metadata's integrity by detecting and correcting violations of the metadata structures' invariant properties.
  - The update order can be controlled by performing each metadata update as a *synchronous write*. That is, the file system actually writes the updated metadata block to disk immediately, rather than buffering the write in RAM for later.

– The update order can be controlled by buffering the updated metadata blocks in RAM for later writing, but with specific annotations regarding the dependencies among them. Before writing a block to disk, the system must write the other blocks upon which it depends. If the same blocks are updated repeatedly before they are written to disk, cyclic dependencies may develop, necessitating additional complications in the mechanism. This approach is known as using *soft updates*.

The strategy of update ordering through synchronous writes was once quite popular. Linux's ext2fs uses this approach, for example. However, performance considerations have removed this approach from favor, and it is unlikely ever to return. The problem is not only that synchronous writes slow normal operation. Far more fatally, as typical file systems sizes have grown, the consistency repair process necessary after each crash has come to take unacceptably long. Because synchronous writes are expensive, even systems of this kind use them as sparingly as possible. The result is that while all inconsistencies after a crash will be reparable, some may be of the critical kind that need immediate repair. Thus, the time-consuming consistency repair process must be completed before returning the crashed system to service.

Contemporary file systems have almost all switched to the journaling strategy; examples include Linux's ext3fs, Microsoft Windows' NTFS, and Mac OS X's HFS Plus. After rebooting from a crash, the system must still do a little work to undo and redo disk-block updates in accordance with the write-ahead log. However, this is much faster, as it takes time proportional to the amount of activity logged since the last checkpoint, rather than time proportional to the file system size.

Shadow paging remains a marginal player in the marketplace. One example is the WAFL file system used in Network Appliance's storage servers. Network Appliance's choice of this design was motivated primarily by the additional functionality shadow paging provides. Because disk blocks are not overwritten, but rather superseded by new versions elsewhere on disk, WAFL naturally supports *snapshots*, which keep track of prior versions of the file system's contents. Moreover, because Network Appliance was designing entire hardware/software systems, they were able to work around some of shadow paging's difficulties. In particular, it seems to be much harder to get acceptable performance from shadow paging if the disk is the only nonvolatile storage; Network Appliance uses some battery-powered RAM. Still, there is more hope for shadow paging than for either form of ordered updates (synchronous writes and soft updates). In some future technological setting, shadow paging could conceivably challenge journaling for dominance.

The soft updates strategy is another marginal player, generally confined to the BSD versions of UNIX. Its main selling point is that it provides a painless upgrade path from old-fashioned synchronous writes. (The on-disk structure of the file system can remain identical.) However, it shares the biggest problem of the synchronous write strategy, namely, the need for post-crash consistency repair that takes time proportional to the file system size.

Admittedly, soft updates somewhat ameliorate the problem of consistency repair. Because soft updates can enforce update ordering restrictions more cheaply than synchronous writes can, file systems using soft updates can afford to more tightly control the inconsistencies possible after a crash. Whereas synchronous write systems ensure only that the inconsistencies are reparable, soft update systems ensure that the inconsistencies are of the noncritical variety, safely reparable with the system up and running. Thus, time-consuming consistency repair need not completely hold up system operation. Even still, soft updates are only a valiant attempt to make the best of an intrinsically flawed strategy.

Because the only strategy of widespread use in contemporary designs is journaling, which I discussed in Section 5.4, I will not go into further detail here. However, it is important that you have a high-level understanding of the different strategies and how they compare. If you were to go further and study the other strategies, you would undoubtedly be a better-educated computer scientist. The notes section at the end of this chapter suggests further reading on shadow paging and soft updates, as well as on a hybrid of shadow paging and journaling that is known as a *log-structured file system*.

8.8 Polymorphism in File System Implementations

If you have studied modern programming languages, especially object-oriented ones, you should have encountered the concept of *polymorphism*, that is, the ability of multiple forms of objects to be treated in a uniform manner. A typical example of polymorphism is found in graphical user interfaces where each object displayed on the screen supports such operations as "draw yourself" and "respond to the mouse being clicked on you," but different kinds of objects may have different methods for responding to these common operations. A program can iterate down a list of graphical objects, uniformly invoking the draw-yourself operation on each, without knowing what kind each is or how it will respond.

In contemporary operating systems, the kernel's interface to file systems is also polymorphic, that is, a common, uniformly invokable interface of operations that can hide a diversity of concrete implementations. This polymorphic interface is often called a *virtual file system* (*VFS*). The VFS defines a collection of abstract datatypes to represent such concepts as directory entry, file metadata, or open file. Each datatype supports a collection of operations. For example, from a directory entry, one can find the associated file metadata object. Using that object, one can access or modify attributes, such as ownership or protection. One can also use the file metadata object to obtain an open file object, which one can then use to perform read or write operations. All of these interface operations work seamlessly across different concrete file systems. If a file object happens to belong to a file on an ext3fs file system, then the write operation will write data in the ext3fs way; if the file is on an NTFS file system, then the writing will happen the NTFS way.

Operating systems are typically written in the C programming language, which does not provide built-in support for object-oriented programming. Therefore, the VFS's polymorphism needs to be programmed more explicitly. For example, in Linux's VFS, each open file is represented as a pointer to a structure (containing data about the file) that in turn contains a pointer to a structure of file operations. This latter structure contains a pointer to the procedure for each operation: one for how to read, one for how to write, and so forth. As Figure 8.18 shows, invoking the polymorphic **vfs_write** operation on a file involves retrieving that file's particular collection of file operations (called **f_op**), retrieving the pointer to the particular **write** operation contained in that collection, and invoking it. This is actually quite similar to how object-oriented programming languages work under the hood; in C, the mechanism is made visible. (The **vfs_write** procedure writes a given count of bytes from a buffer into a particular position in the file. This underlies the POSIX **pwrite** and **write** procedures I described earlier.)

```
ssize_t vfs_write(struct file *file, const char *buf,
                  size_t count, loff_t *pos){
  ssize_t ret;

  ret = file->f_op->write(file, buf, count, pos);
  return ret;
}
```

Figure 8.18   Linux's **vfs_write** procedure, shown here stripped of many details, uses pointers to look up and invoke specific code for handling the write request.

8.9 Security and Persistent Storage

When considering the security of a persistent storage system, it is critical to have a clear model of the threats you want to defend against. Are you concerned about attackers who will have access to the physical disk drive, or those who can be kept on the other side of a locked door, at least until the drive is taken out of service? Do disclosures after the fact matter, or do only contemporaneous ones matter? Will your adversaries have sufficient motivation and resources to use expensive equipment? Are you concerned about authorized users misusing their authorization, or are you concerned only about outsiders? Are you concerned about attackers who have motivations to modify or delete data, or only those whose motivation would be to breach confidentiality?

As I explained in Section 7.6, if unencrypted data is written to a disk drive and an attacker has physical access to the drive, then software-based protection will do no good. This leads to two options for the security conscious:

- Write only encrypted data to the disk drive, and keep the key elsewhere. This leads to the design of *cryptographic file systems*, which automatically encrypt and decrypt all data.

- Keep the attacker from getting at the drive. Use physical security such as locked doors, alarm systems, and guards to keep attackers away. This needs to be coupled with careful screening of all personnel authorized to have physical access, especially those involved in systems maintenance.

Keeping security intact after the disk is removed from service raises further questions. Some data rapidly loses its value; for example, a company must closely guard its earnings reports until they are made public but need not worry about them thereafter. Other data should be kept confidential even when the disk drive containing it has served its useful life and is removed from operation. In this latter case, selling the drives as scrap can be a very risky proposition, even if the files on them have been deleted or overwritten.

File systems generally delete a file by merely updating the directory entry and metadata to make the disk blocks that previously constituted the file be free for other use. The data remains in the disk blocks until the blocks are reused. Thus, deletion provides very little security against a knowledgeable adversary. Even if no trace remains of the previous directory entry or metadata, the adversary can simply search through all the disk blocks in numerical order, looking for interesting data.

Even overwriting the data is far from a sure thing. Depending on how the overwriting is done, the newly written data may wind up elsewhere on disk than the original, and hence not really obscure it. Even low-level software may be unable to completely control this effect, because disk drives may transparently substitute one block for another. However, carefully repeated overwriting by low-level software that enlists the cooperation of the disk drive controller can be effective against adversaries who do not possess sophisticated technical resources or the motivation to acquire and use them.

For a sophisticated adversary who is able to use magnetic force scanning tunneling microscopy, even repeatedly overwritten data may be recoverable. Therefore, the best option for discarding a drive containing sensitive data is also the most straightforward: physical destruction. Even more straightforward, you could choose not to discard obsolete drives and instead lock them up in a secure place.

Having talked about how hard it is to remove all remnants of data from a drive, I now need to switch gears and talk about the reverse problem: data that is too easily altered or erased. Although magnetic storage is hard to get squeaky clean, if you compare it with traditional paper records, you find that authorized users can make alterations that are not detectable by ordinary means. If a company alters its accounting books after the fact, and those books are real books on paper, there will be visible traces. On the other hand, if an authorized person within the company alters computerized records, who is to know?

The specter of authorized users tampering with records opens up the whole area of auditability and internal controls, which is addressed extensively in the accounting literature. Recent corporate scandals have focused considerable attention on this area, including the passage in the United States of the Sarbanes-Oxley Act, which mandates tighter controls. As a result of implementing these new requirements, many companies are now demanding file systems that record an entire version history of each file, rather than only the latest version. This leads to some interesting technical considerations; the end-of-chapter notes provide some references on this topic. Among other possibilities, this legal change may cause file system designers to reconsider the relative merits of shadow paging and journaling.

Authorized users cooking the books are not the only adversaries who may wish to alter or delete data. One of the most visible forms of attack by outsiders is vandalism, in which files may be deleted wholesale or defaced with new messages (that might appear, for example, on a public web site). Vandalism raises an important general point about security: security consists not only in reducing the risk of a successful attack, but also in mitigating the damage that a successful attack would do. Any organization with a significant dependence on computing should have a contingency plan for how to clean up from an attack by vandals.

Luckily, contingency planning can be among the most cost-effective forms of security measures, because there can be considerable sharing of resources with planning for other contingencies. For example, a backup copy of data, kept physically protected from writing, can serve to expedite recovery not only from vandalism and other security breaches, but also from operational and programming errors and even from natural disasters, if the backup is kept at a separate location.

Exercises

8.1 In the introduction to this chapter, I gave an example of a database table, including what the columns would be and what a typical row might contain. Give a corresponding description for another example table of your own choosing.

8.2 Suppose the POSIX API didn't use integer file descriptors, but rather required that the character-string file name be passed to each procedure, such as `mmap`, `read`, or `write`. Discuss advantages and disadvantages of this change.

8.3 Given that the POSIX API uses integer file descriptors, it clearly needs the `open` procedure. But what about `close`? Discuss advantages and disadvantages for eliminating `close` from the API.

8.4 I mentioned that a defragmentation program rearranges files so that the free space on the disk is contiguous. Consider my parallel-parking analogy for external fragmentation, where as a result of smaller cars taking spots opened up by larger ones, there may be enough total free space along a block for another car, but no place that will accommodate the car. What would be the physical analog of the defragmentation program's action?

8.5 Defragmenting parking, as in Exercise 8.4, would make it harder for people to find their cars. The same problem arises for files on disk, but computer programs are not as flexible as people are. After defragmenting a disk, the file system must still be able to unambiguously locate each file. How can a defragmentation program arrange for that?

8.6 Describe in your own words the difference between a directory and an index.

8.7 The Spotlight search feature of Mac OS X can find files rapidly by using indexes. However, this feature may have other undesirable consequences for system performance. Based on the description in this chapter, what would you expect the performance problem to be?

8.8 Show that if a file system uses 4-KB disk blocks and 128-MB block groups, the bitmap for a block group fits within a single block.

8.9 Best-fit allocation sounds superior to first-fit, but in actuality, either may work better. By placing a new allocation into the smallest workable space, best-fit leaves the larger spaces for later. However, if the best fit is not an exact fit, but only an extremely close one, the leftover space may be too small to be useful.

Demonstrate these phenomena by creating two example sequences of extent allocations and deallocations (using an unrealistically small disk), one in which best-fit succeeds but first-fit at some point gets stuck, and the other in which first-fit succeeds but best-fit gets stuck.

8.10 Assume an inode contains 12 direct block numbers, as well as single, double, and triple indirect block numbers. Further, assume that each block is 4 KB, and that each block number is 4 bytes. What is the largest a file can be without needing to use the triple indirect block?

8.11 Draw two alternative "after" pictures for Figure 8.12 on page 299, one showing what would happen if 7 were inserted instead of 16, and the other showing what would happen if 10 were inserted instead of 16.

8.12 Using Figure 8.13 on page 300, translate the following file block numbers into disk block numbers: 3, 9, 76, 251.

8.13 Insertion into a B-tree node that is full to its capacity of N always behaves the same way, whether the node is a leaf or not. The node is split, with $N/2$ keys in each new node, and the median key inserted into the parent node. The situation with B^+-trees is somewhat different. Insertions into leaf nodes use a variant rule. You can work an example starting from Figure 8.13 on page 300. Assume that the leaf nodes have room for up to four records of information, each describing one extent, and that the nonleaf nodes have room for four keys and the associated pointers to subtrees.

(a) Initially insert information about two 100-block extents, starting at file blocks 300 and 400, with respective starting disk blocks 3000 and 4000. These insertions should make one of the leaf nodes full, but not yet require any splitting.

(b) Now insert another 100-block extent, with starting file block 500 and starting disk block 5000. This should require splitting a leaf node. Because all records of information about the extents need to remain in leaf nodes, you should put two records in the first node resulting from the split, and three in the second. Unlike with a pure B-tree, no information is removed from the leaf level and relocated to the parent. However, you do insert into the parent a copy of one of the keys (that is, one of the starting file block numbers). Which one?

8.14 I explained two different ways that Figure 8.15 on page 306 could arise: starting with **alpha** or starting with **beta**. What would a third option be?

8.15 While I was co-authoring a previous book, a system administrator accidentally deleted all our files and then admitted not having made backups for months. (This system administrator no longer works for the college.) He immediately took the drive out of service. Why was this a smart thing to do? What do you think we then did to recover the files containing the book?

▣ Programming Projects

8.1 Modify the `file-processes.cpp` program from Figure 8.2 on page 277 to simulate this shell command:

```
tr a-z A-Z </etc/passwd
```

8.2 Read the documentation for the `fstat` procedure and modify the `fstater.cpp` program of Figure 8.3 on page 278 to print out more comprehensive information. You may want to incorporate some of the code from the `stater.cpp` program of Figure 8.14 on page 302.

8.3 Write a program that opens a file in read-only mode and maps the entire file into the virtual-memory address space using `mmap`. The program should search through the bytes in the mapped region, testing whether any of them is equal to the character **x**. As soon as an **x** is found, the program should print a success message and exit. If the entire file is searched without finding an **x**, the program should report failure. Time your program on files of varying size, some of which have an **x** at the beginning, while others have an **x** only at the end or not at all.

8.4 You have seen that

```
(ls; ps) >information
```

puts both a listing of files and a listing of processes into `information`. Suppose you have an executable program, `./mystery`, such that

```
(ls; ./mystery; ps) >information
```

results in only the process listing being in `information`, without any list of files. How might the program accomplish this? Write such a program.

8.5 Write a program in C or C++ that can be used to rename a file. However, rather than using the `rename` procedure, your program should use `link` and `unlink`.

◯ Exploration Projects

8.1 Section 8.2 makes at least eight quantitative claims about typical contemporary disk drives. Use current literature to verify or update my values for each of the quantities in the following list. Cite the sources you use. In general, the answers need only be order of magnitude approximations.

(a) sector size

(b) sustained transfer rate with optimal access pattern

(c) sustained transfer rate with random accesses

(d) rotational speed

(e) proportion between head switch and single-track seek times

(f) proportion between seek times for large and small seeks

(g) data transferable in time needed for a single-track seek

(h) proportion between rotation time and seek time for a large seek

8.2 Research and write a short paper on persistent storage technologies that were used before moving-head magnetic disks. When and why did they fall out of use?

8.3 Find historical examples of persistent storage technologies that were originally expected to displace magnetic disks, but then failed to do so. Summarize what happened in each case.

8.4 Find examples of persistent storage technologies other than magnetic disks that are currently in use in specific niches. What makes them particularly suited to those niches, but not to the broader application areas where magnetic disks are used? Do they have performance characteristics sufficiently different from disks to invalidate any of the design decisions presented in this chapter?

8.5 Find examples of experimental or proposed storage technologies that have been suggested as possible future replacements for magnetic disks. Do they have performance characteristics sufficiently different from disks to invalidate any of the design decisions presented in this chapter?

8.6 UNIX and Linux file systems generally place ordinary files near their parent directory, and, with the introduction of the new Orlov allocator, even often place subdirectories near the parent directory. You can find out how important these forms of locality are by modifying Linux's ext2 or ext3 file system to scatter the files and directories across the disk and then measuring how much worse the performance gets. (Ext3 is used more today, but ext2 might provide results that are simpler to understand because there would be no journaling activity to factor in.)

The Linux source file `fs/ext2/ialloc.c` (or `fs/ext3/ialloc.c`) contains a procedure `ext2_new_inode` (or `ext3_new_inode`). Near the top of this procedure, you will find code that calls `find_group_dir`, `find_group_orlov`, or `find_group_other` in order to select a block group for the new inode. Normal files always use `find_group_other`, which tries to place the file in the same block group as its parent directory. Depending on an option selection, directories either use the new Orlov allocator or the old `find_group_dir`, which tended to spread directories more widely. (This difference is discussed in Section 8.4.3.)

Change the code to always use `find_group_dir`, whether the inode is for a subdirectory or not, and irrespective of option settings. Build a kernel with this modified code. You should set your system up so that you can boot either the normal kernel or the modified one. (Make sure that there is no other difference between your two kernels. This implies you should have built the normal kernel yourself as well.)

Repeatedly reboot the system with one kernel or the other, and each time do a timing test such as unpacking a software distribution and then removing it.

Write a report in which you explain what you did, and the hardware and software system context in which you did it, carefully enough that someone could replicate your results. How large a performance difference do you find between the two kernels? Is the difference consistent enough, across enough trials, to not to be explainable as chance?

8.7 Find, or generate yourself, some data showing the performance impact of Mac OS X's hot file clustering feature. Report these results and summarize how hot file clustering works. (Be sure not to plagiarize: cite your sources, and don't follow them too closely.)

8.8 If you have a Linux or Mac OS X system, read the documentation for **debugfs** or **hfsdebug**, respectively, and use that tool to examine the structure of a file system. (Linux systems generally include **debugfs**, whereas for Mac OS X, you will need to download the third-party **hfsdebug** from the web.) At a minimum, report for each of several files how many disk blocks are used to store the file, how many extents those disk blocks constitute, and how densely packed together the extents are on disk. As a measure of density, you can divide the number of disk blocks by one more than the difference between the highest and lowest block numbers.

8.9 On a POSIX system (such as Linux or Mac OS X), read the documentation for **ln** and then show how by using it you can create the situation of Figure 8.15 on page 306 using shell commands, without needing to write a custom program. What does the output from **ls -l** show after you have done this? Next, use **rm** to remove **beta**, and then re-create it with different content. What does **ls -l** show afterward? Does **alpha** have the old or new content?

8.10 On a POSIX system (such as Linux or Mac OS X), demonstrate a program continuing to make use of an open file after all names for that file have been removed. You can remove the names using **rm** in a shell, rather than needing to write a program that uses unlink. Similarly, the program using the file can be an existing program such as **cat** or **tail**—no programming is needed. Make sure, however, that the program actually reads or writes the file after the names are removed, rather than just continuing to use data it has in memory that it read from the file previously. You may find this easiest if you have not one but two programs concurrently making use of the file: one writing to it and the other reading from it.

8.11 On a POSIX system (such as Linux or Mac OS X), read the documentation for `ln` and then show how by using it you can create the situation of Figure 8.17 on page 307 using shell commands, without needing to write a custom program. What does the output from `ls -l` show after you have done this? Next, use `rm` to remove `beta`, and then re-create it with different content. What does `ls -l` show afterward? Does `alpha` have the old or new content?

8.12 You have seen two forms of links: symbolic links and hard links. UNIX originally had only one of these; the other was added later. Research the history of UNIX to find out which kind was the original. Moreover, UNIX was based on the earlier Multics system, which only offered one kind of link. Research Multics to find out which kind it offered. Was it the same as UNIX's original kind?

8.13 Even though journaling file systems do not need to run a consistency repair program after each crash, they normally have a consistency repair program available anyway. Speculate on why this might be useful, then see if your explanation matches the one in the article about XFS cited in the end-of-chapter notes.

Notes

In this chapter, I have assumed the use of a single disk; disk arrays and volume managers introduce another layer of interesting questions. The most popular form of disk array is a RAID; see the survey by Chen et al. [27]. For an interesting example of using an adaptive policy to manage RAIDs, see the paper by Wilkes et al. on HP's AutoRAID [135].

Two accessible tutorials on disk technology and performance are those by Anderson [4] and by Anderson, Dykes, and Riedel [5]. These articles also quantify the performance benefits that can be gained by queuing multiple requests with a disk controller and allowing its internal scheduler to process the requests in an appropriate order.

For more complete information on the POSIX API, see *http://www.opengroup.org/*. For the original UNIX API from which POSIX evolved (as did later UNIX versions, for that matter), see the 1974 article by Ritchie and Thompson [104]. That paper also sketches the internal structure of the initial UNIX file system. Other specific file systems I mentioned include NTFS [109], HFS Plus [7], XFS [124], and WAFL [68].

Internal and external fragmentation were distinguished in a 1969 article by Randell [102]. The conclusions reached in that paper were quickly called into question, but the vocabulary it introduced has become standard.

Orlov's heuristic for where to allocate directories has been mostly documented in source code, posts to email lists, and so forth. Moreover, there have been multiple variants; the "Orlov allocator" included in Linux's ext3fs is not quite what Orlov proposed. The closest to a published version of Orlov's work is his web site, *http://www.ptci.ru/gluk/dirpref/old/dirpref.html*. Many other allocation ideas go back much further; the classic work, which includes a comparison of best-fit and first-fit allocation, is by Knuth [81].

I mentioned that the analogs of inodes in Microsoft's NTFS are large enough to contain the entire extent maps for most files. In the rare case that the extent map does not fit in a single 1-KB record, NTFS expands the metadata into multiple 1-KB records, but unlike other file systems, it continues to use a linear extent map rather than a B^+-tree.

B-trees were introduced by Bayer and McCreight [10]. A later survey by Comer [33] explained the B^+-tree variant.

Two historical file systems well worth studying are those from Multics [37] and TENEX [22]. The Multics system originated hierarchical directories. One of TENEX's important innovations was automatic versioning of files. Versioning was incorporated into several other systems, but because neither UNIX nor NTFS included it, this feature faded from prominence. A recent upsurge in concern for auditability has helped bring versioning back to the fore. Some interesting related papers include those by Santry et al. [112], by Quinlan and Dorward [101], and by Soules et al. [120].

Regarding alternatives to journaling, the WAFL paper cited previously provides a good example of shadow paging. Soft updates are presented by Ganger et al. [54]. Rosenblum and Ousterhout's design for a log-structured file system (LFS) [106] essentially amounts to a shadow-paging scheme, because new versions of data and metadata blocks occupy previously free locations on disk, rather than overwriting the prior versions. However, LFS also has some commonality with journaling file systems, in that the written blocks constitute a log.

Gutmann [61] provides information on how hard it is to truly delete data from a disk.

Networking

9.1 Introduction

The overarching theme of this book is how computations interact with one another with support from operating systems and middleware. In Chapter 8 you saw that computations running at different times can interact by using persistent storage. In this chapter, you will see that computations can be distributed in space as well as time by sending messages across networks.

Networking is a topic that merits its own courses and textbooks. My goal here is to give an overview or review, depending on whether you have studied the topic before. I particularly highlight the ways in which networking ties in with the division of responsibilities between operating systems, middleware, and application software. Chapter 10 goes into more depth on the middleware commonly used to support distributed applications.

Because black boxes are inimical to education, I provide more detail about networking than is absolutely necessary for the development of distributed systems. However, my objective is not to make you a network engineer, capable of monitoring congestion and configuring routers, or even to give you a start towards that goal. (Though if you do pursue that goal, my overview of networking should not hurt you.) Instead, I am trying to explain the foundations that underlie distributed systems. In this chapter, not only do I spend a lot of time on the foundations, but also some time on such higher-level structures as the web and distributed file systems. Chapter 10 moves completely away from networking per se and into the middleware most commonly used to build distributed systems.

9.1.1 Networks and Internets

Before going any further, I should be clear about the meaning of three closely related terms: "a network," "an internet," and "the Internet." I will start by describing what networks and internets have in common and then describe the essential difference. Once you understand the general concept of an internet, I will be able to define the Internet as one specific internet.

A network is a collection of *links* and *switches*; so is an internet. Links are communication channels, such as wires, optical fibers, or radio channels. Switches are devices that connect links together and forward data between them. Some switches are known by more specific names; for example, those that connect radio links to wired links are known as *access points*, and those that connect the constituent networks of an internet are known as *routers*, as I will discuss subsequently.

Both networks and internets have computers interfaced to some of the links, as shown in Figure 9.1, with each interface identified by an address. Any interfaced computer can transmit data tagged with a destination address, and under normal circumstances the data will make its way through the appropriate links and switches so as to arrive at the specified destination. (As a simplification, I will ignore *multicast*, in which a single message can be delivered to more than one destination interface.)

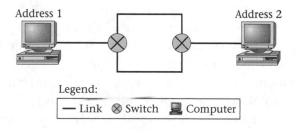

Figure 9.1 This network (or internet) contains four links, two switches, and two interfaced computers. Two alternative paths connect the two computers. As described in the text, more information would be needed to determine whether this is a picture of a single network or an interconnected group of networks, that is, an internet.

For a single *network*, as opposed to an internet, the preceding description is essentially the entire story. Data injected into the network is tagged only with the destination address, not with any information about the route leading to that address. Even the word "address" may be misleading; addresses on a network do not convey any information about physical location. If you unplug a computer from one place on a network and plug it in somewhere else, it will still have the same address.

Thus, a packet of data with a network address is not like an envelope addressed to "800 W. College Ave., St. Peter, MN 56082, USA," but rather like one addressed to "Max Hailperin." The network needs to figure out where I am, as well as what path through the links and switches leads to that location. As such, the switches need to take considerable responsibility.

In part, switches within networks shoulder their responsibility for delivering data by keeping track of each interface's last known location. In part, the switches take the simpler approach of forwarding data every which way, so that it is sure to run into the destination interface somewhere. (However, the forwarding must not be so comprehensive as to cause data to flow in cycles.) Neither approach scales well. As such, networks are normally confined to a limited number of interfaces, such as one workgroup within a company. When the network's scale is small geographically as well as in number of interfaces, it is called a *local area network* (*LAN*). Conversely, a *wide area network* (*WAN*) ties together interfaces that are far apart, though they are generally still few in number, perhaps even just two.

Multiple networks can be linked together into an *internet* by using *routers*, which are switches that connect to more than one network, as shown in Figure 9.2. In order to distinguish internets from networks, I still need to explain why linking networks together doesn't just result in a single larger network.

The distinguishing feature of an internet is that the destination addresses for the the data it conveys are two-part internet addresses, identifying both the destination network and the specific computer interface on that network. Returning to my real-world analogy, a packet of data with an internet address is like an envelope addressed to "Max Hailperin, Gustavus Adolphus College." There are people all over the world (analogous to routers) who could figure out how to forward the envelope to Gustavus Adolphus College. Once the envelope was on my college campus, people (analogous to switches within my local network) could forward the envelope to me.

Internets work similarly. Each router figures out what the next router should be in order to reach the destination network, independent of the specific computer on that network. The data is forwarded from each router to the next using the ordinary

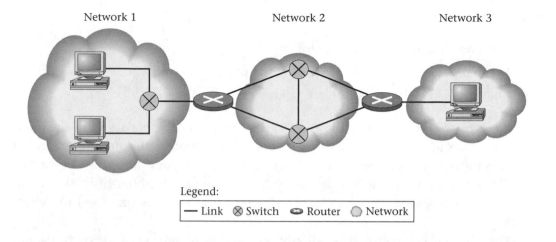

Figure 9.2 This internet was formed by connecting three networks. Each connection between networks is provided by a router, which is a switch interfaced to links belonging to two or more networks.

mechanisms of each constituent network, and likewise is forwarded from the last router to the destination computer using the destination network's mechanisms.

The two-part structure of internet addresses comes with a cost; when a computer is unplugged from one network and plugged into another, it must be assigned a new internet address. However, in return for this cost, an internet can scale to a much larger size than an individual network. In particular, one internet now connects such a large fraction of the world's computers that it is simply known as "the Internet."

9.1.2 Protocol Layers

Network communication is governed by sets of rules, known as *protocols*, which specify the legal actions for each partner in the dialog at each step along the way. For example, web browsers communicate with web servers using HTTP (Hypertext Transfer Protocol), which specifies the messages the browser and server can legally send at each step. In Section 9.2.1, I will show what those messages actually look like. For now, however, I will paraphrase the messages in plain English in order to illustrate the notion of a protocol.

When a web browser asks a web server to download a particular web page only if it has changed since the version the browser has cached, the server may legitimately respond in several different ways, including:

- "It changed; here is the new version."
- "No change, so I won't bother sending the page."
- "I have no clue what page you are talking about."

However, the web server is not allowed to give any of those responses until the question is asked, and it is also not allowed to give other responses that might be legal in other circumstances, such as "I created that new page per your upload." Not surprisingly, HTTP also forbids the web server from responding with something like "mailbox full" that would be appropriate in a different protocol, the one used to deliver email.

When humans converse, they talk not only about the subject of the conversation ("We could sure use some rain."), but also about the conversation itself ("I didn't catch that, could you say it again?"). Similarly, computers use not only *application protocols*, like the ones for downloading web pages and sending email messages, but also *transport protocols*, which control such matters as retransmitting any portions of the message that get lost.

An application protocol can be viewed as layered on top of a transport protocol, because the designers of the application protocol take for granted the services provided by the transport protocol. With the most common transport protocol, TCP (Transmission Control Protocol), the application protocol designers assume the transport protocol will take care of reliably sending a stream of bytes and having them arrive in order, without duplication or loss. All that need concern the application protocol designer is what the bytes should be to encode the various messages and responses. Meanwhile, the transport protocol designer doesn't worry about what bytes need streaming from one computer to another, just about the mechanisms for packaging chunks of bytes with sequence numbers, retransmitting lost chunks, and assembling the chunks together at the receiving end based on their sequence numbers. Thus, the layering of the two protocols results in a separation of concerns; each protocol can be designed without concern for the details of the other.

The transport layer is also responsible for allowing each pair of computers to engage in more than one conversation, a feature known as *multiplexing*. For example, a web browser on my desktop computer can be requesting web pages from the college's main server at the same time as my email program is delivering outgoing email to that same server. Each transport-layer connection is identified not only by the internet addresses of the two computers, but also by a *port number* on each end, which identifies a specific communication endpoint. My web browser connects to one port number on the server while my email program connects to another. The transport-layer software on the receiving computer delivers the data for each port number to the appropriate application-layer software, that is, it *demultiplexes* the arriving data.

The transport protocol can in turn be simplified by assuming that it has a *network protocol* under it, which makes its best effort to deliver a chunk of data to an internet address. The transport protocol may use this service for sending fresh chunks of application data, handed to it from the application layer, or for sending retransmissions. It may also use it for its own internal purposes, such as sending acknowledgments indicating what data has been received versus what needs retransmission. Regardless, from the perspective of the network protocol, these are all just packets to deliver. Meanwhile, from the perspective of the transport layer, delivery just happens; details like routing need not concern it.

The network layer is actually something of a misnomer, in that it is responsible for routing data through an internet. In fact, the most common network protocol is called the Internet Protocol (IP). This protocol is used to attempt to deliver data to any internet address, possibly by way of intermediate routers. Underneath it are two more layers, which are genuinely concerned with individual networks: the link and physical layers. I'll say more about these layers in Section 9.5. For now, it suffices to say that these are the layers implemented by networking hardware, such as Ethernet or Wi-Fi network cards, for wired or wireless LANs, respectively.

Counting up from the bottom of the stack, the physical, link, network, and transport layers are frequently referred to as layers 1, 2, 3, and 4. You might think that the application layer is 5, but in fact there are two layers I omitted, the session and presentation layers, which are layers 5 and 6. Therefore, the application layer is layer 7. The only reason you need to know these numbers is because they frequently show up in discussions of networking devices such as firewalls. For example, someone may tell you that their firewall does "filtering based on level 7 content." What this says is that the firewall looks at the specific contents of web page requests or email transmissions.

The listing of seven layers, illustrated in Figure 9.3, is known as the *OSI (Open Systems Interconnection) reference model*. I omit layers 5 and 6 from my subsequent discussions because they are not part of the architecture of the Internet, which was developed prior to the OSI reference model. In the Internet architecture, the application layer takes on the additional responsibilities, such as character set encoding and the establishment of network connections, that are assigned to the presentation and session layers in the OSI reference model. I will also largely fold together layers 1 and 2, because the difference doesn't matter unless you are engineering network hardware. As such, the bulk of this chapter is divided into four sections, one each for the application layer (9.2), the transport layer (9.3), the network layer (9.4), and the combination of link and physical layers (9.5). Those four sections are followed by my usual section on security (9.6), and by exercises, projects, and notes.

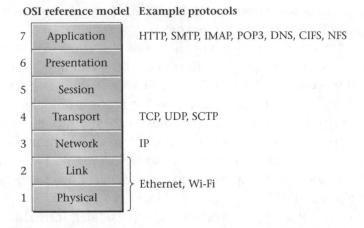

Figure 9.3   This diagram of the seven protocol layers in the OSI reference model provides examples for the layers I discuss.

9.1.3 The End-to-End Principle

Traditionally, the Internet has been based on the *end-to-end principle*, which states that considerable control and responsibility should be in the hands of the endpoint computers interfaced to the Internet's periphery, with the routers and other devices interior to the network providing very simple packet delivery service. In terms of the protocol layering, this means that only end computers have traditionally concerned themselves with the transport and application protocols.

One virtue of the end-to-end principle is that two users can agree upon a new application protocol without needing the cooperation of anyone else. The ability to try new application protocols at the grassroots, and see whether they become popular, was very important in the evolution of the Internet up through the introduction of the web.

However, the Internet has been progressively moving away from the end-to-end principle. I already alluded to one example: firewalls that filter at the application layer. I will mention firewalls again in Section 9.6.2. However, there have also been other non-security-related forces leading away from the end-to-end principle; I will examine one in Section 9.4.3. One upshot of this is that today it may no longer be possible to just start using a new application protocol with its associated port number. Traffic on the new port number might well be blocked as it traverses the Internet.

This helps explain a popular use of web services, which I explain in Chapter 10. This form of communications middleware is often configured to package application programs' messages into web traffic, in effect layering yet another protocol on top of the web's application-layer protocol. This approach helps circumvent obstacles to new application-layer protocols within the Internet. For this chapter, I will stick with the traditional layers, topping out at the application layer.

9.1.4 The Networking Roles of Operating Systems, Middleware, and Application Software

Just as network protocols are layered, so too is the software that communicates using those protocols. However, the layering of networking software does not always correspond directly to the major divisions that I focus on in this book, between application software, optional middleware, and an operating system.

The most common division of roles in systems without middleware has application software responsible for the application-layer protocol, while the operating system handles everything from transport layer on down. That is, the API that operating systems present to application programs usually corresponds to the services of the transport layer. This transport-layer API is normally described as providing a socket abstraction; I will discuss socket APIs in Section 9.3.1.

In keeping with this division of roles, most application-layer protocols are the responsibility of application software. (For example, web browsers and email programs take responsibility for their respective application protocols.) There are a few interesting exceptions, however:

- The *Domain Name System* (*DNS*) maps names such as *www.gustavus.edu* into numerical internet addresses such as 138.236.128.22 using an application-layer protocol. Although it uses an application-layer protocol, it plays a critical supporting role for many different applications. In most systems, you can best think of the DNS software as a form of middleware, because it runs outside of the operating system kernel but supports application software.

- Distributed file systems run at the application protocol layer but need to be visible through the operating system's normal support for file systems. Often this means that at least some of the distributed file system software is part of the operating system kernel itself, contrary to the norm for application-layer protocols.

- In Chapter 10, you will see that many applications are expressed in terms of more sophisticated communication services than the socket API. For example, application programmers may want to send messages that are queued until received, with the queuing and dequeuing operations treated as part of atomic transactions. As another example, application programmers may want to invoke higher-level operations on objects, rather than just sending streams of bytes. In either case, middleware provides the necessary communication abstractions at the application layer, above the transport services provided by operating systems.

9.2 The Application Layer

Typical application-layer protocols include HTTP, which is used for browsing the web, SMTP (Simple Mail Transfer Protocol), which is used for sending email, POP3 (Post Office Protocol–Version 3), which is used for retrieving email, and IMAP (Internet Message Access Protocol), which is also used for accessing email. Rather than examining each of these, I'll present HTTP as an example in Section 9.2.1. Then I'll turn to some less-typical application protocols that play important roles behind the scenes: the Domain Name System, which I explain in Section 9.2.2, and various distributed file systems, which I explain in Section 9.2.3.

9.2.1 The Web as a Typical Example

When you use a web browser to view a web page, the browser contacts the web server using an application-layer protocol known as *HTTP (Hypertext Transfer Protocol)*. This protocol has a request-response form; that is, after the browser connects to the appropriate port on the server (normally port number 80), it sends a request and then awaits a response from the server. Both the request and the response have the same overall format:

1. An initial line stating the general nature of the request or response
2. Any number of header lines providing more detailed information
3. A blank line to separate the header from the body
4. Any number of lines of message body

The message body is where the actual web page being downloaded (or uploaded) appears. For ordinary web browsing, it is empty in the request and non-empty in the response. The most common case where a request has a non-empty body is when you fill in a form and submit it.

To take a concrete example, let's see how you could retrieve my home page, *http://www.gustavus.edu/+max/*, without the benefit of a web browser. You can use the program called `telnet` to connect to the web server's port 80 using the command

```
telnet www.gustavus.edu 80
```

Then you can type in the following three lines, the last of which is blank:

```
GET /+max/ HTTP/1.1
Host: www.gustavus.edu
```

The first of these is the request line stating that you want to get my home page using version 1.1 of the protocol. The second is a header line, indicating which web host you want to get the page from. This is necessary because some web servers have different aliases and may serve different content depending on which host name you are using. The blank line indicates that no more header lines are being specified.

At this point, the server should respond with a large number of lines of output, of which the first ones will look something like

```
HTTP/1.1 200 OK
Date: Sun, 16 Jan 2005 01:18:19 GMT
Server: Apache
Last-Modified: Sun, 16 Jan 2005 01:18:25 GMT
ETag: W/"30ba07-b94-21857f40"
Accept-Ranges: bytes
Content-Length: 2964
Connection: close
Content-Type: text/html; charset=UTF-8

<!DOCTYPE HTML PUBLIC "-//W3C//DTD HTML 4.01 Transitional//EN"
        "http://www.w3.org/TR/html4/loose.dtd">
<html lang="en">
<head>
<title>Max Hailperin's home page</title>
</head>
<body>
<h1>Max Hailperin</h1>
```

and the last two will be

```
</body>
</html>
```

The first line of the response says that the request was OK and will be satisfied using HTTP version 1.1. (The number 200 is a status code, which indicates that the request was successful.) The server then sends quite a few header lines; you can probably figure out what several of them mean. For example, the Content-Length header indicates that my home page contained 2964 bytes at the time I tried this example.

The Content-Type line describes how the web browser should interpret the message body. In this case, it is a text file written using *HTML* (*HyperText Markup Language*) and with the character set being an international standard known as UTF-8 (Unicode Transformation Format 8). The boundary between the headers and the message body is formed by the blank line. If you are familiar with the syntax of HTML, you can see that the body is indeed written in HTML. The HTML format is independent of the HTTP protocol, which can be used for transferring any kind of file; the most familiar other formats on the web are those used for images.

The HTTP standard includes many features beyond those shown in this one simple example. To illustrate just one more, consider sending another request, similar to the first but with one additional header:

```
GET /+max/ HTTP/1.1
Host: www.gustavus.edu
If-none-match: W/"30ba07-b94-21857f40"
```

This time, the reply from the web server is much shorter:

```
HTTP/1.1 304 Not Modified
Date: Sun, 16 Jan 2005 01:19:55 GMT
Server: Apache
Connection: close
ETag: W/"30ba07-b94-21857f40"
```

This corresponds with the scenario described in Section 9.1.2. The browser (or a human using `telnet` to simulate a browser) is asking "please send this web page only if it has changed since the version I previously downloaded." The version is identified using the *ETag* (*entity tag*) the server provided when it sent the previous version. In this case, the version on the server still is the same (matches the provided tag), so the server just sends a short reply to that effect. A browser could use this to validate continuing to use a cached copy.

9.2.2 The Domain Name System: Application Layer as Infrastructure

The network layer takes responsibility for routing a packet of data to a specified internet address. However, the internet addresses that it understands are numbers, encoding the destination network and the specific interface on that network. Humans don't generally want to use these numeric addresses; instead, they prefer to use names such as *www.gustavus.edu*. Thus, no matter whether you are using HTTP to browse the web or SMTP to send email, you are probably also using an additional application-layer protocol behind the scenes, to translate names into numerical addresses. This protocol is known as the *Domain Name System* (*DNS*), because the hierarchically structured names such as *www.gustavus.edu* are known as *domain names*.

The Domain Name System is actually a general facility that allows machines distributed around the Internet to maintain any arbitrary mappings of domain names to values, not just mappings of computers' names to their numerical internet addresses. However, for the sake of this overview, I will concentrate on how DNS is used in this one particularly important context.

The use of domain names to refer to internet addresses is quite analogous to the use of pathnames to refer to files, a topic I addressed in Section 8.6.3. In the following paragraphs, I will describe four aspects of this analogy. First, both kinds of names are hierarchical. Second, both kinds of names can be either absolute or relative. Third, both naming systems allow one object to directly have multiple names. And fourth, both naming systems also allow a name to indirectly refer to whatever some other name refers to.

A domain name such as *www.gustavus.edu* specifies that *www* should be found as a subdomain of *gustavus*, which is in turn a subdomain of *edu*. Thus, the structure of the name is similar to a pathname from a POSIX file system, which might be `edu/gustavus/www` for the file `www` within the subdirectory `gustavus` of the directory `edu`. The only two differences are that the components of a domain name are separated with dots instead of slashes, and that they are listed from most specific to least specific, rather than the other way around.

In POSIX pathnames, the difference between `edu/gustavus/www` and `/edu/gustavus/www` (with an initial slash) is that the former starts by looking for `edu` in the current working directory, whereas the latter starts from the root directory of the file system. These two options are called relative and absolute pathnames. One little-known fact about the DNS is that domain names also come in these two varieties. The familiar domain name *www.gustavus.edu* is relative, and so may or may not refer to my college's web server, depending on the context in which it is used. If you want to be absolutely sure what you are talking about, you need to use the absolute domain name *www.gustavus.edu.* complete with the dot on the end. On the other hand, only a cruel system administrator would set up a system where *www.gustavus.edu* was interpreted as *www.gustavus.edu.horrible.com.* rather than the expected site. The real reason for relative domain names is to allow shorter names when referring to computers within your own local domain.

My discussion of file linking in Section 8.6.3 explained that the simplest form of linking is when two names directly refer to the same file. Similarly, two domain names can directly refer to the same internet address. In the DNS, a domain name can have multiple kinds of information, or *resource records*, each with an associated type. The domain name has a directly specified internet address if it has a resource record of type A. (The letter A is short for address.) As an example, the domain names *gustavus.edu.* and *ns1.gustavus.edu.* both have type A resource records containing the address 138.236.128.18, so both of these domain names are referring directly to the same internet address.

Recall that symbolic links (or soft links) are pathnames that do not refer directly to a file, but rather indirectly to whatever another pathname refers to. Similarly, the DNS supports domain names that are aliases for other domain names. As an example, the domain name *www.gustavus.edu.* currently has no type A resource record. Instead, it has a type CNAME resource record, showing that it is an alias for *www.gac.edu.* Looking this second name up in the DNS, I find that it too is an alias, with a CNAME record referring to *charlotte.gac.edu.* Only this third domain name has the actual type A record, specifying the internet address 138.236.128.22. This internet address will be returned by a lookup operation on any of the three alternative domain names. The domain name at the end of a chain of aliases is known as the *canonical name*, which explains why the resource record type is called CNAME.

In order to translate a name into an address, an application program such as a web browser uses a system component known as the *resolver*. The resolver communicates using the DNS application-layer protocol with a name server, which provides the requested information. In most systems, the resolver is not part of the operating system kernel. Instead, it is linked into each application program as part of a shared library. From the operating system's perspective, the application program is engaged in network communication with some remote system; the fact that the communication constitutes DNS lookups is invisible. From the perspective of the application programmer, however, the resolver is part of the supporting infrastructure, not something that needs programming. As such, the resolver constitutes middleware in the technical sense of that word. However, it is conventionally marketed as part of the same product as the operating system, not as a separate middleware product.

The protocol used between the resolver and name server is a request-response protocol. The resolver indicates what information it is looking for, such as an internet address (type A resource record) for a particular domain name. The name server responds with the requested information, an error report, or a referral to another name server better able to answer the question.

The details of the DNS protocol are somewhat complicated for three reasons. One is that the system is designed to be general, not just suitable for internet address lookups. The second is that the system is designed to reliably serve the entire Internet. Therefore, it contains provisions for coordinating multiple name servers, as I outline in the next paragraph. The third is that the DNS protocol does not use ordinary lines of text, unlike the HTTP example I showed earlier. Instead, DNS messages are encoded in a compact binary format. As such, you cannot experiment with DNS using `telnet`. Exploration Projects 9.1 and 9.2 suggest some alternate ways you can experiment with DNS.

No one name server contains all the information for the complete DNS, nor is any given piece of information stored in only a single name server. Instead, the information is both partitioned and replicated, in the following three ways:

- The hierarchical tree is divided into zones of control that are stored independently. For example, my college maintains the information about all domain names ending in *gustavus.edu.* and *gac.edu.* on name servers we control. Additional resource records within the DNS itself indicate where the dividing lines are between zones.

- Authoritative information about names in each zone is stored on multiple name servers to provide failure tolerance and higher performance. Secondary servers for the zone periodically check with a master server for updates. Resource records within the DNS itself list all the authoritative name servers for each zone.

- Name servers cache individual pieces of information they receive from other name servers in the course of normal operation. Thus, when I repeatedly access *www.nytimes.com.*, I don't have to keep sending DNS queries all the way to the *New York Times*'s name server. Instead, my local name server acquires a non-authoritative copy of the information, which it can continue using for a specified period of time before it expires.

9.2.3 Distributed File Systems: An Application Viewed Through Operating Systems

Using HTTP, you can download a copy of a file from a remote server. Depending on how the server is configured, you may also be able to upload the file back to the server after editing it. Given that the file I am currently editing (containing this chapter) is stored on a centralized server, I could be making use of this download-edit-upload process. Instead, I am taking advantage of a more convenient, more subtle kind of application-layer protocol, a distributed file system. In order to edit this chapter, or any other file stored on the central server, I simply access it by pathname, just the same way I would access a file on the local disk drive. Through some behind-the-scenes magic, certain parts of the file system directory tree are accessed over the network from the server. Ordinary file system operations, such as reading and writing, turn into network messages using the appropriate application-layer protocol.

Distributed file systems are most commonly used within the boundaries of a particular organization, unlike the protocols previously discussed. Perhaps for this reason, several different distributed file system protocols have remained viable, rather than a single standard dominating. Two of the most popular are *CIFS* (*Common Internet File System*) and *NFS* (*Network File System*). CIFS has primarily been championed by Microsoft and is commonly found in organizations with a substantial number of Microsoft Windows systems. It frequently is still referred to by its previous name, the *SMB* (*Server Message Block*) protocol. (The individual messages sent by CIFS continue to be called Server Message Blocks.) NFS was developed by Sun Microsystems and is primarily used at sites where UNIX and Linux systems dominate. To confuse nomenclature further, one specific feature of CIFS is called DFS, for Distributed File System. I won't discuss that feature here and will continue to use the phrase with lower-case letters to refer to distributed file systems in general.

As I will describe shortly, the designs of CIFS and NFS differ in some important regards. However, they also have quite a bit in common. In particular, in each case the client software needs to be at least partially located within the operating system kernel. When you use a pathname that extends into a directory tree supported by CIFS or NFS, the operating system kernel needs to recognize this fact and transfer control to the appropriate network client code, rather than the code that handles local file systems. The kernel can do this using a general purpose VFS (virtual file system) mechanism, as described in Section 8.8. The VFS mechanism delegates responsibility for file operations (such as reading or writing) to kernel code specific to the distributed file system. That kernel code may itself carry out the appropriate application-layer protocol exchange with a remote server, or it may just capture the details of the attempted file operation and pass them up to a specialized process outside the kernel, which actually does the network communication.

NFS is a pure request-response protocol, in the same sense as HTTP and DNS are: each interaction between client and server consists of the client sending a request first, then the server sending a response. CIFS, on the other hand, has a more complicated communication structure. Ordinary operations (such as reading from a file) are accomplished through messages paired in request-response form. However, the server can also spontaneously send a message to the client, without any request, to notify the client of some event of interest, such as that a file has changed or that another client wishes to access the same file. These notifications allow CIFS clients to cache file contents locally for performance, without needing to sacrifice correctness.

Another key difference in the two systems' designs concerns the amount of information servers maintain about ongoing client operations. The difference is most clear if you consider reading a file. In CIFS, the client invokes an operation to open the file for reading, then invokes individual read operations, and then invokes a close operation. These operations are much like the `open`, `pread`, and `close` operations described in Section 8.3. By contrast, NFS has no open and close operations; each read operation stands completely on its own, specifying the file that should be read as well as the position within it. One virtue of this "stateless" design is that the interaction between client and server can naturally tolerate either party crashing and being rebooted. On the other hand, a stateless design cannot readily support file locking or keeping client-side file caches up to date.

9.3 The Transport Layer

As mentioned earlier, the transport layer provides port numbers so that multiple communication channels can share (be multiplexed on) each internet address. Of the two transport-layer protocols common on the Internet, one provides essentially no services other than this multiplexing. This primitive transport protocol is called *UDP* (*User Datagram Protocol*). Like the underlying Internet Protocol, it makes an effort to deliver a chunk of data to a destination anywhere on the Internet, but does not guarantee reliability or that ordering will be preserved.

The other major transport-layer protocol—the one at work every time you browse a web page or send an email message—is the *Transmission Control Protocol* (*TCP*). This protocol does far more than provide port numbers; it provides the application layer with the ability to open reliable connections through which bytes can be streamed. A program using TCP opens a connection from a local port number to a remote port number at a specified internet address. Once the connection is open, each side can transmit bytes of data into its end of the connection and know that they will be received at the other end in order, without duplications or omissions. When the two parties are done communicating, they close the connection. In the HTTP examples of Section 9.2.1, the `telnet` program was used to open a TCP connection to the web server's port 80. The characters typed in for the request were streamed over the connection and hence received intact by the web server. Similarly, the web server's response was received by `telnet` and displayed.

The services provided by these transport-layer protocols are not so convenient for application programming as the higher-level messaging and distributed-object services I will present in Chapter 10. However, they are convenient enough to be widely used in application programming, and they are generally what operating systems provide. Therefore, in Section 9.3.1, I will present an overview of the socket application programming interfaces used to take advantage of these services. Thereafter, in Section 9.3.2, I will explain the basics of how TCP works. Finally, in Section 9.3.3 I will sketch the evolution of TCP into more modern versions, proposed future versions, and possible outright replacements.

9.3.1 Socket APIs

A *socket* is an object used as an endpoint for communication. Several different APIs revolve around the socket abstraction, each forming a variation on a common theme. The most important three are the POSIX socket API, the Windows socket API (known as Winsock), and the Java socket API. I will discuss all three briefly, but will give programming examples only for Java, as it is the easiest to use.

Ordinarily, each socket is associated with a local internet address and port number; that is, the socket knows its own computer's address and its own port number. If the socket is being used for a TCP communication stream, it will also be associated with a remote internet address and port number, identifying the communication partner. The local association is known as a *binding*; the socket is bound to its own address and port number. The remote association is known as a *connection*; the socket is connected to a partner.

Sockets used for UDP are not connected to partners; each time a packet of data, known as a *datagram*, is communicated using the socket, a remote internet address and port number need to be provided specifically for that datagram. As a convenience, if the same remote internet address and port number are to be used repeatedly, socket APIs generally allow the information to be provided once and for all using the connect operation, even though no real connection is formed. The address and port number are simply stored as default values for further datagram operations.

Each socket can be in any of several different states. The diagrams in Figures 9.4, 9.5, and 9.6 show three different life cycles through the states: one for datagram sockets (used with the UDP protocol), one for client-side stream sockets (initiating TCP connections), and one for server-side stream sockets (accepting incoming TCP connections). Several of the transitions, marked in the diagrams with dashed lines, do not require explicit operations in the Java API. The states are as follows:

- When freshly created, the socket may be *unbound*, with no address or port number. In this state, the socket does not yet represent a genuine communication endpoint but is just a hollow shell that has the potential to become an endpoint once bound. In the POSIX and Winsock APIs, all sockets are created unbound and are then bound using a separate operation. In the Java API, you can create an unbound socket if you really want to (and then later bind it), but the normal constructors for the socket classes do the binding at the time the socket is created, saving a step.

- A socket can be *bound* but neither connected nor listening for incoming connection attempts. For UDP, datagrams can be sent or received in this state. For stream sockets, this state is only used as a stepping stone to the connected or listening state. In the Java API, the transition to the connected or listening state is generally

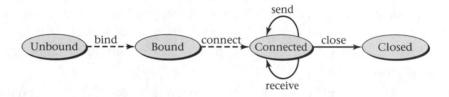

Figure 9.4   This state diagram shows the life cycle of datagram sockets used for sending or receiving UDP datagrams. In the Java API, the class `java.net.DatagramSocket` is used for this purpose, and binding happens automatically as part of the constructor.

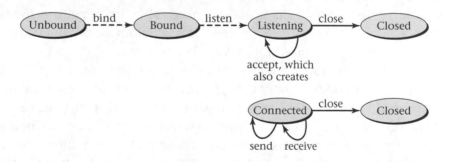

Figure 9.5   This state diagram shows the life cycle of client-side stream sockets used to initiate TCP connections. In the Java API, the class `java.net.Socket` is used for this purpose, and binding and connection ordinarily both happen automatically as part of the constructor.

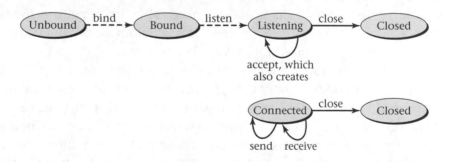

Figure 9.6   This state diagram shows the life cycle of server-side stream sockets used to accept TCP connections. In the Java API, the class `java.net.ServerSocket` is used for this purpose, and the bind and listen operations ordinarily are performed automatically as part of the constructor. Each time the accept operation succeeds, a new connected socket is returned, which in the Java API is an instance of `java.net.Socket`.

accomplished at the time the socket is created, whereas in the POSIX and Winsock APIs, the connect and listen operations are explicit.

- A bound socket can be *connected* to a remote address and port number, forming a TCP connection over which bytes can be streamed in each direction.

- Alternatively, a bound socket can be *listening* for incoming connection attempts. Each time the application program accepts an incoming connection attempt, the socket remains in the listening state. A new socket is spawned off, bound to the same local address and port number as the original listening socket, but in the connected state rather than the listening state. The new connected socket can then be used to communicate with the client that initiated the accepted connection.

    A server program can in this way wind up with lots of sockets associated with the same local port number—one listening socket and any number of connected sockets. The TCP connections are still kept distinct, because each TCP connection is identified by four numbers: the internet addresses and port numbers on both ends of the connection.

- Finally, a socket should be *closed* when it is no longer needed. The socket data structure becomes a vestige of the former communication endpoint, and no operations can be legally performed on it.

To illustrate how a TCP server accepts incoming connections and then communicates using the resulting connected sockets, consider the Java program in Figure 9.7. This server contains an infinite loop that accepts only one connection at a time, reading from that connection, writing back to it, and then closing it before accepting the next connection. This would not be acceptable in a performance-critical setting such as a web server, because a slow client could hold all others up, as you can demonstrate in Exploration Project 9.5. In Programming Project 9.1, you will modify the server to spawn off a concurrent thread for each incoming client. Even sticking with the unmodified code, though, you can see that there may be many sockets associated with port 2718 as the program runs: one listening socket (of class `ServerSocket`) that exists the whole time the server is running, and a whole succession of connected sockets (of class `Socket`), one for each time a client connects. In a multithreaded version, several connected sockets could be in existence at the same time, all on port 2718.

If you compile and run the Java code from Figure 9.7, you can test out the server in the same way as shown in Section 9.2.1 for HTTP. That is, you can use the `telnet` program to connect to port 2718 on whatever machine is running the server, just as there I connected to port 80 on *www.gustavus.edu*. Once you connect with `telnet`, type in a line of text. You should see the `nothing yet` response and then see the

```
import java.io.*;
import java.net.*;

class Server {
  public static void main(String argv[]) throws Exception {
    String storedMessage = "nothing yet";
    ServerSocket listeningSocket = new ServerSocket(2718);
    while(true) {
      Socket connectedSocket = listeningSocket.accept();
      BufferedReader fromClient = new BufferedReader
        (new InputStreamReader(connectedSocket.getInputStream()));
      PrintWriter toClient = new PrintWriter
        (connectedSocket.getOutputStream());
      String newMessage = fromClient.readLine();
      toClient.println(storedMessage);
      storedMessage = newMessage;
      toClient.close();
      fromClient.close();
      connectedSocket.close();
    }
  }
}
```

Figure 9.7 This message-storage server listens on port 2718 for connections. Each time it gets one, it reads a line of text from the connection to use as a new message to store. The server then writes the previous message out to the connection. For the first connection, the message sent out is **nothing yet**, because there is no previous message to deliver.

connection close. Connect again (from the same or a different machine) and repeat the procedure. This time you should see the line of text you previously entered come back to you.

Rather than using **telnet** for the client side of this interaction, you could use a program written specifically for the purpose. This would demonstrate the other way TCP sockets are used, to connect from within a client program to a server's port. The program in Figure 9.8 directly forms a connected socket, bound to an arbitrary system-chosen port on the local host but connected to the specified host's port 2718. To try this program out, you could compile it and then run a command like

```
java Client localhost test-message
```

You should see in response whatever previous message was stored in the server. Moreover, repeating the command with a new message should retrieve **test-message**.

```
import java.io.*;
import java.net.*;

class Client {
  public static void main(String argv[]) throws Exception {
    if(argv.length != 2){
      System.err.println("usage: java Client hostname msgToSend");
      System.exit(1);
    }
    String hostname = argv[0];
    String messageToSend = argv[1];
    Socket connectedSocket = new Socket(hostname, 2718);
    BufferedReader fromServer = new BufferedReader
        (new InputStreamReader(connectedSocket.getInputStream()));
    PrintWriter toServer = new PrintWriter
        (connectedSocket.getOutputStream(), true);
    toServer.println(messageToSend);
    String retrievedMessage = fromServer.readLine();
    System.out.println(retrievedMessage);
    toServer.close();
    fromServer.close();
    connectedSocket.close();
  }
}
```

Figure 9.8   This client program receives a hostname and a textual message string as command line arguments. It connects to the server running on the specified host's port 2718 and sends it a line of text containing the message. It then reads a reply line back and prints it out for the user to see.

The preceding Java examples send only a single line of text in each direction over each connected socket. However, this is just a feature of the example I chose; in effect, it defines the nonstandard application-layer protocol being used. The same TCP transport layer (accessed through Java's socket API) could equally well carry any number of lines of text, or other sequences of bytes, in each direction. You would just need to insert a loop at the point in the program that reads from or writes to the connected socket. For example, you could write an HTTP client or server in Java using this sort of code.

9.3.2 TCP, The Dominant Transport Protocol

You now understand how TCP can be used, through a socket API, to provide reliable transport of a byte stream in each direction over a connection between ports. Now I can take you behind the scenes and give you a brief overview of some of the techniques TCP uses to support reliable ordered byte streams. This will help you appreciate some of the difficult performance-critical issues. In this subsection, I will sketch TCP in its most well-established form; these TCP mechanisms are generally implemented within each operating system's kernel. Recent enhancements, as well as proposals for further change, are the topic of Section 9.3.3.

As the application program uses the kernel's socket API to send bytes, the kernel stores those bytes away in an internal buffer. From time to time, it takes a group of consecutive bytes from the buffer, adds a header of identifying information to the beginning, and sends it over the network to the receiver using the network layer, that is, IP. The chunk of bytes with a header on the front is called a *segment*. Each connection has a maximum segment size, typically no larger than 1460 bytes, exclusive of header. Thus, if the application program is trying to send a large number of bytes at once, the kernel will break it into several segments and send each. If the application program is sending only a few bytes, however, the kernel will wait only a little while for more bytes, and failing to get any, will send a small segment. One performance bottleneck is the copying of bytes from the application program to the kernel's buffer, and generally at least once more before reaching the network interface card. Systems optimized for network performance go to great lengths to reduce the number of times data is copied.

The header on each segment provides the port number for each end of the connection. It also specifies the position the segment's bytes occupy within the overall sequence being transmitted. For example, the first segment header might say "these are bytes 1 through 1000," and then the second segment header would say "these are bytes 1001 through 2000." The receiving code (also part of an operating system kernel) needs to pay attention to these sequence numbers and use them to deliver the bytes correctly to the application program that is using the socket API to read the data. Segments may arrive over the network out of order, for example, by taking two different routes. Thus, the kernel needs to store the arriving data in a buffer and return it to the application program in the order of sequence numbers, not in the order it arrives. As on the sending side, the trick is to do this without spending too much time copying data from one place to another.

In addition to arriving out of order, some segments may not arrive at all, because the network layer may occasionally lose a packet. To overcome that problem, TCP has mechanisms for retransmitting segments. The sender must continue to buffer each segment until its receipt is acknowledged, in case it needs to be retransmitted. Also, a segment believed to be lost may be retransmitted, and then turn out to not have been lost after all, but only delayed. Thus, the receiver needs to cope with duplicate segments.

Performance would be unacceptable if TCP transmitters sent only one segment at a time, waiting for acknowledgment before sending another. However, it would not be a good idea to allow arbitrarily many segments to be sent without waiting for acknowledgment. If a fast computer were sending to a slow computer, the receive buffer space could easily be overwhelmed. Thus, one of the many features TCP provides behind the scenes is *flow control*, which is to say, a receiver-controlled limit on how much unacknowledged data the sender is allowed to have outstanding at any time.

In traditional TCP, each acknowledgment contains a single number, n, to indicate that bytes 1 through n have been successfully received and that byte $n + 1$ hasn't been. This style of acknowledgment, known as *cumulative acknowledgment*, is rather limited. Suppose the sender transmits seven segments of 1000 bytes each and only the first, third, fifth, and seventh arrive. The receiver will see four incoming segments and will send four acknowledgments, all saying bytes 1 through 1000 have been received. The sender will know that those bytes were received and have a pretty good clue that bytes 1001 through 2000 were not. It will also have a clue that three of the subsequent five segments were received, but it will have no idea which three.

The preceding example illustrates one scenario under which a TCP sender will retransmit a segment. Having received an acknowledgment of the first 1000 bytes and then three duplicates of that same acknowledgment, the sender is justified in assuming the second segment was lost and retransmitting it. The rules of TCP specify waiting for three duplicate acknowledgments, because one or two can easily occur simply from segments arriving out of order. That is, any duplicate acknowledgment indicates a hole has opened up in the sequence number order, but if segments are arriving out of order, the hole may quickly get filled in without needing retransmission.

Unfortunately, to provoke the triple duplicate acknowledgment, subsequent segments need to be transmitted. If the sender has no more segments to transmit, or is not allowed to send any more due to flow control restrictions or the congestion control restrictions I will describe shortly, then no duplicate acknowledgments will be triggered. Thus, TCP senders need to fall back on some other means of detecting lost segments; they use a timer. If no acknowledgment is received in a conservatively long time, then the segment is assumed lost. This conservative waiting period can cause substantial performance degradation.

A final challenge for TCP is controlling congestion that occurs at the switches (including routers) within the Internet. Each link leading out from a switch has a particular rate at which it can receive new data. Data destined for a particular outbound link may be coming into the switch from any number of the inbound links. If the total rate at which that data is flowing into the switch exceeds the rate at which it can be sent on the outbound link, then the switch will start to build up a queue of data awaiting forwarding. If the imbalance is only temporary, the queue will build up a little, then drain back down. However, if the imbalance persists, then the queue will grow long, creating lengthy delays, and then eventually get so full that the switch starts discarding packets. This phenomenon is known as *congestion.*

Congestion is not good, because it causes packets of data to be delayed or lost. Because TCP interprets unreasonably long delays as packet losses, either delays or outright losses can cause TCP to retransmit segments. This might even make the problem worse by sending more data to the already congested switch. Thus, TCP contains congestion-control features, which act to throttle back the rate at which it sends segments (new or retransmitted) when it detects packet losses. The theory is that most packet loss is caused by switches with full queues and therefore can be interpreted as a sign of congestion.

The details of congestion control are somewhat complicated. The most important facts to know are that it occurs independently in each TCP connection, and that newly opened connections start with a very low transmission rate, ramping up until the rate that causes congestion is detected. Thus, application performance can be improved by using multiple TCP connections in parallel and by sending a lot of data over each connection rather than repeatedly opening new connections for a little data apiece. Modern web browsers obey both these rules, using parallel and persistent connections. Parallel connections are a mixed blessing, because they constitute an attempt to unfairly compete with other Internet users, creating the potential for an arms race.

9.3.3 Evolution Within and Beyond TCP

Traditional TCP detects data loss through a combination of timeouts and triple duplicate cumulative acknowledgments. This detected data loss serves as the sign of congestion. TCP also responds to the detected data loss with retransmissions in order to ensure that all data is reliably delivered. Every one of these three design decisions has been challenged by networking researchers. That is, there are systems that detect loss in other ways, that detect congestion other than through loss, and that ensure reliability other than through retransmission. Some of the results are already partially deployed, whereas others remain research proposals. Some innovations also discard TCP's basic service model of the bidirectional byte stream. In this subsection, I will briefly overview a few of these trends in order to make the point that network protocols are not timeless truths, but rather are designs that are subject to change.

As network hardware has improved, the rate at which bits can be transmitted has greatly increased. However, the time needed for those bits to travel to the other side of the world and for acknowledgment bits to travel back has not shrunk. The consequence is that a computer may now transmit quite a few bits before getting any acknowledgment back. As a result, it is now common to have large numbers of unacknowledged TCP segments. In this situation, the weakness I mentioned for cumulative acknowledgment starts to become significant. There may well be more than one lost segment, and it would be nice to know exactly which ones were lost. For this reason, a *selective acknowledgment* feature was added to TCP, in which the receiver can provide the sender more complete information about which bytes have been received. This provides a new way to detect data loss.

In whatever manner data loss is detected, it likely stems from congestion. That does not mean, however, that the TCP sender needs to wait for a lost segment in order to sense congestion. If it could sense the congestion sooner, it could avoid the loss entirely. One way this can be done, deployed in some parts of the Internet, is for the routers to provide *Explicit Congestion Notification* (*ECN*). That is, they send an overt signal to the TCP transmitters to throttle back, rather than needing to implicitly code that signal by discarding a packet. Another approach, which has been experimented with, is for the TCP sender to notice that acknowledgments are starting to take longer and infer that a queue must be building up. This is called *TCP Vegas*.

Lost segments don't just signal congestion; they also prevent data from being delivered, necessitating retransmissions. However, there is another approach to ensuring that all data is delivered, even if some packets are lost. Namely, the data can be encoded into a redundant format, in which any sufficiently large subset of the packets contains enough information to allow all the data to be reconstructed. This concept is best explained by a highly simplified example, shown in Figure 9.9. This general approach is known as *forward error correction* using an *erasure code*. More sophisticated versions have been used to build high-performance systems for streaming large files, such as videos, using UDP.

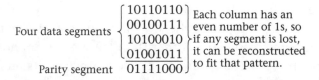

Figure 9.9 Sending redundant data allows loss to be tolerated. Suppose four segments of data are to be sent; for simplicity, here each segment is only 1 byte long. Suppose the loss rate is low enough that it is unlikely two segments will be lost. Rather than waiting to see which one segment is lost, and then retransmitting it, a sender can transmit the four data segments and a parity segment, each with a sequence number in the header. Any one of the five can be lost, and yet all four data segments will be deliverable, because the lost segment can be reconstructed.

One final area of change is in the service provided by TCP. An alternative transport protocol known as *SCTP* (*Stream Control Transmission Protocol*) is a proposed Internet standard that would offer similar reliable delivery and congestion control to TCP, but would go beyond the single bidirectional byte stream. An SCTP sender can transmit a stream of messages, that is, entire chunks of data akin to UDP datagrams, and have them delivered not only reliably and in their correct order, but also with the boundaries between them preserved, rather than all run together into an undifferentiated byte stream. Moreover, the SCTP connection can carry more than one stream in each direction. The messages on each individual stream are delivered in order, but a lost message on one stream doesn't hold up the delivery of messages on other streams. Unlike the trends mentioned previously, which affect only low-level details, if SCTP becomes popular, it will be necessary to rethink the APIs that constitute the interface between application programs and operating systems.

9.4 The Network Layer

The network layer delivers a packet of data to the appropriate destination computer on an internet. In this section, I will highlight a few aspects of this layer. First, I will explain the difference between the two versions of IP and explain how addresses are structured for the currently dominant version, IPv4. Second, I will give an overview of how routers forward packets along appropriate paths to reach their destinations. Finally, I will explain Network Address Translation (NAT), a technology that has considerable utility, but which is at odds with the original end-to-end architectural principle of the Internet.

9.4.1 IP, Versions 4 and 6

Each packet of data sent on the Internet starts with a header formatted in accordance with the *Internet Protocol* (*IP*). If the packet contains a TCP segment or UDP datagram, the TCP or UDP header follows the IP header. The most important pieces of information in the IP header are as follows:

- The version of IP being used, which governs the format of the remaining header fields; currently version 4 is dominant and version 6 is in limited use (version 5 does not exist)
- The internet address from which the packet was sent

- The internet address to which the packet should be delivered
- A code number for the transport-layer protocol, indicating whether the IP header is followed by a TCP header, UDP header, or whatever else

Among the other header fields I will not discuss are some that support optional extensions to the basic protocol.

The next-generation protocol, IPv6, differs from the currently dominant IPv4 in two principle ways. First, the source and destination internet addresses are much larger, 128 bits instead of 32. This should greatly ease assigning internet addresses to ubiquitous devices such as cell phones. Second, IPv6 was designed to support security features, protecting packets from interception, alteration, or forgery. However, these features have in the meantime become available as an optional extension to IPv4, known as *IPsec*. Partially for this reason, the transition to IPv6 is happening exceedingly slowly, and IPv4 is still by far the dominant version.

As I explained in Section 9.1.1, an internet address contains two components: an identifier for a particular network and an identifier for a specific interface on that network. (My analogy in that section was with "Max Hailperin, Gustavus Adolphus College.") Given that IPv4 addresses are 32 bits long, you might ask how many of these bits are devoted to each purpose. For example, does the address contain a 16-bit network number and a 16-bit interface number? Unfortunately, the answer to this question is not so simple.

Each internet address has a prefix, some number of bits long, that identifies the network, with the remainder of the 32 bits identifying the interface within the network. However, the length of the network prefix varies from network to network, so that internet addresses are not partitioned into their two components in a uniform way. The motivation for this awkward design is that the Internet needs both to support a large number of networks (more than 2^{16}, for example) and also some large networks (some containing more than 2^{16} interfaces, for example).

The conceptually simple solution to this problem would be to use larger fixed-format addresses, perhaps containing a 32-bit network number and a 32-bit interface number. However, the designers of IPv4 decided to stick with a total of 32 bits, because this address size was already in place from an early fixed-format version of internet addressing, in which the network identifier was always 8 bits long and the interface identifier 24 bits. The designers considered it more important to stick with their prior address size, 32 bits, than with their prior design concept, that the bits be partitioned in a uniform way. Thus, they made the design choice to cram all addresses into 32 bits by allowing a flexible division. This allows both for a small number of large networks (with short network prefixes) and a large number of small networks (with long network prefixes).

Internet addresses are conventionally written in *dotted decimal* format, in which the 32-bit address is divided into four 8-bit components, and each of the 8-bit components is translated into a decimal number. The four decimal numbers are written with dots between them. As an example, my computer's internet address is 138.236.64.64. Translating 138, 236, 64, and 64 from decimal to binary produces 10001010, 11101100, 01000000, and 01000000. Thus, my internet address in binary is 10001010111011000100000001000000.

Of these 32 bits, the first 21 identify the network for my college's department of mathematics and computer science, whereas the remaining 11 identify my specific computer on that network. My computer's operating system kernel is aware not only of its own internet address, but also of this division into 21 bits and 11. The latter fact is stored as a *mask*, which in my case is 255.255.248.0. If you translate that from dotted decimal to binary, you will see that the first 21 bits are 1s, whereas the last 11 bits are 0s.

The kernel uses this information whenever it sends out an internet datagram. It compares the destination address to its own address, paying attention only to the prefix specified by the mask. Thus, in my case, the kernel checks whether the first 21 bits of the destination address are the same as my own. If so, the destination is on my own network, and my computer's kernel should send the data directly, using my network's own link-layer addressing mechanism.

If, on the other hand, the destination is outside my network, then the kernel should send the datagram to the *gateway router* leading from my local network to the outside world. At the link layer, the kernel will send the datagram out with the gateway router's network address, though it will still have the ultimate destination's internet address within the IP header.

9.4.2 Routing and Label Switching

In the ordinary functioning of the Internet, no entity actually selects a route for a packet of data to follow, in the sense of planning the entire route in advance. Instead, each time the packet arrives at a router, that router decides which neighboring router to forward the packet to. The overall route emerges as the composite result of all these local decisions.

When a router needs to forward a packet, it decides which neighboring router should be next by consulting its forwarding table. Each entry in the forwarding table specifies an internet address prefix and what the next router should be for that prefix. Given this large table, the router's forwarding decision can be made rather rapidly, because it just requires a table lookup. The one problem is that the entries in the table are keyed by variable-length prefixes, making the lookup operation more complicated than would be the case with fixed-length keys.

One other limitation of traditional internet routing, beyond the need to look up variable-length prefixes, is that all traffic for the same destination network gets forwarded to the same next router. Large service providers in the core of the Internet would prefer more flexible traffic engineering with the ability to send some of the traffic through each of several alternative routes. These same core providers are also the ones for whom expensive lookup operations on variable-length prefixes are most burdensome, because their routers need to switch traffic at a very high rate.

In order to address both these issues, some Internet service providers, particularly in the core of the Internet, are moving away from traditional IP routers to *label switching routers* using *Multiprotocol Label Switching* (*MPLS*). A label switching router looks up the next router, not using a variable-length prefix of the destination address, but instead using a fixed-length label that has been attached to the packet; MPLS specifies the standard format for this labeling.

When an IP packet first reaches a label switching router, the router attaches a label to it based on both the destination address and any traffic engineering considerations. Once the packet is labeled, it can be forwarded from label switching router to label switching router any number of times, based only on the label. When the packet is finally passed to a traditional router, the label gets stripped off.

With either approach, the performance-critical task of a router is forwarding individual packets based on a table lookup operation. However, the routers are also engaged in another less time-sensitive activity. Namely, the routers are constantly rebuilding their forwarding tables to reflect the most recent information they have about the Internet. They exchange information with one another using routing protocols. The study of routing protocols, and of approaches to generating forwarding table entries, is quite interesting, but I will leave it for networking texts.

9.4.3 Network Address Translation: An End to End-to-End?

Like many people, I have a network within my home, which uses the Internet Protocol. Moreover, from any of the computers on this network, I can open a TCP connection to any computer on the Internet. For example, I can browse any web site. However, my home network is not a constituent network of the Internet. This situation, which is actually quite typical for home networks, results from my use of *Network Address Translation* (*NAT*) within the router that connects my home network to my service provider's network. NAT is a technology that allows an entire network (or even an entire private internet) to pose as a single computer on the Internet. No matter which of my home computers connects to an external site, the external site will see the same source internet address, the one address that represents my whole network.

Each computer on my home network has its own private IP address; for example, one is 192.168.0.100 and another is 192.168.0.101. All packets on my home network use these addresses. However, as the router forwards packets out from the home network to the service provider, it modifies the packets, replacing these private IP addresses with the single public internet address my service provider assigned me, which is 216.114.254.180.

If all the NAT router did was to change the packets' source addresses, chaos would result. Recall that each TCP connection is uniquely identified by the combination of four values: the source and destination addresses and port numbers. Suppose I start browsing *www.gustavus.edu* on one home computer at the same time my wife does so on another of our home computers. Each of us is therefore opening a TCP connection with destination address 138.236.128.22 and destination port number 80. My source address starts out as 192.168.0.100, and my computer picks a source port number it is not otherwise using, perhaps 2000. My wife's source address starts out as 192.168.0.101, and her computer also picks a source port. Perhaps by coincidence it also picks 2000. Within our home network, our two TCP connections are distinguishable because of our two different IP addresses. However, outside the home network is another issue. If the NAT box rewrites our packets so both have source address 216.114.254.180 and leaves both our port numbers as 2000, then it will have combined what should have been two separate TCP connections into one.

To get around this problem, the NAT router rewrites our packets' source port numbers (in the TCP headers) as well as the source addresses (in the IP headers). Internally to our network, we have distinct addresses but may have coincidentally identical port numbers. Externally, we share a common address, but the NAT router makes sure we use different port numbers. For example, it might assign me port number 3000 and my wife port number 4000. Thus, the router would make two entries in a table for its own later reference. One entry would show that it should map all internal packets destined for the web server from address 192.168.0.100 and port number 2000 into external packets with address 216.114.254.180 and port number 3000. The other entry would show that traffic to the web server from internal address 192.168.0.101 with port number 2000 maps into external address 216.114.254.180 with port number 4000. Figure 9.10 illustrates this scenario.

Luckily, port numbers are not a scarce resource. The TCP header fields for source and destination port numbers are each 16 bits in size, yet computers do not ordinarily use anywhere near 2^{16} ports apiece. Therefore, the NAT router has no problem assigning distinct external port numbers for all the ports in use by any of the computers on the home network.

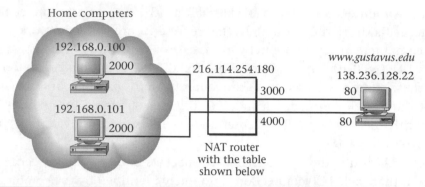

Internal address	Internal port	External address	External port	Remote address	Remote port
192.168.0.100	2000	216.114.254.180	3000	138.236.128.22	80
192.168.0.101	2000	216.114.254.180	4000	138.236.128.22	80

Figure 9.10   A NAT router rewrites port numbers as well as addresses so two computers can share a single public address.

The NAT router has one further essential function. It must also rewrite in the reverse manner each packet coming in from the Internet at large to the private network. For example, if a packet arrives with source address 138.236.128.22, source port 80, destination address 216.114.254.180, and destination port 3000, then the NAT's table will show that this belongs to my connection, and so the NAT will modify the packet to show destination 192.168.0.100 with port 2000. By the time the packet reaches my computer, it will look as though the web server was directly communicating with me using my private address.

What happens if an external computer wants to initiate a TCP connection to one of my home computers? In the particular case of my home, it is out of luck. My NAT router is configured to forward only inbound packets that come as part of a connection initiated from the private network. However, the answer might be somewhat different on another network using a NAT router. Consider, for example, a business that chooses to use a NAT router. The business would allow outgoing connections from all its computers, just as I do at home. These outgoing connections would create temporary entries in the router's table of rewriting rules, just like in my router. However, the business would also allow incoming connections to port 80 (the standard HTTP port) for its main web server and to port 25 (the standard SMTP port) for its main email server. It would do this by configuring the NAT router with two permanent rewriting rules. Any packets coming to the business's public address on port 80 should get rewritten to the web server's private address, while retaining port 80. Any packets coming to the public address on port 25 should get rewritten to the email server's private address, while retaining port 25.

This example illustrates one of the problems with NAT routing, stemming from its violation of the end-to-end principle. Suppose someone within the business wants to start offering a new kind of Internet service using a new application-layer protocol that listens on a new port number. For this to work, the corporate network administrator would need to make a new entry in the NAT router's table, like the two for the web and email servers. This is a significant stumbling block for introducing new services. This is one reason why many services today are packaged inside HTTP traffic, directed to the usual port 80.

NAT routing has other problems as well. One of the fundamental ones is that IPsec is designed to prevent packets from being altered in transit, but NAT relies on doing exactly that. A technique for working around this difficulty has recently been developed, but it does at least introduce additional complexity.

Despite these problems, NAT routing is heavily used and becomes more so every day. The principle reason is that internet addresses are expensive and so are worth sharing. The negative consequences are ameliorated by the fact that most network administrators would prefer to put most internal computers off limits to external access anyhow, for security reasons.

9.5 The Link and Physical Layers

When you plug an Ethernet cable into a socket, the plug snaps into the socket because it is the right size. When your computer starts sending high and low voltages over that cable, they are high enough and low enough to be recognized as 1 and 0 by the equipment on the other end, but not so extreme as to fry that equipment. These are examples of issues addressed by the physical layer. Various physical-layer standards exist for Ethernet over fiber optics, Ethernet over twisted pairs of copper wires, and so forth.

Even granted that the physical layer can get bits from one end of a link to the other, there are still problems to solve. For example, how do computers on the local network address data to each other? Presumably, each chunk of data (known as a *frame*) needs to have a header that specifies a source address and destination address. However, suppose you plug a computer into a network, and it starts immediately hearing 1s and 0s, having come in on the middle of a frame. It should start paying attention at the start of the next frame. How can it recognize the boundary between frames? Perhaps there is some definite minimum space of silence between frames, some recognizable signal at the beginning of each frame, or some error-detecting code at the end which will be correct only if the frame boundaries were correctly guessed. Shared links (like radio channels) pose another problem: how can the various computers take turns, rather than all transmitting at once? These issues of addressing, framing, and taking turns are concerns at the link layer, which is also sometimes known as the data link layer.

Computer systems have hardware devices that support both the link and physical layers. The operating system kernel provides this hardware with a frame of data to deliver, complete with the address of the recipient on the local network. The hardware does the rest. Conversely, the hardware may interrupt the operating system to report the arrival of an incoming frame.

Most of the issues at the link and physical layer have no direct bearing on operating systems or other software. The biggest exception is addressing. The two common kinds of networks (Ethernet and Wi-Fi) use 48-bit addresses that are totally independent from the 32-bit internet addresses. Thus, whenever the operating system sends out a packet of data to an internet address, and the address's prefix shows that it is on the local network, the kernel needs some mechanism for looking up the corresponding 48-bit hardware address, commonly known as a *MAC (Media Access Control) address*.

The kernel discovers MAC addresses using a network protocol called *ARP* (*Address Resolution Protocol*). The kernel broadcasts a request to all machines on the local network asking if any of them knows the MAC address corresponding to a particular IP address. The operating system kernels on all the receiving machines compare the requested address to their own. The one that sees its own IP address responds, providing its own MAC address. The requesting kernel stores the information away in a table for later reuse, so that it won't need to bother all other computers repeatedly.

Lots of network technologies have been developed, but two account for the bulk of networks today. Most networks that use wires or fiber optics use some version of the Ethernet standard, whereas most networks that use radio signals use some version of the Wi-Fi standard. (Wi-Fi is also frequently known by the less-catchy name 802.11, which is the identifying number of the working group that standardizes it.) Because these two use the same high-level interface, they can be integrated into combined networks, in which any device can communicate with any other device by MAC address, even if one is on the Ethernet portion of the network and the other on the Wi-Fi portion. Internet routing is not required. The switching devices that link Ethernet and Wi-Fi in this way are known as *access points*.

9.6 Network Security

Just as networking is a large field that I can only survey in this chapter, network security is a large area. My purpose in addressing it here is twofold. First, I want to impress upon you how important it is; if I remained silent, you might think it was unimportant.

Second, by scratching the surface, I can give you some feel for some of the constituent topics.

Data security must extend beyond security for the systems on which the data is persistently stored. In today's world, the data is frequently also in transit over networks. For example, my students' grades are not only stored on the college's computer, they are also transmitted over the Internet every time I do grading from home. Thus, to be comprehensive, data security must include network security.

There are two key differences between persistent storage and network communication, however:

- Large amounts of data are available for long periods of time in persistent storage. Networks, on the other hand, generally carry any particular piece of data very fleetingly. Contrast gaining access to a merchant's database, containing all its customers' credit card numbers, with tapping into the network connection and snagging the few numbers that pass through during the time your interception is in operation.

- Persistent storage is directly accessible only to a very limited number of people who have physical access and who are subject to the risks of being physically apprehended. The Internet, on the other hand, is accessible to an entire world worth of malefactors, many of whom may be beyond effective reach of law enforcement.

When the Internet was less pervasive, the first of these factors was the dominant one, and network security was not such a major concern. Today, the second factor must be considered the dominant one. Keep in mind also that network adversaries are not limited to eavesdropping on, or modifying, data already passing through the network. They can also send messages that might trigger additional data flows that would not otherwise occur. Many computers (typically in homes) today are "owned" by network intruders. That is, the intruder has obtained complete control and can remotely command the computer to carry out any action, as though it were his or her own computer, including accessing any of the persistently stored data. The only way organizations such as companies and government agencies prevent their computers from being similarly "owned" is by devoting large amounts of attention to network security.

9.6.1 Security and the Protocol Layers

Security vulnerabilities and threats exist at each layer of the protocol stack. Similarly, defensive measures are possible at each level, whether to protect the confidentiality of transmitted data, or to ensure the authenticity and integrity of arriving data.

Many of the most notorious network security problems have been at the application layer. Examples include forged email and the SQL Slammer worm, which propagated by overflowing the memory space a particular application program used for incoming messages. Some of the application-layer vulnerabilities stem from fundamental protocol design decisions (such as that email can claim to come from anyone), whereas others come from implementation flaws (such as a program not checking whether it was putting more data into a buffer than it had room for).

These vulnerabilities can be combated directly by using better designs and more careful programming. However, it is unrealistic to expect perfection in this area, any more than in other human endeavors. Therefore, indirect methods should also be used to minimize risk. Section 9.6.2 mentions the role well-configured firewall and intrusion detection systems can play. To take one example, there was essentially zero need for organizations to allow traffic to come in from the Internet at large to the particular port number used by the SQL Slammer worm. This application-layer vulnerability ought to have been shielded by a firewall.

The application layer also provides plenty of opportunity to actively enhance security. For example, the email protocols can be retrofitted with cryptographic techniques to ensure that messages really come from their stated sender, have not been modified in transit, and are read only by their intended recipient; *PGP* (*Pretty Good Privacy*) and *S/MIME* (*Secure/Multipurpose Internet Mail Extensions*) do exactly that. To take another example, there is no reason why web browsers and web servers need to directly send HTTP messages over vulnerable TCP connections. Instead, they can interpose a layer of encryption known as the *Secure Sockets Layer* (*SSL*). Every time you visit a secure web site and see the padlock icon click shut, it means that SSL is in use. Conceptually this is between the main HTTP application layer and the TCP transport layer, but strictly speaking it is an application-layer protocol.

At the transport layer, TCP is subject to its own set of vulnerabilities. Many of the denial-of-service attacks on network servers take place at this level; the server under attack is flooded by initial connection-establishment requests that are never followed up on. Proposals for fixing that problem in fundamental ways run into the difficulty of changing any protocol that is so widely deployed.

One example of a security-enhancement technology at the transport layer is an optional TCP feature for message authentication. This feature is particularly used by routers in order to secure their communication with neighboring routers. If it were possible for an intruder to inject bogus routing information, the Internet could be rendered unusable. Therefore, routers "sign" their routing update messages, using the optional TCP feature, and check the signatures on the updates they receive from neighboring routers.

One of the biggest security vulnerabilities at the network layer is that packets may have incorrect source addresses. The typical response to this problem is filtering at routers. For example, no packets should be allowed out of my college campus onto the Internet at large if the source address is not a legitimate one from the range assigned to this college. That would prevent someone here from pretending to be elsewhere.

I already mentioned that IPsec is a security technology at the network layer. The most common application of IPsec is when an organization has computers at several physical locations (including, frequently, within workers' homes) and wants to allow them all to communicate securely with one another, even though the traffic between locations is carried on the public Internet. IPsec supports this kind of *virtual private network* (*VPN*) by making sure every packet of data sent is encrypted, so as to be completely opaque to eavesdroppers, and so as to stymie any active intruder who would attempt to modify or inject packets.

Finally, the lowest layers of the protocol stack, the link and physical layers, are not immune from security issues. I will mention just two. One is that the ARP protocol, used to translate internet addresses into MAC addresses, was designed without any serious consideration of security issues. As a result, it is easy for any computer on a local network to take over an internet address that ought to belong to another computer on the same network. This is an attack more readily detected and responded to than prevented. To take a second example, Wi-Fi signals for many organizations can be picked up from the street outside. Moreover, the encryption built into early versions of Wi-Fi was faulty and even in newer versions is frequently not turned on. If you use Wi-Fi, you should definitely read one of the widely available tutorials on Wi-Fi security. These systems can be configured much more securely than they usually are.

9.6.2 Firewalls and Intrusion Detection Systems

A *firewall* is a system that imposes some restriction on the Internet traffic crossing a border, for example, between a company and the outside world, or between a particular computer and the rest of the Internet. Security-conscious organizations deploy multiple firewalls, protecting not only the outer perimeter, but also the borders between internal groups and around individual systems. Every computer installation that is hooked up to the Internet, even as small as a single home computer, should have at least one firewall.

A firewall can be a computer (or special-purpose hardware unit) devoted to the purpose, a router that has been configured to filter traffic, or software installed directly on the computer being protected. If the firewall operates correctly, any of these approaches is valid. However, if the firewall software itself is buggy, the consequences are likely to be more severe if it is operating on the same computer that is being protected. The best practice is to use a reputable external firewall at the organizational and workgroup perimeters and then software firewalls on individual computers. Home users should ideally use the same approach. The external firewall in this case may be a NAT router.

The big problem with firewalls is configuring them to let through only traffic that has a good reason to exist while blocking all other traffic. Empirical studies have shown that a large percentage of firewalls are misconfigured. Security-conscious organizations have their firewall configuration files examined by auditors and also have penetration testing performed, in which the auditors make attempts to gain access to the protected network.

In an organizational setting, there is pressure on network administrators to not configure firewalls too restrictively. If traffic necessary to the organization's functioning is blocked, someone will complain. These complaints could cost the administrator a job. In a home setting, on the other hand, you are likely to be complaining to yourself and can presumably stand the heat. Therefore, you should set all firewall settings as restrictively as possible, and wait and see what harm it does you. Loosen up on only those settings that prove to get in your way. This approach compensates for your inability to hire security auditors.

One of the most important steps an organization can take to preserve overall security is to use firewalls to isolate machines that are exposed to attack, so that even if those particular machines are "owned" by attackers, the damage is limited. As an example, consider a web server that does not support interactive transactions (such as shopping), but rather just disseminates information about the organization. A security-conscious configuration is as shown in Figure 9.11.

Suppose that the web server software has some bug, such that by sending some clever, over-long message to the server's normal port 80, an outside attacker can overwrite some critical memory and come to "own" the server, executing arbitrary code. Clearly the attacker can deface the server, replacing the organization's web pages with others. However, the attacker cannot mount any attack from the server to other machines, whether on the internal network or the external, because the firewall prohibits any outbound connections from the server. When employees of the organization want to reconfigure the server or put new information on it, they do so using connections they initiate from within the internal network.

In addition to firewalls, all organizational networks should also include an *intrusion detection system* (*IDS*). This system monitors all network traffic looking for activity that does not fit the usual, legitimate patterns. The IDS can play two roles, both alerting the network administrators to the existence of a problem and capturing forensic evidence useful in crafting an appropriate response. The response can be both technical (such as removing an infected machine from the network) and non-technical (such as cooperating with law-enforcement officials). A properly configured IDS should protect

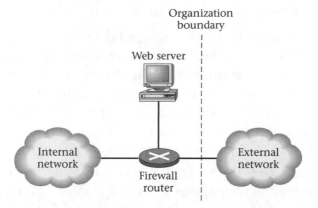

Configuration of the firewall router:

Initiator	Target	Allowed ports
external network	web server	80
internal network	web server	a few needed for operation
internal network	external network	none
external network	internal network	none
web server	any	none

Figure 9.11 This firewall configuration allows an organization's web server to provide static content to the outside world but allows for no other interaction. An organization with other needs would have other equally security-conscious modules added to this one.

not only against intrusions that breach the organizational perimeter, but also against attacks mounted by insiders.

9.6.3 Cryptography

Cryptography consists of mathematical techniques for transforming data in order to assure confidentiality or integrity and authenticity. Cryptography underlies much of network security, ranging from application-layer secure email and web browsing to link-layer encryption within the Wi-Fi protocol. Unlike techniques such as blocking access through a firewall, cryptography provides the means for legitimate communication to continue even as adversaries are thwarted. However, you should be aware that most practical security problems are outside the scope of cryptography. Rarely is there a report of encryption being broken, whereas misconfigured firewalls and systems vulnerable to buffer overflows are everyday occurrences.

Cryptographic techniques can be categorized in two independent ways:

- Some techniques rely on both the sender and the receiver knowing a *shared secret*, that is, a secret key that the two of them both know but intruders don't. Other techniques use a *key pair*, with one component known to the sender and the other to the receiver. These two options are known as *symmetric-key cryptography* and *asymmetric-key cryptography*. Because in many applications one half of a key pair can be made publicly known while the other is kept secret, asymmetric-key cryptography is also known as *public-key cryptography*.

- Some techniques *encrypt* the message, that is, transform the message so that it is not readable without the appropriate key, whereas other techniques leave the message itself alone but append a *Message Authentication Code* that allows the possessor of the appropriate key to verify that the message really comes from the legitimate sender and was not modified. Note that the abbreviation *MAC* is used in this context independently from its use in describing features of link-layer protocols, such as MAC addresses.

The more bits long a cryptographic key is, the more work the legitimate sender and receiver need to do, but also the more work any intruder needs to do. The goal in designing a cryptographic system is to make the legitimate parties' work scale up only modestly with key size, whereas the intruder's work scales up much more rapidly. That way, a key size can be chosen that is infeasible for an intruder to break, yet still practical for use. Unfortunately, none of the computational hardness results used in practical cryptosystems have been proved. Thus, the possibility remains that a sufficiently clever intruder could find a way to break the system that does not scale up so rapidly with key size.

Symmetric-key systems of reasonable security are more computationally efficient for the legitimate parties than asymmetric-key systems are. However, giving each potential pair of communicating parties a shared secret in advance is impractical. Thus, many practical systems (such as PGP and SSL) combine the two types of cryptography, using asymmetric-key cryptography to establish a secret key and then switching to symmetric-key cryptography for the bulk of the communication.

The present standard technique for symmetric-key encryption is *AES* (*Advanced Encryption Standard*), also known as *Rijndael*. Many applications still use the prior standard, the *Data Encryption Standard* (*DES*). However, DES is now considered not very secure, simply because the key size is too small. A more secure variant, *3DES*, uses the basic DES operation three times. Best practice for new applications is to use AES.

The most well-known technique for asymmetric-key encryption is the *RSA* system, named for the initials of its three developers, Rivest, Shamir, and Adleman. Data transformed with one half of the RSA key pair can be transformed back to the original using the other half of the key pair; the two specify inverse functions. Thus, a user who wants to receive encrypted messages can make one half the key pair public for any sender to use, while keeping the other half private so that no one else can read the messages.

The standard technique for computing a MAC using a shared secret is known as a *Hashed Message Authentication Code* (*HMAC*). The shared secret and the message are combined together and fed into a *cryptographic hash function*, also known as a *message digest function*. This function is designed so that adversaries cannot realistically hope to find another input that produces the same output. Thus, if the recipient's copy of the message and shared secret result in the same HMAC code, the recipient can be confident that the message is legitimate, because it came from someone else who knew the same two ingredients. As an additional safeguard against certain possible flaws in the cryptographic hash function, the standard HMAC technique (used in IPsec, for example) applies the hash function twice, as shown in Figure 9.12.

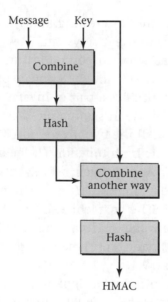

Figure 9.12 An HMAC can be computed as shown here. Both the sender and the receiver use this computation, each with its own copy of the shared secret key. The sender uses the message it is sending and transmits the resulting HMAC along with the message. The receiver does the computation using the (hopefully unchanged) message it received. If all is well, the receiver computes the same HMAC as it received along with the message.

HMAC codes are commonly based on one of two cryptographic hash functions, *MD5* (*Message Digest 5*) and *SHA-1* (*Secure Hash Algorithm 1*). Unfortunately, neither of these widely deployed functions turns out to be as secure as previously thought. Unlike DES, which simply used an insufficiently long key, MD5 and SHA-1 have fallen prey to fundamental mathematical progress. The computational problem faced by adversaries does not scale up as rapidly with hash size as had been conjectured, especially for MD5. No one has yet found a way to exploit these functions' vulnerabilities within the context of HMAC. However, the fact that the underlying cryptographic hash functions are weaker than previously thought is worrisome enough that new systems should definitely at a minimum use SHA-1 rather than MD5, as MD5's vulnerabilities are more pronounced. System developers should monitor further news from the cryptography research community and should consider using successors to SHA-1, such as SHA-512. Existing systems using MD5 (particularly in non-HMAC contexts) should be reconsidered, and many of them should be converted to SHA-1 or successor functions with deliberate speed. Practical exploits have been found for MD5's vulnerabilities in some non-HMAC contexts; the same is not currently true for SHA-1.

The most common technique for creating an asymmetric-key MAC combines a cryptographic hash function with the RSA system. These MACs are also known as *digital signatures*, because they share some important features with real signatures, as I will discuss in the next paragraph. First, though, let me explain how they are computed. Recall that each RSA key pair specifies a pair of inverse functions. A sender can keep one half the key pair secret, for use in signing messages, and make the other public, for use in checking messages. Call the two inverse functions S and C, for signing and checking, and the cryptographic hash function H. Then a sender can use $S(H(m))$ as a signature for the message m. Any recipient who wants to check this signature runs it through the function C, producing $C(S(H(m)))$, which is the same as $H(m)$, because C is the inverse function of S. The recipient also runs the received message through H, and verifies that the same value of $H(m)$ results. This provides evidence that the message wasn't tampered with, and was signed by the one person who knew S. This system is summarized in Figure 9.13.

The key difference between a digital signature and an HMAC is that the recipient is in no better position to forge a digital signature than any one else would be. Thus, digital signatures offer the feature known as *non-repudiation*. That is, if you have an embarrassing email signed by me, you could show it to a third party and I couldn't convincingly claim that you forged it yourself. An HMAC, on the other hand, would offer no evidence to a third party regarding which of the two of us wrote the message.

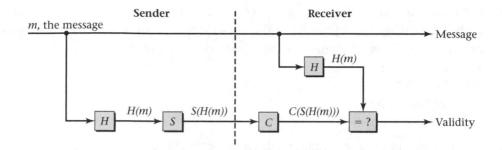

Figure 9.13 A digital signature is computed and verified as shown here. The signing and checking functions S and C are inverses, one kept private and the other publicly known. The role of the cryptographic hash function, H, is simply to efficiently reduce the amount of data that S and C need to process.

Exercises

9.1 Under the end-to-end principle, which protocol layers are processed by devices within the Internet, excluding the endpoint computers?

9.2 List at least five types of header lines that can be used in the HTTP protocol. What is the function of each?

9.3 What is one reason a domain name might take much longer to resolve the first time it is used than on subsequent uses?

9.4 Figure 9.9 on page 348 illustrates how parity can be used as a primitive form of erasure coding for forward error correction. Show how the third segment could be reconstructed if it were missing. Also, suppose the parity segment were 01100001. What would the missing third data segment then have been?

9.5 TCP and UDP headers contain port numbers used by the transport-layer software to demultiplex incoming data to the appropriate application-layer consumer. What analogous number is in the IP header, allowing the network layer to demultiplex to the appropriate transport-layer consumer?

9.6 Express the IP address 10100011000101000110000100001111 in dotted decimal.

9.7 Express the IP address 194.79.127.10 in binary.

9.8 If a network mask is 255.255.192.0, how many bits long is the network prefix?

9.9 If a network mask is 255.255.224.0, how many bits long is the network prefix?

9.10 What would the network mask be for a 20-bit network prefix?

9.11 What would the network mask be for a 22-bit network prefix?

9.12 My computer has IP address 138.236.64.64 and mask 255.255.248.0. For which of the following destination IP addresses does my computer send the packet directly, and for which does it send by way of the gateway router?

(a) 138.236.71.64

(b) 138.236.72.64

(c) 138.236.64.72

(d) 216.114.254.180

9.13 Identify by name and number which layer of the OSI reference model corresponds to each of the following specific protocols, technologies, or functions:

(a) UDP

(b) retrieving email

(c) Ethernet MAC addresses

(d) IP

(e) congestion control

(f) fiber optics

(g) TCP

(h) routers

(i) delivering bytes in their proper sequence

(j) DNS

(k) end-to-end flow-control

(l) HTTP

(m) retransmitting data for which no acknowledgment is received

(n) CIFS

(o) verifying that a cached web page is up to date

(p) port numbers

(q) NFS

🖳 Programming Projects

9.1 Modify the message storage server from Figure 9.7 on page 343 so that each accepted connection is handled in a separate thread, with the main thread immediately looping back around to accept another connection. Using `telnet`, show that a client that is slow providing its line of text does not prevent other clients from being served. Your program should use a synchronized method that atomically stores a newly arrived message and retrieves the previously stored message.

9.2 Write a program that can retrieve a single file from a web server using HTTP, given the hostname of the server and the name of the file on the server. (For example, given *www.gustavus.edu* and `/+max/`, it would retrieve my home page.) You should directly use a socket API, rather than any higher-level mechanism that already implements HTTP for you. Your handling of errors and other exceptional circumstances can be very primitive, at least initially.

9.3 The Java class **java.net.Socket** provides two methods, **getLocalAddress()** and **getInetAddress()**, that can be used to find the local and remote internet addresses associated with a connected socket. Write a server program that accepts connection requests and, each time it receives a connection, writes out on the connection a line of text containing the string form of the remote address from which the connection was received. Write a client program that connects to the server, displays the string the server sends, and also displays the client's own local address. Show how you can use this pair of programs to test whether the client is connected to the server through a NAT router or not.

Exploration Projects

9.1 Most UNIX and Linux systems have a program named **dig** that can be used to send DNS queries and show the responses in human-readable form. Use this tool to explore the DNS. For example, find the internet addresses of some of your favorite computers, check whether the CNAME chain leading from *www.gustavus.edu.* still has the same structure as I reported, and use the zone transfer function to display the contents of your local zone. What aspects of the DNS do you find that were not mentioned in my description?

9.2 Use the freely available network packet capture and analysis tool named **ethereal** to study DNS. Capture packets while you are accessing a web site you have not previously accessed. Look at just the DNS packets and for each one expand out the DNS portion of the display. In what regards do you see confirmation of my description of DNS? What aspects of the DNS do you find that were not mentioned in my description?

9.3 Use the freely available network packet capture and analysis tool named **ethereal** to study either CIFS or NFS. Capture packets while you are accessing a file provided by a server. Look at just the CIFS or NFS packets and for each one expand out the CIFS or NFS portion of the display. In what regards do you see confirmation of my description of this system? What aspects of the system do you find that were not mentioned in my description?

9.4 I mentioned that NFS does not have operations for opening or closing files. With regard to closing, this is inarguably true, whereas with regard to opening, my claim might be only a half-truth. The NFS protocol includes a lookup operation, which is similar to a file open. Find information about the NFS lookup operation and explain how looking up a file is similar to and different from opening a file.

9.5 Compile and run the message storage server from Figure 9.7 on page 343. Using **telnet**, show that a client that is slow providing its line of text prevents other clients from being served.

9.6 Find your own IP address and network mask. On a Microsoft Windows system, you can do this with the **ipconfig** command. On most UNIX or Linux systems, you can do this using the **ifconfig** command; a typical example of its use would be **ifconfig eth0**.

From the network mask, how many bits long is your network prefix? Using this information together with the IP address, what is your actual network prefix?

9.7 Explore some of the resources and sample policies on *www.sans.org*. Write a summary of something interesting you find.

9.8 Read the paper by Pang et al. on "Characteristics of Internet Background Radiation," which you can find on the web. Write a summary no longer than one page.

Notes

Most of the topics in this chapter are covered in more detail in standard networking textbooks, such as the one by Tanenbaum [128] and the one by Kurose and Ross [83]. The ultimate source of information on the various protocols are the corresponding standards documents, which can be found at such sites as *www.rfc-editor.org*. A good compromise, providing almost as much technical detail as the standards and almost as much tutorial clarity as the textbooks, is Stevens's book [122]. If you want to delve into the kernel implementation details, you could look at books on the FreeBSD [93] or Linux [67] implementations. Regarding the frequency of firewall misconfiguration, see the study by Wool [136]. One area of research I mentioned is the use of erasure coding for forward error corrections; see, for example, the paper by Byers, Luby, and Mizenmacher [25]. The paper by Pang et al. that serves as the basis for an exploration project is reference [98].

10

Messaging, RPC, and Web Services

10.1 Introduction

Application programmers who create distributed systems of communicating processes fundamentally rely upon the support for networking provided by operating systems; this support was described in Chapter 9. Sometimes this reliance is direct; for example, the application programs may use sockets to open connections between TCP ports and then send byte streams that encode application messages. Increasingly, however, this reliance is indirect because a middleware layer comes between the application program and the socket API. The application programmer works in terms of the middleware-supported abstractions, such as message queues and remotely accessible objects. The middleware provides those abstractions by making use of the more fundamental operating system–supported facilities.

In this chapter, I will present two distinct styles of communication middleware. Messaging systems, discussed in Section 10.2, support the one-way transmission of messages. Application programmers can choose to use those messages in request-response pairs, but the middleware remains oblivious to this pairing and treats each message individually. Sending a request and receiving a response happen in separate transactions, potentially at quite different times. For more tightly coupled interactions, Remote Procedure Call (RPC) systems provide an alternative style of communication, as presented in Section 10.3. Each time a process invokes an RPC operation, it sends a request and then immediately waits for a response as part of the same transaction. The RPC system makes the request-response pair appear to the application program as a normal procedure call and return.

After presenting each of these styles of communication, I turn in Section 10.4 to their connection with web services. Web services use standardized communication mechanisms to make programmed functionality available over the Internet. Most web services fit the RPC model, though they can also use one-way messaging or (in theory) more general message exchange patterns.

Finally, the chapter concludes, as usual, with a look at security issues in Section 10.5 and then exercises, projects, and notes.

10.2 Messaging Systems

Applications based on one-way transmission of messages use a form of middleware known as *messaging systems* or *message-oriented middleware* (*MOM*). One popular example of a messaging system is IBM's WebSphere MQ, formerly known as MQSeries. One popular vendor-neutral API for messaging is the Java Message Service (JMS), which is part of J2EE.

Messaging systems support two different forms of messaging: *message queuing* and *publish/subscribe messaging*. I already introduced message queuing in Section 5.2.2. Here I will build on that introduction to message queuing and also provide an introduction to publish/subscribe messaging.

Figure 10.1 illustrates the difference between the two forms of messaging. Message queuing strongly decouples the timing of the client and the server, because the queue will retain the messages until they are retrieved. (Optionally, the client can specify an expiration time for unretrieved messages.) The server need not be running at the time a message is sent. On the other hand, the client is only weakly decoupled from the server's identity. Although the client doesn't send the message to a specific server, it does send it to a specific queue, which still creates a *point-to-point* architectural structure, because each queue normally functions as the in-box for a particular server. A point-to-point structure means that if the message is of interest to multiple servers, the client needs to send it to multiple queues. The publish/subscribe architecture, in contrast, strongly decouples publishers from any knowledge of the subscribers' identities. Each message is sent to a general topic and from there is distributed to any number of subscribers that have indicated their interest in the topic. However,

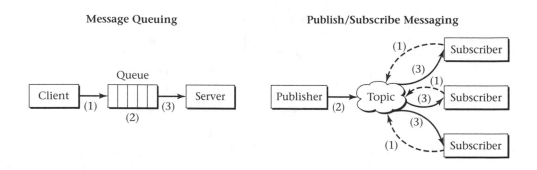

Figure 10.1 Message queuing involves three steps: (1) the client sends a message to a queue, (2) the queue retains the message as long as necessary, (3) the server retrieves the message. Publish/subscribe messaging involves a different sequence of three steps: (1) each subscriber subscribes with one of the messaging system's "topic" objects, (2) the publisher sends a message to the topic, (3) the message is distributed to all current subscribers.

publish/subscribe messaging usually does not decouple timing. Messages are usually only sent to current subscribers, not retained for future subscribers.

The portion of a messaging system managing topic objects for publish/subscribe messaging is known as a *broker*. The broker is responsible for maintaining a list of current subscribers for each topic and for distributing each incoming publication to the current subscribers of the publication's topic.

Section 5.2.2 explained the relationship between message queuing and transactions. A transaction can retrieve messages from queues, do some processing, such as updating a database, and send messages to queues. When the transaction commits, the input messages are gone from their queues, the database is updated, and the output messages are in their queues. If the transaction aborts, then the input messages remain in their queues, the database remains unchanged, and the output messages have not entered their queues.

This transactional nature of message queuing has an important consequence for systems in which request messages are paired with response messages and will help me explain the difference between messaging and RPC systems. Consider a client and server coupled through request and response queues, as shown in Figure 10.2. The client can generate a request message in one transaction and then in a second transaction wait for a response message. However, it cannot do both in a single transaction, or it will wait forever, having deadlocked itself. Until the transaction commits, the request message doesn't enter the request queue. As a result, the server has nothing to respond to and won't generate a response message. Therefore, the client will continue

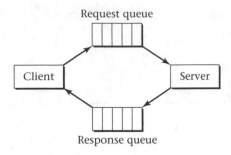

Request queue

Response queue

Figure 10.2 A client and server can engage in a request-response protocol using two message queues. Typically, the client tags each request message with a unique identifying string, known as a *correlation ID*. The server copies this ID into the resulting response message so that the client knows to which request the response corresponds.

waiting for the response message and so the transaction won't commit, completing the deadlock. If your goal is to have the client make use of the server as one indivisible step within a transaction, then you need to use RPC rather than messaging.

Publish/subscribe messaging can participate in transactions as well, but the results are less interesting. Publishing is just like sending to a queue, in that the message isn't actually sent until the transaction commits. However, receipt of messages by subscribers is handled differently. If a subscriber receives a message within a transaction and then aborts the transaction, it cannot count on the message being redelivered when the transaction is retried.

In either messaging model, a consumer may want to receive only selected messages that are of interest to it. For example, it may want to receive stock ticker messages with updated prices, but only for IBM stock and only if the price is less than 75 or more than 150. The program could receive all stock ticker messages (by reading from a queue to which they are sent or by subscribing to a topic to which they are published) and ignore those that are uninteresting. However, for the sake of efficiency, messaging systems generally provide mechanisms to do the filtering prior to message delivery.

In the publish/subscribe model, the selection of just IBM stock might be accomplished simply by having a sufficiently specific topic. Messaging systems generally allow topics to be hierarchically structured, much like files in directory trees or Internet domains within the DNS. Thus, a topic for IBM stock prices might be `finance/stockTicker/IBM`. A subscriber interested only in this one stock could subscribe to that specific topic, whereas a subscriber interested in all stock prices could subscribe to `finance/stockTicker/+`, where the wildcard + indicates any one subtopic. Another wildcard, #, is fancier than needed in this case but can be useful in other circumstances. A subscription to `finance/stockTicker/#` would receive not only messages about each individual stock, such as IBM, but also general messages, directed to `finance/stockTicker` itself, and more specialized messages, directed to descendant subtopics any number of levels below `finance/stockTicker/IBM` and its siblings.

This hierarchy of topics is limited, however. It fits the publish/subscribe model but not the message queuing model, and it addresses only qualitative selection criteria that naturally lead to distinct topics. In the example I gave earlier, it is unlikely that a system architect would create three subtopics of `IBM` for `under75`, `between75and150`, and `over150`. Among other reasons, there may be other subscribers interested in other price ranges.

Therefore, messaging systems allow message consumers to specify more general selection criteria. In the JMS API, for example, if `s` is a messaging `Session` and `d` is a messaging `Destination`, that is, either a `Queue` or a `Topic`, then executing

```
s.createConsumer(d, "Symbol = 'IBM' AND " +
                    "(Price < 75 OR Price > 150)")
```

will produce a `Consumer` object with the specified selector. Any `receive` operation performed on that `Consumer` (or any `MessageListener` registered with that `Consumer`) will see only those messages satisfying the selection criterion.

10.3 Remote Procedure Call

The goal of *Remote Procedure Call* (*RPC*) middleware is to make request-response communication as straightforward for application programmers to program as ordinary procedure calls. The client application code calls a procedure in the ordinary way, that is, passing in some arguments and obtaining a return value for its further use. The procedure it calls just happens to reside in a separate server. Behind the scenes, the middleware encodes the procedure arguments into a request message and extracts the return value from the response method. Similarly, the server application code can take the form of an ordinary procedure. By the time it is invoked, the procedure arguments have already been extracted from the request message, freeing it from that responsibility. Section 10.3.1 explains further the principles upon which RPC operates. Section 10.3.2 provides a concrete example of using RPC in the particular form of Java RMI (Remote Method Invocation). The subsequent section, 10.4, is devoted to web services but also provides additional information on how RPC plays out in that context.

10.3.1 Principles of Operation for RPC

To understand how RPC middleware functions, it is helpful to think about the fact that different procedures can present the same interface. For example, consider procedures for squaring a number. You could have several different procedures that take a numeric argument, compute the square, and return it. One might work by multiplying the number by itself. Another might use a fancy calculation involving logarithms. And a third might open up a network instant-messaging connection to a bored teenager, ask the teenager what the square of the number is, then return the value it receives, correctly extracted from the textual instant-messaging response. This third procedure is known as a *proxy* for the teenager. The proxy's method of squaring the number involves neither multiplication nor logarithms, but rather delegation of responsibility. However, the proxy still is presenting the same interface as either of the other two procedures.

Figure 10.3 shows how RPC middleware uses a proxy to put the client in the position of making a normal procedure call. The client application code actually does make a normal procedure call; that much is no illusion. However, it only gives the illusion of calling the server procedure that does the real computation. Instead, the called procedure is a proxy standing in for the server procedure; the proxy is often known as a *stub*. The stub proxy discharges its responsibility not by doing any actual computation itself, but by using request and response messages to communicate with the server.

The stub proxy suffices to hide communication issues from the application programmer writing the client code. In some cases, that is all that is needed, and the server is written by a networking expert who can directly write code to handle request and response messages. More typically, however, the server code is written by another

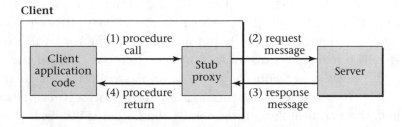

Figure 10.3 In Remote Procedure Call, application code makes a normal procedure call to a stub proxy, which doesn't carry out the requested computation itself, but rather sends a request message to the server and then turns the response message into the procedure return value.

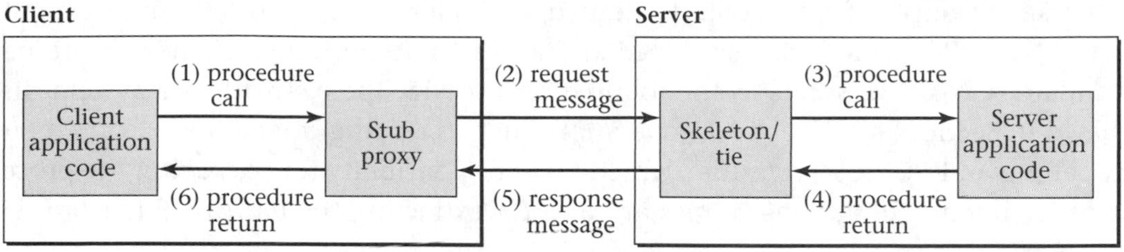

Client   **Server**

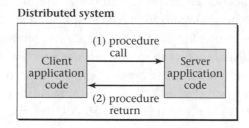

Figure 10.4   In order for the server application code to be free from communication details, it can be a normal procedure invoked by a portion of the RPC runtime sometimes called a skeleton or a tie.

Distributed system

Figure 10.5   The application programmer's view of an RPC system has the client code apparently making a direct call to the server procedure; the RPC proxy mechanism is invisible.

application programmer who appreciates middleware support. As shown in Figure 10.4, the server application code can be a normal procedure, called the same way it would be if it were running on the same machine with the client. Once again, the illusion is only partial. The server application code really is being called with an ordinary procedure call. The only illusion concerns what code is doing the calling. From an application standpoint, the caller seems to be the client. However, the caller really is a dedicated portion of the RPC runtime system, known as a *skeleton* or a *tie*, the purpose of which is to call the procedure in response to the request message. See Figure 10.5 for the application programmer's view of the result; the middleware communication disappears from view and the client application code seems to be directly calling the server application procedure, as though they were part of a single system.

Early versions of the RPC communication model were based on ordinary procedure calls, whereas more recent versions are based on the object-oriented concept of method invocation. The basic principles are the same, however, and the name RPC is commonly understood to include method invocation as well as procedure calling.

A key example of a non-object-oriented RPC standard is Open Network Computing (ONC) RPC, which was developed at Sun Microsystems and became an Internet standard. ONC RPC serves as the foundation for NFS, the Network File System discussed in Section 9.2.3. Each NFS operation, such as reading from a file, is carried out by calling an RPC stub procedure, which takes responsibility for packaging the procedure arguments into a request message and for extracting the return value from the response message.

In object-oriented versions of RPC, the stub proxy is an object presenting the same interface as the server object. That is, the same repertoire of methods can be invoked on it. The stub uses a uniform strategy for handling all methods: it translates method invocations into appropriate request messages.

Two significant object-oriented RPC standards are *CORBA* and *RMI*. CORBA (*Common Object Request Broker Architecture*) is a complicated language-neutral standard that allows code written in one language to call code written in another language and located elsewhere in a distributed system. RMI (*Remote Method Invocation*) is a considerably simpler mechanism included as part of the Java standard API; part of its simplicity comes from needing to support only a single programming language. Because RMI can optionally use CORBA's communication protocol, the Internet Inter-Orb Protocol (IIOP), the two systems can interoperate.

One important feature of object-oriented RPC systems such as RMI is that the values communicated as method arguments and return values can include references to other objects. That is, a remotely invoked method can operate not only on basic values, such as integers or strings, but also on user-defined types of objects. One remotely accessible object can be passed a reference that refers to another remotely accessible object. In fact, this is the way most objects find out about other objects to communicate with after getting past an initial startup phase.

To initially get communication started, client objects typically look up server objects using a *registry*, which is a specialized server that maintains a correspondence between textual names and references to the remotely accessible objects. (These correspondences are known as *bindings*.) The registry itself can be located, because it listens for connections on a prearranged port. When an application server object is created that a client might want to locate, the server object is bound to a name in the registry. The client then presents the same textual name to the registry in a lookup operation and thereby receives a reference to the initial server object it should contact.

After this initial contact is made, the objects can use the arguments and return values of remote method invocations to start passing each other references to additional objects that are not listed in the registry. Pretty soon any number of client and server objects can have references to one another and be invoking methods on each other.

Section 10.3.2 is occupied by an RMI programming example designed to reinforce the aforementioned point, that remote objects are located not only using the registry, but also by being passed as references. This example illustrates the way in which an application programmer uses RMI and thereby complements the preceding general discussion of how RPC stubs and skeletons work. I do not provide any more detailed information on the inner workings of RMI. However, in Section 10.4, I show how RPC messages are formatted in the web services environment.

10.3.2 An Example Using Java RMI

Using RMI, it is possible to develop an implementation of the publish/subscribe messaging model, in which publishers send messages to topic objects, which forward the messages along to subscribers. The code in this section shows such an implementation in the simplest possible form. In particular, this code has the following limitations; to address each limitation, there is at least one corresponding Programming Project:

- The message delivery is fully synchronous. That is, the publisher asks the topic object to deliver a message; control does not return to the publisher until the message has been delivered to all the subscribers. Programming Projects 10.2 and 10.3 address this.

- The example programs support only a single topic. Programming Projects 10.4 and 10.5 address this.

- In the example code, there is no way for a subscriber to explicitly unsubscribe from a topic. However, the code does support subscribers that terminate, lose communication, or otherwise fail. Programming Project 10.6 provides explicit unsubscription.

- The example code includes simple command-line interfaces for sending textual strings as messages and for displaying received messages on the terminal. These suffice to demonstrate the communication but do not have the appeal of a chat-room application or multi-player game. Programming Project 10.7 provides the opportunity to address this shortcoming.

When using RMI, each object that is remotely accessible must implement a Java interface that extends **java.rmi.Remote**. Each method in that interface must be declared as potentially throwing **java.rmi.RemoteException**. This potential for an exception is necessary because even if the underlying operation cannot possibly fail,

```
import java.rmi.Remote;
import java.rmi.RemoteException;

public interface MessageRecipient extends Remote {
  void receive(String message) throws RemoteException;
}
```

Figure 10.6 The `MessageRecipient` interface describes the common feature shared by subscribers and the central topic objects that redistribute published messages to subscribers: any of these objects can receive a message.

```
import java.rmi.RemoteException;

public interface Topic extends MessageRecipient {
  void subscribe(MessageRecipient subscriber)
    throws RemoteException;
}
```

Figure 10.7 The `Topic` interface provides an operation for subscribers to use to register their interest in receiving messages. By extending the `MessageRecipient` interface, the `Topic` interface is also prepared to receive messages from publishers.

the remote invocation of that operation can fail in myriad ways, such as through a network disconnection or a crash of the machine on which the remote object is located. Figure 10.6 shows the source code for a simple remote interface implemented by subscribers and also by topic objects. The reason why these two categories of participants in the publish/subscribe model implement this same interface is that they have something in common: they both receive messages.

Subscribers directly implement the `MessageRecipient` interface, as you will see later. However, topic objects need to implement an extension of the interface, because they can do more than receive messages; they can also add subscribers. Figure 10.7 shows the `Topic` interface, which extends `MessageRecipient` through the addition of a `subscribe` method. Notice that the argument passed to `subscribe` is itself a `MessageRecipient`. This allows a reference to one remotely accessible object (the subscriber) to be passed to another (the topic) for its later use.

Having seen these two interfaces for remotely accessible objects, you are now ready to see an example of code that makes use of such an object. Figure 10.8 contains a simple program for sending a textual message (given as the first command-line

```
import java.rmi.registry.LocateRegistry;
import java.rmi.registry.Registry;

public class Publisher {

  public static void main(String[] args) {
    if(args.length < 1 || args.length > 2){
      System.err.println("Usage: java Publisher message [host]");
      System.exit(1);
    }
    String message = args[0];
    String hostname = args.length > 1 ? args[1] : null;
    try {
      Registry registry = LocateRegistry.getRegistry(hostname);
      Topic topic = (Topic) registry.lookup("topic.1");
      topic.receive(message);
    } catch (Exception e) {
      System.err.println("caught an exception: " + e);
      e.printStackTrace();
    }
  }
}
```

Figure 10.8 This program uses the registry to locate the remote object that is named `topic.1` and that implements the `Topic` interface. The program then asks that object to receive a message.

argument) to a remote object implementing the `Topic` interface. The specific remote object is looked up with the aid of a registry, that is, a service within RMI that records name/object pairs. The registry is located on a server computer whose hostname is specified as the second command-line argument or on the local computer if no hostname is given.

Let's turn next to an example of how a remotely accessible object can be created and listed in the registry. The `TopicServer` class, as shown in Figures 10.9 and 10.10, implements the `Topic` interface. Each `TopicServer` keeps track of its current subscribers; additions happen in the `subscribe` method, and deletions happen when a message cannot be successfully delivered. Because the RMI infrastructure is allowed to invoke each operation in its own thread, the remote operations are marked as `synchronized` so as to provide mutual exclusion. This prevents any races in the manipulations of the list of subscribers. When the `TopicServer` program is run from the command line, the `main` method creates an instance of the class, exports it for

```java
import java.rmi.registry.Registry;
import java.rmi.registry.LocateRegistry;
import java.rmi.RemoteException;
import java.rmi.server.UnicastRemoteObject;
import java.util.List;
import java.util.ArrayList;

public class TopicServer implements Topic {

  private List<MessageRecipient> subscribers;

  public TopicServer(){
    subscribers = new ArrayList<MessageRecipient>();
  }

  public synchronized void receive(String message)
    throws RemoteException {
    List<MessageRecipient> successes =
      new ArrayList<MessageRecipient>();
    for(MessageRecipient subscriber : subscribers) {
      try {
        subscriber.receive(message);
        successes.add(subscriber);
      } catch(Exception e) {
        // silently drop any subscriber that fails
      }
    }
    subscribers = successes;
  }
```

Figure 10.9 The `TopicServer` class continues in Figure 10.10. The `receive` method shown here is remotely invoked by publishers and itself remotely invokes the `receive` method of subscribers.

remote access, and places it in the local registry, using the same `topic.1` name as the `Publisher` class looks up.

The final component of the example publish/subscribe system is the `Subscriber` class, as shown in Figure 10.11. This class provides a simple test program which displays all the messages it receives. Like the `Publisher` class, it uses the registry on a specified host or on the local host if none is specified. Also like the `Publisher` class, it looks up the name `topic.1` in that registry, thereby obtaining a reference to some remote object implementing the `Topic` interface. The reference will actually be to

```
public synchronized void subscribe(MessageRecipient subscriber)
  throws RemoteException {
  subscribers.add(subscriber);
}

public static void main(String args[]) {
  try {
    TopicServer obj = new TopicServer();
    Topic stub =
      (Topic) UnicastRemoteObject.exportObject(obj, 0);
    Registry registry = LocateRegistry.getRegistry();
    registry.rebind("topic.1", stub);
    System.err.println("Server ready");
  } catch (Exception e) {
    System.err.println("Server exception: " + e.toString());
    e.printStackTrace();
  }
}
}
```

Figure 10.10 This continuation of the `TopicServer` class, begun in Figure 10.9, shows how remote objects are created, exported (that is, made remotely accessible), and bound to a name in the registry.

a proxy that implements the interface. However, the proxy will be communicating with an instance of the `TopicServer` class. Unlike the `Publisher`, the `Subscriber` is itself a remotely accessible object. It is created and exported just like the `Topic-Server` is. However, it is not bound in the registry; the `TopicServer` does not locate its subscribers by name.

Before you can successfully run the `TopicServer` and test it using the `Publisher` and `Subscriber` programs, you will probably need to run the `rmiregistry` program that comes as part of the Java system. The details of how you run this program are system-specific, as is the mechanism for ensuring that all components of the overall RMI system have access to your classes. Therefore, you are likely to need to consult the documentation for your specific Java system in order to successfully test the sample code or complete the programming projects. Once you get over these technical hurdles, however, you will be able to communicate among multiple machines, so long as they are all running Java and so long as no network firewalls impede communication among them. In the following section, you will see how web services provide an alternate RPC mechanism that can allow communication between an even wider assortment of machines.

```java
import java.rmi.registry.LocateRegistry;
import java.rmi.registry.Registry;
import java.rmi.RemoteException;
import java.rmi.server.UnicastRemoteObject;

public class Subscriber implements MessageRecipient {

  public synchronized void receive(String message)
    throws RemoteException {
    System.out.println(message);
  }

  public static void main(String[] args) {
    if(args.length > 1){
      System.err.println("Usage: java Subscriber [hostname]");
      System.exit(1);
    }
    String hostname = args.length > 0 ? args[0] : null;
    try {
      Registry registry = LocateRegistry.getRegistry(hostname);
      Topic topic = (Topic) registry.lookup("topic.1");
      Subscriber obj = new Subscriber();
      MessageRecipient stub = (MessageRecipient)
        UnicastRemoteObject.exportObject(obj, 0);
      topic.subscribe(stub);
    } catch (Exception e) {
      System.err.println("caught an exception: " + e);
      e.printStackTrace();
    }
  }
}
```

Figure 10.11 Instances of the `Subscriber` class are created and exported the same way as `TopicServers` are, so that they can be remotely accessed. However, they are not bound in the registry. Instead, the stub referring to the `Subscriber` is passed to the `subscribe` method so the `TopicServer` can store the reference away for later.

10.4 Web Services

A *web service* is a communicating component that complies with a collection of Internet standards designed to share as much as possible with the standards used for ordinary web browsing. This allows web services to take advantage of the web's popularity, hopefully making communication between programmed components as ubiquitous as the communication with humans facilitated by the web.

The web services standards are based on *XML* (*Extensible Markup Language*), a form of structured textual document. All XML documents have nested components with explicitly indicated types and attributes. The specific kinds of nested components depend on the XML application. For example, where XML is used for request messages, the component parts indicate what operation is being invoked and what arguments are being supplied to it. By contrast, where XML is used not to invoke an operation but to define an interface, the component parts enumerate what the interface's operations are, what kinds of messages should be exchanged to invoke those operations, and so forth.

Web service interfaces are described using an XML notation known as *WSDL* (*Web Services Description Language*). This notation is rather verbose and is not usually read or written by humans. Instead, the humans normally use user-friendly tools to process the WSDL, which serves as a common interchange format accepted by all the tools. However, you can get a feel for WSDL by looking at the excerpts shown in Figure 10.12. The GoogleSearch API, from which these are taken, provides operations for searching for web pages. However, it also provides an operation for suggesting spelling corrections, as shown here. The operation involves two message types, one for request messages and one for response messages. Request messages contain two string arguments; one is an access control key that Google demands so as to limit use of their service,

```
<message name="doSpellingSuggestion">
  <part name="key"              type="xsd:string"/>
  <part name="phrase"           type="xsd:string"/>
</message>

<message name="doSpellingSuggestionResponse">
  <part name="return"           type="xsd:string"/>
</message>

<operation name="doSpellingSuggestion">
  <input message="typens:doSpellingSuggestion"/>
  <output message="typens:doSpellingSuggestionResponse"/>
</operation>
```

Figure 10.12 These excerpts from the WSDL definition of the GoogleSearch API show the two messages used to ask for and receive a spelling suggestion and the operation that combines those two messages.

and the other is the phrase to correct. The response message contains just the returned value, a string containing the suggested correction.

Notice that in Figure 10.12, the `doSpellingSuggestion` operation is explicitly specified as using an input request message and an output response message. Because WSDL provides this detailed specification of how operations exchange messages, it can be used for patterns of communication other than RPC. The most common usage is for RPC, as with the GoogleSearch API. However, an operation can have only an input message, in which case the web service fits the messaging model instead of the RPC model. In theory, an operation could also specify a more extended message exchange pattern, with multiple input and output messages; however, I am unaware of any use of this feature.

The WSDL standard allows providers of web services to make their interfaces known to potential users without concern for what programming language or implementation technology they use. For example, I cannot tell from the WSDL excerpted in Figure 10.12 whether Google is using J2EE, Microsoft's .NET, or some other technology. I am free to use whichever I choose in writing my client.

For this goal of interoperability to be realized, the service providers and users need to agree on more than just WSDL as a means of specifying interfaces. They also need to agree upon the specific format for transmitting the request and response messages. For this purpose, web services use a second XML format, known as *SOAP*. (SOAP once stood for Simple Object Access Protocol but no longer does.) Each SOAP document is a message and should match one of the message descriptions from the WSDL interface description. For example, you saw WSDL message descriptions for the two message types `doSpellingSuggestion` and `doSpellingSuggestionResponse`. Figures 10.13 and 10.14 show specific SOAP messages that fit these two descriptions. The first one is a message asking for suggestions as to how "middlewear" should really be spelled, and the second is a message responding with the suggestion of "middleware."

Some transport mechanism needs to underlie SOAP. That mechanism delivers the string of bytes shown in Figure 10.13 to the server and then delivers the bytes shown in Figure 10.14 back to the client. The most common transport mechanism for SOAP is HTTP, the application-layer protocol normally used to access web pages. Notice that in web services terminology, HTTP is referred to as a transport, because it conveys the SOAP messages, whereas in traditional networking terminology, the transport layer is one layer lower, where TCP operates. In effect, web services are building a super-application-layer on top of the application layer, thereby treating the HTTP application layer as though it were only a transport layer. As mentioned in Chapter 9, one advantage of this arrangement is that it circumvents obstacles such as firewalls that

```
<?xml version="1.0" encoding="UTF-8"?>
<env:Envelope
 xmlns:env="http://schemas.xmlsoap.org/soap/envelope/"
 xmlns:xsd="http://www.w3.org/2001/XMLSchema"
 xmlns:xsi="http://www.w3.org/2001/XMLSchema-instance"
 xmlns:enc="http://schemas.xmlsoap.org/soap/encoding/"
 xmlns:ns0="urn:GoogleSearch"
 env:encodingStyle="http://schemas.xmlsoap.org/soap/encoding/">
  <env:Body>
    <ns0:doSpellingSuggestion>
      <key xsi:type="xsd:string">GoogleAccessControlKeyHere</key>
      <phrase xsi:type="xsd:string">middlewear</phrase>
    </ns0:doSpellingSuggestion>
  </env:Body>
</env:Envelope>
```

Figure 10.13 This example SOAP message asks Google for spelling suggestions on the string `middlewear`. This message has been broken into indented lines for legibility and has a place-holder where a real message would contain an access-control key issued by Google, which I am not allowed to divulge.

```
<?xml version='1.0' encoding='UTF-8'?>
<SOAP-ENV:Envelope
 xmlns:SOAP-ENV="http://schemas.xmlsoap.org/soap/envelope/"
 xmlns:xsi="http://www.w3.org/1999/XMLSchema-instance"
 xmlns:xsd="http://www.w3.org/1999/XMLSchema">
  <SOAP-ENV:Body>
    <ns1:doSpellingSuggestionResponse
     xmlns:ns1="urn:GoogleSearch"
     SOAP-ENV:encodingStyle=
       "http://schemas.xmlsoap.org/soap/encoding/">
      <return xsi:type="xsd:string">middleware</return>
    </ns1:doSpellingSuggestionResponse>
  </SOAP-ENV:Body>
</SOAP-ENV:Envelope>
```

Figure 10.14 This example SOAP message returns `middleware` as a spelling suggestion in response to `middlewear`. (Line breaks and indentation changed for legibility.)

stand in the way of deploying new application-layer protocols. Almost any Internet connection is open to HTTP traffic.

When HTTP is used for a request-response message pair, as in the spelling suggestion example, the client opens a connection to the server exactly as it would to an ordinary web server, providing a URL that represents the particular web service, known as an *endpoint address*. The client then sends the SOAP request message as the body of a POST method, the kind of HTTP transaction more traditionally used for filled-in forms. The server sends the SOAP response message in the body of its HTTP response.

Although SOAP is most commonly used with HTTP, the web services architecture is intentionally neutral with regard to transport. SOAP messages can equally well be sent as the bodies of email messages, using SMTP, or as messages in a reliable message-queuing system, such as WebSphere MQ.

If you remember that the goal of communication middleware is to ease application programmers' burdens, it should be obvious that SOAP and WSDL are not intended to be used without the aid of automated tools. You could, in principle, read the GoogleSearch API's WSDL specification yourself and based on it write code that sent the SOAP message shown in Figure 10.13 over HTTP. You could do this by using nothing more than the ability to open up a TCP socket and send bytes through it. Then you could read in from the socket the bytes constituting Figure 10.14's response and arduously extract from it the spelling suggestion being returned. However, this would be making a distributed system harder to construct, not easier.

Luckily, there are a variety of language-specific and vendor-specific tools that make web services much easier to construct. In particular, both .NET and J2EE have support for web services. As an example, let's look at *JAX-RPC (Java API for XML-Based RPC)*, a component of J2EE.

In Programming Project 10.10, you can use a JAX-RPC tool to automatically translate the GoogleSearch WSDL file into a Java interface that contains ordinary Java-callable methods for each of the web service's operations. For example, it contains

```
public String doSpellingSuggestion(String key, String phrase);
```

Using this, you can set a variable to the suggested spelling with just this code:

```
suggestion = aGoogleSearch.doSpellingSuggestion(
                    "GoogleAccessControlKeyHere",
                    "middlewear");
```

The Java object named **aGoogleSearch** is a stub proxy implementing the interface created from the WSDL file; a few prior lines of code would set it up. This proxy takes care of generating the big, messy SOAP request message, sending it, reading in the response, and picking the suggestion out from amid all its SOAP wrappings. You, the application programmer, don't need to do any of that.

The WSDL and SOAP facilities described thus far provide the core facilities for web services, but there are many other standards, and proposed standards, for less central aspects. The entire area is in considerable flux with many competing draft standards. However, one other standard is approximately as solid as WSDL and SOAP are. That standard, *UDDI* (*Universal Description, Discovery, and Integration*), provides a way for web service providers to list their services in a registry and for potential users to discover them by looking in the registry for services matching a description. UDDI registries are themselves web services, accessed via SOAP messages in accordance with a WSDL specification.

10.5 Security and Communication Middleware

Messaging systems and RPC servers often use ACLs to control access, much like file systems do. For example, a broker with a hierarchy of publish/subscribe topics can associate two ACLs with each topic in the hierarchy: one specifying the users or groups that may publish, and the other specifying those that may subscribe. ACLs on subtopics take precedence over those on more general topics. Thus, security can be specified as precisely as necessary for those subtopics where it matters while allowing most subtopics the convenience of inheriting an ancestor topic's ACL.

An ACL lists the users or groups that should be granted access, but this still leaves open one of the most difficult aspects of security in a distributed system. Namely, how should a server know which user's access rights apply for each incoming connection? Any robust solution to this problem relies on the cryptographic mechanisms described in Section 9.6. I can illustrate this using an example from web services.

Recall that the exchange of SOAP messages between a client and web service normally takes place using the same HTTP protocol as is used for browsing the web. As such, the same cryptographic security mechanisms are used by interposing the Secure Sockets Layer, SSL, between HTTP and the underlying TCP connection.

Just as with a secure web site, a secure web service identifies itself by using a *certificate*, which is a document attesting to the server's identity and to the public half of the server's asymmetric key pair. This public key can be used by the client to check the server's digitally signed messages and also to send the server a secret key for confidential communication. The certificate itself is digitally signed by some trusted *Certification Authority* (*CA*), an organization that has made its public key well known and that can be counted on to check out the legitimacy of another organization's or individual's identity claim before issuing a certificate.

The server's certificate allows the client to trust that it is communicating with the real server and not an impostor. However, the server still has no idea which user identity to associate with the client. Two options exist for solving that problem, one that continues to follow the lead of ordinary web sites used by humans and another that may be better suited to widespread deployment of web services. I will present the solution first that you are probably familiar with from your own use of the web and then the more robust alternative.

When you connect to a secure web site, your browser checks the server's certificate and if all is well signals this fact by showing you a locked padlock. The server then typically asks you to enter a username and password for the site. The strings that you enter are sent over the SSL-encrypted communication channel and so are not subject to eavesdropping or tampering in transit. Moreover, because your browser checked the server's certificate, you can be sure you aren't sending your password to a con artist. The server gets the strings in decrypted form and checks them against its user database. This style of authentication relies on you and the site having a shared secret, the password. In general, each client/server pair requires a shared secret established in advance.

This first style of client authentication, which is provided by HTTP under the name *basic authentication*, can be a workable method for web services that are not widely deployed, especially for those that are deployed only internally to an enterprise. In that context, the various web services will ordinarily be controlled by the same administrators and as such can all share a common authentication server that keeps track of users with their passwords. Thus, a secret password needs to be established for each user, but not for each user/service pair. Even across enterprise boundaries, basic authentication may suffice for web services that have only a small number of users, such as a web service used to facilitate one particular relationship between a pair of enterprises.

Before I move on to the more sophisticated alternative, it is worth contrasting the first alternative, basic authentication using SSL, with weaker password-based authentication. Consider, for example, the GoogleSearch API's spelling suggestion operation, which was shown in Section 10.4. This operation takes a secret access-control key as an argument in the request message itself. The access-control key is issued by Google and essentially acts as a combination of username and password in a single string. However, the GoogleSearch web service does not use SSL; it uses ordinary unencrypted HTTP directly over TCP. One consequence is that the access control keys are subject to eavesdropping and so could be captured and then reused. However, there is a second way in which a malefactor could capture a key.

Recall that with SSL, the client program receives a certificate of the server's identity, protecting it against impostors. Because GoogleSearch is not using SSL, you could be sending your misspellings to an impostor, perhaps someone who wants to embarrass you. Moreover, because you send your key along, you could also be sending your key to an impostor. This helps explain the significance of SSL's server authentication. It not only protects the client from rogue servers, but also protects the server from misuse through password capture. Even if you don't care whether your misspellings become public knowledge, Google presumably cares that their service isn't used indiscriminately. Otherwise they would not have established access-control keys.

What can you conclude, then, about Google's security design? Presumably they decided that their service was valuable enough to make some attempt to discourage casual misuse, but not so valuable that they were willing to pay the price of SSL cryptography to keep determined adversaries away. Also, their main concern is not with the actual identity of the user, but with limiting the number of searches made by any one user. If someone captures your GoogleSearch key, they will simply share your daily limit on searches, not imposing any extra burden on Google. Thus, Google's design stems from a well thought-out cost-benefit analysis, paradigmatic of how security decisions ought to be made. They did not make a mistake in using passwords without SSL. However, you would be making a mistake to blindly emulate their security mechanism on a web service of greater value.

Let us return, then, to security mechanisms suitable for high-value targets that are likely to attract serious attackers. Recall that the problem with using HTTP's basic authentication over SSL is that it requires a shared secret password for each pair of client and server. If web services are to form a ubiquitous Internet-wide economy, as some prognosticators suggest, this will not be workable. Any client must be able to securely access any web service without prearrangement.

To solve this problem, web services can use the *mutual authentication* feature of SSL, which is almost never used for ordinary human-oriented web sites. In mutual authentication, both the client and the server have digitally-signed certificates obtained from trusted Certification Authorities. They exchange these certificates in the initial setup handshake that starts an SSL connection. Thus, without needing any usernames or passwords, each knows the identity of its communication partner for the entire duration of the connection. Mutual authentication is impractical for ordinary consumer-oriented web browsing, because merchants don't want to require all their customers to go to the trouble and expense of getting certificates. However, for the business-to-business communications where web services are expected to play their major role, mutual authentication seems well suited. It does, however, still have limitations, as I explain next.

The use of SSL, sometimes with mutual authentication, is widely deployed in practical web service applications. It also is incorporated in the most mature standards for web services; the Web Services Interoperability Organization's Basic Profile specifies that web service instances may require the use of HTTP over SSL and, in particular, may require mutual authentication. However, this approach to web service security has a fundamental limitation, with the result that more sophisticated, less mature standards take a different approach. The fundamental limitation is that SSL secures communication channels, rather than securing the SOAP messages sent across those channels.

To understand the difference between securing a channel and securing a message, consider the fact that several SOAP messages, originated by different users running different applications, may be sent across a single network connection. Consider also the fact that a single SOAP message may be relayed through a whole succession of network connections on its way from its originator to its ultimate destination. In both cases, SSL allows each computer to be sure of the authenticity of the neighboring computer, but it doesn't provide any direct support for associating the SOAP message with its author.

Therefore, the Web Services Security standard provides a mechanism whereby the XML format of a SOAP message can directly contain a digital signature for the message. Standards also govern the transmission of XML in encrypted form and the use of XML to send certificates. Using these mechanisms, the Web Services Interoperability Organization's Basic Security Profile, currently only a working draft, provides requirements for SOAP messages to be encrypted and digitally signed. Because the signature is on the message itself, it can be forwarded along with the message through relay channels and has sufficient specificity to allow messages of varying origins to share a network connection.

One final advantage of the Web Services Security approach compared with SSL is that SOAP messages that have been digitally signed support non-repudiation, as described in Section 9.6. That is, because the recipient is in no better position to forge a message than anyone else would be, the recipient can present the message to a third party with a convincing argument that it came from the apparent sender. Today, web services are largely used within organizations and between close business partners with a high degree of mutual trust. However, as web services spread into more arms-length dealings between parties that have no established relationship, non-repudiation will become more important. Moreover, even if the communicating enterprises have a trust relationship, individual employees may be corrupt; digital signatures limit the scope of investigation that is needed if tampering is suspected.

Exercises

10.1 How does messaging differ from sending bytes over a TCP connection?

10.2 How does messaging differ from sending an email message?

10.3 How does messaging differ from RPC?

10.4 Does using response messages turn a message-queuing system into the equivalent of an RPC system? Why or why not?

10.5 Are web services an alternative to messaging and RPC systems, that is, a third kind of communication middleware? Why or why not?

10.6 For each of the following communication methods, give one example application scenario where you think it would be appropriate: message queuing, publish/subscribe messaging, RPC. In each case, justify your choice of communication method.

10.7 Recall that in publish/subscribe topic hierarchies, the wildcard + represents one component topic, whereas # represents a sequence of zero or more components separated by slashes. Suppose a publish/subscribe system has topics a, b, a/c, a/d, b/c, b/e, a/c/e, and a/d/e. For each of the following subscriptions, specify which of those topics would be included: a, a/+, a/#, a/c/+, a/+/e, #/e.

10.8 Suppose s is a JMS messaging session and d is a JMS messaging destination. Show how to create a Consumer that would receive all messages sent to d containing a Symbol of IBM and that would also receive all those containing a Price of 0, independent of their Symbol.

10.9 In the RMI programming example, suppose several Subscriber objects are all subscribed to a single TopicServer and that several Publisher objects send messages to that TopicServer. Will all the Subscribers necessarily print the messages in the same order? Explain why or why not.

10.10 In the TopicServer implementation shown in Figures 10.9 and 10.10 on pages 380 and 381, the receive method invokes each subscriber's receive method. This means the TopicServer's receive method will not return to its caller until after all of the subscribers have received the message. Consider an alternative version of the TopicServer, in which the receive method simply places the message into a temporary holding area and hence can quickly return to its caller. Meanwhile, a separate thread running in the TopicServer repeatedly loops, retrieving messages from the holding area and sending each in turn to the subscribers. What Java class from Chapter 4 would be appropriate to use for the holding area? Describe the pattern of synchronization provided by that class in terms that are specific to this particular application.

10.11 The text shown in Figure 10.15 has the right form to be a legal SOAP message, but it would not be legitimate to send this message to the GoogleSearch web service. Why not?

10.12 Section 10.5 mentions one reason why mutual authentication using certificates is not common in the human-oriented web: merchants don't want to

```
<?xml version="1.0" encoding="UTF-8"?>
<env:Envelope
 xmlns:env="http://schemas.xmlsoap.org/soap/envelope/"
 xmlns:xsd="http://www.w3.org/2001/XMLSchema"
 xmlns:xsi="http://www.w3.org/2001/XMLSchema-instance"
 xmlns:enc="http://schemas.xmlsoap.org/soap/encoding/"
 xmlns:ns0="urn:GoogleSearch"
 env:encodingStyle="http://schemas.xmlsoap.org/soap/encoding/">
  <env:Body>
    <ns0:doSpellingSuggestion>
      <key xsi:type="xsd:int">314159</key>
      <phrase xsi:type="xsd:string">middlewear</phrase>
    </ns0:doSpellingSuggestion>
  </env:Body>
</env:Envelope>
```

Figure 10.15 This is a legal SOAP message but is not legitimate for sending to the GoogleSearch web service.

turn customers off by requiring them to get certificates. One item of context here is that most consumers do business with only a small number of merchants. This is starting to change, as more businesses develop online presences and as consumers start branching out and shopping online for more than just books, music, videos, and airline tickets. Can you see any reason why this change might affect consumers' willingness to acquire certificates rather than use passwords?

▣ Programming Projects

10.1 Create an RMI analog of the message-storage server of Figure 9.7 on page 343 and its companion client of Figure 9.8 on page 344.

10.2 Modify the **TopicServer** class shown in Figures 10.9 and 10.10 on pages 380 and 381 as described in Exercise 10.10. Be sure to correctly synchronize access to the list of subscribers.

10.3 Exercise 10.10 describes one way to modify the **TopicServer** class so that the **receive** method does not need to wait for each subscriber's **receive** method, at least under normal circumstances. An alternative design to achieve that same goal would be for the **TopicServer**'s **receive** method to create a new thread for each incoming message. The thread would deliver that one message to the subscribers. Modify the `TopicServer` class shown in Figures 10.9 and 10.10 on pages 380 and 381 in this alternate way. Be sure to correctly synchronize access to the list of subscribers.

10.4 In the RMI example code given in Section 10.3.2, only a single topic is used, bound in the registry to the name `topic.1`. Show how the `Publisher`, `TopicServer`, and `Subscriber` programs can be generalized to take a topic name as an additional command line argument, with each topic separately bound in the registry. Demonstrate the concurrent execution of two different topic objects on the same host, each with its own subscribers.

10.5 In Programming Project 10.4, you accommodated multiple publish/subscribe topics by having a separate `TopicServer` for each and by registering each in the registry. An alternative design would be to have a single `TopicServer` object, but with the `receive` and `subscribe` methods taking an extra argument that is the topic name. Develop and demonstrate the code for this approach. You may want to include extra methods for such purposes as adding topics and obtaining a list of the current topics.

10.6 The publish/subscribe system provided as an RMI example in Section 10.3.2 does not include a method for unsubscribing from a topic. Arguably, such a method would be redundant, because the `TopicServer` class is prepared for subscribers that fail. A subscriber that wishes to unsubscribe could simply arrange to intentionally fail. However, the design might be cleaner and more flexible if the `Topic` interface and `TopicServer` class did support an `unsubscribe` method. Add one and demonstrate its use.

10.7 Section 10.3.2 shows how RMI can be used to convey textual messages from publishers to subscribers by way of intermediate topic objects. If you have the requisite skill in building user interfaces in Java, you could use this RMI mechanism as the foundation for a chat-room application or a multi-player game. Write such a program. Depending on your design, you may want to incorporate some of the features from earlier programming projects; for example, multiple topics could support multiple chat rooms. You are also welcome to change the message type; an application-specific class of game moves might be more appropriate than textual strings.

10.8 The `Publisher` class in Figure 10.8 on page 379 makes use of the `Topic` interface even though the `MessageRecipient` interface would suffice. Change the class to use the more general interface and demonstrate that, with appropriate changes elsewhere, the `Publisher` can wind up communicating either directly with a `Subscriber` or with an intermediary `TopicServer` as before.

10.9 The `Topic` interface in Figure 10.7 on page 378 extends `MessageRecipient` and also uses that same interface as the argument type for the `subscribe` method. Demonstrate how this allows one `TopicServer` to function as a subscriber to another `TopicServer`.

10.10 Acquire an access control key for GoogleSearch from Google and download the software associated with the *J2EE 1.4 Tutorial*. After working through the JAX-RPC portion of the tutorial, modify one of the example clients so that it gets a spelling suggestion from GoogleSearch instead of accessing the example Hello web service. You can use *http://api.google.com/search/beta2* as the endpoint address and *http://api.google.com/GoogleSearch.wsdl* as the WSDL location. Optionally, you can use a packet capture program such as `ethereal` to verify that the web service is being accessed through ordinary HTTP, without the use of SSL, and that the SOAP messages are essentially as shown in Figures 10.13 and 10.14.

Exploration Projects

10.1 Read about message-driven beans in the *J2EE 1.4 Tutorial* and write a concise explanation of what they are and why they are more convenient than directly using JMS.

10.2 Work through the examples in Chapters 28 and 33 of the *J2EE 1.4 Tutorial*, "A Message-Driven Bean Example" and "The Java Message Service API."

Notes

The topics in this chapter are subject to particularly rapid technical developments. As such, your best source of information is likely to be the web sites. The Java web site, *http://java.sun.com*, has information both on RMI and on J2EE, which includes JMS and JAX-RPC. The Web Services Activity web site, *http://w3c.org/2002/ws/*, has information on WSDL, SOAP, and web services in general. Other important sites for web services standards are the Web Services Interoperability Organization, *http://www.ws-i.org/*, and OASIS, *http://www.oasis-open.org/*, which tends to have more specialized, advanced standards. The information on these sites—and in many published books for that matter—tends to emphasize the technical details over the big picture of how to use the technology. One book that does provide a lot of big-picture advice on the use of messaging is by Hohpe and Woolf [70].

11

Security

11.1 Introduction

I have addressed security issues in each preceding chapter because security is a perva-sive design issue, the same way performance is. Just as one can't discuss virtual memory mechanisms or persistent storage as though performance didn't exist and then devote a later chapter solely to performance, it would have been wrong to treat security as an add-on. On the other hand, there has been such sustained attention to security from so many talented researchers that a rich, coherent body of security concepts has resulted, worthy of a chapter of its own.

Section 11.2 recapitulates and amplifies on Chapter 1's definition of security and statement of security objectives. It also lists a number of high-level security principles, many of which were illustrated in particular cases throughout the book.

Sections 11.3 and 11.4 discuss the two most well-developed areas of security tech-nology: the authentication of user identities and the provision of access control and information-flow control to limit the authority of users. The latter topic builds on Chapter 7's introduction to protection. (Another well-developed area of security tech-nology, cryptography, was addressed in Chapter 9.)

Section 11.5 describes viruses and worms, some of the most prevalent security threats, which fall largely outside of the scope of conventional authentication and authorization controls. Because worms often propagate by exploiting buffer-overflow vulnerabilities, I also describe this widespread form of vulnerability in the same section.

Security measures are subject to imperfection, just like all other human endeavors. Sections 11.6 and 11.7 describe two responses to this reality: (1) assurance techniques used to assess the quality of security measures and (2) monitoring techniques used to collect information on attacks, particularly any that are not thwarted.

Finally, Section 11.8 closes the book on a practical note by providing a summary of key security best practices. Many of these have already been mentioned in earlier chapters or will be mentioned in the course of Sections 11.2–11.7. However, by bringing all of them together in one place, I hope to provide something of a checklist for your guidance. After this summary, the chapter ends with exercises, programming and exploration projects, and notes.

11.2 Security Objectives and Principles

Security is best understood as one aspect of overall system quality. Like quality in general, it refers to how well the system meets the objectives of its owner or other primary stakeholders. If you think about all the factors that can stop a system from meeting those objectives, it should be clear that quality stems from a combination of proper design, implementation, and operation. Similarly, security spans all these areas. Before examining what makes security different from other aspects of quality, I would like to pin down the definition of quality a bit more carefully.

A tempting first definition of a quality system is that it is one that is designed, implemented, and operated so as to meet the objectives of its owner. However, this definition is somewhat unrealistic because it fails to acknowledge that decisions, particularly regarding design, need to be made without complete knowledge of how they will affect the system's suitability. Therefore, I would refine the definition to say that a quality system is one that is designed, implemented, and operated to reduce to an appropriate level the risk that it will fail to meet the objectives of its owner.

A system's risk has been reduced to an appropriate level if it is preferable to accept the remaining risk than to incur the costs of further reducing the risk. This definition makes risk management sound like a straightforward economic calculation, like deciding whether to continue paying high fire-insurance premiums for an old warehouse or instead build a new, more fire-resistant warehouse. Unfortunately, the decisions regarding system development and operation are not so precisely calculable.

An insurance company has a good estimate of how likely the warehouse is to burn down; the probability a computer system will fail to meet objectives is far fuzzier. In addition, the insurance company has a good estimate of how large a loss would result from the fire, denominated in dollars. In contrast, the consequences of a low-quality computer system may be difficult to predict, and in some cases may not be adequately translatable into financial terms. Consider, for example, a computer system that is essential to national security.

Nonetheless, however imperfect the risk-management approach to system quality may be, it provides the correct conceptual framework. The management goal should be to expend resources in a way that provides a commensurate reduction in risk. This requires keeping in view all three factors: cost, likelihood of failure, and consequences of failure. Moreover, all three factors may be manipulable. For example, rather than building a new warehouse, it may be preferable to reduce the amount of material stored in the warehouse, thus reducing the possible loss. Similarly, rather than making a computer system less likely to fail, it may be preferable to reduce reliance on the system so that its failure would not be so significant. That reliance may be reduced through the use of redundant computer systems as well as through the use of noncomputerized systems.

Having provided this background on quality in general, I can define system security similarly. A system is secure if it is designed, implemented, and operated so as to reduce to an appropriate level the risk that it will fail to meet the objectives of its owner, even in the face of adversaries. An *adversary* is someone with objectives so contrary to those of the owner as to strive to make the system fail.

One mildly interesting consequence of this definition is that security is irrelevant for low-quality systems, because they will fail to meet their owners' objectives even without intervention by adversaries. However, the more interesting consequence is that the risk-management approach to system quality needs to be extended to include the actions of adversaries.

A secure system need not be impervious to attack by adversaries. In fact, it need not even be especially difficult for adversaries to interfere with. Instead, what is needed is that the likelihood an adversary will choose to mount an attack, the likelihood that the attack will succeed, and the damage likely to be done to the system owner's objectives by a successful attack all combine to produce an appropriate level of risk relative to the cost of available countermeasures.

Generally, an acceptable level of risk will not be achievable if the system offers no resistance to attack. However, at some point further reduction in the system's vulnerability will be a less appropriate risk-management approach than reducing the threats the system faces and the consequences of a successful attack.

Some of these risk-management actions may be nontechnical. For example, if the organization can avoid creating disgruntled employees, its systems will not face such severe threats, independent of how vulnerable they are. As another example, a company might choose to accept the cost of repeated data entry rather than store its customers' credit-card numbers online. Doing so will both reduce threats (because adversaries will have less motivation to break into the system) and reduce the consequences of successful attacks (because the company will lose less customer goodwill).

However, it would be wrong to equate technical efforts with only the reduction of vulnerabilities and assume that all efforts to reduce threats or the consequences of failure are nontechnical in nature. In fact, one of the most active technical areas today is the monitoring of systems' operation; I discuss this in Section 11.7. This monitoring does nothing to reduce a system's inherent vulnerability. However, it both deters adversaries (especially adversaries internal to the organization), thereby reducing threats, and allows rapid-response incident-handling teams to quickly and efficiently get systems operational again after attacks, thereby reducing losses.

So, what might the owner's objectives be that an adversary could seek to thwart? There is no end to the specific objectives an owner might have. However, there are four broad classes of objectives that commonly arise in discussions of security:

- The owner may wish to maintain the *confidentiality* of information stored in the computer system. That is, the information should not be disclosed to any person who has not been authorized to receive it.

- The owner may wish to maintain the *integrity* of information stored in the computer system. That is, the information should not be modified or deleted by any person who has not been authorized to do so.

- The owner may wish to preserve the *availability* of the services provided by the computer system. That is, persons authorized to use the system should be able to do so without interference from adversaries. The adversaries should not be able to cause a *denial of service*.

- The owner may wish to ensure *accountability*. That is, it should be possible to determine how users have chosen to exercise their authority, so that they can be held responsible for the discretionary choices they made within the limits set by the security controls.

All four of these objectives have a common prerequisite, user *authentication*. That is, the system must verify that each user is correctly identified. Without reliable user identities, there is no way the system can enforce a restriction on which users can retrieve or modify information and no way it can keep records of who has done what. Even availability relies on authentication, because without a way to determine whether a user is a bona fide system administrator, there is no way to control the use of commands that shut the system down.

To increase the chance that these objectives are achieved, system designers have found it useful to have a guiding set of principles. These are more specific than the overall risk-management perspective sketched earlier, but less specific than individual technical measures. Most of these principles came to prominence in a 1975 paper by Saltzer and Schroeder, though they date back yet further. The following list largely echoes Saltzer and Schroeder's:

Economy of mechanism: Simple designs that consistently use a small number of general mechanisms are more likely to be secure. An example would be Chapter 5's point that a general-purpose transaction-processing infrastructure is more likely to be secure than individual ad hoc mechanisms for atomicity.

Fail-safe (and fail-noisy) defaults: A security system should be designed to withhold access by default. If anything goes wrong in the granting of authority, the result will be too little authority, rather than too much. This makes the problem more likely to be fixed, because legitimate users will complain. An example from Chapter 7 is Microsoft's mechanism for resolving conflicts between ACL entries. That mechanism governs the case when one entry says to allow a permission and another says to deny it. The kernel itself is not fail-safe, because it gives precedence to whichever entry is listed first. However, the higher-level API used by the GUI is fail-safe, because it always gives precedence to denying permission.

Complete mediation: Ideally, every access should be checked for authority. Processes should not be allowed to continue accessing a resource just because authority was checked at some earlier point. An example from Chapter 7 is the change IBM made in deriving the AS/400 design from the System/38. The original design used ACLs to decide whether to grant capabilities, but then allowed the capabilities to be retained and used without any further reference to the ACLs. The revised design causes the ACLs' record of authorization to be checked more consistently.

Open design: The only secret parts of the security mechanism should be cryptographic keys and passwords. The design should be inspected by as many parties as possible to increase the chance of a weakness coming to light. An example would be Chapter 9's description of openly standardized cryptographic algorithms. In particular, that chapter mentioned that the MD5 algorithm was found to be weak. I would not have been able to give you that warning without the public scrutiny MD5 has received.

Separation of privilege: No one individual should be authorized to carry out any particularly sensitive task. Instead, the system should be designed so that two authorized users need to collaborate. Among other benefits, this defends against the corruption of persons in positions of authority.

Least privilege: Each process should operate with only the authority it needs so that even if an adversary makes something go wrong in the process's execution, there will be many kinds of damage it can't do. In Chapter 4, I described a case where adversaries exploited a Time Of Check To Time Of Use (TOCTTOU) vulnerability to trick a mail delivery program into writing into sensitive files. I highlighted the failure to use proper synchronization, resulting in the vulnerable race condition. However, I could equally well point to that mail program as a failure to honor the principle of least privilege. The mail program needed authority only to write in each user's mail file, not authority to write in all files whatsoever. Because UNIX provided no easy way to grant it just the requisite authority, it was given way too much, and hence its vulnerability was rendered far more dangerous.

Psychological acceptability: All security mechanisms must have sufficiently well-designed user interfaces that they will be used correctly. An example is the graphical user interface Microsoft Windows provides for ACLs, as shown in Chapter 7. As I pointed out there, the user interface design includes such features as hiding unnecessary complexity.

Work factor: Just as you reason about the cost and benefit of security countermeasures, you should reason about your adversaries' cost/benefit trade-offs. You should make sure that breaking into your systems takes more time and trouble than it is worth. An example would be the discussion of cryptographic key length in Chapter 9. Keys are not completely secure, in that they can be figured out with sufficient trial and error. However, the usual key lengths are such that adversaries will not have the resources necessary to find the keys in this way.

Compromise recording: If the system's security is breached, information about the breach should be recorded in a tamper-proof fashion. This allows an appropriate technical and legal response to be mounted. An important example of this principle, described in Chapter 9, is the use of network intrusion detection systems.

Defense in depth: An adversary should need to penetrate multiple independent defenses to be able to compromise a system's functioning. For example, Chapter 9 suggested the use of multiple firewalls, such as hardware firewalls at the organizational and workgroup perimeters and a software firewall on each desktop machine.

Alignment of authority and control: The same person should control what a process will do and supply the authorization credentials for the process's action. In Chapter 7, I described the risk of Trojan horse programs, which combine their executors' authority with their authors' control, and setuid programs, which may combine their executors' control with their authors' authority. Many network server programs have problems similar to setuid programs, in that they allow anonymous individuals elsewhere on the Internet some degree of control over their actions while using a local user's authority.

Physical security: The system's owner should control physical access to computer equipment and unencrypted data. An example from Chapter 8 is that disk drives must be protected from physical theft. Otherwise, confidentiality can not be ensured. As another example, I once visited an organization that was in the business of printing and mailing out lots of checks to individuals. Much to my shock, their computer room was wide open. Here the threat is to integrity rather than confidentiality. An adversary could exploit physical access to change the list of recipients for the checks—an attractive proposition.

Before leaving this section of generalities and diving into technical specifics, I want to return to the topic of adversaries. Adversaries can be outside your organization, but they can also be inside. Either way, they may exploit technical vulnerabilities, misuse authority they have been granted, or engage in *social engineering*, that is, tricking others who may have greater authority into cooperating. For this reason, I generally use the word adversary rather than such alternative terms as intruder and cracker. The word *intruder* implies an external adversary, and *cracker* implies one who uses technical means. The largest danger is that if you use one of these terms, you may blind yourself to significant threats. For example, protecting your organization's network perimeter may be a fine defense against intruders—but not against all adversaries.

Occasionally I will call an adversary an intruder or cracker, when appropriate. However, I will never call one a hacker, contrary to what has become common usage. Decades before crackers co-opted the word, it meant someone who had a deep, creative relationship with systems. Many of the technologies taken for granted today were developed by people who described themselves as hackers. Today, I would no longer dare call such a person a hacker outside a knowledgeable circle of old-timers, for fear of being misunderstood. However, just because I no longer use the word in its traditional sense does not mean I would use it for crackers.

11.3 User Authentication

You are probably most familiar with user authentication in a very basic form: logging into a computer system using a password at the start of a session of usage. This authentication mechanism suffers from several potentially serious weaknesses:

- Because the authentication takes place only at the beginning of the session, the computer system at best knows who was seated at the keyboard then. No attempt is made to notice whether you have walked away and someone else has taken your place.

- Because you identify yourself by using something intangible (your knowledge of a password), there is nothing to discourage you from sharing it with someone else. You wouldn't need to give up your own knowledge to let someone else also have it.

- Similarly, someone can steal the password without depriving you of it, and hence without drawing attention to themselves. As an example, if you have written the password down, the adversary can copy it yet leave you your copy.

- Because the same password is used each time you log in, anyone who observes you using it can then reuse it. This is true whether they physically observe your typing (known as *shoulder surfing*) or use technical means to capture the password, either with covert software on the computer where you are typing (a *keylogger*) or with a network packet capture program (a *sniffer*). The use of network encryption prevents sniffing but not the other techniques.

- Either the password is easy for you to remember, in which case it is also probably easy for an adversary to guess, or you wrote it down, thereby exposing it.

In addition, there are several other pitfalls that, though not unavoidable, are common in actual password systems:

- If you type in your password without the computer system having first authenticated itself to you, then you could fall prey to a *spoofing* attack, in which the adversary sets up a fake system to capture passwords and then presents them to the real system.

- If the system checks your password by comparing it with a copy it has stored, then any exposure of its storage would reveal your password and probably many others.

- If you have to choose your own passwords for many different systems and are like most people, you will use the same password for several different systems. This means any weakness in the security of one system, such as the use of stored passwords, will spread to the others.

With such a long list of weaknesses, you can be sure that security specialists have devised other means of authentication. I will discuss those in Section 11.3.4. Nonetheless, I would first like to explain how you can make the best of password authentication because it is still widely used. I will start with the most avoidable weaknesses, which are those listed most recently: spoofing, storing passwords, and choosing the same passwords for several systems.

11.3.1 Password Capture Using Spoofing and Phishing

One form of spoofing attack is to write a program that puts the correct image on the screen to look like a logged-out system prompting for username and password. Thus, when someone comes up to the computer and sees what looks like a login screen, they will enter their information, only to have it recorded by the program. The program can avoid detection by displaying a realistic error message and then logging itself out, returning to the genuine login window. To defend against this version of a spoofing attack, there needs to be something the genuine login window can do to authenticate itself to users that no other program could do. Microsoft Windows can be configured to take this approach by requiring users to press the CTRL+ALT+DEL key combination at the start of a login. The reason Microsoft chose this combination is that Windows allows programmers to draw anything at all to the screen and to respond to any other key combination, but not that one particular key combination. Thus, so long as Windows is running, you can be sure that CTRL+ALT+DEL is being responded to by Windows itself, not by a spoofing program. The one hitch is that a spoofer could have installed software other than Windows. To defend against that, you would need to use physical security, which is important for other reasons anyhow.

Another style of spoofing has become more problematic lately. A web site may be set up to look like a password-protected site, but really be in the business of capturing the passwords. Users can be directed to the fake site using sophisticated network manipulations, but more commonly they are simply tricked into accessing it using a misleading email message, a technique known as *phishing*. One important countermeasure in this case is user education. Users need to be much less credulous of emails they receive.

However, there is also a technical dimension to the problem of web spoofing. As described in Chapter 10, the SSL protocol used for encrypted web communication allows your browser to verify the identity of the web server by using a public-key certificate. Spoofing is made much less likely if you type your password in only to web pages that have authenticated themselves in this way. Unfortunately, some web site designers are conditioning users to ignore this principle. These web sites use non-SSL connections to display the form into which users type their passwords. The form then submits the information back using SSL. The designers probably think all is well, because the actual password transmission is SSL-encrypted. However, unless the user looks at the HTML source of the web form, there is no way to be sure where the password will be sent. To protect against spoofing, the login form itself should be sent using SSL. That way, the user will have seen the server's authentication before typing the password.

11.3.2 Checking Passwords Without Storing Them

To avoid storing passwords, a system should use a cryptographic hash function, such as the SHA-1 function described in Chapter 9. Recall that these functions are designed not to be easily invertible and in practice to essentially never have two inputs produce

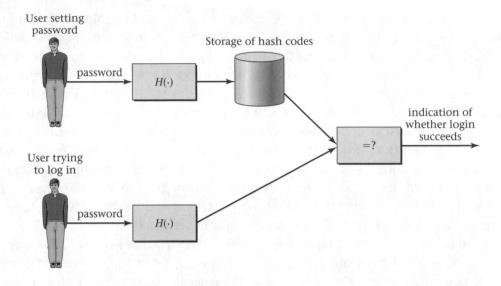

Figure 11.1 The system stores a cryptographic hash of the password when it is set, and compares that with the hash of the attempted password. Because the hash function is collision-resistant, equal hashes mean the password was almost surely correct. Because the hash function is difficult to invert, disclosure of the stored hash codes would not reveal the passwords.

the same output. Therefore, the system can feed a newly chosen password through the hash function and store the hash value. When a user tries to log in, the system feeds the proffered password through the same hash function and compares the resulting value with the stored hash code, as shown in Figure 11.1. If the two hash codes are equal, then for all practical purposes the system can be sure the correct password was entered. However, if the stored hash values are disclosed, no one can recover the passwords from them other than by trial and error. One cost to user convenience is that the system cannot support a function to "remind me of my password," only one to "assign me a new password." In most settings, that is a reasonable price to pay.

11.3.3 Passwords for Multiple, Independent Systems

In principle, you can easily avoid the problems stemming from using the same password on multiple systems. You just need to train yourself not to pick the same password for shopping on Sleazy Sam's Super Saver Site as you use to guard your employer's confidential records. In practice, however, picking a new password for every system would lead to an unmemorizable array of different passwords. Even one password for each general category of system may be difficult. Therefore, an active area of development today is *password wallet* systems, which store a range of passwords under the protection of one master password. The stored passwords constitute a security vulnerability; this vulnerability is hopefully not so severe as the alternatives.

Another technique that can help users cope with multiple systems also makes use of a master password but does not use it to protect storage of individual passwords. Instead, the individual passwords are generated algorithmically from the master password and the sites' names. As an advantage compared with a password wallet, nothing at all needs to be stored on the client machines. As a disadvantage, there is no easy way to change the master password.

11.3.4 Two-Factor Authentication

Even if a system is designed and operated so as to avoid the pitfalls of spoofing, password storage, and password reuse, if it relies on password-controlled login as its sole authentication method, it will still possess the more fundamental vulnerabilities listed earlier. Some of those can be overcome with sufficient user education or mitigated in other ways. For example, a system can be designed so as to issue passwords (or pass phrases) that are random, and hence difficult to guess, but are constructed out of real syllables or words so as to be easily memorizable—an example of psychological acceptability. To avoid problems with users walking away, a system can demand reentry of the password before any particularly sensitive operation or after any sufficiently long period of inactivity. All these countermeasures to password threats are valuable but still leave something to be desired. Thus, I will turn now to other authentication methods.

Rather than relying on something the authorized user knows (a password), an authentication mechanism can rely on something the user physically possesses, such as a card or small plug-in device. These physical devices are generically called *tokens*. The big problem with tokens is that they can be lost or stolen. Therefore, they are normally combined with passwords to provide *two-factor authentication*, that is, authentication that combines two different sources of information. Another way to achieve two-factor authentication is by combining either a password or a token with *biometric authentication*, that is, the recognition of some physical attribute of the user, such as a fingerprint or retinal pattern.

The most familiar two-factor authentication system is that used for bank automated teller machines (ATMs), in which you insert a card carrying a magnetic stripe and also type in a four-digit personal identification number (PIN), which is essentially a short password. Magnetic-stripe cards are rather weak tokens, because they carry fixed information rather than engaging in a cryptographic authentication protocol and because they are easily copied. However, in the ATM application, they provide sufficient security. In part, this stems from other aspects of the system design, such as a limit on how much money a customer can withdraw in a day.

One important difference between biometric authentication and other techniques is that it is inextricably tied with actual human identity. A password-protected or token-protected account can be issued to a person known only by a pseudonym, and it will never be possible to ascertain the true identity of the user. By contrast, even if a biometric authentication user is initially enrolled without presenting any proof of true identity (such as a passport), the user's identity could later be deduced from matching the fingerprint (or other biometric) with other records. This is both an advantage and a disadvantage. Where the highest standards of accountability are necessary, it can be advantageous. However, it also cuts into personal privacy. For many purposes, pseudonymity is desirable, so that people can dissociate some portion of their life from another unrelated, perhaps earlier, portion.

When a user logs in using biometric authentication, some physical device scans the user's fingerprint or other attribute and then transmits a digitally coded version of the scan to a computer for checking. If an attacker can capture the digital version and later replay it, the system's security will be breached, just as would be the case if a password were captured and replayed. One crucial difference, however, is that a user can be issued a new password but not a new fingerprint. Therefore, the design of any biometric authentication system needs to be particularly resistant to such replay attacks.

Biometrics can be used for *identification* as well as *authentication*. That is, a user's physical attributes can play the role of a username (selecting a specific user) as well as of a password (providing evidence that the selected user is actually present). However, biometric identification is a harder problem than biometric authentication, as it requires searching an entire database of biometric information, rather than only the information for a specific user. This broader search space increases the chance for error. Therefore, the most reliable systems still require the user to enter some other identifier, such as a textual username.

11.4 Access and Information-Flow Controls

In Chapter 7, I briefly made the distinction between Discretionary Access Control (DAC), in which the creator or other "owner" of an object can determine access rights to it, and Mandatory Access Control (MAC), in which organizational policy directly governs the access rights. In that chapter, I then went into some depth on capabilities and access control lists (ACLs), which are the two mechanisms commonly used to implement DAC. Therefore, I will now focus on MAC in order to round out the picture.

The most well-developed MAC policies and mechanisms are geared to protecting the confidentiality of information in national security systems, where formal policies regarding the flow of information predated the introduction of computer systems. My discussion in this section will be based on the policies of the United States government, as is much of the published literature. The general principles, however, apply equally well to other similar systems of information classification and user clearance. In particular, after discussing government classification systems, I will briefly remark on a currently popular application to commercial web servers. The goal there is to limit the damage if an attacker achieves control over the web server.

The United States military sponsored research, particularly in the early 1970s, with the goal of allowing a single computer system to be shared by principals operating on data of varying sensitivity and running programs written by authors who are not fully trusted. This sort of system is known as a *Multi-Level Security* (*MLS*) system. In this context, the technical security mechanism must enforce *information-flow control* rather than only *access control*. That is, the system must protect sensitive information from indirect disclosure rather than only from direct access by unauthorized principals.

To appreciate the need for information-flow control in an MLS system, consider the simplest possible system: one handling information of two different levels of sensitivity. Suppose objects containing high-level information are labeled H and those containing low-level (less sensitive) information are labeled L. There are some principals, those with H clearance, who may read and modify all objects. There are others, with L clearance, who may only read L objects. So far, access control would suffice, granting each class of principals access to specific objects. Now consider one further requirement: an untrusted program run by an H principal must not be allowed to copy data out of an H object and into an L object where an L principal could retrieve it. Ideally, the program must also not leak the information any other way, though as you will see, this is a challenging requirement. I can summarize the requirements by saying that information initially contained in an H object must not flow to an L principal, even through means other than the L user accessing the object.

Real MLS systems handle more than two categories of information. The information is categorized in two ways. First, there is an overall *classification level*, indicating the degree to which disclosure could damage national security. In the United States, four classification levels are used: unclassified, confidential, secret, and top secret. (Technically, unclassified is not a classification level. However, it is handled like a level below the lowest true classification level, which is confidential.) Second, there are *compartments*, which indicate topics, such as nuclear weapons or international terrorism. A principal may be cleared for access to data all the way up to top

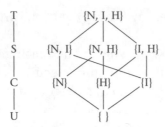

Figure 11.2 The classification levels top secret (T), secret (S), confidential (C), and unclassified (U) form a total order, as shown on the left. Sets of compartments, on the other hand, form only a partial order, namely the subset order in which one set of compartments is below another if it has a subset of the other's compartments. This is illustrated on the right with three hypothetical compartments: nuclear weapons (N), international terrorism (I), and human intelligence (H). Someone cleared for {I, H}, for example, could read documents labeled with {I, H}, {I}, {H}, or {}.

secret classification, but be limited to a specific compartment, such as nuclear weapons only.

Each object is labeled with exactly one classification level but can be labeled with any set of compartments because (for example) a document might concern the acquisition of nuclear weapons by international terrorists. Figure 11.2 shows how each of the two kinds of labels forms a partially ordered set, and Figure 11.3 shows how combining them results in another partially ordered set, known mathematically as their Cartesian product.

In a partial order, two elements may be ordered relative to one another, with $x < y$ or $y < x$, or they may be unordered. For example, {I} and {H} are unordered, because neither is a subset of the other. In security applications, a principal with clearance p is allowed to view information with label i only if $p \geq i$, a condition known as p dominating i in the partial order. This rules out disclosing information to principals with too low a clearance level, but also to those who aren't cleared for all the necessary compartments.

Whenever an untrusted subject (that is, a process running an untrusted program) has read from an object with label l_1 and then modifies an object with label l_2, an unauthorized information flow may result unless $l_2 \geq l_1$. That is, information is only allowed to flow into an object whose consumers could all have directly accessed the source information. Strictly speaking, the information flow results not from the modification of an l_2 object *after* accessing the l_1 object, but rather from the modification of an l_2 object *based on* the earlier access to the l_1 object. However, it is extremely difficult to test whether an earlier access has had some influence on a later modification. In particular, the earlier access can have a subtle influence on whether the later

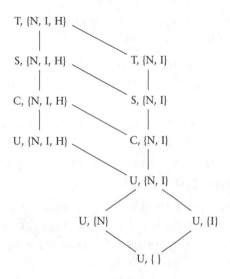

Figure 11.3 Forming the Cartesian product of the two partial orders from Figure 11.2 results in a 32-element partial order, each element of which pairs one of the four classification levels (T, S, C, or U) with one of the eight sets of compartments (ranging from {N, I, H} down to {}). Of those 32 elements, only 11 are shown here in order not to clutter the diagram. What you should note in the diagram is the definition of ordering in the Cartesian product: a pair ($level_1$, $compartments_1$) is above ($level_2$, $compartments_2$) only if both $level_1 \geq level_2$ and $compartments_1 \supseteq compartments_2$.

modification occurs, as well as an overt influence on the nature of that possible later modification. Therefore, practical MLS systems generally take the simpler, more conservative approach of forbidding any subject from modifying an object that does not dominate all previously accessed objects in the security label partial order.

The best-known information-flow control policy is known as the *Bell-LaPadula model*, after the two MITRE Corporation researchers who developed it in the early 1970s.[1] The key idea of the Bell-LaPadula model is to associate with each subject a current level chosen by the principal running the subject process. The current level must be dominated by the principal's security clearance, but can be lower in the partial order if the principal chooses. This flexibility to run at a lower current level allows a principal to run subjects that modify low-level objects and other subjects that read from high-level objects, but not to have any one subject do both. These restrictions

---

1. LaPadula's name was spelled La Padula on the original publications and therefore is cited that way in the end-of-chapter notes and the bibliography. However, in this section I will use the spelling LaPadula for consistency with most published descriptions, as well as with LaPadula's own current spelling of his name.

are enforced by two rules, each based on a formal property from Bell and LaPadula's mathematical model, as follows:

- A subject running with current level c may read only from objects with level r such that c dominates r, that is, $c \geq r$. This corresponds to Bell and LaPadula's *simple security property*.

- A subject running with current level c may modify an object with level m only if m dominates c, that is, $m \geq c$. This can be derived from Bell and LaPadula's **-property* (pronounced *star-property*), which prevents untrusted programs from transferring information into inappropriate objects.

In order for these two rules to effectively regulate information flow, the Bell-LaPadula model also includes tight restrictions on how a subject may change current levels. In practical systems, the current level is selected when a principal logs in and then is left unchanged until the principal logs out.

You can gain some appreciation for the role of untrusted subjects in the Bell-LaPadula model by considering that a principal may be simultaneously logged in at two adjacent terminals, one set to a high current level (as high as the principal is allowed) and the other set to a low current level (unclassified, with no compartments). The human principal may display highly sensitive material on one terminal and type it into an unclassified file on the other. However, no untrusted subject (that is, no process running an untrusted program) may do the same information transfer. The idea is that the human principal is granted a high-level clearance only upon providing evidence of trustworthiness. Moreover, the principal can be monitored to detect suspicious meetings, an excess of cash, and other signs of corruption. The author of the untrusted program, on the other hand, is beyond reach of monitoring, and the group of low-clearance principals who could be reading the leaked data is too large to monitor.

Mandatory Access Control of the Bell-LaPadula variety can also be combined with Discretionary Access Control using a mechanism such as access control lists. In fact, Bell and LaPadula themselves recommended this. The underlying security principle is *Need-To-Know*; that is, the possessor of sensitive information ought not to disclose it to all principals of appropriately high clearance level, but rather only to those with a specific need to know. Compartments provide a crude approximation to the Need-To-Know principle, but many people cleared for a particular compartment will not have a need to know any one specific document within that compartment. Therefore, it is wise to give the owner of an object the ability to further restrict access to it using an ACL. However, unlike in a pure DAC system, the ACL restrictions serve only to further refine the access limits set by the simple security and *-properties. An otherwise cleared subject may be denied access for lack of an appropriate ACL entry. However, adding an ACL entry cannot grant access to a subject running at an inappropriate current level.

Even with the Bell-LaPadula simple security and *-properties, an untrusted subject may not be completely stopped from leaking sensitive information. Rather than leaking the information through a file, network connection, or other legitimate storage or communication object, the subject could disclose the sensitive information by way of a *covert channel*. A covert channel is a mechanism not intended to be used for communication, but which can be manipulated by one subject and observed by another, thus achieving communication. An example would be if a subject with access to highly sensitive information varied the demands it placed on the CPU or disk based on the sensitive information, and another subject, run at a lower clearance level, was able to detect the changes in system utilization. Complete protection against covert channels is impractical, but if processes' resource utilization is tightly controlled, the risk can be reduced.

Moving outside the area of military classification levels, one currently popular MAC system is *Security-enhanced Linux* (*SELinux*), a version of the Linux kernel. This system is quite flexible and can enforce a wide variety of rules regarding which objects each subject can read and write. Objects are tagged with type labels, which are a generalization of classification levels and compartments. Subjects are assigned to domains, which are a generalization of clearance levels. One popular configuration tags the files containing web pages with a specific label and assigns the Apache web server to a domain that is allowed to read those files but not to write them nor to read any other files. That way, even if an attacker can exploit some bug in the web server to obtain control over it and make it execute arbitrary code, it cannot leak confidential information or damage the system's integrity. This is an example of the principle of least privilege.

11.5 Viruses and Worms

As the Bell-LaPadula model and SELinux illustrate, security mechanisms need to limit the actions not only of users, but also of programs. Limiting programs' actions is important because they may be under the control of untrusted programmers as well as because they may have exploitable bugs that allow them to be misused. In this section, I will address two particular kinds of adversarial programs, or *malware*, that pose especially widespread security threats. The common feature of viruses and worms, which distinguish these two kinds of malware from garden-variety Trojan horses, is that one of the actions they are programmed to take is to propagate themselves to other systems. Thus, an adversary can effectively attack all the computers on the Internet, not by directly connecting to each one, but rather by attacking only a few initial systems and programming each attacked system to similarly attack others. Through their sheer ubiquitousness, viruses and worms constitute significant threats.

Both worms and viruses strive to replicate themselves. The difference is in how they do this. A *virus* acts by modifying some existing program, which the adversary hopes will be copied to other systems and executed on them. The modified program will then run the inserted viral code as well as the original legitimate code. The viral code will further propagate itself to other programs on the infected system as well as carrying out any other actions it has been programmed to perform. A *worm*, on the other hand, does not modify existing programs. Instead, it directly contacts a target system and exploits some security vulnerability in order to transfer a copy of itself and start the copy running. Again, the worm can also be programmed to take other actions beyond mere propagation. Even propagation alone can be a significant problem if carried out as fast as possible, because the rapid propagation of worm copies can constitute a denial-of-service attack.

Viruses were a greater problem in the days when the major communication channel between personal computers was hand-carried diskettes. As the Internet has become dominant, worms have become the more common form of self-propagating malware. However, because of the earlier prominence of viruses, many people inaccurately use the word virus to refer to worms.

Any network-accessible vulnerability that a human intruder could exploit can in principle be exploited by a worm in order to propagate. Historically, for example, worms have used password guessing. Also, as mentioned in Chapter 7, email worms are common today; these worms arrive as email attachments and are run by unwary users. However, the most serious means of worm propagation has come to be the exploitation of buffer-overflow vulnerabilities. Therefore, I will explain this common chink in systems' defenses.

Most programs read input into a contiguous block of virtual memory, known as a buffer. The first byte of input goes into the first byte of the buffer, the second into the second, and so forth. Often, the program allocates a fixed-size buffer rather than allocating progressively larger ones as more and more input arrives. In this case, the programmer must test the amount of input against the size of the buffer and take some defensive action if an unreasonably large amount of input is presented, which would otherwise overflow the buffer. Unfortunately, programmers perennially omit this checking. Therefore, adversaries are perennially able to find programs that, when presented with unusually large inputs, try to write the input data into addresses beyond the end of the buffer. This is particularly problematic for network server programs, which can be provided input by an adversary elsewhere on the Internet.

The consequences of a buffer overflow depend heavily on the programming language implementation, operating system, and computer architecture. In modern languages such as Java, any attempt to write past the end of an array is detected. Often, the detected error will cause the attacked server program to crash. In some cases, this is victory enough for an adversary. However, it is minor compared with the damage an adversary can do when exploiting a buffer overflow in a program written using more primitive technology, such as typical implementations of the programming language C. In those settings, the extra input data may be written to addresses beyond the end of the buffer, overwriting other data assigned to those later addresses.

One possible tactic an adversary could use is to look for a server program in which a buffer is followed by some particularly sensitive variable, such as a Boolean flag indicating whether a password has been successfully checked yet. However, buffer-overflow exploits typically take a different approach, which allows the adversary to inject entirely new instructions for the process to execute, which it ordinarily would not even contain. In this way, the server process can be made to take any action whatsoever, within the limits of the authority it has been granted. This an extreme example of misalignment between authority and control.

To understand how a buffer overflow can lead to the execution of arbitrary code, you need to consider some facts about typical runtime stacks, which are described in Appendix A. Often, program variables such as buffers are allocated their space within the stack. The stack also typically contains the return address for each procedure invocation, that is, the address of the instruction that should be executed next when the procedure invocation returns. If the stack grows downward in virtual memory, expanding from higher addresses down into lower ones, then the return address will follow the buffer, as shown in Figure 11.4(a).

In this circumstance, which arises on many popular architectures, a buffer overflow not only can overwrite data values, as shown in Figure 11.4(b), but also can overwrite the return address, as shown in Figure 11.4(c). This form of buffer overflow is commonly called *smashing the stack*. When the current procedure invocation completes, the overwritten return address causes the processor to jump to an adversary-specified instruction address. On its own, this would allow the adversary only to choose which existing code to execute. However, when taken together with one other factor, it provides the means to execute code provided by the adversary.

Many architectures and operating systems provide virtual memory mechanisms that allow each page of virtual memory to be independently read-protected or write-protected, but that do not allow a distinction between reading data and fetching instructions. In this circumstance, the pages holding the stack, which need to be readable for data, can also contain executable code—even though extremely few programs legitimately write instructions into the stack and then jump to them.

An adversary can exploit this situation by writing a large input that not only overflows the buffer and overwrites the return address, but also contains the bytes

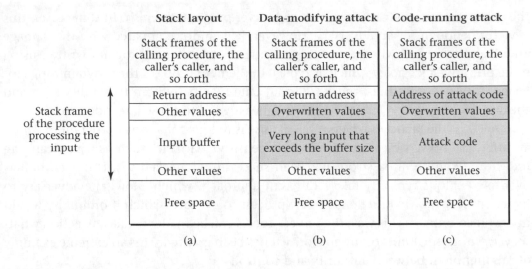

Figure 11.4 If input is allowed to overflow the amount of memory allocated on the stack for an input buffer, it can overwrite other data values, as shown in part (b), or the return address, as shown in part (c). In the latter case, the modified return address can point to attack code included in the oversized input.

constituting the adversary's choice of machine language instructions. These machine language instructions are labeled as attack code in Figure 11.4(c). The overwritten return address is used to jump into the buffer itself, thereby executing the provided instructions.

Because these exploits are so prevalent, there has been considerable interest recently in modifying virtual memory mechanisms so as to allow stack space to be readable (and writable) but not executable. Other than techniques such as this for preventing malware from entering, the major countermeasure has been the use of antivirus scanning programs, which commonly scan for worms as well. These programs look for distinctive patterns of bytes, known as *signatures*, found in known viruses and worms. As such, scanners need to be frequently updated with signatures for newly emerging threats.

11.6 Security Assurance

Organizations directly influence their systems' security through the manner in which the systems are installed and operated, as well as through the design of components developed in-house. However, the organizations also exercise more indirect control by choosing to procure security-critical components from vendors that demonstrate that the components are suited to the organizations' needs. In this section, I will explain how this kind of security assurance is provided by vendors and interpreted by consumers. The component in question may be an operating system, middleware system, or a network device such as a firewall or intrusion detection system, among others. In the security assurance field, any of these may be referred to as a *Target of Evaluation* (*TOE*), because the assurance derives from an independent evaluation of how well the TOE satisfies stated security requirements.

The assurance of security-related products is governed by an international standard called the *Common Criteria,* because it was developed to harmonize previously independent national standards. The Common Criteria are also sometimes known by their International Standards Organization number, ISO 15408. The Common Criteria define a process in which a vendor contracts with a qualified independent assessor to evaluate how well a product meets a set of security requirements known as a *Security Target* (*ST*).

Each ST is an individual requirements document specific to the particular product under evaluation, that is, specific to the TOE. However, because consumers can more easily compare products whose STs share a common basis, the STs are built in a modular fashion from common groups of requirements. A published group of requirements, intended to be used as the basis for multiple STs, is called a *Protection Profile* (*PP*).

Just as STs are built from standard PPs, each PP is assembled by choosing from a standard menu of potential requirements. Extra custom requirements can be added at either stage, but the bulk of any ST's requirements will come from the standard list by way of one of the standard PPs. Thus, consumers are in a better position to learn their way around the landscape of potential requirements. This is critical, because a product certified by an independent assessor to meet its ST is worthless if that ST does not contain requirements appropriate to a particular consumer's needs.

The requirements contained in PPs and STs fall into two general categories: functional requirements and assurance requirements. An example of a functional requirement would be a mandate for a spoofing-resistant login method. (Microsoft Windows would satisfy this requirement, using CTRL+ALT+DEL.) An example of an assurance requirement would be a mandate that detailed design documents, testing reports, and samples of security-critical code be reviewed by outside evaluators.

The assurance requirements are summarized by a numerical *Evaluation Assurance Level* (*EAL*), in the range from EAL1 to EAL7. For example, an ST based on EAL4 will contain moderately rigorous demands regarding the evidence that the system actually meets its functional requirements, but none that go beyond ordinary good development practices outside the security field. At EAL5 and above, specific security-oriented

EAL	Rubric
EAL1	functionally tested
EAL2	structurally tested
EAL3	methodically tested and checked
EAL4	methodically designed, tested, and reviewed
EAL5	semiformally designed and tested
EAL6	semiformally verified design and tested
EAL7	formally verified design and tested

Figure 11.5 This table shows brief rubrics for the Common Criteria Evaluation Assurance Levels; expanded descriptions are available in the Common Criteria documentation.

assurance practices need to be incorporated into the development process, including progressively increasing use of semiformal and formal methods. Figure 11.5 gives a brief rubric for each EAL, taken from the Common Criteria documentation.

Although each EAL includes a whole package of sophisticated assurance requirements, the EALs can be easily understood in a comparative way: a higher-numbered EAL is stricter. This makes it tempting to focus on the EALs. However, you need to remember that an EAL, even a very strict one, tells only how thorough a job the vendor has done of demonstrating that the TOE meets the functional requirements that are in the ST. It tells nothing about how demanding those functional requirements are. More importantly, the EAL tells nothing about how well-matched the requirements are to your needs.

As an example, Microsoft contracted for a Common Criteria evaluation of one particular version of Windows, relative to an ST that included the assumption that the only network connections would be to equally secure systems under the same management and that all authorized users would be cooperative rather than adversarial. Thus, it gave no indication how well the system would fare if confronted with serious adversaries, either within the user population or out on the Internet. These issues arise from the functional requirements in the ST, completely independent of the EAL. Figure 11.6 shows the relevant language from Microsoft's ST.

The weakness of these small excerpts from one particular ST may leave you wondering about the value of the Common Criteria process. The lesson you should take away is not that the Common Criteria process is worthless, but rather that it relies upon educated consumers. To benefit from the process, you need to understand its vocabulary, such as what the difference is between an EAL and an ST.

> - Any other systems with which the TOE communicates are assumed to be under the same management control and operate under the same security policy constraints. The TOE is applicable to networked or distributed environments only if the entire network operates under the same constraints and resides within a single management domain. There are no security requirements that address the need to trust external systems or the communications links to such systems.
>
> - Authorized users possess the necessary authorization to access at least some of the information management [sic] by the TOE and are expected to act in a cooperating manner in a benign environment.

Figure 11.6   These excerpts are from the Windows 2000 Security Target, ST Version 2.0, 18 October 2002, prepared for Microsoft Corporation by Science Applications International Corporation.

11.7 Security Monitoring

System operators have at least three reasons to monitor for attacks, both successful and unsuccessful:

- By gaining a better understanding of adversaries' behavior, you can develop better countermeasures.

- By putting adversaries on notice that you may gather enough evidence to allow successful prosecution or other punishment, you may deter attacks. This tends to work better against adversaries within your organization than against adversaries on the other side of the Internet. You should coordinate in advance with legal counsel on appropriate policies and notices.

- By quickly detecting a successful attack, you can limit the damage, and by obtaining accurate information about the extent of the damage, you can avoid overly conservative responses, such as reinstalling software on uncompromised systems. Overly conservative responses not only take time and money, they also require system downtime. Thus, an overly conservative response magnifies the damage done by an attack.

For all these reasons, security professionals have been very active in developing monitoring techniques. I already mentioned one in Chapter 9, namely network intrusion detection systems (IDSes). Others that I will summarize here include robust logging facilities, integrity checking software, and honeypots.

Intrusion detection systems are perhaps best thought of as anomaly detectors for network traffic. Many IDSes can be configured to spot anomalous traffic even if it results from an adversary internal to your network, rather than an intruder. Thus, the name IDS is somewhat misleading. An IDS may look for specific attack signatures or may respond to deviations from past patterns of activity. For example, if a normally quiet desktop machine starts spewing out UDP packets at the maximum rate the network can carry (as it would if infected with the SQL Slammer worm), even an IDS that had no signature for the specific worm ought to raise a warning about the sudden traffic.

Other anomalous events may be detected internal to a particular system, rather than in network traffic. For example, an operating system may be programmed to note repeated failed attempts to log in as the system administrator, which could constitute a particularly dangerous password-guessing attack, worthy of notice even if unsuccessful. These sorts of anomalies are routinely logged by systems into a chronological event log, which can be used to reconstruct a break-in after the fact as well as serving as a source to drive real-time alerts. The biggest technical challenge is that a successful attack may give the adversary the necessary access privileges to clean up the log, covering traces of the attack. High-security systems therefore use append-only logging devices. Log entries can also be sent over the network to a centralized, heavily-protected logging server.

Another non-network monitoring approach is to periodically check the integrity of a system's configuration, such as whether any of the system programs have been modified. Successful attackers will frequently modify programs or configuration files so as to give themselves a *back door*, that is, a second way in to use even if the initial vulnerability is fixed. Thus, a periodic check may turn up signs of a successful break-in since the previous check, even if the break-in was sufficiently stealthy to otherwise go unnoticed.

In addition to periodic checks, the same integrity checking can be done after any break-in that comes to notice through other means. Without integrity checking, a system administrator has little choice but to treat the whole system as compromised, scrub it clean, and reinstall from scratch. Thus, integrity checking not only allows successful attacks to be detected, it also guides the mounting of an appropriate response.

An example of an integrity monitoring system is *Tripwire*. The basic principle of operation is that a cryptographic hash of each critical file is computed and stored in a tamper-resistant database, such as on a CD that is writable only once. The Tripwire program itself is also stored in tamper-resistant form. To check the system, the known-good copy of Tripwire recomputes the cryptographic hashes and compares them with the stored copies.

The final form of security monitoring I will mention is the use of honeypots. A *honeypot* is a decoy system used specifically to monitor adversaries. It is configured to appear as realistic as possible but is not used for any genuinely valuable purpose other than monitoring. It is subject to extreme but clandestine monitoring, so as to fully record adversaries' behavior but not tip them off. Because no legitimate user will ever have reason to connect to the honeypot, the monitoring can be comprehensive— no anomaly detection filtering is needed to distinguish legitimate traffic from attack traffic.

By letting an adversary take over the system, rather than immediately repelling the attack, you can learn more about the attack techniques beyond the initial connection and thus learn more about vulnerabilities you need to repair on other systems, as well as other countermeasures you need to take. However, because the adversary is allowed to take over the honeypot, it must be thoroughly firewalled against outbound attacks so that you don't provide the means to launch attacks on further systems. Humans should also monitor the honeypot continuously and be ready to intervene. These considerations help explain why honeypots, although quite in vogue, are best left to large organizations with experienced security professionals. Smaller organizations can still benefit because honeypots largely provide epidemiological evidence about what worms are circulating, which can serve the whole Internet community.

11.8 Key Security Best Practices

Appropriate security practices depend on many factors, including whether you are defending your home computer or an employer's high-value system and whether you are engaging in custom application-software development or only procuring, installing, configuring, and operating existing systems. However, I will attempt a unified list of best practices with the understanding that some may be more applicable than others to any one context:

- Consult others. Everybody, even home users, should at least read the web site of the SANS (SysAdmin, Audit, Network, Security) Institute, *http://www.sans.org*. Organizations should also hire reputable consultants, as well as engage in conversations with legal counsel, those responsible for noncomputer security, and the human resources department.

- Adopt a holistic risk-management perspective. Consider how much you have to lose and how much an adversary has to gain, as well as how likely an adversary is to be caught and punished. Are any of these factors more manipulable than the inherent vulnerability of your system?

- Deploy firewalls and make sure they are correctly configured. The best approach combines hardware firewalls guarding organizational and workgroup perimeters with software firewalls guarding individual machines. Even a home can use this approach, often with a NAT router serving as the hardware firewall.

- Deploy anti-virus software. An organization should have server-based software that scans all incoming email so as not to be at risk should an individual client machine fail to scan. However, the individual client machines should also have protection for defense in depth and in particular to guard against infections that sneak past the network perimeter by being carried in on a portable computer or storage device.

- Keep all your software up to date. This includes not only system software such as the operating system, but also any application software that may be exposed to data from the network. Today, that includes nearly everything.

- Deploy an IDS, integrity checking software such as Tripwire, and a robust logging platform. These steps are not very practical for typical home users yet.

- Assume all network communications are vulnerable; use end-to-end encryption rather than relying on the security of network infrastructure. The same principle applies if storage media are physically shipped between locations.

- Use two-factor user authentication, as described in Section 11.3.4.

- Maintain physical security over computer equipment and be vigilant of service personnel or others with extraordinary physical access.

- Do what you can to stay on good terms with employees and to part from them cleanly. When hiring for particularly sensitive positions, such as system administrators, candidly disclose that you will be checking background and do so. Establish realistic expectations that do not encourage people to work nights or weekends when no one else is around. Have employees cross-train one another and take vacations.

- Establish and clearly communicate policies on acceptable use and on monitoring.

- Beware of any security-relevant phone calls and emails that you do not originate, as well as of storage media that arrive by mail or courier. A "vendor" with a critical patch you need to install could be a con artist. The same is true of a law-enforcement agent or a member of your organization's upper management; being cooperative should not preclude taking a minute to politely confirm identity and authority.

- Examine closely any case where the user whose authority is exercised by a process is not the same as the user who controls the process's actions:
  - If at all possible, never run a program from an untrusted source. Failing that, run it with the least possible authority and the greatest possible monitoring.
  - If you need to write a setuid program, check very carefully what it does with all user input. Might any buffer overflow? Might any input be interpolated into a shell command or otherwise allowed to exert control? Did a programmer insert an intentional "trapdoor," whereby a particular input can trigger the program to bypass normal security controls? Are there any TOCTTOU races? Also, have the program owned by a special-purpose user account that is granted only the necessary authority. More generally, review the principles listed in Section 11.2.
  - Examine any program that communicates over the network according to the exact same standards as a setuid program.

Exercises

11.1 To keep certain individuals from flying on commercial airliners, a list is maintained that airlines must check before issuing a boarding pass. The pass may be issued over the web, as well as at the airport. The pass must be presented to a human at the airport along with an identifying document. The human, who uses no computer technology, checks that the name on the pass matches that on the identifying document and that the photo on the identifying document matches the appearance of the person presenting it. This check is done at the perimeter of the secured portion of the airport as an admission condition. You may assume that identifying documents are hard to forge and that getting past the perimeter control without going through the check is difficult.

(a) How could an adversary get admitted to the secure area despite being on the no-fly list?

(b) Is the vulnerability you identified in part (a) one that could be explained by inattention to any of the security principles listed in Section 11.2?

(c) Can you design a countermeasure to deter the exploitation of the vulnerability you identified? Would the use of additional computer technology help you do so without sacrificing desirable properties of the current system?

11.2 An organization's checks are preprinted with a statement that checks for $100 or more require a handwritten signature, whereas smaller checks are valid with a printed signature. How is this explainable in terms of the general principles of security enumerated in Section 11.2?

11.3 Section 11.2 contains a long list of general security principles. For each of the following audiences, suppose you had time to explain only a few of the principles. Which few would you explain? Why?

(a) software developers designing and programming new systems

(b) information technology staff who will be purchasing, configuring, and administering systems

(c) the Chief Information Officer, who is the executive supervising both of the above groups

11.4 Another weakness of password security is that there is always an administrator to whom a user can turn upon forgetting a password. That administrator has the ability to reset the password. This person may be gulled by a con artist (who tells a pitiful tale of woe) into resetting a password without first authenticating the user in some alternate manner, for example, by using a photograph on an ID card.

(a) What is the name for the general category of threat of which this is an example?

(b) Even if the human customer-service staff can't be stopped from resetting passwords like this, the system can be programmed to print out a letter acknowledging the password change, which is mailed by ordinary postal mail to the registered address of the user. Why would this enhance security, even though it wouldn't prevent the adversary from obtaining access?

11.5 What is two-factor authentication? Give an example.

11.6 Why should a blank web form to be filled in with a password be downloaded to the browser via SSL, rather than using SSL only to send the filled-in form back to the server?

11.7 Draw the following partially ordered sets:

(a) One based on the subset ordering for sets of compartments, as in Figure 11.2 on page 408, but using only the N and I compartments.

(b) The full Cartesian product of your answer from part (a) and the total ordering of {T, S, C, U}. Unlike Figure 11.3 on page 409, no elements should be left out.

11.8 Figure 11.7 shows the full 32-element Cartesian product of the 4-element and 8-element partial orders shown in Figure 11.2 on page 408. However, the elements are not labeled with their security classification levels and sets of compartments; instead, they are shown just as circles. What should the labels be for the eight circles shown in black? (Note that this diagram is arranged differently than the 11-element excerpt in Figure 11.3 on page 409. Do not expect to find those 11 elements in the same positions here.)

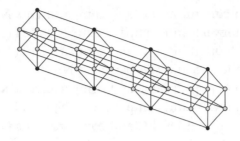

Figure 11.7 This is an unlabeled version of the Cartesian product of the partial orders shown in Figure 11.2 on page 408.

11.9 Using the Bell-LaPadula model, with the compartments {N, I, H} and classification levels {T, S, C, U}, which of the following statements are true?

(a) A subject with current level C and compartments N and H may read from an object with level C and compartments N and H.

(b) A subject with current level C and compartments N and H may read from an object with level C and compartment N.

(c) A subject with current level C and compartments N and H may read from an object with level C and compartments N, I, and H.

(d) A subject with current level C and compartments N and H may read from an object with level C and compartments N and I.

(e) A subject with current level C and compartments N and H may read from an object with level S and compartments N and H.

(f) A subject with current level C and compartments N and H may read from an object with level S and compartment N.

(g) A subject with current level C and compartments N and H may read from an object with level S and compartments N, I, and H.

(h) A subject with current level C and compartments N and H may read from an object with level U and no compartments.

(i) A subject with current level C and compartments N and H may write into an object with level C and compartments N and H.

(j) A subject with current level C and compartments N and H may write into an object with level C and compartment N.

(k) A subject with current level C and compartments N and H may write into an object with level C and compartments N, I, and H.

(l) A subject with current level C and compartments N and H may write into an object with level C and compartments N and I.

    (m) A subject with current level C and compartments N and H may write into an object with level S and compartments N and H.

    (n) A subject with current level C and compartments N and H may write into an object with level S and compartment N.

    (o) A subject with current level C and compartments N and H may write into an object with level S and compartments N, I, and H.

    (p) A subject with current level C and compartments N and H may write into an object with level U and no compartments.

11.10 In the Bell-LaPadula model, under what conditions may a subject read from an object and then modify the object to contain new information that is derived from the old?

11.11 Why, in the Bell-LaPadula model, is it important that a principal can run a subject at a current security level below the one the principal is cleared for?

11.12 In the Bell-LaPadula model, a subject running at a high current level may read from an object that is labeled with a lower level. In a system with readers-writers locks, this could block a subject running at a lower level from writing the object. Explain why this could compromise the design goals of the Bell-LaPadula model.

11.13 Viruses have historically been a problem primarily on systems designed with little regard for the principle of least privilege. Explain why this would be expected. Keep in mind the distinction between viruses and worms.

11.14 A Common Criteria assessment includes inspection not only of the system design and code, but also of documentation intended for system administrators and users. Why is this relevant?

11.15 Explain the difference in the Common Criteria between a PP, an ST, and an EAL.

11.16 Is a system certified at a high EAL necessarily more secure than one certified at a low EAL? Explain.

11.17 Distinguish honeypots from IDSes.

11.18 Why should the code of network server programs be audited for correct processing of received input in the same way a setuid program's processing of user input is audited?

▣ Programming Projects

11.1 Write a program that runs all strings of six or fewer lowercase letters through a library implementation of SHA-1. Report how long your program takes, with enough details of the hardware and software context that someone could approximately replicate your result.

Consider the system shown in Figure 11.1 on page 404 in which the hash function can be SHA-1. The point of this system is to increase an adversary's work factor if the stored value is disclosed. Based on your experiment, you should have some indication of how much the work factor increases by, given an assumption that users pick passwords of the sort your program checked. Under what sorts of circumstances would this increase in work factor be sufficient?

11.2 On a Linux system, you can read cryptographically-strong random bytes from `/dev/random` and can generally read a list of words (one per line) from a file such as `/usr/share/dict/words`. Other systems are likely to have similar information available. Write a program that randomly chooses four words, each of which is four letters long, and prints them out with hyphens between them to serve as a passphrase. For example, you might get the output **mean-chef-pour-pubs**. On the Linux distribution on my computer, there are 2236 four-letter words. How many four-word passphrases can be formed from them? How long would a random string of lowercase letters need to be to have a comparable number of possibilities? Which seems to be more memorizable?

Exploration Projects

11.1 User authentication systems are successfully attacked all the time, usually without generating much publicity. However, when the user in question is a celebrity, the newspapers sit up and take notice. Write a summary of a user-authentication failure involving Paris Hilton in February of 2005. Your sources should include at least the article that month by Brian McWilliams in *MacDev Center* as well as the article by Brian Krebs in the May 19, 2005, issue of *The Washington Post*; both articles are cited in the end-of-chapter notes. As these articles contain contradictory information, presumably they should be taken with a grain of salt. Nonetheless, are there any lessons you can draw, both for designers of authentication systems and for users?

11.2 The website *http://www.sans.org* contains a list of top-twenty vulnerabilities. Look at the information given on how to remedy each problem. How many of these correspond to the best practices listed in this chapter?

11.3 Research and write a paper about the role that Trojan horses reportedly played in a 2004 unauthorized access to Cisco Systems and in a 2005 unauthorized access to LexisNexis's Seisint unit. In the first, the Trojan horse was reportedly a version of the **ssh** program, whereas in the second, the Trojan horse reportedly masqueraded as a display of nude photos of a teenage girl. Setting that difference aside, what commonality and what other differences can you find in the way the two attacks worked? What more general lessons for computer system security can be gained from these two incidents?

11.4 Most UNIX and Linux systems include a program called **sudo**. Read the documentation for it on your system or on the web at *http://www.sudo.ws*. Write a description of how this program's design reflects several of the principles explained in this chapter.

Notes

The single most important source of practical information about security is *http://www.sans.org*. There are also a number of good books on practical security matters, such as those by Garfinkel, Spafford, and Schwartz [55]; Cheswick, Bellovin, and Rubin [29]; and Northcutt et al. [97].

Saltzer and Schroeder presented most of Section 11.2's general security principles in their 1975 tutorial paper [111]. That paper also described capabilities and access control lists, along the lines of Chapter 7's presentation.

One example of a system that generates multiple passwords from a single master password was described by Ross et al. [108].

The Bell-LaPadula model was described by Bell and La Padula in a series of MITRE Corporation technical reports in the early 1970s. Their best summary is in a later "unified exposition," which was also published only as a technical report [13]. A more sophisticated, but less influential, information-flow model was published by Dorothy Denning [39]. Both of these and other formal models were surveyed by Landwehr [86]. The problem of covert channels was described by Lampson [84]. Another important survey of the state of security research in the highly-productive 1970s was published by Dorothy and Peter Denning [40].

I mentioned that although most buffer-overflow attacks overwrite return addresses, an attacker could instead arrange to overwrite some security-critical variable, such as a Boolean flag used to control access. Chen et al. [28] showed that such attacks are in fact realistic, even if not currently popular. As defenses are put in place against current-generation stack-smashing attacks, these alternate forms of attack are likely to gain in popularity.

Information about the Common Criteria is available from *http://www. commoncriteriaportal.org*. A good overview is in the introductory document [125]. The specific ST that I use for illustration is the one for Windows 2000 [113]. It was also used by Shapiro to make similar points about the importance of functional requirements [117].

Exploration Project 11.1 mentions a user authentication failure involving Paris Hilton. Many published accounts at the time included some information about the attack; the one specifically mentioned in the project assignment is by McWilliams [94]. Information about the attack seems to have shifted over time; the project assignment also mentions an article a few months later by Krebs [82].

Stacks

Most compilers for higher-level programming languages produce machine-language object code that makes crucial use of a stack stored in the computer's memory. This stack is used to allocate space whenever a procedure is called and then deallocate the space when the procedure returns. That is, the space is associated with a particular activation of a procedure, and as such, is called an *activation record*. For this reason, the stack is called an *activation record stack*. Another name for the same stack is the *runtime stack*, because it plays a central role in the *runtime environment*, which is to say, the supporting structures the compiler expects to be present at the time the object code is run. Even programs written in assembly language generally make use of an activation record stack, because assembly programmers normally write their procedures following the same conventions as are used by compilers.

You may have studied activation record stacks in a course on programming languages, compilers, or computer organization; you may even have learned something about them in an introductory computer science course. If you have not previously studied this topic, this appendix should suffice. For the purposes of understanding operating systems, you do not need to know all the details of how activation records are used. However, you do need some understanding of how the stack space is allocated in order to understand Chapter 2's explanation of thread switching and also as background for one of the security issues discussed in Chapter 11. Therefore, in Section A.1, I provide an overview of what stack-allocated storage is, and in Section A.2, I explain how this storage is represented using memory and a register. Then, in Section A.3, I sketch how this is used to support procedure activations.

A.1 Stack-Allocated Storage: The Concept

Like most authors writing about computer systems, I use the word *stack* to refer to stack-allocated storage, which is a generalization of the simpler variety of stack used in the mathematical study of algorithms. I will first describe the simpler kind of stack, and then I will explain how stack-allocated storage goes beyond it.

The simple kind of stack is a modifiable object supporting two operations: *push* and *pop*. Each of these operations modifies the stack's state, which can be thought of as a sequence of values arranged in chronological order according to when they were added to the stack. When a new stack is created, it does not hold any values. The push operation adds one new value as the most recent one. The pop operation removes the most recent value and returns it. Because the pop operation changes the stack's state, the next pop will generally produce a different result. You can think of pop as returning the most recently pushed value that has not yet been popped. This value is said to be at the top of the stack. Note that it is illegal to pop from an empty stack.

As an example of how this simple kind of stack operates, suppose a new stack is created, and then the values 3 and 1 are pushed on it, in that order. If a pop operation is done, the top element, 1, is returned. After this pop operation, the 1 is no longer on the stack, and so a second pop would return the 3 that is now on top. A third pop would be illegal, because the first two pops leave the stack empty.

Stack-allocated storage provides a collection of memory locations that can be individually loaded from or stored into, much like the elements of an array. However, the collection of locations can expand and contract in a stack-like fashion.

I can now explain the operations available on a stack, in the sense of a stack-allocated storage structure. Each newly created stack starts with a size of zero. That is, while the underlying representation may already be occupying memory space, there are no memory locations valid for loading and storing. The stack at this point is much like a zero-length array.

The size of the stack can be expanded using an allocate operation, which takes a parameter specifying how many new memory locations should be made available. The newly allocated memory locations are guaranteed to be located at consecutive addresses, and the allocate operation returns the smallest of these addresses. Thus, each location within the allocated block of storage can be loaded or stored using an address calculated as some offset from the base address returned by the allocation.

The size of the stack can be decreased using a deallocate operation, again with a parameter specifying the number of locations to be removed. Because the storage is managed in a stack-like fashion, a deallocate operation frees up the most recently allocated storage locations that have not already been deallocated. Once storage locations are deallocated, it is illegal to use their addresses for loading or storing.

Normally the size of each deallocation request matches the size of a corresponding allocation request. For example, one might allocate 16 locations, allocate 48 more, deallocate the top 48, and finally deallocate the remaining 16. A single deallocation request can also combine the sizes from several allocations. For instance, all 64 locations in the preceding example could be deallocated at once. The only complicated kind of deallocation request is one that frees up some, but not all, of a block of memory locations that were allocated together. In that case, the stack implementation needs to specify which locations in the partially deallocated block remain valid. I will not pursue this issue further, as it isn't relevant to the matters at hand. Instead, I will turn to the realities of how stacks are represented within computer hardware.

A.2 Representing a Stack in Memory

The standard representation of a stack is a large region of consecutive memory locations together with a *stack pointer* register that indicates how many of the locations are in use. The size of the region is chosen to be large enough that the stack normally will not overflow it. The virtual memory system (described in Chapter 6) can enforce this limit and can also expand the size of the region if necessary, provided the adjoining addresses are not in use for another purpose.

The allocated locations within the stack are all at one end of the region of memory. One possibility is that the allocated locations occupy the lowest addresses in the region and that each allocation request expands the stack upward into the higher addresses. The other possibility is that the allocated locations occupy the highest addresses in the region and that allocation requests expand the stack downward into lower addresses. The latter arrangement is the more common in practice, and so I will assume it for the remainder of my explanation.

The stack pointer register indicates how much of the memory region is in use. It does this not by containing a count of how many locations are currently allocated, but by holding the address of the most recently allocated location. This location is

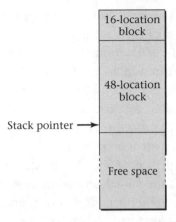

Figure A.1 A stack grows downward, occupying the highest addresses in the region used to store it. The stack pointer points at the "top" of the stack, that is, the most recently allocated block of space. In this example, blocks of size 16 and 48 were allocated, so the stack pointer points at the 64th location from the end of the memory region.

conceptually the "top" of the stack, though because the stack grows downward, the word "top" is misleading. The stack pointer contains the numerically smallest memory address of any currently allocated location. Figure A.1 shows a stack after allocating 16 locations and then 48; the stack pointer contains the 64th largest memory address in the region.

Given this representation, an allocate operation decreases the stack pointer by the number of locations requested and returns the new stack pointer value as the base address of the allocated block. A deallocate operation increases the stack pointer by the number of locations to be freed. For example, deallocating 48 locations in Figure A.1 would leave the stack pointer pointing at the lowest-numbered address of the 16 locations in the remaining block of storage.

At this point, you should understand the basic management of stack space, but not the purpose to which that space is put. Therefore, I will provide a brief synopsis of how programming-language implementations make use of stack space.

A.3 Using a Stack for Procedure Activations

When one procedure calls another, the caller executes an instruction that jumps to the beginning of the called procedure. That instruction also stores a *return address*, which is the address of the calling procedure's next instruction after the procedure call. That way, when the called procedure is ready to return, it can jump to the return address and thereby resume execution of the calling procedure.

Computer architectures differ in where they store the return address. One approach is for the procedure call instruction to push the return address on the stack. This approach is used in the popular IA-32 architecture, which is also known as the x86 architecture, and is implemented by processors such as those in the Pentium family. Thus, the very first element of a procedure activation record may be the return address, pushed by the procedure call instruction itself.

In other architectures, such as MIPS, the procedure call instruction places the return address in a register. If the called procedure does not execute any further procedure calls before it returns, the return address can remain in the register. The return instruction jumps to the address stored in the register. In this case, when there are no further procedure calls, the procedure activation is termed a *leaf*.

However, this register-based approach to return addresses does not directly support nesting of procedure activations, with the called procedure in turn calling a third procedure, which may call a fourth, and so on. To support that nesting, a whole chain of return addresses is needed; the innermost procedure activation must be able to return to its caller, which in turn must be able to return to its caller, and so forth. One register cannot hold all these return addresses simultaneously. Therefore, any nonleaf procedure activation must store the return address register's value into the activation record and later retrieve it from there. As a result, the activation records hold return addresses, even on architectures that don't directly push the return address onto the stack in the first place.

Each procedure activation also needs some storage space for local variables and other values that arise in the course of the procedure's computation. Some of this storage may be in registers rather than in memory. When one procedure calls another, there must be some agreement regarding how they will share the registers. Typically the agreement specifies that the called procedure must leave some registers the way it found them, that is, containing the same values at procedure return as at procedure entry. The calling procedure can leave its values in these registers when it executes the procedure call. Other registers can be freely modified by the called procedure; the calling procedure must not leave any important values in them.

Either kind of register is likely to be saved into the stack. If the called procedure promises to leave a register as it found it, but wants to use that register for its own storage, it will reconcile this conflict by saving the register to the stack before modifying it and then restoring the saved value before returning. Thus, the caller will never know that the register was temporarily modified. This approach is known as *callee saves*, because the callee saves the register into its activation record.

For registers that the callee may overwrite without compunction, the situation is somewhat different. For these registers, it is the caller that may want to save them into its own activation record. The caller saves the registers before the procedure call and restores them upon resumption. Therefore, this approach is known as *caller saves*.

Each architecture has some convention for which registers are preserved using the caller-saves approach and which are preserved using the callee-saves approach. That way, any two procedures will correctly interoperate. The details don't matter for the purposes of this book; what matters is that activation records hold saved registers. As such, the stack is also a natural place for saving registers upon thread switching, as described in Chapter 2.

Some values local to a procedure activation cannot be stored in registers. For example, suppose that a procedure makes use of a local array, which is allocated when the procedure is entered and deallocated when the procedure returns. This array will be stored in memory so that the array elements can be accessed with load and store instructions. Because the lifetime of the array corresponds with a procedure activation, the array will be part of the activation record. In Chapter 11, I explain that this can create a security risk if input is read into the array without checking the amount of input versus the array size. As I explain there, if the input runs past the end of the array, it can overwrite other parts of the procedure's activation record, or the activation records of the caller, the caller's caller, and so forth, with potentially dangerous results.

Bibliography

[1] Atul Adya, Barbara Liskov, and Patrick E. O'Neil. Generalized isolation level definitions. In *Proceedings of the 16th International Conference on Data Engineering*, pages 67–78. IEEE Computer Society, 2000.

[2] Alfred V. Aho, Peter J. Denning, and Jeffrey D. Ullman. Principles of optimal page replacement. *Journal of the ACM*, 18(1):80–93, 1971.

[3] AMD. *AMD64 Architecture Programmer's Manual Volume 2: System Programming*, 3.09 edition, September 2003. Publication 24593.

[4] Dave Anderson. You don't know jack about disks. *Queue*, 1(4):20–30, 2003.

[5] Dave Anderson, Jim Dykes, and Erik Riedel. More than an interface—SCSI vs. ATA. In *Proceedings of the 2nd Annual Conference on File and Storage Technology (FAST)*. USENIX, March 2003.

[6] Apple Computer, Inc. *Kernel Programming*, 2003. Inside Mac OS X.

[7] Apple Computer, Inc. HFS Plus volume format. Technical Note TN1150, Apple Computer, Inc., March 2004.

[8] Ozalp Babaoglu and William Joy. Converting a swap-based system to do paging in an architecture lacking page-referenced bits. In *Proceedings of the Eighth ACM Symposium on Operating Systems Principles*, pages 78–86. ACM Press, 1981.

[9] Gaurav Banga, Peter Druschel, and Jeffrey C. Mogul. Resource containers: A new facility for resource management in server systems. In *Proceedings of the Third Symposium on Operating Systems Design and Implementation*, pages 45–58. USENIX, 1999.

[10] R. Bayer and E. McCreight. Organization and maintenance of large ordered indexes. *Acta Informatica*, 1(3):173–189, 1972.

[11] L. A. Belady. A study of replacement algorithms for a virtual storage computer. *IBM Systems Journal*, 5(2):78–101, 1966.

[12] L. A. Belady, R. A. Nelson, and G. S. Shedler. An anomaly in space-time characteristics of certain programs running in a paging machine. *Communications of the ACM*, 12(6):349–353, 1969.

[13] D. E. Bell and L. J. La Padula. Secure computer system: Unified exposition and Multics interpretation. Technical Report ESD-TR-75-306, MITRE, March 1976.

[14] A. Bensoussan and C. T. Clingen. The Multics virtual memory: Concepts and design. *Communications of the ACM*, 15(5):308–318, May 1972.

[15] Hal Berenson, Phil Bernstein, Jim Gray, Jim Melton, Elizabeth O'Neil, and Patrick O'Neil. A critique of ANSI SQL isolation levels. In *Proceedings of the 1995 ACM SIGMOD International Conference on Management of Data*, pages 1–10. ACM Press, 1995.

[16] Philip A. Bernstein. Middleware: A model for distributed system services. *Communications of the ACM*, 39(2):86–98, 1996.

[17] Philip A. Bernstein and Nathan Goodman. Concurrency control in distributed database systems. *ACM Computing Surveys*, 13(2):185–221, 1981.

[18] Philip A. Bernstein and Nathan Goodman. Multiversion concurrency control—theory and algorithms. *ACM Transactions on Database Systems*, 8(4):465–483, 1983.

[19] Philip A. Bernstein and Eric Newcomer. *Principles of Transaction Processing*. Morgan Kaufmann Publishers, 1997.

[20] Viktors Berstis. Security and protection of data in the IBM System/38. In *Proceedings of the 7th Annual Symposium on Computer Architecture*, pages 245–252. IEEE Computer Society Press, May 1980.

[21] Mike Blasgen, Jim Gray, Mike Mitoma, and Tom Price. The convoy phenomenon. *SIGOPS Operating Systems Review*, 13(2):20–25, 1979.

[22] Daniel G. Bobrow, Jerry D. Burchfiel, Daniel L. Murphy, and Raymond S. Tomlinson. TENEX, a paged time sharing system for the PDP-10. *Communications of the ACM*, 15(3):135–143, 1972.

[23] Per Brinch Hansen. Structured multiprogramming. *Communications of the ACM*, 15(7):574–578, 1972.

[24] Per Brinch Hansen. Monitors and Concurrent Pascal: A personal history. In *HOPL-II: The Second ACM SIGPLAN Conference on History of Programming Languages*, pages 1–35, New York, NY, USA, 1993. ACM Press.

[25] J. W. Byers, M. Luby, and M. Mitzenmacher. A digital fountain approach to asynchronous reliable multicast. *IEEE Journal on Selected Areas in Communications*, 20(8):1528–1540, October 2002.

[26] Jeffrey S. Chase, Henry M. Levy, Michael J. Feeley, and Edward D. Lazowska. Sharing and protection in a single-address-space operating system. *ACM Transactions on Computer Systems*, 12(4):271–307, 1994.

[27] Peter M. Chen, Edward K. Lee, Garth A. Gibson, Randy H. Katz, and David A. Patterson. RAID: High performance, reliable secondary storage. *ACM Computing Surveys*, 26(2):145–185, 1994.

[28] Shuo Chen, Jun Xu, Emre C. Sezer, Prachi Gauriar, and Ravishankar K. Iyer. Non-control-data attacks are realistic threats. In *14th USENIX Security Symposium*, pages 177–192, 2005.

[29] William R. Cheswick, Steven M. Bellovin, and Aviel D. Rubin. *Firewalls and Internet Security*. Addison-Wesley, 2nd edition, 2003.

[30] E. F. Codd, E. S. Lowry, E. McDonough, and C. A. Scalzi. Multiprogramming STRETCH: Feasibility considerations. *Communications of the ACM*, 2(11):13–17, November 1959.

[31] E. G. Coffman, M. Elphick, and A. Shoshani. System deadlocks. *ACM Computing Surveys*, 3(2):67–78, 1971.

[32] Ellis Cohen and David Jefferson. Protection in the Hydra operating system. In *Proceedings of the Fifth ACM Symposium on Operating Systems Principles*, pages 141–160. ACM Press, 1975.

[33] Douglas Comer. The ubiquitous B-tree. *ACM Computing Surveys*, 11(2):121–137, 1979.

[34] Fernando J. Corbató, Marjorie Merwin Daggett, and Robert C. Daley. An experimental time-sharing system. In *Proceedings of the Spring Joint Computer Conference*, pages 335–344. Spartan Books, 1962.

[35] P. J. Courtois, F. Heymans, and D. L. Parnas. Concurrent control with "readers" and "writers". *Communications of the ACM*, 14(10):667–668, 1971.

[36] R. J. Creasy. The origin of the VM/370 time-sharing system. *IBM Journal of Research and Development*, 25(5):483–490, September 1981.

[37] R. C. Daley and P. G. Neumann. A general-purpose file system for secondary storage. In *Proceedings of AFIPS Fall Joint Computer Conference*, volume 27, pages 213–229. Spartan Books, 1965.

[38] Robert C. Daley and Jack B. Dennis. Virtual memory, processes, and sharing in MULTICS. *Communications of the ACM*, 11(5):306–312, 1968.

[39] Dorothy E. Denning. A lattice model of secure information flow. *Communications of the ACM*, 19(5):236–243, 1976.

[40] Dorothy E. Denning and Peter J. Denning. Data security. *ACM Computing Surveys*, 11(3):227–249, 1979.

[41] Peter J. Denning. The working set model for program behavior. *Communications of the ACM*, 11(5):323–333, 1968.

[42] Peter J. Denning. Virtual memory. *ACM Computing Surveys*, 2(3):153–189, 1970.

[43] Jack B. Dennis. Segmentation and the design of multiprogrammed computer systems. *Journal of the ACM*, 12(4):589–602, 1965.

[44] Jack B. Dennis and Earl C. Van Horn. Programming semantics for multiprogrammed computations. *Communications of the ACM*, 9(3):143–155, 1966.

[45] E. W. Dijkstra. Solution of a problem in concurrent programming control. *Communications of the ACM*, 8(9):569, 1965.

[46] Edsger W. Dijkstra. Cooperating sequential processes. Published as [47]; manuscript identified as EWD123, 1965.

[47] Edsger W. Dijkstra. Cooperating sequential processes. In F. Genuys, editor, *Programming Languages: NATO Advanced Study Institute*, pages 43–112. Academic Press, 1968.

[48] Edsger W. Dijkstra. Hierarchical ordering of sequential processes. In *Operating Systems Techniques*, pages 72–93. Academic Press, 1972.

[49] Cort Dougan, Paul Mackerras, and Victor Yodaiken. Optimizing the idle task and other MMU tricks. In *Proceedings of the 3rd Symposium on Operating Systems Design and Implementation*, pages 229–237. USENIX 1999.

[50] K. P. Eswaran, J. N. Gray, R. A. Lorie, and I. L. Traiger. The notions of consistency and predicate locks in a database system. *Communications of the ACM*, 19(11):624–633, 1976.

[51] R. S. Fabry. Capability-based addressing. *Communications of the ACM*, 17(7): 403–412, 1974.

[52] Renato Figueiredo, Peter A. Dinda, José Fortes, et al. Special issue on virtualization technologies. *Computer*, 38(5):28–69, May 2005.

[53] John Fotheringham. Dynamic storage allocation in the Atlas computer, including an automatic use of a backing store. *Communications of the ACM*, 4(10): 435–436, 1961.

[54] Gregory R. Ganger, Marshall Kirk McKusick, Craig A. N. Soules, and Yale N. Patt. Soft updates: A solution to the metadata update problem in file systems. *ACM Transactions on Computer Systems*, 18(2):127–153, 2000.

[55] Simson Garfinkel, Gene Spafford, and Alan Schwartz. *Practical Unix and Internet Security*. O'Reilly, 3rd edition, 2003.

[56] J. N. Gray. Notes on data base operating systems. In R. Bayer, R. M. Graham, and G. Seegmüller, editors, *Operating Systems: An Advanced Course*, chapter 3.F, pages 393–481. Springer-Verlag, 1979. Originally published as Lecture Notes in Computer Science, Vol. 60, 1978.

[57] Jim Gray. The transaction concept: Virtues and limitations. In *Proceedings of the Seventh International Conference on Very Large Datatabases*, pages 144–154, September 1981.

[58] Jim Gray, Raymond A. Lorie, Gianfranco R. Putzolu, and Irving L. Traiger. Granularity of locks and degrees of consistency in a shared data base. In *IFIP Working Conference on Modelling in Data Base Management Systems*, pages 365–394, 1976. Reprinted in *Readings in Database Systems*, ed. Michael Stonebraker, Morgan Kaufmann Publishers, 1988.

[59] Jim Gray, Paul McJones, Mike Blasgen, Bruce Lindsay, Raymond Lorie, Tom Price, Franco Putzolu, and Irving Traiger. The recovery manager of the System R database manager. *ACM Computing Surveys*, 13(2):223–242, 1981.

[60] Jim Gray and Andreas Reuter. *Transaction Processing: Concepts and Techniques*. Morgan Kaufmann Publishers, 1993.

[61] Peter Gutmann. Secure deletion of data from magnetic and solid-state memory. In *Sixth USENIX Security Symposium*, pages 77–90, 1996.

[62] A. N. Habermann. Prevention of system deadlocks. *Communications of the ACM*, 12(7):373–377, 385, 1969.

[63] Theo Haerder [Härder] and Andreas Reuter. Principles of transaction-oriented database recovery. *ACM Computing Surveys*, 15(4):287–317, 1983.

[64] Michael A. Harrison, Walter L. Ruzzo, and Jeffrey D. Ullman. Protection in operating systems. *Communications of the ACM*, 19(8):461–471, 1976.

[65] J. W. Havender. Avoiding deadlock in multitasking systems. *IBM Systems Journal*, 7(2):74–84, 1968.

[66] Joseph L. Hellerstein. Achieving service rate objectives with decay usage scheduling. *IEEE Transactions on Software Engineering*, 19(8):813–825, August 1993.

[67] Thomas F. Herbert. *The Linux TCP/IP Stack: Networking for Embedded Systems*. Charles River Media, 2004.

[68] Dave Hitz, James Lau, and Michael Malcolm. File system design for an NFS file server appliance. In *USENIX Technical Conference*, pages 235–246, 1994.

[69] C. A. R. Hoare. Monitors: An operating system structuring concept. *Communications of the ACM*, 17(10):549–557, October 1974.

[70] Gregor Hohpe and Bobby Woolf. *Enterprise Integration Patterns: Designing, Building, and Deploying Messaging Solutions*. Addison-Wesley, 2003.

[71] Richard C. Holt. Some deadlock properties of computer systems. *ACM Computing Surveys*, 4(3):179–196, 1972.

[72] Merle E. Houdek and Glen R. Mitchell. Hash index helps manage large virtual memory. *Electronics*, 52(6):111–113, March 15, 1979.

[73] Merle E. Houdek, Frank G. Soltis, and Roy L. Hoffman. IBM System/38 support for capability-based addressing. In *Proceedings of the 8th Annual Symposium on Computer Architecture*, pages 341–348. IEEE Computer Society Press, 1981.

[74] Jerry Huck and Jim Hays. Architectural support for translation table management in large address space machines. In *Proceedings of the 20th Annual International Symposium on Computer Architecture*, pages 39–50. ACM Press, 1993.

[75] Intel Corporation. *Intel Itanium Architecture Software Developer's Manual*, 2.1 edition, October 2002.

[76] Eike Jeseen [misspelling of Jessen]. Origin of the virtual memory concept. *IEEE Annals of the History of Computing*, 26(4):71–72, October–December 2004.

[77] J. Kay and P. Lauder. A fair share scheduler. *Communications of the ACM*, 31(1): 44–55, January 1988.

[78] Tim Kempster, Colin Stirling, and Peter Thanisch. Diluting ACID. *SIGMOD Record*, 28(4):17–23, 1999.

[79] R. E. Kessler and Mark D. Hill. Page placement algorithms for large real-indexed caches. *ACM Transactions on Computer Systems*, 10(4):338–359, November 1992.

[80] T. Kilburn, D. B. C. Edwards, M. I. Lanigan, and F. H. Sumner. One-level storage system. *IRE Transactions*, EC-11(2):223–235, April 1962.

[81] Donald Ervin Knuth. *The Art of Computer Programming*, volume 1 (Fundamental Algorithms). Addison-Wesley, 3rd edition, 1997.

[82] Brian Krebs. Paris Hilton hack started with old-fashioned con. *The Washington Post*, May 19, 2005. *http://www.washingtonpost.com/wp-dyn/content/article/ 2005/05/19/AR2005051900711.html*.

[83] James F. Kurose and Keith W. Ross. *Computer Networking: A Top-Down Approach Featuring the Internet*. Addison-Wesley, 3rd edition, 2005.

[84] Butler W. Lampson. A note on the confinement problem. *Communications of the ACM*, 16(10):613–615, 1973.

[85] Butler W. Lampson and Howard E. Sturgis. Crash recovery in a distributed data storage system. This paper was circulated in several drafts, but it was never published. Much of the material appeared in *Distributed Systems—Architecture and Implementation*, ed. Lampson, Paul, and Siegert, Lecture Notes in Computer Science 105, Springer, 1981, pages 246–265 and pages 357–370, June 1, 1979.

[86] Carl E. Landwehr. Formal models for computer security. *ACM Computing Surveys*, 13(3):247–278, 1981.

[87] Nancy G. Leveson and Clark S. Turner. An investigation of the Therac-25 accidents. *Computer*, 26(7):17–41, July 1993.

[88] Henry M. Levy and Peter H. Lipman. Virtual memory management in the VAX/VMS operating system. *Computer*, 15(3):35–41, March 1982.

[89] Theodore A. Linden. Operating system structures to support security and reliable software. *ACM Computing Surveys*, 8(4):409–445, 1976.

[90] Tim Lindholm and Frank Yellin. *The Java Virtual Machine Specification*. Addison-Wesley, 2nd edition, 1999.

[91] C. L. Liu and James W. Layland. Scheduling algorithms for multiprogramming in a hard-real-time environment. *Journal of the ACM*, 20(1):46–61, January 1973.

[92] R. Mattson, J. Gecsei, D. Slutz, and I. Traiger. Evaluation techniques for storage hierarchies. *IBM Systems Journal*, 9(2):78–117, 1970.

[93] Marshall Kirk McKusick and George V. Neville-Neil. *The Design and Implementation of the FreeBSD Operating System*. Addison-Wesley, 2005.

[94] Brian McWilliams. How Paris got hacked? *MacDev Center*, February 22, 2005. *http://www.macdevcenter.com/pub/a/mac/2005/01/01/paris.html*.

[95] R. A. Meyer and L. H. Seawright. A virtual machine time-sharing system. *IBM Systems Journal*, 9(3):199–218, 1970.

[96] R. M. Needham and R. D.H. Walker. The Cambridge CAP computer and its protection system. In *Proceedings of the Sixth ACM Symposium on Operating Systems Principles*, pages 1–10. ACM Press, 1977.

[97] Stephen Northcutt, Lenny Zeltser, Scott Winters, Karen Kent, and Ronald W. Ritchey. *Inside Network Perimeter Security*. Sams, 2nd edition, 2005.

[98] Ruoming Pang, Vinod Yegneswaran, Paul Barford, Vern Paxson, and Larry Peterson. Characteristics of Internet background radiation. In *IMC '04: Proceedings of the 4th ACM SIGCOMM Conference on Internet Measurement*, pages 27–40. ACM Press, 2004.

[99] R. P. Parmelee, T. I. Peterson, C. C. Tillman, and D. J. Hatfield. Virtual storage and virtual machine concepts. *IBM Systems Journal*, 11(2):99–130, 1972.

[100] John E. Pomeranz. Note on an anomaly in paging. *Communications of the ACM*, 13(7):451, 1970.

[101] Sean Quinlan and Sean Dorward. Venti: A new approach to archival storage. In *Proceedings of the Conference on File and Storage Technologies*, pages 89–101. USENIX Association, 2002.

[102] B. Randell. A note on storage fragmentation and program segmentation. *Communications of the ACM*, 12(7):365–369, 372, 1969.

[103] John Regehr. Inferring scheduling behavior with Hourglass. In *Proceedings of the USENIX Annual Technical Conference FREENIX Track*, pages 143–156, Monterey, CA, June 2002.

[104] Dennis M. Ritchie and Ken Thompson. The UNIX time-sharing system. *Communications of the ACM*, 17(7):365–375, July 1974.

[105] Kay A. Robbins and Steven Robbins. *Unix Systems Programming: Communication, Concurrency and Threads*. Prentice Hall, 2003.

[106] Mendel Rosenblum and John K. Ousterhout. The design and implementation of a log-structured file system. *ACM Transactions on Computer Systems*, 10(1):26–52, 1992.

[107] Daniel J. Rosenkrantz, Richard E. Stearns, and Philip M. Lewis, II. System level concurrency control for distributed database systems. *ACM Transactions on Database Systems*, 3(2):178–198, 1978.

[108] Blake Ross, Collin Jackson, Nick Miyake, Dan Boneh, and John C. Mitchell. Stronger password authentication using browser extensions. In *14th USENIX Security Symposium*, pages 17–32, 2005.

[109] Mark E. Russinovich and David A. Solomon. *Microsoft Windows Internals: Microsoft Windows Server 2003, Windows XP, and Windows 2000*. Microsoft Press, 4th edition, 2004.

[110] Jerome H. Saltzer. Protection and the control of information sharing in Multics. *Communications of the ACM*, 17(7):388–402, 1974.

[111] Jerome H. Saltzer and Michael D. Schroeder. The protection of information in computer systems. *Proceedings of the IEEE*, 63(9):1278–1308, September 1975.

[112] Douglas S. Santry, Michael J. Feeley, Norman C. Hutchinson, Alistair C. Veitch, Ross W. Carton, and Jacob Ofir. Deciding when to forget in the Elephant file system. In *Proceedings of the Seventeenth ACM Symposium on Operating Systems Principles*, pages 110–123. ACM Press, 1999.

[113] Science Applications International Corporation. Windows 2000 security target. Technical report, Microsoft Corporation, October 18, 2002. ST Version 2.0.

[114] L. H. Seawright and R. A. MacKinnon. VM/370—a study of multiplicity and usefulness. *IBM Systems Journal*, 18(1):4–17, 1979.

[115] Lui Sha, Ragnathan Rajkumar, and Shirish S. Sathaye. Generalized rate-monotonic scheduling theory: A framework for developing real-time systems. *Proceedings of the IEEE*, 82(1):68–82, January 1994.

[116] Lui Sha, Ragunathan Rajkumar, and John P. Lehoczky. Priority inheritance protocols: An approach to real-time synchronization. *IEEE Transactions on Computers*, 39(9):1175–1185, September 1990.

[117] Jonathan S. Shapiro. Understanding the Windows EAL4 evaluation. *Computer*, 36(2):103–105, February 2003.

[118] Frank G. Soltis. Design of a small business data processing system. *IEEE Computer*, 14(9):77–93, September 1981.

[119] Frank G. Soltis. *Inside the AS/400*. Duke Press, 2nd edition, 1997.

[120] Craig A. N. Soules, Garth R. Goodson, John D. Strunk, and Gregory R. Ganger. Metadata efficiency in versioning file systems. In *Proceedings of the Conference on File and Storage Technologies*, pages 43–58. USENIX Association, 2003.

[121] Richard E. Stearns and Daniel J. Rosenkrantz. Distributed database concurrency controls using before-values. In *Proceedings of the 1981 ACM SIGMOD International Conference on Management of Data*, pages 74–83. ACM Press, 1981.

[122] W. Richard Stevens. *TCP/IP Illustrated: The Protocols*, volume 1. Addison-Wesley, 1994.

[123] W. Richard Stevens and Stephen A. Rago. *Advanced Programming in the UNIX Environment*. Addison-Wesley, 2nd edition, 2005.

[124] Adam Sweeney, Doug Doucette, Wei Hu, Curtis Anderson, Mike Nishimoto, and Geoff Peck. Scalability in the XFS file system. In *USENIX Technical Conference*, pages 1–14, 1996.

[125] Syntegra. Common criteria: An introduction. *http://www.commoncriteriaportal.org/public/files/ccintroduction.pdf*.

[126] M. Talluri, M. D. Hill, and Y. A. Khalidi. A new page table for 64-bit address spaces. In *Proceedings of the Fifteenth ACM Symposium on Operating Systems Principles*, pages 184–200. ACM Press, 1995.

[127] Madhusudhan Talluri. *Use of Superpages and Subblocking in the Address Translation Hierarchy*. Ph.D. thesis, Computer Sciences Department, University of Wisconsin–Madison, 1995. Also Technical Report 1277.

[128] Andrew S. Tanenbaum. *Computer Networks*. Prentice Hall PTR, 4th edition, 2003.

[129] Ken Thompson. Reflections on trusting trust. *Communications of the ACM*, 27(8):761–763, August 1984. Turing Award lecture.

[130] Rollins Turner and Henry Levy. Segmented FIFO page replacement. In *Conference on Measurement and Modeling of Computer Systems*, pages 48–51. ACM Press, 1981.

[131] Carl A. Waldspurger. Memory resource management in VMware ESX Server. In *Proceedings of the 5th Symposium on Operating Systems Design and Implementation*, pages 181–194, December 2002.

[132] Carl A. Waldspurger and William E. Weihl. Lottery scheduling: Flexible proportional-share resource management. In *Proceedings of the First Symposium on Operating System Design and Implementation (OSDI)*, pages 1–11, 1994.

[133] Carl A. Waldspurger and William E. Weihl. Stride scheduling: Deterministic proportional-share resource management. Technical Memorandum MIT/LCS/TM-528, Laboratory for Computer Science, Massachusetts Institute of Technology, 1995.

[134] Gerhard Weikum and Gottfried Vossen. *Transactional Information Systems: Theory, Algorithms, and the Practice of Concurrency Control and Recovery*. Morgan Kaufmann Publishers, 2002.

[135] John Wilkes, Richard Golding, Carl Staelin, and Tim Sullivan. The HP AutoRAID hierarchical storage system. *ACM Transactions on Computer Systems*, 14(1):108–136, February 1996.

[136] Avishai Wool. A quantitative study of firewall configuration errors. *IEEE Computer*, 37(6):62–67, June 2004.

[137] W. Wulf, R. Levin, and C. Pierson. Overview of the Hydra operating system development. In *Proceedings of the Fifth ACM Symposium on Operating Systems Principles*, pages 122–131. ACM Press, 1975.

Index

Note:

- Page numbers in bold type indicate term introductions/definitions.
- Page numbers in italic type indicate illustrations.
- Page numbers followed by *q* indicate quotations.
- Page numbers followed by *(2)* indicate two separate discussions.
- Cross-reference targets beginning with ":——" indicate the current main heading in cross-references from one subheading to another.